Political Elites in Canada

COMMUNICATION
STRATEGY
AND POLITICS

Communication, Strategy, and Politics

THIERRY GIASSON AND ALEX MARLAND, SERIES EDITORS

Communication, Strategy, and Politics is a ground-breaking new series from UBC Press that examines elite decision making and political communication in today's hyper-mediated and highly competitive environment. Publications in this series look at the intricate relations between marketing strategy, the media, and political actors and explain how this affects Canadian democracy. They also investigate such interconnected themes as strategic communication, mediatization, opinion research, electioneering, political management, public policy, and e-politics in a Canadian context and in comparison to other countries. Designed as a coherent and consolidated space for diffusion of research about Canadian political community, the series promotes an inter-disciplinary, multi-method, and theoretically pluralistic approach.

Other volumes in the series are

Political Marketing in Canada, edited by Alex Marland, Thierry Giasson, and Jennifer Lees-Marshment

Political Communication in Canada: Meet the Press and Tweet the Rest, edited by Alex Marland, Thierry Giasson, and Tamara A. Small

Framed: Media and the Coverage of Race in Canadian Politics, by Erin Tolley

Brand Command: Canadian Politics and Democracy in the Age of Message Control, by Alex Marland

Permanent Campaigning in Canada, edited by Alex Marland, Thierry Giasson, and Anna Lennox Esselment

Breaking News? Politics, Journalism, and Infotainment on Quebec Television, by Frédérick Bastien

See also

Canadian Election Analysis 2015: Communication, Strategy, and Democracy, edited by Alex Marland and Thierry Giasson. Open access compilation available at http://www.ubcpress.ca/canadianelectionanalysis2015.

Political Elites in Canada

Power and Influence in Instantaneous Times

•••••• Edited by Alex Marland,
Thierry Giasson, and
Andrea Lawlor

UBCPress · Vancouver · Toronto

27 26 25 24 23 22 21 20 19 18   5 4 3 2 1

Printed in Canada on FSC-certified ancient-forest-free paper
(100% post-consumer recycled) that is processed chlorine- and acid-free.

Library and Archives Canada Cataloguing in Publication

Political elites in Canada : power and influence in instantaneous times / edited by Alex Marland, Thierry Giasson, and Andrea Lawlor.

(Communication, strategy, and politics)
Includes bibliographical references and index.
Issued in print and electronic formats.
ISBN 978-0-7748-3793-4 (hardcover). – ISBN 978-0-7748-3794-1 (softcover)
ISBN 978-0-7748-3795-8 (PDF). – ISBN 978-0-7748-3796-5 (EPUB)
ISBN 978-0-7748-3797-2 (Kindle)

1. Communication in politics – Technological innovations – Canada. 2. Digital media – Political aspects – Canada. 3. Social media – Political aspects – Canada. 4. Elite (Social sciences) – Canada. 5. Power (Social sciences) – Canada. I. Marland, Alexander J., 1973-, editor II. Giasson, Thierry, editor III. Lawlor, Andrea, 1982-, editor IV. Series: Communication, strategy, and politics

P95.82.C3P65 2018   320.01'4   C2018-902157-8
                                                                 C2018-902158-6

Canada

UBC Press gratefully acknowledges the financial support for our publishing program of the Government of Canada (through the Canada Book Fund), the Canada Council for the Arts, and the British Columbia Arts Council.

This book has been published with the help of a grant from the Canadian Federation for the Humanities and Social Sciences, through the Awards to Scholarly Publications Program, using funds provided by the Social Sciences and Humanities Research Council of Canada.

Printed and bound in Canada by Friesens
Set in Alternate Gothic, Scala, and Minion by Artegraphica Design Co. Ltd.
Copy editor: Dallas Harrison
Proofreader: Alison Strobel
Indexer: Judy Dunlop
Cover designer: David Drummond

UBC Press
The University of British Columbia
2029 West Mall, Vancouver, BC V6T 1Z2
www.ubcpress.ca

Contents

..... Figures and Tables

Foreword

Susan Delacourt

Early in the 1990s, when I had been reporting on Parliament Hill for about five years, one of my political contacts told me about an illuminating incident aboard a flight from Toronto to Ottawa. An instant-win contest, based on a random draw of seat assignments on the plane, set off an uproar among the passengers. The people in economy class were outraged that the prize on the flight went to someone sitting up front, in the premium, executive-class seats. They booed loudly when the winner came forward to claim his prize. Class warfare on a flight to Canada's capital – what was going on in this country?

I used the incident to write a feature for the *Globe and Mail*, for which I worked at the time, about how political elites were falling out of fashion (Delacourt 1992). The Meech Lake Accord had been defeated in 1990, fuelled by public outrage against what critics called deals made by "men in suits" "behind closed doors." Two years later, with another constitutional accord poised to go down in the flames of populist opposition, my article was an attempt to describe a recent trend in Canadian politics, on the eve of the Charlottetown Accord referendum in 1992.

The headline of the story was "Loss of Faith" – as in loss of faith in elites – and the story opened with the anecdote from the Toronto–Ottawa flight. "This is Canada in the midst of the referendum campaign," I wrote. "A victory for the executive class is not a victory for everyone. Canada's politicians may be happy with their prize – a constitutional compromise in the Charlottetown accord – but voters are reluctant to share in the enthusiasm" (Delacourt 1992).

Nowadays, of course, an editor would laugh at any reporter who proposed to write a feature on such an obvious, daily fact of life in our politics – the disconnect between the public and the political "elites." What was new and startling in the latter years of the twentieth century is now just another day at the office for the country's political class and those who report on them in the twenty-first century. Our political coverage, as well as the conduct of politics itself, has evolved in many ways since the 1990s to take account of a trend called, variously, the rise of political cynicism, the decline of deference, and the democratization of the public sphere.

That is why this book is so necessary. Although the fundamental structure of the government endures, political communications and conduct of politics have been in the midst of a radical upheaval in the past few decades.

* * * * *

When one has been reporting on Parliament Hill for thirty years, as I have, people often ask about what has changed in the culture – what are the biggest shifts that I and others have witnessed? I have several answers, many of them revolving around the subjects of this book: political elites and how they communicate with both the media and the public.

One significant change has been the regard in which political elites are held by the voting public. Political journalists have long been seen as defenders and promoters of political elites, if not elites themselves, and in the past few decades they too have not been spared the tumble in public esteem or deference.

Another significant change that I have seen in the business simultaneously captures the issues of elites and technological innovation. And it has nothing to do with what happens during the work week; rather, it concerns what happens – or more correctly does not happen – on the weekend.

When I first started reporting for the *Globe and Mail,* widely regarded as the newspaper for political and business elites, there was no such thing as online political coverage, of course. (Web editions and media blogs were not seen as serious destinations for political reporting until the mid-2000s at the earliest.) There was also no Sunday edition of the newspaper. Many political events took place on the weekends: leadership conventions, for instance. Here is how journalists would approach coverage of these events. On Friday, we would file a story at the end of the working day, setting up for our readers what was expected to take place over the weekend. On Sunday, when the momentous event was all over, we would write long stories or even special sections to run in the Monday papers. In the forty-eight hours between those two deadlines, we would observe, interview, and take notes, cultivating sources and insights. Broadcast reporters might have been doing wall-to-wall coverage on Saturday and Sunday, but print journalism, especially at the *Globe and Mail,* was the medium in which more contemplative, con-sidered analysis could be conducted over a whole weekend.

Compared with the typical working life of a political journalist nearly two decades into the 2000s, this seems like an unimaginable luxury of time and depth. There were no stories to file online throughout the weekend, no bul-letins to send out on social media, and no pressure to take photos or videos of the action unfolding on the convention floor. When we wanted to talk to someone, we had to do so in person or maybe by cellphone – we did not have BlackBerries or other smartphones to send text messages back and forth at the event or to our editors and readers.

I recognize that the above description comes dangerously close to wistful nostalgia, akin to the people whom I viewed as out-of-touch old-timers back in the 1980s when they complained how television had ruined the House of Commons. I can assure you that is not the intention of the backward look. Without question, some of the innovations in communications since the 1980s have made it possible to talk to a wider range of people, in terms of distance and perspective, than one could ever have approached within forty-eight hours in the past. Journalists are in better touch with their readers. Now, thanks to those constant updates on social media or online, reporters can give their audiences access to the same array of information that they receive in real time. News consumers can make up their own minds about which sources are the most credible or persuasive. So the same online media sources, making huge demands on reporters' time, also relieve journalists of some of their old jobs as curators or gatekeepers, or even analysts, in the process chipping away at the elite status that these roles conferred on the media. What I saw as forty-eight hours of doing my job in depth, telling readers on Monday what I thought they needed to know, could well have seemed to the public like an exclusive, weekend retreat for politicians and the people who cover them, giving them the impression that "we will tell you later, in our own good time, what you need to know."

All-news television channels arrived in the past thirty years as well, and they contributed to the erosion of journalism's gatekeeping function, spe-cifically as it used to exist within the confines of Parliament Hill. When I first arrived on the Hill, my editors were aware of daily events only as they were transmitted to them by bureau chiefs or reporters. By the mid-1990s, all of our bosses kept televisions on their desks, tuned in to all-news cover-age on CBC, CTV, or CPAC, able to see the same events and news confer-ences that we were seeing, and making their own judgments on which developments were the most newsworthy. They could even assess, at long distance, whether their reporters were asking the right questions of politicians. In this way, again, the ongoing conversation between political elites and reporters became less closed or clubby. Moreover, in the past decade, news consumers were similarly empowered through media such as Twitter and Facebook to measure journalists' on-the-job performance in real time, even suggesting questions to be asked of politicians as the scrums or news conferences were under way.

In short, the walls between political journalism and its audience have been knocked down by television and digital technology, as surely as the barriers have been falling down between the electors and the elected. It has been bracing and democratizing, but the speed at which this new era has arrived makes it all the more essential that books such as this one force us to slow down, stop, and reflect on how our civic culture has been transformed.

A key question, now and in the future, revolves around the interactivity of all the new channels of communication in politics. Twitter and Facebook have given political elites some powerful new channels to speak directly to citizens, detouring around traditional media altogether. But when these tools are used as simply another method of one-way broadcasting, the innovations lose some of their democratizing lustre. The arrival of BlackBerries and then other smartphones on Parliament Hill made it much easier to talk to political people and journalists with rapid-fire exchanges of information. They also made it easier for communications directors, public relations (PR) people, and consultants to deliver mere soundbites or spin or talking points, without the bother of follow-up questions or conversations.

Moreover, political journalism, for the most part, is still covering only half the story of these social media innovations, tracking what the political actors transmit online but not the intelligence or data that they might receive from citizens. We know that political parties are increasingly fond of using Facebook for communications, for instance, because messages can be shaped or targeted to sought-after demographic groups. We rarely know who those groups are and why the parties have chosen them. Sophisticated parties can gather intelligence on where their messages are landing with approval and where they need work on Facebook or Twitter. Journalism does not have access to that information, at least not at the same level.

Big-data politics, in effect, is a whole new level of interaction between politicians and public opinion. But while political journalism was adept at keeping up with how more traditional polling transformed the culture of government and politics – with the media eventually commissioning and designing their own polls in the 1980s – it has not yet done the same in trying to keep up with what politicians are learning about voters through the new tools of campaigning and governance. As long as that gap continues, people sophisticated in the ways of big-data politics might well become the new political elites, plying their skills in a realm different from that of voters or journalists who cover politics.

I first met the editors and many of the authors in this book at a Canadian Political Science Association seminar on political marketing in 2009. The presentations and the whole subject itself were revelations to this former student of political science. Finally, political scientists were breaking down a wall that I had observed between my education and the on-the-job learning that I had been doing as a reporter, the gap between theory and practice. Political science, as I had studied it, was more about rules, history, and tradition and less about the day-to-day operation of politics and its ongoing conversation with the public. In many ways, the research that I saw in 2009 was part of the bigger trend that I have written about in this foreword: questions about and reflections on what technological change has meant for how things have always been done, including a democratizing and popularizing process in the academic realm. I have said on a number of occasions that the kind of work to be found in these pages represents the future of political science. As a bonus, to my knowledge, it required no expression of outrage or class warfare on airline flights to Ottawa.

REFERENCE
Delacourt, Susan. 1992. "Loss of Faith." *Globe and Mail,* October 24, D1.

...... Acknowledgments

This book originated from discussions among like-minded scholars who study political elites in Canada and who have noticed change. It was agreed that there is a need for a cohesive forum for new research in this area. The fresh angle? Authors would examine ways that Canadian elites are evolving, or not, as political institutions and political actors adjust to a digital age. It is a political environment characterized by profound societal implications brought about by innovations in communications and information technology.

Political Elites in Canada: Power and Influence in Instantaneous Times is the fourth book in an edited series. *Political Marketing in Canada* (UBC Press, 2012) looked at how political elites are using marketing strategies and tactics to shape their interactions with electors. *Political Communication in Canada: Meet the Press and Tweet the Rest* (UBC Press, 2014) examined how political elites are using different forms of mediated communication to reach Canadians. Then *Permanent Campaigning in Canada* (UBC Press, 2017) considered how political elites are leveraging available public resources to fund a constant state of electioneering. These books appear in the UBC Press series Communication, Strategy, and Politics, dedicated to the publication of innovative scholarly work that investigates the intricate relations among marketing strategy, the media, and political actors, with an emphasis on explaining the implications for Canadian democracy.

The editors wish to thank Susan Delacourt for authoring the foreword. She ranks among the most respected veterans of political journalism in Canada. The author of a number of books herself, including the influential *Shopping for Votes: How Politicians Choose Us and We Choose Them* (Douglas and McIntyre, 2013), and a chapter contributor to *Political Communication in Canada,* she is a big supporter of this series and its community of researchers.

The editors and authors appreciate the insightful suggestions provided by the two referees. Their comments significantly improved the draft manuscript and helped the editors to navigate a complex topic. The authors of the following chapters were a delight to work with, routinely submitting quality work when requested, thereby ensuring that the editorial train ran on time. We would like to thank Alec Dobson, a highly capable student at the University of Western Ontario, who performed a solid copyedit of draft chapters. Amanda Clarke kindly provided some suggestions for the glossary.

Political Elites in Canada has been published with the help of a grant from the Canadian Federation for the Humanities and Social Sciences, through the Awards to Scholarly Publications Program. The authors also wish to acknowledge funding assistance provided by King's University College.

As usual, the enthusiasm, timely communication, and general professionalism of UBC Press personnel is top notch, including Senior Editor Randy Schmidt, Editor Megan Brand, Designer David Drummond, Copy Editor Dallas Harrison, and Indexer Judy Dunlop. The marketing and sales team of Marketing Manager Laraine Coates, Academic Marketing Manager Harmony Johnson, and Publicist and Events Manager Kerry Kilmartin have been a delight to work with on the other books in the Communication, Strategy, and Politics series. We expect they will continue to exhibit their normal high standards with *Political Elites in Canada*.

Abbreviations

ADM	assistant/associate deputy minister
AFN	Assembly of First Nations
CJ	chief justice
CPC	Conservative Party of Canada
CRM	customer relationship management
DBCTs	digitally based communications technologies
DM	deputy minister
ELO	executive legal officer
EX	executive ranks (in government)
GDP	gross domestic product
GP	Green Party
ICTs	information and communications technologies
IS	information services (in government)
LPC	Liberal Party of Canada
MP	Member of Parliament
NDP	New Democratic Party
NPG	New Political Governance
OLO	Office of the Leader of the Official Opposition
PCO	Privy Council Office
PMO	Prime Minister's Office
PR	public relations
PS	public service
SCC	Supreme Court of Canada
TBS	Treasury Board Secretariat

Political Elites in Canada......................................

PART 1

Introduction . . . .

1
Political Elites in the Age of Digital Media

Alex Marland, Andrea Lawlor, and Thierry Giasson

> *Political elites:*
> *Individuals who hold public office, who act as agents of those who do, or who otherwise have greater political influence and power than other citizens do.*
>
> *(from the Glossary)*

Digital media have the potential to revolutionize the relationship between government and the governed. The enhanced information environment, driven by low-cost technology and instantaneous access to information, enables citizens to hold leaders to account in ways previously unimaginable. The speed of communication provides an agile forum for participation. Yet competing political agendas are leveraging digital media, sometimes with negative outcomes for civic engagement. The sheer volume of information can dampen engagement and push citizens toward apathy. In short, society is undergoing an intensification of political competition. Those hoping to maintain the informational status quo are in a power struggle with those seeking to disrupt established institutions.

Elite politics occurs at the intersection of these motivations. *Political Elites in Canada: Power and Influence in Instantaneous Times* focuses on the techniques that elites use to communicate with one another and with the public. It is a timely undertaking given the anti-elitism expressed worldwide and the rise in skepticism toward the use of digital media in political discourse. Many insights presented here about elite communication in Canadian politics are generalizable to democracies everywhere. Studying these behaviours can help us learn more about what it means to be a political elite in today's society and the nature of elite influence.

We set out to explore three overarching themes. We are interested in understanding the nature of *political representation* in a digital environment. Attempts to remove institutional barriers and the ubiquity of digital communications technologies have flattened the once narrow power hierarchy. Traditional elites embedded their status within formal institutions. New ones are informing the policy space using affordable, user-friendly digital technologies such as blogging, social networking, and other modes of online influence. There is a push within existing institutions to diversify representation through formal means, such as a more diverse selection of candidates for election and appointment, and through informal mechanisms, such as broader consultation when making decisions. How do political elites in Canada represent interests using their position and relationship to formal power? How are elites integrating new forms of communication into their offices? Are digital technologies being used to enhance or stymy participation and two-way communication? Which constraints, if any, bind elites in an age of digital media and hypermediatization of politics? These are some of the many questions that we contemplate under the political representation umbrella.

We are also concerned with *political decision making* and the implications of digital communications on elite behaviour. This encompasses the nature of the deliberative process as much as it does the policy outcomes. One measure of elites' ability to represent the public interest is the extent to which societal preferences are reflected in their actions. Historically, citizens have formally passed judgment in elections; increasingly, interelection assessments are rendered through standings in public opinion polls and an ability to win the media cycle. Either way this reflects a belief that democracies require "two-way communication and trust" with citizens (Fenno 1978, 243). An interactive dialogue can be difficult to achieve when the public lacks information about the behaviour of elites. It thus becomes necessary to explore how Canadian elites engage in political or policy decision making, the transparency of these activities, and the role of the public in this process.

Finally, we examine the *political accountability* of elites where digital communications is concerned. Democracy depends on formal structures and processes that shape public policy outcomes (Krane 2007). There are growing expectations that these processes should be out in the open and inclusive, contrary to traditional elite influence, which tended to occur through backroom channels. On occasion, it has even been suggested that elites protect the interests of the public, even when those interests might diverge from public opinion (Converse 1964; Mills 1957). More recent work suggests that leadership can, in fact, lead public opinion, simply by cultivating the list of available alternatives (e.g., Van der Wal 2014). In whatever manner political elites are conceptualized, they are characterized by their access to and influence over those with substantive decision making and representative capacities in the government. Ideally, their activities should be subject to public oversight. However, codes of conduct have been absent from many areas of the government, and conflicts of interest are often difficult to monitor (Stark 2008). For decades, many elites were thought to operate away from the public eye, and the business of the government was presumed to be conducted smoothly enough (Alboim 2012; Presthus 1973; Pross 1992).

What, then, are the corresponding mechanisms to enforce compliance and responsiveness of political elites? To what extent does the presence or absence of accountability impact the practice of representative/responsible government and democracy in Canada? How does the existence of new forms of communication challenge the traditional opaque nature of elite communication? These are some of the many questions that permeate this book, the answers to which are somewhat tempered by the very pace of change that prompts us to ask such questions in the first place. Before embarking on this research undertaking, we need to establish who political elites are.

Elites and Political Elites: The Theoretical Terrain

Whether appointed, elected, hired, or self-proclaimed, elites are individuals in positions of authority who wield influence over citizens. At the broadest level, elites sit atop the economic and social hierarchy. In *The Power Elite*, Charles W. Mills (1957) explained that American society is replete with people who hold positions of authority. They make decisions that affect many lives and can leverage their status to bypass institutional barriers faced by ordinary citizens. Elites are found in the smallest of communities and the largest of metropolises, where family lineage and old money press up against migrants and the nouveau riche. Historically, many of them have risen from an exceedingly narrow segment of society – well-off, white, older, heterosexual, anglophone, Christian, male – meaning that elite structures have generally not mirrored society's diversity. Moreover, public figures ranging from entertainers to elected officials are accorded prestige among their kind and by their followers. They are attuned to the importance of media relations, Mills noted (5), but there is so much interest in celebrities that the masses are distracted from paying attention to those at the top of the power hierarchy with lower profiles (359–60).

Much of this rings true in Canada. Yet there is a more nuanced picture of power structures north of the forty-ninth parallel, heavily influenced by ethnicity and political culture and often pronounced in provinces and small communities. As John Porter (1965) outlined in *The Vertical Mosaic: An Analysis of Social Class and Power in Canada,* positions of authority in Canadian society have historically been held by men of British or French ancestry, while citizens of other heritages have faced barriers to upward mobility. The upper class shaped churches, corporations, media, political parties, the public service, trade unions, and other institutions, each of which had its organizational norms. This led Porter to conclude that ethnicity was the dominant characteristic of Canadian society. Others have observed the influence of regionalism, social class, religion, and education and how some elites switch roles within and between bureaucratic, corporate, and political worlds (e.g., Clement 1975). If Porter were to update his work today, he would surely comment on the ascent of women among elite enclaves, reflect on how the country is attempting to reach reconciliation with Indigenous peoples, and examine the erosion of traditional media gatekeeping. Those who study the Canadian establishment add that, since the 1990s, the globalization of business and the influence of online technologies have been turning the upper echelon into more of a meritocracy (Newman 2013). Furthermore, we struggle to establish the socio-economic characteristics of those who engage in "elite-challenging" behaviour and to define the nature of that behaviour (Painter-Main 2014).

However, no matter their sociodemographic characteristics, elites know the value of leveraging status. Social historians who research the public and private lives of Ottawa elites tell tales about how those with ambition navigate their way to the top (e.g., Gwyn 1984). They are willing to employ personalism and their connections to brush aside institutional barriers (Savoie 2010, 214–15). They tend to congregate in "a very similar set of social circles" (Clement 1975, 262) and are prone to hold convictions disconnected from those of the public, giving rise to populist uprisings that unnerve the established hegemony. Indeed, social diversity in itself does not resolve ideological disconnects: Canadian elites' philosophical orientations are increasingly a function of their occupational positions rather than their class backgrounds (Ornstein and Stevenson 1999).

Analyzing the political power of those with considerable economic and social capital is difficult.[1] Elites do not generally flaunt their ability to access each other. Some of them exert political clout by mingling in private settings with the political class, by offering resources, and by sharing their knowledge and connections. Others hold sway over those who travel in political circles by exploiting their fame and ability to command media attention. Some do both. How can we know in which, if any, political activities Canada's wealthiest families – among them the Thompson, Saputo, Rogers, Irving, and Weston families – are involved? What of the CEOs of Canada's largest companies? The few news reports that identify the Quebec-based Desmarais family (Power Corporation) and the Beaudoins (Bombardier) as heavy donors to Liberals and Conservatives, to identify only a couple of examples, offer limited insights into a hidden world. How can we be definitive about the politicking of the heads of labour unions, many of whom are affiliated with the Canadian Labour Congress, which has ties to the New Democratic Party? Likewise, cursory information about galas and parties at which socialites hobnob with aspirants and office holders offers no insight into the flow of political power. Demystifying the interconnected web of the upper class requires some broader context beyond information available through media coverage, lobbying reports, financial documents released by an elections agency, or an individual's social media posts. Unravelling all of that would be a formidable socio-anthropological undertaking that extends well beyond our present objectives.

Turning to politics and governance, there is not even an agreed way to define the elites who exercise political power. They are traditionally described as individuals "who in any society rank toward the top of the (presumably closely intercorrelated) dimensions of interest, involvement, and influence in politics" (Putnam 1971, 651). An earlier description defines them as "a small stratum of individuals much more highly involved in political thought, discussion, and action than the rest of the population" (Dahl 2005, 90). Understanding the term invokes epithets such as "ruling class, political class, elite, power elite, and leadership group," sometimes applied synonymously, other times working in deliberate opposition to one another (Stanworth and Giddens 1974, 2). As Mills (1957) noted, some are public figures and lauded as celebrities, whereas others are unknowns who toil in obscurity.

How, though, to distinguish political elites from those who occupy high positions in business, the bureaucracy, labour unions, the media, and other aspects of society who might or might not dabble in the political realm? Moreover, the concept has application to new forms of elites. Even as social media enable pan-Canadian mobilization – such as the Idle No More movement, which connected formerly disparate Indigenous voices (see Coates 2015) – those who participate in politicking are themselves elites of some form. The reason is that people involved with political parties, interest groups, and social movements are attuned to public policy in ways that other citizens are not. In whatever manner we conceptualize political elites, we must be mindful that there are different layers of political information among citizens. For instance, through social media, governments are disseminating news content, thereby displacing the fourth estate's role of filtering information (Garland, Tambini, and Couldry 2017). Lobbyists, religious groups, antiglobalization protesters, social movements, trade associations, charities, corporations – these and countless other organizations are producing digital information every day. So are individuals. Political activists and ordinary citizens have been exerting influence online over their fellow citizens for over a decade now (Harmon 2004).

If "only a small minority of politically, socially, and economically privileged Canadians are quite knowledgeable about politics" (Fournier 2002, 93), then it stands to reason that those discussing politics online are prone to be mistaken as a representative sample of the broader public mood. We are left with the muddy waters of trying to differentiate the "higher circles" of the power elite from those who participate in protests and other forms of political expression compared with backroom actors and the "ordinary" people who shun the limelight (Mills 1957). The confusion might be related to the overlapping nature of political processes and concepts. Scholars have many concerns, yet they lack a definitive understanding of the complexities of political power in policy making (e.g., McFarland 2007).

Given this, how can we conclusively determine who warrants the label of a "political elite"? Porter (1965) confined that term to the executive and judicial branches of the government. Certainly, the cabinet and higher courts represent the pinnacle of the political system, particularly when there are bursts of executive federalism or judicial activism. In comparison, *Elite Accommodation in Canadian Politics* (Presthus 1973) afforded this treatment to the legislative branch, the public service, and the heads of interest groups, all of which revolve around cabinet in some way. That study differentiated Canadian elites in the following manner: "The 'political elite' includes legislators and bureaucrats in the official government apparatus and private interest group leaders; the 'government elite' includes only legislators and bureaucrats; while interest group leaders and their representatives will be characterized as 'private elites'" (3). This begs the question of whether interest groups and the mass media ought to be studied because of their roles in political life or excluded because of their corporate ties. To us their exclusion is inconceivable given the transformative social changes brought about, in part, by changes in communications strategies and technologies.

The political elite, then, is an amorphous concept. It encompasses the three branches of the government, the extraparliamentary wings of political parties, and the upper echelon of public administration. Political advisers are included. After that, the political activities of media and interest groups warrant attention. New dynamics mean that everyday citizens who interact online with powerful figures should be studied, as should the implications of digital media for how political elites behave. A wide net must be cast to consider the broadening variety of political actors who wade into and out of circles of influence.

Political Elites in Canada: Who They Are Today

In contemporary Canadian scholarship, conceptions of political elites are often narrowly drawn, limiting the concept to senior politicians, high-powered civil servants or partisans, and partisan-aligned corporate interests (e.g., Lindquist 1992). Although our aim here is not to create a taxonomy, it is helpful to identify the positions of political authority and influencers, including some portrayed as apolitical. Table 1.1 summarizes diverse types in the Canadian political system. That it contains so many positions but is not an exhaustive inventory speaks to the variety of political elites in Canada. There is no mention of those whose power has been waning, such as the church and party financiers, or of those who have a formidable presence in crisis situations, such as the military and police. We do not discuss elites who represent Canada abroad, namely ambassadors and members of foreign missions. As well, there are varied power structures within Indigenous governance and of Indigenous peoples in Canadian society not addressed here. We are also not preoccupied with elites' sociodemographic composition (but see Chapter 5). Rather, we illustrate the use of their power, the relationships among these elites, and how these relationships are changing in a digital era characterized by enhanced communication ability and monitor-

TABLE 1.1

Political elite types in Canadian politics and government

Elite type	Functions	Examples of political actors
Formal executive	Head of state, constitutional and ceremonial duties	Monarch, governor general, lieutenant governors
Political executive	Apex of government decision making; main spokespersons for government	Prime minister, premier, cabinet ministers
Legislators	Representing constituent concerns; voting in the legislature	MPs, senators, members of provincial legislatures, mayors, city/town councillors
Officers and officials of the legislature	Watchdog organizations charged with reviewing, regulating, or overseeing government decisions; annual reports to the legislature	Access to information commissioner, auditor general, chief electoral officer, commissioner of lobbying, conflict of interest and ethics commissioner, official languages commissioner, privacy commissioner, public sector integrity commissioner
Political staff	Agents of senior public officials	Partisans in the PMO, premiers' offices, ministers' offices, opposition offices, legislators' offices
Judiciary	Interpreters of the Constitution and laws; rule on legal matters	Supreme Court justices, lower court and federal judges, crown lawyers
Senior civil service	Senior members of the permanent administration of government; might or might not exhibit partisan leanings	Clerk of the Privy Council, central agency personnel, DMs, ADMs, directors, chairs of boards, officers of the legislature, diplomats and consular officers
Political parties	Senior office holders in the extraparliamentary wing of a party	Leaders, riding association presidents, candidates/nominees
Interest groups and social movements	Groups of people who seek to influence the government and/or society	Leaders or spokespersons of corporations, unions, business organizations, professional organizations, single-issue groups, community groups
Lobbyists and public affairs personnel	Individuals who cultivate relationships with senior political personnel and seek to persuade them about courses of action	Government relations personnel, in-house lobbyists

Elite type	Functions	Examples of political actors
Traditional media	Operators and employees of broadcast and print media; act as the fourth estate to hold the government to account	Publishers, editors, news anchors, television personalities and hosts, syndicated columnists, journalists, broadcast producers, media research teams
Online influencers	Citizen journalists; heavy users of digital media who become opinion leaders	Social media mobilizers, bloggers, media aggregators
Political consultants/ advisers	For-hire or in-house communications strategists and boutique operators	Pollsters, marketers, political strategists
Intelligentsia	Purveyors of informed opinion in the public sphere	Think tanks, academics, pundits, public intellectuals

ing of elite behaviour. It is important to understand that some individuals belong in more than one category. This is instructive: the more roles converge, the more potential influence an individual has over others, and the more power becomes concentrated in one person. This helps to explain why prime ministers and premiers hold so much sway. It suggests that, generally speaking, the most powerful elites are those who simultaneously hold multiple positions of authority.

At the top of Table 1.1 and the elite pyramid is the formal executive. The institution of the Crown is often cited as a relic of a bygone era, playing a meaningful role in the parliamentary process in rare and sometimes obscure cases. The criticism is signalled by Canada's waning British connection, the appointed nature of the monarch's representatives, and a position that rubber-stamps the first minister's requests. Public opinion about Canada's relationship with the British monarchy goes through ebbs and flows, with support for continuance seemingly rooted in strong public approval of Queen Elizabeth II (CTV 2016) and outbursts of anger spurred by reports of dubious financial costs of the Canadian monarchy (Zemanek 2011). Rarely is there anything but nominal public discussion about what a republican head of state might look like – an essential question to resolve given the governor general's role in legislative approval and role as commander-in-chief of the Canadian Forces. Even if largely formal responsibilities are retained by a homegrown head of state, that individual would have to maintain a greater sense of relevance in the contemporary political age and would be subject to greater media scrutiny locally. This does not even delve into matters such as the method of appointment or the nature of its functions. In the absence of significant political pressure for change, the monarchy of Canada busies itself with ceremonial duties, such as award ceremonies and the delivery of throne speeches.

The de facto political executive attracts considerable media and academic attention. The prime minister and the Prime Minister's Office (PMO), along with the heavy hitters on the most powerful cabinet committees, sit at the unquestionable centre of power. With respect to the acting political executive, there is a widening scope of centripetal influence in policy-making and agenda-setting circles, and there are perceptions that everything flows through "the centre" of the government (e.g., Savoie 1999). The growth of communications and marketing practices brings a need for more staff and a confrontation of partisan/political priorities with an apolitical public service. This requires resources. Thus, generally speaking, larger jurisdictions and administrations that have been in office the longest are prone to house the most entrenched central operations. Prime ministers and premiers avail themselves of these supports for priority files. Sometimes this strains the federalist system as premiers lobby on the national stage for elite accommodation that favours their interests. Globalization and the recent dearth of first ministers' conferences, which shower national attention on regional grievances, confound the ability of premiers to become household names whose demands must be placated (e.g., Tossuti 2002).

The debate about centralized authority over departmental communications is a healthy one. Political communicators prioritize urgent directives from the PMO and must work with the public service communications personnel required to uphold written practices established by the Privy Council Office (PCO), Treasury Board Secretariat (TBS), and Public Services and Procurement. This top-down hierarchy contrasts with the precarious nature of some external mechanisms of accountability, such as the parliamentary budget officer and freedom of information requests. Other government watchdog agencies – such as the Offices of the Auditor General, the Chief Electoral Officer, and the Official Languages Commissioner – have periodically set the political agenda over the years.

In the face of institutional barriers, government leaders have advanced their agendas using mainstream and social media as their platforms. This shift toward a personality-driven executive has been a long time in the making, beginning with radio broadcasts and televised debates (Cross 2004). Prime ministers and premiers dominate the mainstream media or manufacture their own coverage through social media platforms. Justin Trudeau and his team have embraced social networking technology, which enhances his celebrity image and connection with ordinary citizens. There is more going on than selfies; the Liberal prime minister has participated in seemingly uncontrolled question-and-answer sessions with everyday Canadians online and in traditional media. Yet the Trudeau administration is the latest to make copious use of government resources for publicity, particularly media events as well as a growing online presence for the prime minister (Boutilier 2016). At the federal and provincial levels, centralization of government power shows no sign of easing off in a 24/7 hybrid media environment in which information is constantly emerging, shared, and discussed in real time across platforms.

When media attention focuses squarely on first ministers, it detracts from the roles of other parliamentarians. What individual legislators had to say mattered more in late nineteenth century, yet representatives have always struggled to balance the public interest with agency for constituents (Franks 1987, 58). As political parties formed, members of Parliament and their provincial counterparts cultivated a tribal loyalty to those sharing their party label, a loyalty that shifted to deference to the leadership circle as broadcast media emerged. Not only did the number of backbenchers grow – there were 180 MPs in the first Parliament, whereas now there are 338 MPs – but so did the size and complexity of the government, in conjunction with the technological ability to coordinate internal messaging. Today parliamentarians are commonly thought to have limited capacities to represent their constituencies or hold the behaviour of the political executive or party leadership to account (Cross 2000). Many of them exercise (presumably meagre) power through committee or constituency work. Even then strong party discipline and message control can severely constrain independent thought. That said, technological advances might counter these effects: through social media and strong local connections, MPs have potent means to develop and communicate with their constituents and with people outside their electoral districts. Politicians can reach out to Canadians with a frequency previously enjoyed only by a select few with a team of employees and large budgets. Problems can be heard and sometimes resolved in real time. Communications and criticism are direct, low cost, and managed by just one or two staffers. But it is unknown at which junctures this transforms into real political influence as opposed to conveying the illusion of strong representation, particularly among backbenchers. They learn early on to fall in line or face the wrath of a party centre that jettisons candidates based on their digital footprints (Daro 2015).

Staffers in political offices appear to be on the rise both in number and in power. Political operatives in the PMO and ministers' offices have access to politically sensitive information. Staff assist ministers in directing the actions of senior public servants at the department level. Those in the PMO have a hand in the complex and interweaving operations of many government ministries and agencies (Esselment and Wilson 2017). Elected and appointed officials are displaced on the spectrum of power by unelected hired hands who represent the prime minister and who employ digital communications to coordinate actions across departments and agencies. It has been a long-standing practice that political staffers stay out of the public eye; however, this norm is changing. These influential individuals are often the subjects of media attention during election campaigns, and they maintain social media profiles after elections. In particular, Prime Minister Trudeau's chief of staff and his principal secretary are active Twitter users, even making news for engaging in policy debates online (Farooq 2016). This strategy is fraught with risk, for ignoring the rules and regulations that govern staffers' actions and advancements could result in misstatement of their authority (Brodie 2012).

Likewise, public engagement by members of the judiciary can be controversial. The prominence of the courts in directing policy as well as receiving and adjudicating the role of interests in policy making drives both criticism and applause. It is marked by a perceived increase in judicial activism that encourages legislatures to revisit policy, particularly with respect to the Supreme Court of Canada's (SCC) interpretation of the Charter of Rights and Freedoms (Macfarlane 2012). Judicial enforcement and interpretation of the Charter significantly constrain the power and composition of elite networks in Canada. The prominence of judicial advocacy extends to the chief justice of the SCC, who periodically delivers public speeches about matters of public policy, or media coverage of the comments of judges on the decisions made by policy makers. Even in the digital age, Canadians continue to rely on news coverage of court decisions that, like all news, is subject to media agendas and biases (Sauvageau, Schneiderman, and Taras 2011).

Moreover, the appointment of judges is a constant source of concern. Prime Minister Harper went from initiating a public hearing process for his first SCC nominee in 2006 to publicly sparring with former Chief Justice Beverley McLachlin over a failed appointment in 2014. Controversial remarks made by a Federal Court justice when he was a provincial judge led the Canadian Judicial Council to hold an inquiry in 2016 about his suitability to serve. In contrast, Prime Minister Trudeau's first appointment to the top bench was smoother, yet his mechanism for appointment supplanted multiparty representation of MPs with an external committee that he appointed (Fine 2016). Ideological and partisan undercurrents flow through the one branch of government positioned as apolitical. The Supreme Court might well be a culmination of the weighing of evidence, but its members are unelected elites with considerable power who can retain their positions until reaching seventy-five years of age.

This type of job security is a feature of many aspects of the Canadian public service. This hearkens back to sociologist Max Weber's criteria for an ideal bureaucracy, namely a division of labour among skilled experts who follow a chain of command and written rules and who collectively operate as an "efficient machine" (Swedberg and Agevall 2016, 20). The influence of top mandarins in the public service, particularly the clerk of the Privy Council, has always been significant (e.g., Granatstein 2015). At times, the urgent stubbornness of political personnel clashes with the process-driven meritocracy and organizational hierarchy of the government. In his introduction of New Political Governance (NPG) associated with the increased politicization of public administrations in Westminster-style democracies, Aucoin (2012) speaks of turf wars between partisan loyalists and civil servants. Changes in the communications environment, increased demands for transparency, and a more competitive and polarized political market are identified as causes of this trend. The phenomenon is depicted as a threat both to an impartial public administration and to managerial performance.

The nature of the influence of the public administration hierarchy has diversified as the government has grown. The proliferation of government surveillance agents such as the auditor general and the parliamentary budget officer is a noteworthy trend. Legislative steps to enhance transparency in the early 2000s included improved freedom of information requests and creation of the positions of conflict of interest and ethics commissioner, lobbying commissioner, and public sector integrity commissioner. As digital technologies became more prevalent in Canadian society, so did the open-government movement. All can be understood as attempts by elites to put representation, decision making, and accountability back at the fore of the relationship between the government and citizens. For instance, executives of businesses and charities seek to mingle with ministers and senior bureaucrats over meals and at events, but now they must register with the lobbying commissioner, and government employees must pay for their own tickets and meals, and these expenses are posted online. Yet top public officials, including Prime Minister Trudeau, have hosted exclusive private events for large donors, something that Minister of Finance Bill Morneau has defended as a mechanism to "support the democratic process" and "good people in public life" (quoted in Payton 2016). Public outrage at the impression of "pay-to-play" fundraising led both the ethics commissioner and the lobbying commissioner to initiate investigations (Thompson 2016). This response demonstrates the important role of officers who report to the legislature to advance matters in the public interest when elected officials themselves do not.

Another area where power is shifting is the composition of membership in political parties. There is decreasing grassroots volunteerism and (paid) party membership numbers. In their place are the centralization of authority in executive offices, increased scrutiny of candidates and grassroots fundraising, and precise control of communications. The party leader has become the face of the party and is generally perceived as being responsible for political successes and failures. Interactivity is predominantly digital as members vote online in leadership contests and as parties fundraise through email and social media. The move by the Liberal Party of Canada to dispense with membership in favour of no-fee registration is a stunning example of how party structures are evolving. Trudeau branded the renewal of the party constitution as part of a "movement" (Bryden 2016), implying that the Liberal organization uses technology to advance the interests of a coalition of everyday Canadians. He did not refer to new clauses for the leader to wrest control over election platform development and campaign committee composition away from party members (Naumetz 2016).

The relevance of membership in political parties is declining as the ability of special interests to mobilize citizens grows. Elite accommodation occurs when interest groups and government officials interact. In a robust democracy, pluralist theory holds that representatives of political interests external to the government will compete to influence public policy and that majority and minority interests are mediated by politicians (Dahl 1956). In Canada, these groups have varied structures, resources, and methods, but all of them have some sort of mission to achieve (Presthus 1973, 117). As with political parties, the power and influence of interest groups and social movements are changing considerably with digital technologies. The prevention of direct contributions to parties and candidates and the increases to third-party spending (see Crandall and Lawlor 2014) force organized interests to find less direct, and often less transparent, ways to influence elite behaviour. Stricter political finance rules result in shifts in advocacy tactics that include increased court challenges, social media campaigns, and organized protests. Social movements build momentum by using inexpensive digital media tools to connect with their audiences. Elites and non-elites alike gather in the virtual sphere to put an issue on the public agenda and to pressure decisions made by public officials.

Other outsiders who seek to influence those with political power include people in the government relations or public affairs business. The activities of registered lobbyists who meet with political decision makers are under-represented both in the media and in the academic literature. Lobbyists and those in the government relations field make it their business to interact with fellow elites (e.g., Bennedsen and Feldmann 2006). In Canada, we lack an understanding of how their role has changed with constraints introduced under new legislation, such as the Accountability Act (2006), and with technological and social changes. This lack of knowledge matters, given that every day parliamentarians are contacted by over a dozen registered lobbyists, and lobbying activity has increased considerably in the Trudeau government (Abma 2016; McGregor, Mayeda, and Kennedy 2010). Relationships between the lobby community and its political clients can change policy and alter the communications tactics used by the government. These relationships typically go unnoticed by citizens but are much more visible through digital tracking of information and emails obtained through freedom of information requests.

The traditional media are among the few providers of information on elite activity and arguably the last body that can hold institutional elites to account. Which people own the media and how political elites try to control coverage have long been objects of study (e.g., Levine 1993; Taras 1990). Media ownership confers control over the dissemination of ideas and how information is presented. Editors and journalists decide what is newsworthy as they balance what politicians publicly disclose and what is in the public interest to report. They are gatekeepers who compete to obtain information, frame news, and set the public agenda (Castelló and Montagut 2011, 517). Thus, the concentration of ownership concerns scholars, particularly when a media organization communicates content over different platforms.

The decentralization of mainstream media amid the rise of social media, civic journalism, and blogging is creating a new category of elites. Parliamentary press galleries are wrestling with accreditation issues (McQuigge 2016) even as the circulation of fake political news on social media illustrates how important fact checking is (Cheadle 2016). Adopting these technologies has enabled mainstream media to grow their research capacities, despite waning demand for print media and tendencies to republish content freely travelling on social media. Yet the challenges are obvious: mainstream media now compete with emergent digital platforms in capturing audiences and selling advertising. The growth of digital media and citizen journalism has far-reaching implications for mainstream news media, as it does for political actors. These implications include a forced presence online, engagement with a broader array of information providers, and a reduced ability to control information. Although mainstream media might still qualify as part of the elite, they are under fire as much as any political actor.

An emerging form of the elite is the everyday citizen who develops an online following. Increasingly, elites include people who wield power through their ability to connect with thousands and even millions of people online. This power ranges from the influence of individuals who have many online followers to lesser knowns whose social media posts abruptly destabilize political agendas (Karlsen 2015; Vaccari and Valeriani 2015). The turn to online communications alters elite-citizen relations given that voices typically sidelined now have a pulpit. Increasingly, online influencers are better positioned to promote political messages than many higher-ranking officials (Small et al. 2014). Digital media have profound repercussions for how political elites are conceptualized and how they operate.

Among the fastest-rising "new" elites are political consultants and advisers. These figures play the roles of part partisan actor and part public servant as they serve as mediators between the public and the government. Pollsters, advertisers, marketing strategists, and communications professionals are receiving unprecedented attention from the media and the public. This profile increases their ability to influence the policy judgments of their clients and to advance their opinions and perspectives through the mass media (Pétry and Bastien 2013). Digital communications technologies enhance the speed and frequency with which they can get their messages out. For instance, the tracking of poll results has gone from an item of interest to a mandatory in-house strategy for political parties (Turcotte and Vodrey 2017). The sphere of influence of pollsters extends to the media when they provide commentary on public impressions of policy and party elites. Pollsters give a voice to ordinary Canadians, confronting elite opinion with public opinion, simultaneously reducing the power of parliamentarians and pundits (Adams 2007, xii). Nevertheless, the concept of political consultants is a more appropriate description of the American arena. In Canada, political strategists are the norm, as this book will show.

In many ways, the role of political strategists is like that of the intelligentsia. The influence of public figures such as academics, think tanks, media personalities, and pundits on policy decisions and agenda setting is not as pronounced as some of their more institutionalized counterparts. Nevertheless, public intellectuals are routinely called on to provide information – and in some cases legitimacy – for the opinions and policy goals of other political actors. Political pundits are often better able to influence public policy and public opinion precisely because of their relative distance from the political process (e.g., Rogstad 2014; Wiseman 2013).

Each set of actors above represents its own locus of power. There is a need for more work in these fields together, particularly as power structures evolve with communications technologies. We lack an overarching understanding of how political elites interact and how their actions can complement, influence, or oppose one another's policy goals. Among the reasons is difficulty gathering data from elites themselves. This volume makes strides in addressing these gaps in knowledge in the digital media environment.

Outline of the Book
This book explores who Canadian political elites are, how they exert power, and how communications in the digital era has changed access to and application of power. Questions of decision making, representation, and accountability are addressed to determine to what extent the range of policy influencers affects our understanding of their role in governance and representation. An overarching research objective is to consider whether the role of political elites in the government or with access to the government is changing in the digital media environment.

The book is organized into four parts. In this first chapter we have provided an overview of the core theoretical underpinnings of the concept of political elites and sought to identify them in Canadian society. In Chapter 2, Alex Marland and Anna Esselment delve into methodological challenges for researchers, including getting access to data from government actors. They conduct a social experiment by contacting a small number of people who interact with political elites and seek suggestions for the best ways to secure interviews with public officials. Their tips and tactics will be useful to emerging and experienced social scientists alike, particularly when the subject matter concerns remote and shadowy political or partisan processes. That guidance lays the groundwork for ensuing chapters and further study.

Part 2 tackles political elites within the government. Contributors explore how political elites navigate interest representation and policy making with government officials and institutions. This section contrasts elites who obtain their positions by election and appointment. It highlights core differences in maintaining accountability. This includes the importance of political staff and their roles with civil servants along with those of PMO staff in influencing political agendas within departments. In Chapter 3, Robert Shepherd and Bryan Evans examine how communications processes intersect with the roles of senior civil servants in policy making. They present insights collected from in-depth interviews with well-placed administrators to describe the implications of changes in the media landscape for public administration. This leads into Chapter 4, by Jennifer Robson and Paul Wilson, who examine the tension and compatibility between political and permanent personnel in the government. They draw on surveys of Canadian federal public servants and in-depth interviews with political staff to understand how they are coping with the direct and indirect pressures of a 24/7 media environment. The next two contributions consider the provincial context. In Chapter 5, Melanee Thomas, Allison Harell, and Tania Gosselin examine online media coverage of premiers in Alberta, British Columbia, and Ontario to ascertain to what extent these leaders attract attention and to what degree media treatment differed on the basis of a premier's gender. J.P. Lewis and Stéphanie Yates build on this examination in Chapter 6 through their study of how all Canadian premiers use social media or at least how their handlers exploit the resources of the premier's office to mount a social media presence. Their review of videos posted to Facebook, Twitter, YouTube, and government websites is a timely understanding of connectivity with citizens in a controlled manner that bypasses news filters. The chapter is buttressed by Erin Crandall, who looks at how SCC judges – perhaps at once the most elitist and egalitarian of all – operate in the digital world. In Chapter 7, she conducts a media analysis of the public dispute between Prime Minister Harper and Chief Justice McLachlin and weighs in on how the courts are adapting to the evolving public environment.

Part 3 turns to political elites who operate outside government. Chapter 8, by Cristine de Clercy, delves into the operations of the Liberal Party caucus. Her analysis of the party constitution, supplemented by information procured from the caucus chair, seeks to understand the relationships among the party leader, the caucus, party members, and the electorate. In Chapter 9, Jamie Gillies and David Coletto investigate the prevalence of political consultants in Canada. Their in-depth interviews with senior political strategists uncover insider/outsider dynamics within the party's inner circle and the implications of digital technologies for traditional approaches to campaigning. Ensuing chapters look specifically at social media. Geneviève Chacon, Andrea Lawlor, and Thierry Giasson's analysis in Chapter 10 moves beyond conventional understandings of elites by researching the diverse informed publics who participated in campaign-related online chatter using the #cdnpoli and #elxn42 hashtags. Likewise, in Chapter 11, Fenwick McKelvey, Marianne Côté, and Vincent Raynauld offer a detailed case study of the use of Twitter by two external, non-traditional political actors and how they helped to shape campaign coverage. Then, in Chapter 12, Julie Killin and Tamara Small examine messages posted to election candidates' Twitter accounts. Their coding for national versus local messages reveals the extent to which party candidates parrot central messaging as opposed to engaging in constituency-level dialogue. In Chapter 13, Rachel Laforest draws on research reports and in-depth interviews to document how Canadian interest groups use digital technologies. Her investigation seeks to get past the chronic resource constraints to identify how non-profits are benefiting from inexpensive technologies.

Finally, in Part 4, we reflect on all of these case studies. In the concluding chapter, we draw out the broader implications for knowledge about political elites and their communications behaviour. We argue that, at a minimum, digital media are disrupting traditional conceptualizations of this powerful class of citizens. However, taken together, the chapters point to a stronger trend in the evolution of who constitutes the elite and what drives their behaviour, linked, in good part, to digital media.

The analyses in these chapters move beyond the question of who is part of the political elite in Canada. They study what elites do to represent groups and interests and how they communicate these perspectives. These analyses account for the greater communication freedom experienced by (most) elites in a digital working environment as well as the challenges of maintaining confidentiality or secrecy. In this way, this volume differs from standard institutionalist approaches. It embarks on a new path of study that focuses on why and when political actors use communication strategies to divert decision making to their advantage. We look at how people in positions of authority can break down traditional hierarchies and circumvent rules to interact directly with other elites and members of the public. This implies reordering traditional distributions of power. As this volume attests, the outcomes of these changes are still unfolding.

NOTE

1 Information in this paragraph was gleaned from CB Staff (2016); Employment and Social Development Canada (2016); and McMahon (2016).

REFERENCES

Abma, Derek. 2016. "Federal Lobbying Activity Heats Up, Reflects Liberals' Friendlier Stance with Consultant Lobbyists." *Hill Times,* March 21, 1.

Adams, Michael. 2007. "Foreword." In *Polling and Public Opinion: A Canadian Perspective,* edited by Peter M. Butler, ix–xv. Toronto: University of Toronto Press.

Alboim, Elly. 2012. "On the Verge of Total Dysfunction: Government, Media, and Communications." In *How Canadians Communicate IV: Media and Politics,* edited by David Taras and Christopher Waddell, 45–54. Edmonton: Athabasca University Press.

Aucoin, Peter. 2012. "New Political Governance in Westminster Systems: Impartial Public Administration and Management Performance at Risk." *Governance: An International Journal of Policy, Administration, and Institutions* 25, 2: 177–99. https://doi.org/10.1111/j.1468-0491.2012.01569.x.

Bennedsen, Morten, and Sven E. Feldmann. 2006. "Lobbying Bureaucrats." *Scandinavian Journal of Economics* 108, 4: 643–68. https://doi.org/10.1111/j.1467-9442.2006.00473.x.

Boutilier, Alex. 2016. "Privy Council Office Wants $600,000 More to Update Trudeau's Website." *Toronto Star,* March 5. https://www.thestar.com/news/canada/2016/03/05/privy-council-office-wants-600000-more-to-update-trudeaus-website.html.

Brodie, Ian. 2012. "In Defense of Political Staff." *Canadian Parliamentary Review* 35, 3: 33–39.

Bryden, Joan. 2016. "Trudeau Promotes Wide-Open Liberal Party, End to Party Membership." *Global News,* April 3. https://globalnews.ca/news/2615587/trudeau-promotes-wide-open-liberal-party-end-to-party-membership/.

Castelló, Enric, and Marta Montagut. 2011. "Journalists, Reframing, and Party Public Relations Consultants: Strategies in Morning Talk Radio." *Journalism Studies* 12, 4: 506–21. https://doi.org/10.1080/1461670X.2010.530969.

CB Staff. 2016. "Canada's Richest People: The Complete Top 100 Ranking." *Canadian Business,* December 7. http://www.canadianbusiness.com/lists-and-rankings/richest-people/100-richest-canadians-complete-list/.

Cheadle, Bruce. 2016. "As Fake News Spreads, MPs Consider Importance of Canada's Local Papers." *CTV News,* November 17. http://www.ctvnews.ca/politics/as-fake-news-spreads-mps-consider-importance-of-canada-s-local-papers-1.3165962.

Clement, Wallace. 1975. *The Canadian Corporate Elite.* Toronto: McClelland and Stewart.

Coates, Ken. 2015. *IdleNoMore and the Remaking of Canada.* Regina: University of Regina Press.

Converse, Philip E. 1964. "The Nature of Belief Systems in Mass Publics." In *Ideology and Discontent,* edited by David Apter, 206–61. New York: Free Press.

Crandall, Erin, and Andrea Lawlor. 2014. "Third Party Election Spending in Canada and the United Kingdom: A Comparative Analysis." *Election Law Journal* 13, 4: 476–92.

Cross, William P. 2000. "Members of Parliament, Voters, and Democracy in the Canadian House of Commons." Parliamentary Perspectives Series, No. 3, Canadian Study of Parliament Group, Ottawa. http://cspg-gcep.ca/pdf/Bill_Cross-e.pdf.

–. 2004. *Political Parties.* Vancouver: UBC Press.

CTV. 2016. "7 in 10 Canadians Still Support Ties to Monarchy: Nanos Survey." *CTV News,* May 14. http://www.ctvnews.ca/canada/7-in-10-canadians-still-support-ties-to-monarchy-nanos-survey-1.2902716.

Dahl, Robert. 1956. *A Preface to Democratic Theory.* Chicago: University of Chicago Press.

–. 2005. *Who Governs? Democracy and Power in an American City.* 1961; reprinted, New Haven, CT: Yale University Press.

Daro, Ishmael N. 2015. "Is Your Online Footprint Clean Enough to Run for Office?" *BuzzFeed,* August 28. https://www.buzzfeed.com/ishmaeldaro/never-tweet.

Employment and Social Development Canada. 2016. "Labour Organizations in Canada 2015." https://www.canada.ca/content/dam/esdc-edsc/migration/documents/eng/resources/info/publications/union_coverage/UnionCoverage_EN.pdf.

Esselment, Anna Lennox, and Paul Wilson. 2017. "Campaigning from the Centre." In *Permanent Campaigning in Canada,* edited by Alex Marland, Thierry Giasson, and Anna Esselment, 222–40. Vancouver: UBC Press.

Farooq, Ramisha. 2016. "Gerald Butts, Trudeau's Principal Secretary, Ignites Twitter Skirmish over ISIS Policy." *CBC News,* February 9. http://www.cbc.ca/news/politics/trudeau-twitter-butts-isis-policy-1.3440155.

Fenno, Richard F. 1978. *Home Style: House Members in Their Districts.* New York: HarperCollins.

Fine, Sean. 2016. "Supreme Court Hearings Provide Transparency, Respect to Process." *Globe and Mail,* October 23. https://www.theglobeandmail.com/news/national/supreme-court-hearings-provide-transparency-respect-to-process/article32486760/.

Fournier, Patrick. 2002. "The Uninformed Canadian Voter." In *Citizen Politics: Research Theory in Canadian Political Behaviour,* edited by Joanna Everitt and Brenda O'Neill, 92–109. Don Mills, ON: Oxford University Press.

Franks, C.E.S. 1987. *The Parliament of Canada*. Toronto: University of Toronto Press.

Garland, Ruth, Damian Tambini, and Nick Couldry. 2017. "Has Government Been Mediatized? A UK Perspective." *Media, Culture, and Society*, 40, 4: 496–513.. https://doi.org/10.1177/0163443717713261.

Granatstein, Jack L. 2015. *The Ottawa Men: The Civil Service Mandarins, 1935–1957*. Oakville, ON: Rock's Mills Press.

Gwyn, Sandra. 1984. *The Private Capital: Ambition and Love in the Age of Macdonald and Laurier*. Toronto: McClelland and Stewart.

Harmon, Amy. 2004. "Survey Finds 'Opinion Leaders' Logging on for Political News." *New York Times*, February 5. http://www.nytimes.com/2004/02/05/us/2004-campaign-internet-survey-finds-opinion-leaders-logging-for-political.html.

Karlsen, Rune. 2015. "Followers Are Opinion Leaders: The Role of People in the Flow of Political Communication on and beyond Social Networking Sites." *European Journal of Communication* 30, 3: 301–18. https://doi.org/10.1177/0267323115577305.

Krane, Dale. 2007. "Democracy, Public Administrators, and Public Policy." In *Democracy and Public Administration*, edited by Richard C. Box, 21–39. Armonk, NY: M.E. Sharpe.

Levine, Allan. 1993. *Scrum Wars: The Prime Ministers and the Media*. Toronto: Dundurn Press.

Lindquist, Evert A. 1992. "Public Managers and Policy Communities: Learning to Meet New Challenges." *Canadian Public Administration* 35, 2: 127–59. https://doi.org/10.1111/j.1754-7121.1992.tb00685.x.

Macfarlane, Emmett. 2012. *Governing from the Bench*. Vancouver: UBC Press.

McFarland, Andrew S. 2007. "Neopluralism." *Annual Review of Political Science* 10, 1: 45–66. https://doi.org/10.1146/annurev.polisci.10.072005.152119.

McGregor, Glen, Andrew Mayeda, and Mark Kennedy. 2010. "Lobbyists Mount Full-Court Press." *Ottawa Citizen*, November 9, A1.

McMahon, Tamsin. 2016. "Which Families Give the Most?" *Globe and Mail*, August 24. https://www.theglobeandmail.com/news/politics/the-top-ten-families-in-canada-who-contribute-to-politicalparties/article26678961/.

McQuigge, Michelle. 2016. "Rebel Ban Sparks Debate over Journalism in the Digital Era." *Global News*, February 18. https://globalnews.ca/news/2524952/rebel-ban-sparks-debate-over-journalism-in-the-digital-era/.

Mills, Charles W. 1957. *The Power Elite*. New York: Oxford University Press.

Naumetz, Tim. 2016. "Justin Trudeau, Party Brass Set to Gain More Power over Campaigns, Policy under New Proposed Liberal Constitution." *Hill Times*, April 15. http://www.hilltimes.com/2016/04/15/justin-trudeau-party-brass-set-to-gain-more-power-over-campaigns-policy-under-new-proposed-liberal-constitution/58608.

Newman, Peter C. 2013. "The Death of the Canadian Establishment." *Maclean's*, March 12. http://www.macleans.ca/economy/business/the-fall-of-the-titans/.

Ornstein, Michael, and H. Michael Stevenson. 1999. *Politics and Ideology in Canada: Elite and Public Opinion in the Transformation of a Welfare State*. Montreal: McGill-Queen's University Press.

Painter-Main, Michael A. 2014. "Repertoire-Building or Elite-Challenging? Understanding Political Engagement in Canada." In *Canadian Democracy from the Ground Up: Perceptions and Performance*, edited by Elisabeth Gidengil and Heather Bastedo, 62–82. Vancouver: UBC Press.

Payton, Laura. 2016. "People at Fundraisers Show Support for Democracy: Morneau." *CTV News*, November 6. http://www.ctvnews.ca/politics/people-at-fundraisers-show -support-for-democracy-morneau-1.3146864.

Pétry, François, and Frédérick Bastien. 2013. "Follow the Pollsters: Inaccuracies in Media Coverage of the Horse-Race during the 2008 Canadian Election." *Canadian Journal of Political Science* 46, 1: 1–26. https://doi.org/10.1017/S0008423913000188.

Porter, John. 1965. *The Vertical Mosaic: An Analysis of Social Class and Power in Canada*. Toronto: University of Toronto Press. https://doi.org/10.3138/9781442683044.

Presthus, Robert. 1973. *Elite Accommodation in Canadian Politics*. Toronto: Macmillan.

Pross, A. Paul. 1992. *Group Politics and Public Policy*. 2nd ed. London: Oxford University Press.

Putnam, Robert D. 1971. "Studying Elite Political Culture: The Case of Ideology." *American Political Science Review* 65, 3: 651–81. https://doi.org/10.2307/1955512.

Rogstad, Ingrid Dahlen. 2014. "Political News Journalists in Social Media: Transforming Political Reporters into Political Pundits?" *Journalism Practice* 8, 6: 688–703. https:// doi.org/10.1080/17512786.2013.865965.

Sauvageau, Florian, David Schneiderman, and David Taras. 2011. *Last Word: Media Coverage of the Supreme Court of Canada*. Vancouver: UBC Press.

Savoie, Donald J. 1999. *Governing from the Centre: The Concentration of Power in Canadian Politics*. Toronto: University of Toronto Press.

–. 2010. *Power: Where Is It?* Montreal: McGill-Queen's University Press.

Small, Tamara A., Harold Jansen, Frédérick Bastien, Thierry Giasson, and Royce Koop. 2014. "Online Political Activity in Canada: The Hype and the Facts." *Canadian Parliamentary Review* 37, 4: 9–16.

Stanworth, Philip, and Anthony Giddens. 1974. *Elites and Power in British Society*. London: Cambridge University Press.

Stark, Andrew. 2008. "Conflict of Interest in Canada." In *Conflict of Interest and Public Life: Cross-National Perspectives*, edited by Christine Trost and Alison L. Gash, 125– 54. New York: Cambridge University Press. https://doi.org/10.1017/CBO9780511 611490.008.

Swedberg, Richard, and Ola Agevall. 2016. *The Max Weber Dictionary: Key Words and Central Concepts*. Stanford, CA: Stanford Social Sciences.

–. 2015. *The Digital Mosaic: Media, Power, and Identity in Canada*. Toronto: University of Toronto Press.

Thompson, Elizabeth. 2016. "Ethics Commissioner Wants Tighter Rules on 'Pay-to-Play' Fundraisers." *CBC News*, October 27. http://www.cbc.ca/news/politics/political -fundraising-liberals-ethics-money-1.3824260.

Tossuti, Livianna. 2002. "Regionalism in an Age of Globalization." In *Regionalism and Party Politics in Canada*, edited by Lisa Young and Keith Archer, 221–41. New York: Oxford University Press.

Turcotte, André, and Simon Vodrey. 2017. "Permanent Polling and Governance." In *Permanent Campaigning in Canada,* edited by Alex Marland, Thierry Giasson, and Anna Esselment, 127–44. Vancouver: UBC Press.

Vaccari, Cristian, and Augusto Valeriani. 2015. "Follow the Leader! Direct and Indirect Flows of Political Communication during the 2013 Italian General Election Campaign." *New Media and Society* 17, 7: 1025–42. https://doi.org/10.1177/1461444 813511038.

Van der Wal, Zeger. 2014. "Elite Ethics: Comparing Public Values Prioritization between Administrative Elites and Political Elites." *International Journal of Public Administration* 37, 14: 1030–43. https://doi.org/10.1080/01900692.2014.928319.

Wiseman, Nelson. 2013. *The Public Intellectual in Canada.* Toronto: University of Toronto Press.

Zemanek, Rick. 2011. "Adrienne Clarkson Must Stop Milking Taxpayers." *Winnipeg Free Press,* September 28. https://www.winnipegfreepress.com/opinion/analysis/adrienne -clarkson-must-stop-milking-taxpayers-130688163.html.

2

Tips and Tactics for Securing Interviews with Political Elites

Alex Marland and Anna Esselment

Researchers interested in gaining insights from political elites in Canada can experience difficulty securing interviews. Requests for sit-downs are often denied or ignored. Some governments are obsessive about message control and micromanagement of media relations. A first minister's office that imposes internal process constraints and the resulting media histrionics stir an operational culture in which many political elites are, and are assumed to be, guarded about granting interviews. This leads to unconventional pathways to obtain data. For instance, to collect information from federal public servants, one group of academics interviewed respondents in locations unlikely to be frequented by their colleagues or political superiors (Jiwani and Krawchenko 2014). Other governments promote an image of transparency and ministerial accessibility, but even then the safety of sticking to approved message lines and avoiding controversial situations remains. In an environment in which private remarks can end up in the online public sphere, political elites are acutely aware of the importance of copiously vetting requests and requesters, and for many it is safer to decline an interview invitation.

Political elites – particularly parliamentarians, cabinet ministers, and public servants – are ideally placed to explain government decisions and share information about the inner workings of the political system and public administration, as are senior political staffers. Both qualitative and quantitative research with them are key methodological approaches in many disciplines, particularly political science, and securing access to them has been a perpetual challenge in Canada. In the early 1970s, Robert Presthus (1973, 356) experienced a 50 percent refusal rate among ministers whom he sought to interview. Soon after, Allan Kornberg and William Mishler set out to interview all members of Parliament. Their determined resolve entailed mailing individual letters, making multiple phone calls, sending follow-up letters, and employing persuasion and pressure tactics via "friendly MPs, cabinet ministers, colleagues in Canadian universities, and even members of the media" (Kornberg and Mishler 1976, 59). They managed to interview 189 of 264 MPs, a formidable 72 percent response rate. Another study conducted in the 1970s employed proportional stratification sampling by party to generate a sample of MPs who were then "approached" a minimum of three times until 80 percent of the sample agreed to be interviewed in their offices (Hall and Washburn 1979, 297). The complications of administering in-depth interviews, and the proliferation of empirical methods, have since led researchers to favour quantitative surveys of political elites – far too many to list here.

Along the way, the techniques for contacting parliamentarians have changed with communications technologies. In the late 1990s, a questionnaire sent by fax to newly elected MPs generated a 57 percent response rate (Black 2000), whereas a survey emailed to all MPs generated a meagre response rate of 11 percent (Barbour 1999). In another study, briefing notes were circulated to MPs other than party leaders and ministers. A panel discussion was held on Parliament Hill, and it was followed up with a short questionnaire, which generated a response rate of approximately 28 percent, which the study author thought "impressive" (Dobell 2000, 35). In the early 2000s, mailing letters to potential respondents on official letterhead outlining the project was a common tip for interviewers (Goldstein 2002; Lilleker 2003). So was carrying a cellphone (Goldstein 2002, 671).

Our focus here is on qualitative research, specifically ways to obtain in-depth interviews with political elites in Canada in the digital environment. Qualitative engagement through interviewing provides rich contexts for data found through other sources, such as surveys, on which theory and quantitative studies are built (Lilleker 2003). Without it, we have a limited understanding of how government and politics actually work. Given the advantaged position of the proposed subjects and the typically high rate of non-response, random sampling in qualitative research is thought to be problematic (Goldstein 2002). Consequently, snowball sampling – in which interviewees offer names of other potential research recruits – has been a popular way of connecting with respondents. Public administration scholar Donald Savoie cites his background as a former senior public servant with helping him to obtain interviews (Jiwani and Krawchenko 2014, 63), generating a success rate that includes interviewing eighty-eight of the ninety former and current government officials whom he contacted for *Governing from the Centre: The Concentration of Power in Canadian Politics* (Savoie 1999, 15). Unfortunately, referrals come at the expense of structured design and randomness, and the resulting introduction of bias (Macdonald and Hellgren 2004) suggests that data cannot be replicated and might not be generalizable. This presents a conundrum in the apparent necessity of snowball sampling since it reduces our confidence in the research even as the exclusivity of the data means that there is no obvious alternative. A further concern about the validity and reliability of data is that political elites wield a fair degree of power during interviews (Aberbach and Rockman 2002; Rivera, Kozyreva, and Sarovskii 2002). Sometimes these power dynamics are to a researcher's advantage. An interviewer belonging to the same political minority group as respondents might generate an atypically high participation rate (e.g., Tremblay 2003). Above all, researchers must establish trust and rapport with their subjects, no matter the characteristics of the interviewer or the respondent (Mikecz 2012; Ostrander 1993).

An acute challenge for researchers is that political executives demand error-free government (Good 2010, 9). As a consequence, many interview subjects approach requests for comments with caution and even reluctance. When a researcher seeks an interview, it is the equivalent of a self-invitation to enter a privileged world. How deeply these elite networks can be penetrated is heavily dependent on the references of past interviewees and the willingness of respondents to grant the interview and talk candidly. In theory, passing through academic research ethics boards and using informed consent forms should act as a surrogate for trust by conveying that privileged information will be treated in confidence. In practice, the ethics process adds a layer of bureaucracy that interferes with data collection. Elites are extremely busy and operate in a fast-paced environment that is accelerating with digital technology. Requiring paperwork introduces a bias in that some who would have otherwise agreed to be interviewed will be turned off by the administrative burden. These are among the reasons why Canadian social scientists are not expected to treat political elites with the same responsibility for informed consent as with other human subjects. Guidance provided by the Canadian Political Science Association (2009) is that research ethics boards must have "sensitivity to the particular circumstances surrounding research on political elites and the more nuanced and open approach to obtaining informed consent." Accordingly, the Government of Canada's Tri-Council Policy Statement about ethical research practices states that,

in cases where the participant holds a position of power, or routinely engages in communicative interactions similar to those involved in the research by virtue of their position or profession (e.g.,
a communications officer or spokesperson for an organization),
consent can be inferred by the participant's agreeing to interact with
the researcher for the purpose of the research. For example, some
political science research focuses on power structures and individuals in positions of power (e.g., a senior partner in a law firm, a
cabinet minister or a senior corporate officer). In this type of research, where a prospective participant agrees to be interviewed on
the basis of sufficient information provided by the researcher, *it
may be sufficient for the participant to signify consent to participate*
in the research. The researcher should record this in an appropriate
way. (Government of Canada 2014, 144; emphasis added)

University ethics boards might not be aware of this special status. What
seems to matter is the proximity to power and respondent experience. Ethics
clearance that might be warranted with election candidates new to politics
should be less strenuous for incumbents.

Digital communications presents new opportunities and challenges for
securing interviews. It is a medium that encourages "conversation, connect-
edness, and participation," though in reality it is most embraced by smaller
opposition parties (Small 2014, 93). For researchers, ascertaining a subject's
relative expertise and aptitudes involves far less guesswork than in the past.
In addition to career-related formalities available on an employer's website,
social media profiles can offer a peek into the subject's recent activities and
personality (Reich 2015). LinkedIn, Facebook, Instagram, Twitter, Wikipedia,
and other such sites offer text and visual information that can range from
revealing the subject's hometown to that individual's current thoughts. Even
if the online profiles of political elites are carefully crafted, pertinent information that would otherwise be private (e.g., away on vacation, policy opinions) can be located, as can personal interests. Moreover, social media are
characterized in large part by homophily, presenting an opportunity to break
into online circles inhabited by the elites whom a researcher wants to target
(Tarbush and Teytelboym 2012). This creates new ways to secure interviews, such as through the direct messaging services on applications, a practice whose salience increases as the success rate of the traditional practice of
sending formal invitations declines (Jiwani and Krawchenko 2014; Rivera,

Kozyreva, and Sarovskii 2002). However, to the potential detriment of the researcher, online vetting can go both ways (Reich 2015). Although finding out information about interviewees predates the digital age (Ostrander 1993), today a researcher's internet and social media footprints are readily available for viewing by those contacted.

The amount of digital information available about any one individual is difficult to comprehend. The practice of mining data from these online platforms to create psychographic profiles of users is a dynamic field facilitated by digital technology (Lambiotte and Kosinski 2014). Businesses, political parties, political movements, and governments are realizing the opportunities that big data offer through the ability to microtarget messages for promotion, persuasion, and mobilization. This is a burgeoning field: where the Harper Conservatives were innovators in political marketing, the Trudeau Liberals are disciples of metrics. Katie Telford, the Liberal PMO chief of staff and 2015 campaign co-chair, has explained that this involves "from eyeballs on Facebook versus YouTube videos, to ratios to door knocks to phone calls, from radio ad buys against TV ad buys, and which baseball game more Canadians might be watching" (quoted in Boutilier 2016). This suggests that researchers should be careful leaving digital tracks – particularly what and whom they "like" on Facebook – lest they be used as a barrier to access among a political class that routinely looks into people's backgrounds. Online information provides a basis for whether or not a potential respondent decides to grant an interview and, if so, how candid to be.

No matter the technological environment, the initial point of contact for a researcher is an agent who determines whether and how to pass along the request to the desired respondent. For elites in general, gatekeeping is a role held by anyone within a closed network, such as "personal assistants, advisers, lawyers, and security guards" (Odendahl and Shaw 2001, 299). In politics and government, this includes desk receptionists, constituency assistants, executive assistants, chiefs of staff, directors of communications, and others. In a fast-paced environment, public officials routinely outsource screening to gatekeepers instructed to follow set procedures and "rigorous rules of thumb" for what warrants the elite's limited time (Walgrave and Dejaeghere 2016, 14). To a researcher, they are either formidable barriers or important allies. But getting past the gatekeeper is only one step toward obtaining good data. A common tip found in most of the literature, even from decades ago, is that a researcher needs an "in" (Goldstein 2002; Ostrander 1993). Leveraging personal connections can be the antithesis of principles of the scientific method, which brings us back to the conundrum of weighing accessibility against random selection. The aim of this chapter is twofold. First, we want to assess the degree of difficulty in accessing elites; we do so with an experiment. Second, we share techniques helpful to researchers pursuing elite interviews in a digital communications environment.

Case Study

METHOD

To identify best practices, we employed a method of data collection that itself was a social experiment in elite research methodology. We are therefore more concerned with an exploratory process that we will apply in future research than we are with generating a large sample. Given the topic, our method is especially germane. We decided to apply maximum variation sampling by collecting tips about getting past gatekeepers from a small number of Canadian political scientists, journalists, and political staff.[1] We chose academics who had recently published qualitative research findings because they had developed ways to reach those within the corridors of power. Conducting interviews is the bedrock of journalism, and speaking with decision makers is part of a political journalist's creed. As gatekeepers, political staff can provide insights into why they would provide a researcher with access to an elected official or why a request for an interview might be ignored. Our objective was to complete a minimum of two semi-structured interviews per cohort. Doing so would enable us to identify a variety of tactics used in the digital age that would supplement our own experiences. We asked about the implications of digital communications and social media for obtaining interviews with political elites. We explored to what respondents attributed their successes and failures in securing interviews. We provided academics and journalists with the choice of written replies or telephone conversations that lasted twenty to forty-five minutes. We required telephone interviews of gatekeepers. Data were collected between May and August 2016.

For each cohort, we devised a randomized sampling method that could be replicated. A random sample should generate different information and more diverse perspectives than if we were to contact people in our existing networks. However, the trade-off is reduced accessibility and disclosure. In all cases, we erred on the side of a simplified informed consent form, leaving it up to the respondent whether or not to complete it. We do not name our respondents, or provide direct quotations from them, in order to focus on the aggregate. Indeed, we made it known that we were not recording the discussions and that instead we would vigorously type notes during the conversations. This commitment was important to political staff, in particular, who otherwise might not have spoken as freely or at all. After each conversation, we followed up by email to reconfirm in writing how the information would be used.

To identify Canadian political scientists who recently published work based on elite interview data, we consulted impact factor metrics that rank Canadian periodicals. Beginning with the first article in the most recent issue of the highest-ranked journal in Canadian political science fields, and working backward through the journal, we methodically searched abstracts to identify those employing depth interviews with political elites. Our capture focused on the appearance of the word *interview* and/or *qualitative* in order to trigger a manual review. We sought one author per journal. Our resulting requests to interview the qualitative researchers who had most recently published in the *Canadian Journal of Political Science* and *Canadian Public Administration* were readily accepted. The respondents were previously unknown to us, and both conducted research in different areas than our own: an anglophone specializing in western Canadian religious politics (telephone interview) and a francophone with expertise in public administration in Quebec (email communication). Their suggestions were combined with those received from discussants and attendees following the presentation of an earlier draft of this text at the Canadian Political Science Association conference.

Our selection process for political reporters began by identifying the three federal electoral districts with the highest, the median, and the lowest number of constituents. We notionally identified the largest community media outlet in each riding. On the media outlet's website, we looked for the news report nearest the top of the webpage that featured an interview with a Canadian political elite. We selected that reporter even if it was a wire service story (i.e., we prioritized randomization over regional representation). Of the eight journalists contacted, four were interviewed. Telephone interviews were held with members of the Canadian Press, the Northern News Service, and the *Oshawa Express,* and email communication was conducted with a journalist with the *Brantford Expositor.* Once again all were unknown to us.

To identify political staff, we consulted the most recent issue of the *Hill Times* (June 8, 2016) and identified the names of the eight MPs who appeared first: Prime Minister Justin Trudeau, Conservative Leader of the Opposition Rona Ambrose, Green Party leader Elizabeth May, Minister of Democratic Institutions Maryam Monsef, and backbenchers affiliated with the Conservatives (two), Liberals, and New Democrats. There are more random ways of identifying MPs' offices, but we carried on with this purposeful sample because it included party leaders, and we wanted to see whether those in the news would be accessible.

In early June 2016, while the House of Commons was sitting, we phoned each MP's Parliament Hill office and asked to speak with the MP or a member of that MP's political staff about the best way for scholars to secure an interview. Uniformly, those who answered the phone said to put the request in an email, sometimes directing us to use a particular staffer's email address rather than the one listed on the Parliament of Canada webpage. For the prime minister and the minister of democratic institutions, we submitted requests through their government online contact forms. An autoreply was received from May's office stating that, because of the high volume, not all messages would receive a response, and Ambrose's office declined participation because of "prior commitments." A second email was sent to nonrespondents in late June, shortly after the House of Commons adjourned for the summer. The NDP MP's office declined because of a lack of "time to participate," and a Green Party staffer sought further information, but nothing came of it. In early July, supplementary phone calls were placed to the three remaining backbenchers' offices. Staffers in the offices of an Ontario Conservative MP and an Atlantic Liberal MP both apologized profusely and were highly amicable, resulting in lengthy telephone interviews held in late summer. In total, eight respondents were interviewed for this chapter (two academics, four journalists, and two political staffers).

Findings

Among the findings of our experiment was a stark reminder of the considerable time, effort, and frustration involved in developing a randomized sample and contacting strangers compared with the relative ease of asking favours from members of a personal network. Our success was meagre with respect to political personnel. Not only do timing, choice of topic, and persistence matter, but also offline reputation matters: our interviews appear to have been secured in part because of the political staffers' familiarity with the researchers.[2] We experienced none of the sunny accessibility and transparency promised by the Liberals, whose outward behaviour was no different from that of their Conservative predecessors. More optimistically, qualitative researchers and some journalists are happy to share their experiences and are potential support networks for others.

The following pages present some tips and tactics for obtaining interviews with political elites in the digital communications environment. Some techniques are summarized in Figure 2.1 for ease of reference. Our objective is to provide a basic roadmap for young scholars as well as anyone grappling with interview research design and non-response.

Our first point of guidance is that a good researcher develops a respondent sample using scientific principles that reduce subjectivity and enable replicability. The method must be clearly communicated to readers, who will need

FIGURE 2.1
___

Suggested tips for interview research design with Canadian political elites

SAMPLING
- Do not let a media narrative about political elites influence the application of scientific principles to design a respondent pool.
- Avail yourself of a variety of online resources to develop a respondent pool.
- Use online sleuthing to track down people who recently held an elite position and may now be more accessible and willing to speak freely.
- Where possible, align research interests with a potential respondent's interests.
- Plan to supplement interviews obtained through random sampling with ones obtained through referrals and vouching, ideally as part of a mixed-method research study.

PLACING THE INTERVIEW REQUEST
- Be cognizant of timing considerations, such as the Parliamentary calendar.
- Where possible, initiate a request through a personal interaction, and immediately follow up with a succinct written request.
- Consider the value of older tactics that may stand out in a digital world, such as telephone calls. Equally, consider newer approaches such as placing requests through social media.
- Prioritize a request for a verbal interview conducted in person, by telephone, or video chat applications, but also provide the option to respond in writing electronically.
- Be respectfully persistent when faced with no response.
- Practice self-reputation management, online and otherwise.
___

to agree to some extent with its suitability. Thus, the temptation to leverage personal contacts must be secondary to developing a matrix based on identified criteria that can be explained. Equally, research must not be unduly influenced by exposure to media coverage of subjects or one's personal political ideology. Selecting respondents on the basis of having chosen to follow them on Twitter, or because they have an intriguing public persona, or rejecting someone because of an aversion to that person's political values lacks the rigour of a research design that uses recognized sampling methods.

The internet offers an abundance of reasonably current information that can be quickly located from almost anywhere. It takes moments to uncover the names and contact details of personnel in a government electronic directory, though email addresses are not always available. Online news media archives are repositories of career information and expertise. Potent sources are business-oriented social media accounts, particularly LinkedIn professional profiles, which identify the user's employment history. A microblog such as Twitter or Instagram is a good way to identify whether a potential respondent is actively engaged in the online sphere as opposed to being off the grid (i.e., inaccessible) at a given moment. Social media also provide opportunities to understand that individual's interests, style of communication, and approaches to public outreach. This has become a new norm in Canadian politics. Until recently, senior personnel in the PMO have kept low profiles and not commented publicly. Unbowed, senior members of Trudeau's inner sanctum have active social media presences. However, to access the full range of social media data, the researcher will need to open an account or obtain the information from someone who has one.

An interview candidate must be confident that it is worthwhile to spend valuable time communicating with a relative unknown about potentially confidential matters. Impressions of a researcher's online reputation – faculty profile, Twitter activity, Facebook page, comments in news stories, publications, student posts to Ratemyprofessors.com, and so on – are a collective proxy of trustworthiness. Reputation management is a multi-pronged process necessary to assure others that the research will be conducted with high standards of professionalism. As one of our interviewees confirmed, political staff conduct an online assessment of a requester's scholarly work, employment history, political affiliation, and social media profile. Doing so helps to explain why, not long after placing an interview request, a researcher might receive a notification from Academia.edu or ResearchGate that someone has just perused the interviewer's profile. In this context, a qualitative researcher who engages in heated philosophical debates on public media ought to consider whether doing so has implications for securing interviews. Disparagement of institutions, occupations, or individuals should not be confused with critical questioning, but this is not always obvious in the political world, and no potential respondent can be compelled to talk with a scholar. Our research revealed that political elites want a reasonable sense of whether they will be treated fairly and dispassionately. What matters most, we were told, is a sense that a student or professor will follow the facts. Elected officials in particular believe that what is said is not necessarily what is publicly conveyed. To address these challenges, if appropriate, a researcher might pair with a co-author to balance the sanctity of scientific rigour with freedom of speech.

Several of our respondents noted that being aware of personal and public interests can provide a window of opportunity for academics seeking insight and information. In other words, matching one's area of research to elected officials with similar interests can be fruitful. We were advised that a researcher ought to seek officials whose portfolios align with the researcher's own subject matter or who might have advocated for the issue to be discussed. It is important to be clear about how a project aligns with the subject's interests, why it might be helpful to the official's constituents, or how it could propel knowledge or a policy forward. Digital technology is a useful resource in this respect. Content searches of Twitter feeds, MPs' websites, local newspapers, committee membership webpages, and more can reveal the projects or areas that an elite personally considers significant. Sometimes academics will carefully seek to set respondents at ease by mentioning shared interests (if publicly known) or identifying people they have already interviewed (if consent was granted). Customizing the nature of requests to connect on a personal level is a seemingly justifiable abrogation from norms of standardization. This variation ought to be mentioned in the study methodology.

Despite the methodological limitations, the timeworn tactic of vouching from people whom elites know and trust can have added importance in the digital age. If appropriate, a researcher should carefully leverage available personal and professional connections, taking care to build new connections, and to blend this tactic with cold calling, to ensure information breadth. Ethical judgments come into play, given that the person asked to make a referral might be placed in a difficult position. Co-authoring with an elite or partnering with a governmental or non-governmental organization is an option worthy of consideration. Prospective respondents might derive comfort by being informed that the research has been sanctioned by their employer, an ethics board, or a professional association. Equally, research affiliated with an advocacy group, a think tank, or a non-partisan organization might open doors among select respondents. For instance, to assist Samara Canada with conducting exit interviews with MPs not returning to Parliament, the Canadian Association of Former Parliamentarians sent a letter of introduction and invitation (Samara 2010). In other instances, a researcher's involvement with a group might close doors, particularly if this involvement indicates competing ideological or partisan leanings.

In all circumstances, our findings make it clear that political elites are bombarded with electronic communications. Parliament Hill offices routinely receive e-petitions and other messages from non-constituents, blended with complaints and spam. The Green Party leader's autoreply cautioned that her office replies to over 400,000 pieces of correspondence annually, approximately 1,100 replies each day, including weekends. The ideal in the digital era is to submit requests that provide extensive information about the nature of the research project and that can be processed with speed. Succinct requests for short interviews are more likely to be read and accepted than long requests for lengthy discussions. To break through, a few of our respondents suggested that a researcher consider the merits of old technology. This tactic would begin with a phone call to establish a personal relationship with a gatekeeper. A phone call stands out, whereas an emailed request without an initial voice contact can more easily be ignored by a busy staffer. A phone call also primes the individual on the other end so that a follow-up email is not left languishing in someone's inbox. Likewise, asking an administrative assistant, or potentially a respondent, for the best email address to use can be productive, as can a carefully chosen subject line and consideration of the time of day that a message is sent. Including a link to a faculty profile page or personal website is considered good practice too. New technology can also provide a last resort; a researcher whose efforts have gone unheeded can publicly press a public official on social media. Parliament Hill staffers informed us that this gets results. When someone authors a public post on an MP's social media account claiming that the MP is inaccessible, the parliamentarian promptly makes a public declaration of accessibility and directs staff to be available. This approach does not guarantee an interview, but at least it does generate a response. However, it is one thing for constituents to do this; for a researcher, it risks crossing the boundaries of research ethics and reputation management.

When seeking an interview with a public official, it behooves a researcher to be aware of parliamentary timetables and cycles. Our interviewees noted that there are times of the year when political elites are so busy with their own responsibilities that inbound communications might be triaged, and making time for an academic researcher is difficult. There is a torrent of demands when a legislature is sitting and relatively little urgency when it is not. Certain weeks in the parliamentary calendar provide a greater window for scheduling a research interview with a parliamentarian. If the objective is to interview political staffers, then the best times might be the designated periods when MPs are in their home ridings to attend to constituency matters. It is as important to consider the nature of impositions during busy periods of the parliamentary cycle as it is to be aware of the inaccessibility of a public figure under duress because of some controversy.

Whether placed in a busy period or not, open-ended or vague requests are less successful than specific requests. Concluding a message by stating when the recipient can expect to be contacted next will convey a sense of focus, efficiency, and perseverance. A respondent should be advised that an interview consent form, a time frame for the interview, a project summary sheet, and discussion questions will be provided. However, given the special nature of political elites, the volume of information provided should not be overbearing. Completion of the consent form can be presented as optional and provided after an initial response. Approaching a potential respondent at a public event and developing a personal rapport can be a successful technique. Equally, mailing a thank-you note at the conclusion of an interview might increase the respondent's likelihood of agreeing to a subsequent interview and vouching for the researcher to others in a closed network. In short, technology should be treated as a supplement to rather than a substitute for in-person relationships.

Accessing former or retired political elites might be an easier task than securing interviews with those who currently hold busy and prominent jobs. Internet searches of names can generate lists of retirees and their current contact details. Many dated government documents are stored online and contain the names of public servants who worked on the file. Searching political staffers' LinkedIn profiles is another option. As the Samara example suggests, former public employees, MPs, ministers, political staffers, and other political elites can be forthcoming and candid. Although they might remain loyal to their former employers – and, in the case of political staff, a confidentiality agreement might have been signed – as time passes most recognize the reduced risk of sharing information. They might even welcome the opportunity to reflect and share knowledge.

For all types of respondents, the richest data are typically obtained from in-person interviews. Text-based and online video technologies (e.g., instant messaging platforms, Skype, FaceTime, and Google Hangout) can offer advantages over telephone interviews because of the nature of informal and visual communications. Responses submitted by email generate a different variety of information with minimal effort for the researcher, albeit with greater opportunities for a respondent to spin responses. The option of emailed responses can offer an additional opportunity if the researcher and respondent have different mother tongues or can collect perfunctory information from an aide to the intended respondent (e.g., Clark, McGrath, and MacDonald 2007).

Whatever the nature of the research design, for a major undertaking a researcher is well advised to draw on multiple sources of data to further discern the validity of collected evidence. Mixed-method research can situate interview data collected from Canadian political elites in comparative perspective (e.g., Marland and Giasson 2013). Scholars who study elites are voracious readers of academic literature, political biographies, journalistic accounts, and political elites' personal collections of papers (private and/or deposited at public archives). Supplementary data accessible online include government reports, open-data repositories, budget documents, court cases, speeches, news releases, election manifestos, campaign finance data, newspaper and magazine articles, and the many other items that can be located on an organization's website or located through search engines.

Access to information requests are another vehicle, either by obtaining completed files archived online or by initiating original requests. By filing, a researcher invokes a legal requirement for public servants to consider the request and respond within an established time frame. Applicants are entitled to a reasonable search for existing records within a specified date range. Documents not otherwise accessible can be procured, such as internal reports, presentation decks, planning materials, and emails. A limitation is that the requested information can be subject to redaction or even withheld; some government offices, notably matters involving the offices of the first minister and ministers, tend to be exempt entirely. Thus, a researcher must craft a request carefully, emphasizing keywords. The compiled files tend to be provided electronically and are then made available online as part of open-government initiatives, such as at http://open.canada.ca/en/. Content analysis of collected data might not be straightforward when files are not machine-readable and because coding of personal communications is complex. Nevertheless, access to information is an outstanding mechanism to obtain internal government data.[3]

Political Elites in Canada in the Digital Age

The study of political elites and the actions that they take while in the government is a critical component of scientific inquiry. This influential group is handed the task of decision making, affecting large swaths of the population. Considering what we set out above, how does the ability to research political elites affect representation, decision making, and accountability?

As representatives of the citizens whom they serve, political actors ought to be reasonably available to communicate with researchers who seek to understand the nature of public sector operations. Conversely, the ability to ignore interview requests, or to be choosy about whom to speak with and what information to disclose, is a function of their position. Elites are busy individuals who must preserve secrecy on select matters. But there is a fine line: those who are the most clandestine, the least studied, and routinely dodge interview requests are the very representatives who arguably warrant the greatest study. What's more, the digital era affects accessibility by imposing constraints on how political elites can communicate, which diminishes being available to constituents (however they are defined), one of many facets of their multifaceted representative role. Although digital technology has opened more ways for political elites to connect with those whom they represent – which does not technically include a researcher in another riding – it has also encouraged a stronger culture of information discipline and self-censorship. In this type of setting, representative capacity is challenged.

Interviewing elites is one of the best ways to understand the nature of their decision-making processes and outcomes, provided that they are willing to speak about it. The ability to judge the transparency of their activities is dependent on our knowledge of such activities. If we rely exclusively on publicly offered information, then we might be missing out on the true roles, behaviours, and motivations of our representatives. This is especially true if the potential exists to manipulate or selectively withhold information. As a consequence, important details of public policy can be either obscured or left unexplored by researchers, which highlights the power that elites can exercise over the academy if and when they refuse to talk. An interview is an excellent way to uncover new terrain and an opportunity for representatives to explain their decisions. Face-to-face meetings are especially valuable considering the degree of message control that is increasingly the norm within the public service. Researcher guarantees of anonymity should also encourage public office holders to be candid with their answers. In our view, data collected by interviewing political elites outside the researcher's normal comfort zone are among the most rewarding. Academics with trustworthy reputations who convey confidence that their mission is not to publicly embarrass the respondent perform a service by collecting privileged information about public institutions and political events. Digital media both facilitate and inhibit this service.

The varied approaches that we have outlined indicate that strong research design, innovative practices, support from other elites, and persistence are necessary to optimize participation. Moreover, sensitivity to external dynamics is essential, for during peak busy periods the ability to reach some elites is understandably limited. The difficulty in accessing them is somewhat at odds with the increasing pressure that public institutions are under to project an image of accountability. For instance, a researcher interested in interviewing a minister might consider that the government's directive on the management of communications is replete with commitments to provide information in either official language. These policies include offering "timely, accurate, clear, objective and complete information about its policies, programs, services and initiatives"; ensuring that "institutions of the Government of Canada are visible, accessible and accountable to the public they serve"; and encouraging "public service managers and employees to communicate openly with the public about policies, programs, services and initiatives they are familiar with and for which they have responsibility" (Treasury Board Secretariat 2016). Unfortunately, too often being turned down or ignored goes with the territory.

As digital media technology advances, Canadians might be better served if the communications policy of the government, as well as the rules of the Canadian Parliamentary Press Gallery, were to identify academics as clients in the same vein as accredited journalists. It is worth questioning whether academics can partly fill the role being vacated by professional muckrakers. Accreditation in press galleries, opening up to bloggers, as well as recognition in the government's communications policy, would lead to better access to public officials. As demand for "evidence-based policy" grows, it is worth considering whether there are better ways to accommodate the requests by scholars who seek to interview political elites.

NOTES

1 An external reviewer of an earlier draft of this text observed that our method did not seek interviews from mid- to lower-level public servants directly involved with public policy development and implementation. These employees are often prevented by communications staff from speaking with researchers. Our own experience is that, even under tight communications management regimes, access to public servants is still possible, such as by stating on an access to information request that, in lieu of releasing documents, an interview with government personnel would be acceptable.

2 The Conservative staffer commented that he was aware that the researcher had testified to a House of Commons committee of which the Conservative MP was a member. The Liberal staffer mentioned that he had checked with a senior member of the Liberal government about participating, and this member had given clearance on the basis of past personal interactions with the researcher.

3 For a good overview of Canadian access to information processes, see Larsen and Walby (2012).

REFERENCES

Aberbach, Joel D., and Bert A. Rockman. 2002. "Conducting and Coding Elite Interviews." *PS: Political Science and Politics* 35, 4: 673–76. https://doi.org/10.1017/S10490965 02001142.

Barbour, Michael K. 1999. "Parliament and the Internet: The Present and the Future." *Canadian Parliamentary Review* 22, 3: 23–25.

Black, Jerome. 2000. "Ethnoracial Minorities in the Canadian House of Commons: The Case of the 36th Parliament." *Canadian Ethnic Studies Journal* 32, 1: 105–14.

Boutilier, Alex. 2016. "Liberals Outline New-Found Digital Muscle." *Toronto Star,* May 28. https://www.thestar.com/news/canada/2016/05/28/liberals-outline-new-found -digital-muscle.html.

Canadian Political Science Association. 2009. "Response by the Canadian Political Science Association to the Draft Second Edition of the Tri-Council Policy Statement on Research Ethics (TCPS II)." March 23. https://www.cpsa-acsp.ca/researchethics.php.

Clark, Daniel, Patrick McGrath, and Noni MacDonald. 2007. "Members' of Parliament Knowledge of and Attitudes toward Health Research and Funding." *Canadian Medical Association Journal* 177, 9: 1045–51. https://doi.org/10.1503/cmaj.070320.

Dobell, Peter. 2000. "Reforming Parliamentary Practice: The Views of MPs." *Policy Matters* 1, 9: 1–44.

Goldstein, Kenneth. 2002. "Getting in the Door: Sampling and Completing Elite Interviews." *PS: Political Science and Politics* 35, 4: 669–72. https://doi.org/10.1017/S1049 096502001130.

Good, David. 2010. "Minority Government: Politics, Planning, and the Public Service." Paper presented at the Conference Governing without a Majority: What Consequences in Westminster Systems?, Université de Montréal, November 12.

Government of Canada. 2014. "Ethical Conduct for Research Involving Humans." Tri-Council Policy Statement. http://www.pre.ethics.gc.ca/pdf/eng/tcps2-2014/TCPS_2_FINAL_Web.pdf.

Hall, Peter, and Peter Washburn. 1979. "Elites and Representation: A Study of the Attitudes and Perceptions of MPs." In *The Canadian House of Commons Observed: Parliamentary Internship Papers,* edited by Jean Pierre Gaboury and James Ross Hurley, 293–325. Ottawa: University of Ottawa Press.

Jiwani, Farzana Nanji, and Tamara Krawchenko. 2014. "Public Policy, Access to Government, and Qualitative Research Practices: Conducting Research within a Culture of Information Control." *Canadian Public Policy* 40, 1: 57–66. https://doi.org/10.3138/cpp.2012-051.

Kornberg, Allan, and William Mishler. 1976. *Influence in Parliament: Canada.* Durham, NC: Duke University Press.

Lambiotte, Renaud, and Michael Kosinski. 2014. "Tracking the Digital Footprints of Personality." *Proceedings of the Institute of Electrical and Electronics Engineers* 102, 12: 1934–39. https://doi.org/10.1109/JPROC.2014.2359054.

Larsen, Mike, and Kevin Walby, eds. 2012. *Brokering Access: Power, Politics, and Freedom of Information Process in Canada.* Vancouver: UBC Press.

Lilleker, Darren G. 2003. "Interviewing the Political Elite: Navigating a Potential Minefield." *Politics* 23, 3: 207–14. https://doi.org/10.1111/1467-9256.00198.

Macdonald, Stuart, and Bo Hellgren. 2004. "The Interview in International Business Research: Problems We Would Rather Not Talk About." In *Handbook of Qualitative Research Methods for International Business,* edited by Rebecca Marschan-Piekkari and Catherine Welch, 264–81. London: Edward Elgar Publishing. https://doi.org/10.4337/9781781954331.00029.

Marland, Alex, and Thierry Giasson. 2013. "Investigating Political Marketing Using Mixed Method: The Case for Campaign Spending Data." *Journal of Public Affairs* 13, 4: 391–402. https://doi.org/10.1002/pa.1492.

Mikecz, Robert. 2012. "Interviewing Elites: Addressing Methodological Issues." *Qualitative Inquiry* 18, 6: 482–93. https://doi.org/10.1177/1077800412442818.

Odendahl, Teresa, and A.M. Shaw. 2001. "Interviewing Elites." In *Handbook of Interview Research: Context and Method,* edited by J.F. Gubrium and J.A. Holstein, 299–316. Thousand Oaks, CA: Sage Publications.

Ostrander, Susan A. 1993. "'Surely You're Not in This Just to Be Helpful': Access, Rapport, and Interviews in Three Studies of Elites." *Journal of Contemporary Ethnography* 22, 1: 7–27. https://doi.org/10.1177/089124193022001002.

Presthus, Robert. 1973. *Elite Accommodation in Canadian Politics.* Toronto: Macmillan.

Reich, Jennifer A. 2015. "Old Methods and New Technologies: Social Media and Shifts in Power in Qualitative Research." *Ethnography* 16, 4: 394–415. https://doi.org/10.1177/1466138114552949.

Rivera, Sharon Werning, Polina M. Kozyreva, and Eduard G. Sarovskii. 2002. "Interviewing Political Elites: Lessons from Russia." *PS: Political Science and Politics* 35, 4: 683–88. https://doi.org/10.1017/S1049096502001178.

Samara. 2010. "MP Exit Interviews." http://www.samaracanada.com/research/political-leadership/mp-exit-interviews.

Savoie, Donald J. 1999. *Governing from the Centre: The Concentration of Power in Canadian Politics*. Toronto: University of Toronto Press.

Small, Tamara. 2014. "The Not-So Social Network: The Use of Twitter by Canada's Party Leaders." In *Political Communication in Canada: Meet the Press and Tweet the Rest*, edited by Alex Marland, Thierry Giasson, and Tamara Small, 92–110. Vancouver: UBC Press.

Tarbush, Bassel, and Alexander Teytelboym. 2012. "Homophily in Online Social Networks." In *Internet and Network Economics, 512–18 Heidelberg*, edited by Paul W. Goldberg, 512–18. Berlin: Springer. https://doi.org/10.1007/978-3-642-35311-6_40.

Treasury Board Secretariat. 2016. "Directive on the Management of Communications." https://www.tbs-sct.gc.ca/pol/doc-eng.aspx?id=30682.

Tremblay, Manon. 2003. "Women's Representational Role in Australia and Canada: The Impact of Political Context." *Australian Journal of Political Science* 38, 2: 215–38. https://doi.org/10.1080/1036114032000092693.

Walgrave, Stefaan, and Yves Dejaeghere. 2016. "Surviving Information Overload: How Elite Politicians Select Information." *Governance* 30, 2: 229–44. http://dx.doi.org/10.1111/gove.12209.

3

The Intersection of Public Policy and Digital Communications: The Federal Government Vantage Point

Robert P. Shepherd and Bryan Evans

The use of digitally based communications technologies (DBCTs) has become pervasive in federal government operations and policy making. Ministers and officials routinely use social media platforms to engage citizens' perspectives and respond to them accordingly. Likewise, public servants increasingly rely on such communications technologies and platforms (Twitter, Facebook, blogs, to name a few) to gather information and inform policy choices. Embedded in these new ways of doing things are important questions about the working relationship between ministers and public servants, whether digital communications fragments or broadens the policy process to more actors, and how policy construction and implementation are affected. From an operational standpoint, government communications functions, enabled and supported by DBCTs, are becoming "integral to developing, implementing and evaluating the government's policies, programs, services and initiatives" (Canada 2016, s. 4.5). Unlike other institutions of the Canadian state, such as the Supreme Court, which does not appear to have been affected by the changing media landscape (see Crandall in this volume), the federal government, as a central political actor and manager, is required to respond and adapt to this disruptive transformation. The work on the evolution of political journalism presented in this volume notes that the "concept of media elite is in transition" (see Chapter 10 by Chacon, Lawlor, and Giasson, this volume). The small elite of political journalists, who have had a monopoly on the reporting (and thus the framing) of political events, actors, and institutions, is now challenged by "new practices and new actors." Consequently, there is a less easily managed environment of information and opinion influencing. Given these implications, our central question is how DBCTs intersect with the public policy process and the work of senior policy officials in the federal government.

Interest in redesigning the policy process with a view to engaging a wider range of non-governmental policy actors has informed the emergence of a body of research concerned with what is termed "New Public Governance" (Osborne 2010). This school of thought contends that the policy process has become more accessible to non-governmental policy actors (Clarke and Margetts 2014; Dunleavy et al. 2006). It proposes that a larger number of policy actors are enabled to access what is viewed as a previously closed policy process. As Rachel Laforest notes in this volume, non-governmental organizations, and specifically non-profit organizations, "are central institutions for the transmission of citizens' interests and preferences into the policy arena." However, DBCTs "have an impact on the political issues that will be advocated to the state" and on which issues the state will address.

Much of the literature has theorized that information technologies have created global shifts of political power between citizens and the state (Margetts and Dunleavy 2013; Meijer and Torenvlied 2016). The broad message is that technology either will or ought to compel the government to invite the public into collaborative arrangements for policy decision making. However, critics of open-source approaches to the government contend that they privilege a few organizations rather than produce a more equitable and accessible process (Hindman 2007). Others challenge the extent to which digital groups are as representative as has been implied, pointing out the tendency for important voices to be excluded from policy deliberations in online discussions (Deschamps 2014; Knox 2016). And others, in particular with respect to the federal government, have observed that, despite the broad potential for Web 2.0 technologies to engage citizens, the reality appears to be one in which such a capability is limited to largely service delivery and information provision rather than authentic deliberation and dialogue (Small 2012). Likewise, the New Political Governance model (Aucoin 2012) challenges the core claim of New Public Governance by arguing that political pressures on governments are manifesting in more responsive public services. It maintains that mass media and communications have put pressure on politicians to be active rather than passive participants in policy development and implementation.

Extending these debates, our argument is that the federal communications function has assumed a much more prominent role in the digital age. Communications is now integral to government operations and has significant effects on the policy process map. These effects are felt in different ways, including by public servants who have seen their roles in policy processes

FIGURE 3.1

The policy process: A communications view

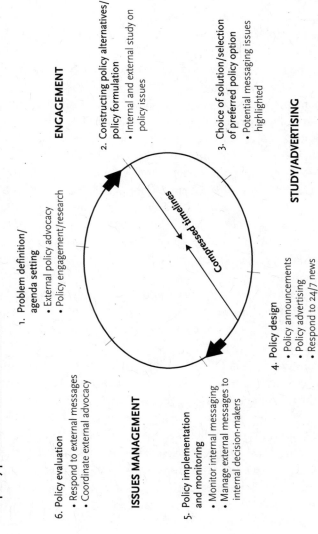

ENGAGEMENT

1. Problem definition/
   agenda setting
   - External policy advocacy
   - Policy engagement/research

2. Constructing policy alternatives/
   policy formulation
   - Internal and external study on
     policy issues

3. Choice of solution/selection
   of preferred policy option
   - Potential messaging issues
     highlighted

STUDY/ADVERTISING

4. Policy design
   - Policy announcements
   - Policy advertising
   - Respond to 24/7 news
     cycle for new ideas

5. Policy implementation
   and monitoring
   - Monitor internal messaging
   - Manage external messages to
     internal decision-makers

ISSUES MANAGEMENT

6. Policy evaluation
   - Respond to external messages
   - Coordinate external advocacy

Compressed timelines

fundamentally redefined. One important effect, for example, has been a shift in the operation of technical or bureaucratic expertise in the traditional policy process because of pressures to respond to public input. We illustrate this dynamic in Figure 3.1.

This figure shows the traditional stages of policy development (Pal 2009), where the internal communications function plays a key role. In this version, we superimpose three major areas of internal communications responsibility on the policy process: engaging stakeholder communities (1 and 2); studying policy problems and advertising possible solutions (3 and 4); and internally managing implementation issues, including mediating external feedback and advocacy relationships (5 and 6). The traditional approach views the policy process as a linear progression of steps. However, the effect of the digital environment on that process is that citizens and stakeholder communities can engage at various points much sooner and more often. They can also quickly mobilize support or opposition. The effect of such engagement is that reaction times become shorter, and political leaders feel compelled to act quickly or face immediate responses. In addition, given shorter reaction times, there is a greater probability that communications messages and processes will transform themselves. In this respect, the internal communications function can engage the policy cycle and refract, deflect, or distract the policy narrative at that point in the process or at a later point to serve the government's purposes. It can shift those narratives in other directions either to avoid responsibility or to alter the policy discussion altogether.

In this view, DBCTs and the flow of information and opinion that they facilitate, tend to reduce timelines for study and feedback, as indicated in the figure by the arrows showing compressed timelines, especially in those study portions of the policy process. Communications, and related inputs, do not negate the important role of policy, strategy, oversight, risk, and other units that support the development and assessment of policy. Rather, they indicate where communications as a function appears to affect policy input. Notably, communications officers are sensitive to the external environment. Their role is to engage with various internal and external actors in the media (social and traditional), federal departments, other jurisdictions, non-profit groups, advocacy groups, labour organizations, and citizens. Consequently, they can quickly gauge the reception of internal and external ideas and messages and then convey to decision makers how such messages resonate with various audiences. The enhanced responsiveness means that their input in policy discussions is critical. Policy development, therefore, can be more responsive than discerning.

The federal communications function provides several roles: it filters information among stakeholder groups, citizens, and the government; it acts as a buffer between outside communicators and government decision makers; it is a policy resource on how messages can be communicated and understood, both internally and externally, with bureaucratic and political officials; it markets ideas; and it manages crises as they arise. Communications units are tasked with bringing competencies to policy making that extend well beyond what traditional centralized policy units were able to offer in the past.

Case Study

METHOD

Our case study provides critical observations on changes emanating from online communications in the Canadian policy process. It also considers the responses of public officials to digitally based communications, and their perspectives on it, and how the policy process has been affected. When interviewing officials, we clarified that digitally based communications referred not simply to external social media and digital media interactions but also to internal communications such as email/text/PIN responses, internal/external performance, and other reporting and hierarchical communications tools that connect ministers' offices with departmental programs and activities. As such, this case provides a broad picture of arguments taken from the literature and key informant interviews with reference to three major questions:

1. How has the policy process been affected by digitally based communications?
2. Has the policy advisory role of the senior public service become more responsive to the political arm of government as a consequence of digital communications?
3. How has the use of online technologies affected policy work at the federal level?

Ten semi-structured anonymous in-person interviews were carried out in Ottawa between January and April 2016. Five federal departments were identified for interviews according to the following criteria: size, extent to which they were likely to have significant external and internal communications, and respondents whose tenures crossed both the Harper government and the Trudeau government. Two large or multi-functional departments, two medium-sized or focused responsibility departments, and one small special purpose agency were selected, based on consultations with two federal government respondents. To protect the confidentiality and anonymity of the key informants, we refrain from directly or indirectly identifying these federal government departments. Obviously, it is a relatively small and well-networked world, and any hint of which departments are represented here would lead to speculation on the identities of the informants.

We attempt to understand how and why each of these departments/ agencies placed high value on the role of internal communications in the policy process; why there might be differences in how communications informs management decisions; how this function contributes to internal policy discussions; and how it manages internal and external boundaries, including central agency directives. An interview guide comprising nine questions, across three thematic areas, was developed. The themes were (1) effects of digital communications on the policy process as they relate to internal decision-making structures and people; (2) shifting relationships between departments and central actors; and (3) discernible changes to internal accountability processes and reporting. Our approach was to convey prevailing thoughts from the literature and then to ask respondents to assess the literature against organizational experience. Another aim was to determine whether departmental approaches to online communications were influenced in any way by political or bureaucratic preferences along the three thematic lines.

Seven of the ten interviews were held with more than one respondent in the same department representing the five departments/agencies. Three of these interviews were undertaken with the deputy minister or a senior communications official. Four of the seven interviews were held with an individual deputy minister, senior communications official, senior policy official, or senior information technology manager. Finally, three of the ten interviews were held with central agency officials, including the current clerk and a former clerk of the Privy Council. All respondents were assured anonymity and confidentiality in their comments. Hence, all quotations are cited as respondent one (R1) and so on.

Findings

Respondents were asked to position the role of the 2014 federal Policy on

Communications in the policy process given the various structural and agency changes observed. The policy provided that public servants should "consult the public ... [and] listen to and take account of people's interests and concerns when establishing priorities, developing policies, and planning programs and services. The government's obligation to reach out and communicate with citizens is concomitant with the right of citizens to address and be heard by their government" (Canada 2014, 2.6). This policy was updated in May 2016 and explicitly recognizes the addition of digital tools and platforms. At the time of the interviews, senior federal public servants implicitly acknowledged the important role of digital communications and anticipated that the new Policy on Communications and Federal Identity expected officials to use these tools. The new policy states that "the Government of Canada considers the views of Canadians when developing policies, programs, services and initiatives. In order to have an effective and open dialogue with an increasingly diverse Canadian public, the government uses innovative digital tools and online platforms" (Canada 2016, 4.2).

This provision entails policy dialogue as an approach that views the communications function as a dynamic process of engagement rather than simply a means to consult or convey information (Canada 2016, 4.1, 4.2). According to respondents, such changes are affecting how government policy is approached. As inputs to policy, e-technologies have fundamentally altered "how business is done in government" (R1) in that governments recognize a duty to consult on policy questions and that a reasonable response is required based on collected information. In addition, technology has made it possible to consult more broadly or to be more focused. Citizens, advocacy groups, lobbyists, pundits, media, and social media actors also know that their relative influence has increased, given that with access there is political power to put pressure on decision makers.

Respondents noted that such shifts in the communications environment ensure that new and more voices are encouraged at various points of intervention in the policy process. However, they said that these voices are still proportionate to the traditional players, whose influence has not changed. Industry, labour, and business organizations have maintained their influence and become more adept at doing so through various media and other public forums. It stands to reason that, "the more voices there are in the room, the louder one has to shout to be heard" (R5). That aside, these voices continue to be sought by decision makers because "they ... still carry much weight in terms of their influence on us" (R6). Voices with power, position, and money still attract attention because they can be used to support the government's aims, or work against them, more so than other voices. All respondents indicated that online technologies can contribute to the exercise of power since the intensity of messages brought to bear on decision makers can be significant. The loudest voices are not always reflected in the volume of communications activity; it is, rather, the strength of the voices behind them. One respondent (R3) indicated that the department "floated an idea in the media" and was met with an "onslaught" by the major business groups, not just in traditional media coverage but also in social media: "The minister got the message loud and clear."

Respondents expressed concerns about the uneven access of vulnerable populations or those that either elect not to engage or cannot engage because of technological or capacity challenges (Bovaird 2003; R1 and R6). The concern is that uneven access can exacerbate inequities between targeted and non-targeted groups (Margetts 2009, 10). Who is heard and responded to can fracture the inclusive ideological foundation of New Public Governance on which the federal communications policy appears to be based. Respondents worried that such considerations raise problems of democratic legitimation since some populations are highly engaged while others are not. One respondent (R1) pointed to the disparate participation of Indigenous populations: some communities have access to reliable digital platforms, whereas many do not. When a technological response to a policy issue is given high priority, some people will not be heard (R6 and R7). Respondents indicated that, though this perspective might be perceptual, in operational terms it is an ongoing concern that an accurate reflection of reality be communicated to ministers. Despite this challenge, two respondents indicated that there is no evidence to suggest that increased access by disadvantaged groups translates into more consideration of their views (R6 and R7).

The communications policy creates the conditions for policy co-creation, which, according to respondents, gives permission to departments to consult more broadly. At the front end of the policy process, "communications are used to affect the behaviour of actors in the agenda-setting and formulation stages, and in the back end the implementation and evaluation stages" (Glenn 2014, 6). Respondents widely agreed that they are using digitally based technologies with greater sophistication and precision, depending on where the policy is in the cycle. However, greater precision means that departments and agencies are having to invest in specialized expertise, which often transcends the functional lines of authority. Furthermore, with greater expertise, there is a much higher value placed on the government's ability to control the message and hold the attention of citizens and the media in the twenty-four-hour news cycle. Creating a culture of openness is difficult to instill in a public service that also values its own policy space and the need for secrecy. According to one official who served before and throughout the Conservative government's mandate, secrecy is a necessary feature of the government so that it can have its own conversation before engaging with others. Given shifts in openness, "it is all the more important to carve out space to think and reflect rather than respond to ministers on a dime" (R3). In this official's view, the current modus operandi appears to be to respond first and reflect later.

Respondents also observed that, despite increased access by citizens and groups, and the potential for more legitimate action, those using social media tools for political and policy objectives can be motivated by private, partisan, or ideological interests. This observation is supported in this volume by Fenwick McKelvey, Marianne Côté, and Vincent Raynauld, who consider "social media elites" not only "non-professional technology experts" who might be citizen journalists and bloggers but also politically motivated partisans. For example, respondents pointed to "astroturfing" (i.e., the act of creating a false grassroots organization and making it appear to represent something popular to promote a specific entity or cause) as exercising undue influence on government officials. They also cited government self-promotion, as in the case of former Conservative Minister of Employment Pierre Poilievre and the vanity videos controversy (CBC 2015). Some highlighted the Economic Action Plan ads of the former Conservative government as an example of promoting a singular policy focus while ignoring all other communications inputs. In the current government context, respondents indicated that a concerted orientation toward digitally based communications creates high public expectations that the government is listening, expectations that can be dashed quickly if they are not met. In other words, technology can create the conditions for engagement quickly and be used to dispel notions of legitimate action just as quickly.

Respondents said that one negative effect of misused online communications is that legitimate and unbiased information is lumped in with illegitimate messages. Such misuse creates a pervasive cynicism that all external messages are staged in order to manipulate decision makers. In essence, the social media universe is not always representative of perspectives given that the many communities of interest residing there respond to different events in different ways. When viewed in this way, social media engagement can actually lead to less engagement by decision makers since public intentions cannot be legitimated.

Several respondents indicated that, despite the advantages of digitally based communications, and the promise of greater public discourse, technology on its own will not lead to greater democratic engagement of citizens. Although technology might not compel outcomes, it can make difficult things easier. Internet and social media tools encourage active communications, as the study of the use of Twitter by local candidates presented in this volume by Julie Killin and Tamara Small demonstrates, but a key threshold for effective public policy making has not yet been achieved; the government's participation remains elusive. This supports Froomkin's view (2004, 15) that not enough has been done "for the direct integration of the popular will into political decision-making processes." For respondents, the view of the government is that public service reliance on technology is ambitious, and the capacity does not yet exist to facilitate internal debates and encourage active citizen involvement. There is a growing willingness to engage, but current technology has only facilitated a greater inflow of information. The bureaucracy is hesitant to engage because expectations of openness require resources and a political culture to support it.

Although bureaucratic decision makers want to be more engaged in and responsive to public discourse, internal policy processes remain more closed than open. "Our policy process is still largely secretive, very little is visible, even to ourselves in many cases," said one respondent (R6), and this orientation has been intensified with e-communications and the engagement of ministers. When political responsiveness becomes central, the net effect is that "every unit sees itself in the policy discussion: everyone has a piece of the story and wants their kick at the can" (R9). Because public servants do not always drive discussions, these units fight to demonstrate their value to ministers, especially in times of austerity. The consequence of such involvement, for some respondents, can be expedient advice to deputies and ministers with multiple evidentiary positions reflected and reduced decision coherence. For other respondents, such conditions force greater coherence by focusing advice on the perspectives of traditional and powerful actors over other policy participants.

Respondents recognized the increased role of internal communications in both policy making and decision making. Every department, large and small, supports internal communications. Respondents also observed that communications officers resemble policy analysts in many respects, to the point that "it is difficult to separate these activities any longer" (R4). In addition to the several roles that communications plays in managing boundary issues, it monitors social media and other discussions on matters that affect the departments and assesses them against critical internal conversations. Communications is regarded as an important contributor to policy inputs, including floating or relaying ideas for policy alternatives internally. At the policy decision stage (stage 3 in Figure 3.1), for example, communications and other officials respond to requests for information from ministers and parliamentarians as debates ensue. The communications function frames memorandums to cabinet, and other decision documents, that move up the line and outward to the public. It is now a fully integrated policy function that supports and even encourages the confidential management of information, and the framing of key outbound messages, consistent with the model of New Political Governance.

According to respondents, digitally based communications technologies facilitate a great deal of traffic, but this places a premium on the buffering role of senior public servants and partisan advisers (Craft 2016, 28). Advisers in particular filter the information provided in a way that aligns with ministers' preferences. In essence, several respondents agreed that political and bureaucratic policy officials resist using techniques/methods that broaden citizen engagement in policy work (see Turnbull and Aucoin 2006). The reasons are manifold: engagement requires that elites relinquish or share power; agendas and outcomes are harder to control; citizens are not adequately informed or sufficiently interested to justify their input; officials are more willing to share power with important organized interests because they can make deals and negotiate behind veils; and parliamentarians believe that direct citizen engagement diminishes their own roles as elected representatives, thereby negating parliamentary democracy. The buffering role of policy officials, both political and bureaucratic, is to filter myriad policy inputs and to separate the useful from the not so useful. Questions of capacity, the simple ability to manage and curate inputs, loom large in the context of technologies, which fragment the policy and communications environment.

In response to the complexity of communications both inside and outside the government, political and bureaucratic elites work to re-establish a semblance of centralized control to ensure consistent and uncomplicated repetition of core information to specific constituencies. Messaging mistakes can go viral quickly and often elicit speedy responses in aggressive communications campaigns, such as the controversial announcement that the federal government had approved defence contracts with Saudi Arabia (CBC 2016). The result of this announcement was reluctance by the Department of Global Affairs to publicly discuss future arms or other controversial deals (Dobbin 2016).

Respondents said that they have observed increased coordination and control being exercised by the Privy Council Office under the Liberal government than under the Conservative government, which had managed its communications roles out of the Prime Minister's Office. The PCO has been increasingly tasked with triaging issues coming from line departments and determining critical messages supported by political decision makers. Despite promises that the PMO would "loosen its grip" (Delacourt 2016), respondents indicated that the PCO has assumed many of the roles once held in the Conservative PMO. Because the PCO is staffed by public servants, control by that agency provides some degree of legitimate cover for political control of government communications and messaging. Politically based, results-based management regimes serve to support a coordinated approach, including the federal government's "deliverology" initiative (Barber, Moffit, and Kihn 2010). Departments are now under constraints and deadlines to respond to central inquiries in ways that adhere to new political-level delivery directives, as per the new Policy on Results 2016. Deliverology is a manifestation of results-based management that highlights political results and their measurement from the centre of government and emphasizes a whole-of-government approach. Political results are gathered through delivery units that coordinate with other results measurement functions, such as internal audit and program evaluation.

Respondents noted departmental confusion about the roles of political staffers in the policy process. Whereas there were noted instances of direct interference in bureaucratic decision making in the Harper era (Craft 2016; Savoie 2010, 209), the challenge facing respondents now is that, though it has become common for staffers to participate in the policy process, their roles and authorities are unclear. Staffers were used by the Conservative government to direct bureaucratic action, whereas under Trudeau there appears to be recognition of boundaries and specific responsibilities of the public service for technical advice. Some respondents indicated that staffers are learning the limits of their responsibilities but that sometimes the line between ministerial direction and public service responsibility is crossed. It is becoming clear to respondents that, in essence, a second source of bureaucratic responsibility has been created with particular expertise in political communications and messaging. Public service staff are expected to include such expertise in their policy calculations, and this is welcome to some and unwelcome to others. According to one official (R1), this indicates the growing importance of digitally based communications attached to policy questions.

From a departmental perspective, a critical operational question for respondents is how to rationalize divergent views in the form of useful advice to ministers in a timely way, especially given the roles of staffers. Identifying which voices are given priority is a political and operational challenge, requiring much political acuity. Being responsive to ministers can often mean, according to respondents, ignoring some pertinent perspectives on a question over others. With a greater volume of information and perspectives, the risk of selective advice, whether purposeful or not, increases. Although these challenges have always existed, the risk to ministers of "losing control of discussions" is greater now (R7).

In addition, though digitally based communications provides a means for the expansion of participants in the process, respondents said that the usefulness and quality of that input can be uneven. A great deal of what is communicated in social media is regarded as having little or no value in policy terms. Respondents expressed concerns not only about the volume and quality of digitally based communications but also about its attribution. It is difficult to validate whether all of this communication relates to the questions of concern to policy makers and whether such messages provide anything other than the fact that there are different opinions on broadly defined issues. For one official (R5), this has implications for democratic deliberation in that political officials might ultimately elect to ignore input from communications officials or attach more weight to it in the absence of technical evidence.

Finally, almost all respondents indicated that digitally based communications places a high priority on governments to respond to public messages and other information inputs. However, public bureaucracies believe that they have an obligation to study those inputs, validate them, and provide balanced and representative advice to ministers. Such processes take time, and ministers are not always willing to wait, leading to greater direction provided to public officials to respond in ways that they believe are appropriate. The challenge for senior officials, however, is that they might be unable to push back on ideas that they believe to be inappropriate, unfeasible, or ineffective. Given the many cuts to research and data functions since the mid-1990s, the capacity of the public service to generate evidence-based policy advice has been hampered (R6). Although there is a move toward injecting more input from the public service in policy making, such as a move toward greater experimentation (Canada 2015), this will take time and significant resources. Respondents raised concerns that results-based evidence in policy making is founded on information management systems and the creation of reliable data: "The rubber hits the road with good information" (R8). There have been some investments in these areas under the Liberal government, but building expertise that fits with current preferences will take time.

Equally important, pressure to respond quickly places public officials in a short-term frame of mind. The system becomes singularly focused on responding to immediate needs at the expense of the long view: "The public service is the voice of the long game, and it is a voice that is increasingly difficult to make heard" (R1). Policy announcements are a regular occurrence in the government, most of which serve its permanent campaigning efforts

TABLE 3.1

Summary of the contribution of digital communications (DC) to the policy process

Finding	Benefits	Constraints
Inputs to policy making		
There is an increased "duty" to consult.	More voices are heard in the policy process.	The larger number of voices (policy actors) forces all to work harder to be heard above the cacophony.
	There are more focused consultations.	With more voices, policy actors pay more attention to traditional sources of power.
	There is more effort to reach vulnerable populations.	There is uneven access by vulnerable populations unwilling or unable to use DC.
DC can expand or narrow policy legitimacy.	The government can get messages out quickly.	Messages can be self-interested.
	DC can rally support publicly.	Illegitimate use can displace legitimate policy action.

Finding	Benefits	Constraints
Increased role of DC		
A merging of the communications and policy functions of the government is discernible.	The public service is no longer the sole creator of knowledge in the policy process.	With less protected policy space, the public service could further entrench secrecy internally.
	There is more policy co-creation.	There is greater pressure internally to demonstrate public value.
Senior public servants serve to a greater degree than before as a buffer, filtering and curating information to make it policy relevant/usable.	There is pressure to build the capacity within the public service to better utilize DC.	Building capacity can be constrained with more controls on tools.
	There are more policy positions reflected in internal and external discourse.	DC can create conditions for selective buffering and channelling of information upward.
	There is greater policy capacity with the addition of communications analysts.	DC can take a priority role in policy decisions.
Policy coordination		
DC has contributed to the greater centralization of coordination and control in the PCO and PMO.	DC can create the conditions for improved policy coordination.	Coordination can be onerous.
	Central agencies can better focus key messages.	The pressure to control messages increases.
DC carves out a role for political staffers in managing policy messages.	DC increases the ability and manageability of ministers' offices to receive and understand policy messages.	DC can confuse political and public service staff policy roles.
		Staffers can use DC to refine and simplify messages that suit ministerial preferences.
There is increased pressure to move policy advice quickly up the line.	There is the promise of improved public service policy responsiveness.	Data quality might be uneven, and the potential for errors in evidence increases.

to stimulate electoral fortunes and the twenty-four-hour news cycle. Such pressures are out of step with regulations and other processes that rely on due diligence and public consultation. Respondents said that democratic imperatives for due diligence can be contrary to political and public pressures for immediate responses. Given the breadth of findings from this case, we have summarized the key messages, with critical benefits and constraints noted for each in Table 3.1.

Political Elites in Canada in the Digital Age

A major change in the federal policy process is that public service influence and inputs are no longer sacrosanct. The federal public service is undergoing its own rationalization, including, most notably, whether it has a role in policy construction. It is coming to terms with being a co-producer of policy positions, evidence, and implementation. What this means, in practical terms, is that senior officials, including the clerk of the Privy Council, have had to rationalize the relevance of the public service in the policy process, including how it fits within the larger digital environment (May 2016). It is no longer the sole creator of knowledge, if it ever was, and it is not always the authoritative voice on a given problem.

A perverse effect is that the public service might see itself as being "off the hook on governmental decisions, because advice may not always be attributed to public servants" (R2). Such advice can come from many sources. Respondents concluded that the role of the public bureaucracy is being recast in light of shifts toward greater responsiveness to political and social media inputs. Questions are raised about whether the public service can maintain the idea of being merit based, professional, and non-partisan in light of greater responsiveness. Although this is a much larger discussion, bureaucratic roles are being rationalized in the policy process as focusing on consolidating evidence, confirming positions, and ensuring fairness and due diligence in validating evidence.

The increasing prominence of political staff points to a major shift in how the Canadian system of government operates. They play a critical role in connecting with citizens and voters, who express their views in multiple ways, including via digital communications. Respondents appear to recognize the role that staffers play in gathering and synthesizing digital communications inputs. The challenge from a bureaucratic perspective is how to weight these perspectives against various forms of technical or research evidence. Staffers are capable of and responsible for conveying what is happening at the moment. Although important, the bureaucracy can become swept up in crisis management that responds to digital communications at the expense of longer-term policy imperatives. Internal communications functions can amplify short-term thinking, which – when combined with electoral priorities supported by reporting manifestations such as deliverology – potentially reduce the prevalence of long-term policy thinking. That said, the same stated preferences for experimentation and technical evidence in policy choices and implementation can temper or mitigate these risks, assuming that there remains the political will to do so.

With respect to the policy process itself, the traditional cycle appears to be intact despite the rise of digital communications. Although counterintuitive, the agenda-setting and engagement stages of public policy making are showing signs of democratization, but the internal churning of documents, studies, and advice to ministers remains stubbornly closed, albeit compressed. Although there is evidence of greater consultation and solicitation of views, especially evident in the new Policy on Communications and Federal Identity (Canada 2016), it will take time for the internal capacity for engagement to catch up to a point where participative democracy is possible. Senior officials continue to adhere to systems of accountability that value confidence to ministers over open engagement with various publics. Equally important, ministers still value evidence informed by economic power over civil society or advocacy positions. This is unlikely to change since political fortunes are often driven by economic gains.

E-government, e-technologies, and e-governance are helping to transform the policy process. However, such arguments are regarded as being oblivious of the control frameworks that permeate bureaucratic processes, including access to information, privacy, lobbying, official languages, communications, and other policies. According to respondents, open communications must be fashioned according to accepted rules of practice, which limit the ability of the government to communicate outwardly. The government is held to a higher standard of engagement than that imposed by social media. In this respect, conversations tend to be strategically focused with key actors on policy questions in order to limit noise that cannot be attributed to the questions themselves. Such focused conversations also ensure that stakeholders are actively consulted. Therefore, technology has enabled departments and agencies to be more precise in targeting key policy actors, but its use remains governed by internal accountability and control frameworks. Technology will have an effect on the next generation of public servants, who will regard digital communications as an essential tool for gathering evidence and working horizontally.

Although online communications contributes to centralization and political responsiveness, one cannot ignore both personal and structural factors, which also contribute to the drive for greater centralization of control. Although greater attention is being focused on ministers in the Trudeau era, there is still a preference for central control over government messages. The old adage "the dance is the same, it's just a different tune," applies. Ministers, and their departments and agencies, still take their direction from the PMO. Digital communications, and the immediacy with which missteps are reported, will reinforce a centralized approach to the government's messaging and communications. The bureaucracy might have greater flexibility to contribute to policy making under the Liberal government, but central control and coordination are unlikely to be decreased. From a democratic perspective, this could limit the exploration of policy options at the departmental level despite greater external policy discussion.

Technologies aside, the internal communications function has assumed prominence federally. It is used to assert control over internal policy discussions not simply by central agents and political actors but also by bureaucrats. It plays an important buffering role between external actors and internal discussions, and it translates internal messages that play with external audiences. Internal communications maintains the insider-outsider relationship and preserves the confidential advice demanded by ministers. It also supports the preservation of the traditional policy process and wrestles some responsibilities for diligence away from traditional policy units that value comprehensive evidence over timely advice.

Constructing appropriate systems to support engagement is in its infancy. In practical terms, information generation and analysis capability are critical, along with building appropriate information management systems and policies that can support them. The current government shows a willingness to engage public service advice. However, restoring policy analysis capability will take investment and patience.

Aside from systems that have to be built or reinforced, senior officials are under pressure to respond more quickly and with greater reliability. The challenge is that bureaucracies are large and subject to several competing authorities, regulations, and procedural constraints. Digitally based communications is placing great pressure on bureaucracies to reform for the future, all the while living in a house under intense renovation. The need to change has always been omnipresent for bureaucracies; online communications has simply accelerated that need and laid bare the challenges of working in a large system that is often slow but resilient in its response.

ACKNOWLEDGMENTS: The authors would like to acknowledge the research contributions of Diane Simsovic (PhD candidate, Carleton University), Ryan Deschamps, and Stephen Fleet (MA candidates, Ryerson University).

REFERENCES

Aucoin, Peter. 2012. "New Political Governance in Westminster Systems: Impartial Public Administration and Management Performance at Risk." *Governance: An International Journal of Policy, Administration, and Institutions* 25, 2: 177–99. https://doi.org/10.1111/j.1468-0491.2012.01569.x.

Barber, Michael, Andy Moffit, and Paul Kihn. 2010. *Deliverology 101: A Field Guide for Educational Leaders.* Thousand Oaks, CA: Corwin.

Bovaird, Tony. 2003. "E-Government and E-Governance: Organisational Implications, Options, and Dilemmas." *Public Policy and Administration* 18, 2: 37–56. https://doi.org/10.1177/095207670301800204.

Canada. Prime Minister's Office. 2015. "President of the Treasury Board of Canada Mandate Letter." https://pm.gc.ca/eng/president-treasury-board-canada-mandate-letter.

–. Treasury Board Secretariat. 2014. *Communications Policy of the Government of Canada.* http://www.tbs-sct.gc.ca/pol/doc-eng.aspx?id=12316.

–. 2016. *Policy on Communications and Federal Identity.* https://www.tbs-sct.gc.ca/pol/doc-eng.aspx?id=30683.

CBC. 2015. "Pierre Poilievre Rejects Criticism over Taxpayer-Funded 'Vanity Videos.'" *CBC News,* May 15. http://www.cbc.ca/news/politics/pierre-poilievre-rejects-criticism-over-taxpayer-funded-vanity-videos-1.3076240.

–. 2016. "Stéphane Dion Approves Export Permits for $11B in LAVs to Be Sent to Saudi Arabia." *CBC News,* April 13. http://www.cbc.ca/news/politics/saudi-arms-deal-documents-1.3533082.

Clarke, Amanda, and Helen Margetts. 2014. "Governments and Citizens Getting to Know Each Other? Open, Closed, and Big Data in Public Management Reform." *Policy and Internet* 6, 4: 393–417. https://doi.org/10.1002/1944-2866.POI377.

Craft, Jonathan. 2016. *Backrooms and Beyond: Partisan Advisors and the Politics of Policy Work in Canada.* Toronto: University of Toronto Press.

Delacourt, Susan. 2016. "Will Justin Trudeau Keep His Promise to Loosen PMO's Grip?" *Toronto Star,* January 1. https://www.thestar.com/news/insight/2016/01/01/will-justin-trudeau-keep-his-promise-to-loosen-pmos-grip-delacourt.html.

Deschamps, Ryan. 2014. "What Potential for YouTube as a Policy Deliberation Tool? Commenter Reactions to Videos about the Keystone XL Oil Pipeline." *Policy and Internet* 6, 4: 341–59. https://doi.org/10.1002/1944-2866.POI376.

Dobbin, Murray. 2016. "Saudi Arms Deal Signals Mideast Betrayal." *Tyee,* April 29. https://thetyee.ca/Opinion/2016/04/29/Canadian-Saudi-Arms-Deal/.

Dunleavy, Patrick, Helen Margetts, Simon Bastow, and Jane Tinkler. 2006. *Digital Era Governance: IT Corporations, the State, and E-Government.* Oxford: Oxford University Press. https://doi.org/10.1093/acprof:oso/9780199296194.001.0001.

Froomkin, Michael. 2004. "Technologies for Democracy." In *Democracy Online: The Prospects for Political Renewal through the Internet,* edited by Peter Shane, 3–20. New York: Routledge.

Glenn, Ted. 2014. "The Management and Administration of Government Communications in Canada." *Canadian Public Administration* 57, 1: 3–25. https://doi.org/10.1111/capa.12057.

Hindman, Matthew. 2007. "Open-Source Politics Reconsidered: Emerging Patterns in Online Political Participation." In *Governance and Information Technology: From Electronic Government to Information Government,* edited by Viktor Mayer-Schönberger and David Lazer, 183–207. Cambridge, MA: MIT Press.

Knox, Claire Connolly. 2016. "Public Administrators' Use of Social Media Platforms: Overcoming the Legitimacy Dilemma?" *Administration and Society* 48, 4: 477–96. https://doi.org/10.1177/0095399713503463.

Margetts, Helen Z. 2009. "The Internet and Public Policy." *Policy and Internet* 1, 1: 1–21. https://doi.org/10.2202/1944-2866.1029.

Margetts, Helen, and Patrick Dunleavy. 2013. "The Second Wave of Digital-Era Governance: A Quasi-Paradigm for Government on the Web." *Philosophical Transactions of the Royal Society A: Mathematical, Physical, and Engineering Sciences* 371, 1987: 1–17. https://doi.org/10.1098/rsta.2012.0382.

May, Kathryn. 2016. "PS Needs to Pick Up Pace of Reforms: Privy Council Clerk." *Ottawa Citizen,* March 25. http://ottawacitizen.com/news/local-news/ps-needs-to-pick-up-pace-of-reforms-privy-council-clerk.

Meijer, Albert Jacob, and René Torenvlied. 2016. "Social Media and the New Organization of Government Communications: An Empirical Analysis of Twitter Usage by the Dutch Police." *American Review of Public Administration* 46, 2: 143–61. https://doi.org/10.1177/0275074014551381.

Osborne, Stephen P. 2010. *The New Public Governance: Emerging Perspectives on the Theory and Practice of Public Governance.* London: Routledge.

Pal, Leslie. 2009. *Beyond Policy Analysis: Public Issue Management in Turbulent Times.* 4th ed. Toronto: Nelson.

Savoie, Donald. 2010. *Power: Where Is It?* Montreal: McGill-Queen's University Press.

Small, Tamara. 2012. "E-Government in the Age of Social Media: An Analysis of the Canadian Government's Use of Twitter." *Policy and Internet* 4, 3–4: 91–111. https://doi.org/10.1002/poi3.12.

Turnbull, Lori, and Peter Aucoin. 2006. *Fostering Canadians' Role in Public Policy: A Strategy for Institutionalizing Public Involvement in Policy.* Ottawa: Canadian Policy Research Networks.

4

Political Staff and Permanent Public Servants: Still Getting Along

Jennifer Robson and R. Paul Wilson

Cabinet ministers in Canada are undoubtedly elite actors. Collectively responsible under the prime minister for exercising executive power and for proposing the government's budget and legislative agenda to Parliament, ministers are the driving force behind law, public policy, and politics. But today ministers face unprecedented challenges because of multiple and often interacting forces: the prominence of wicked policy problems, with no clear or easy resolution within jurisdictional boundaries; public and media distrust of institutions and the decline of deference; the decline of party loyalty among voters; unprecedented public expectations for openness and accountability; and, perhaps above all, the speed with which events unfold in the full glare of 24/7 journalism and social media.

Ministers have always had assistance in carrying out their duties. Traditionally, this assistance largely came from civil servants who, in the British tradition, were permanent, expert, and politically neutral, capable of loyally serving whichever political masters formed the government of the day. Since the 1960s, prime ministers and ministers in Canadian governments of all stripes have increased their reliance on partisan political staffers. These staffers act as a "counterweight" (Aucoin 2010, 77) to permanent public servants, and they are employed to play a political challenge role on departmental advice; to increase officials' responsiveness to the government's agenda; and, by exchanging information and even negotiating between political offices, to further ministers' policies and political agendas. Ministerial staffers view the world in a way fundamentally different from that of public servants since, as political actors, they are driven by the pressures of the permanent campaign, and the heightened concern for brand management, both of which are enabled and necessitated by digital technology (Marland 2016).

According to the Privy Council Office, the relationship between federal ministerial staff and departmental public servants should be "characterized by mutual respect, cooperation, and the sharing of information where it is relevant or needed for their respective work." Although political staff may "transmit the minister's instructions," they "do not have a role in departmental operations," "have no legal basis for exercising the delegated authority of ministers," and "have an obligation to inform themselves about the appropriate parameters of public service conduct" (PCO 2015, 47). Sometimes the relationship is smooth and complementary, but this is not always the case, and ministerial political staff have been central to political scandals in Canada – such as the Rivard Affair in the Pearson government, the sponsorship scandal of the Chrétien government, and the senate expenses scandal of the Harper government – as well as in other Westminster countries, including Australia, New Zealand, and the United Kingdom. Although stricter controls over ministerial staffers' behaviour (notably, in Canada, provisions in the 2006 Federal Accountability Act and the new 2015 Code of Conduct) have helped to allay concerns, the continuing perception is that ministerial staffers exercise power without commensurate accountability.

What, however, do we know about the relationship between ministerial staffers and permanent public servants, the two elite groups serving ministers? How do these two elite groups interact under the pressures of too little time and far more information technology in the digital age? Is the relationship generally adversarial? Does it tend to undermine the neutrality of public servants? Or is there evidence of a creative tension, and even a partnership, in meeting the needs of their elected masters?

Academics have reached different conclusions about the relationship. Some have found that ministerial staffers can help to insulate public servants from partisan politics, spur public servants to improve their service to ministers, and facilitate relationships and exchange of resources within the core executive (e.g., Connaughton 2010; Craft 2016; Eichbaum and Shaw 2008; Maley 2011). More often, however, the literature harbours concerns about the potential for ministerial staff to subvert the expert, politically neutral public service because of their personal connections and direct access to ministers, which can lead to politicization by bringing inappropriate political pressure to bear on aspects of program implementation and administration, by funnelling out politically unwanted advice, by influencing the appointment and tenure of senior public servants, and generally by facilitating greater concentration of power at "the centre" of government (e.g., Aucoin 2012; Benoit 2006; Tiernan 2007). Indeed, Peter Aucoin (2012, 186) views ministerial staffers as integral to the reality of New Political Governance: they will risk "the continuous trashing of traditional public service values and structures" in order to promote and protect the governing party at all costs. In the context of permanent campaigning and the centralization of information and communications management (Kozolanka 2012; Thomas 2013), ministerial staffers replace public servants as the principal strategists with respect to proactive communications, detecting risk and defending the government's reputation in real time in mainstream media as well as on social media platforms, especially Twitter (Esselment and Wilson 2017).

Often, however, judgments about ministerial staff have been based more on media commentary than on detailed study. A former UK cabinet secretary, Andrew Turnbull (2005), noting "the thinly disguised hostility" in much of the writing about ministerial aides, encouraged critics to "go and visit some departments to see how special advisers are working day to day." Academics have begun, figuratively, to take this advice, and the empirical evidence of the relationship between public servants and ministerial staffers is growing in several Westminster countries.

Chris Eichbaum and Richard Shaw (2007, 462) found, through empirical survey-based research, that the relationship between ministerial staffers and public servants in New Zealand was "relatively healthy." Scholars have reached similar positive conclusions in the United Kingdom (Yong and Hazell 2014), Ireland (Connaughton 2010), and Australia (Maley 2002), though Anne Tiernan (2004, 246) also found "significant problems in the relationship between ministerial staff and public servants," especially with respect to their understanding of roles and responsibilities. Jonathan Craft's recent qualitative study (2016) fits into this emerging pattern, finding substantial evidence of cooperation between ministerial staffers and public servants in the Canadian government, observing that deputy ministers view ministerial staffers as "complementary rather than adversarial" to public servants and regard them in a "positive" manner (151–52).

Craft analyzed the state of affairs toward the end of the Harper government. No empirical research is yet available to illuminate the relationship between political staffers and public servants in the Trudeau government. However, following a 2011 Institute of Public Administration of Canada survey of federal, provincial, and municipal deputy ministers/chief administrative officers, the study's authors concluded that many thought "that 'the Political/Bureaucratic relationship was under strain,' with insufficient levels of trust and mutual respect" (IPAC 2012, 14).[1] The authors mused that this "could be [as one respondent phrased it] 'because political staff employs a political calculus while the bureaucracy is oriented toward substantive influence of policy" (14). According to data provided by the Institute of Public Administration, compared with 2007, a declining share of responding deputy ministers or equivalents thought that ministerial staff understood their role and that of public service: 34.4 percent in 2011 versus 44.7 percent in 2007. Finally, the 2011 survey asked respondents to comment on the following statement: "In Canada the political/bureaucratic relationship is under strain and there is insufficient trust and mutual respect." Although at least fifteen of the sixty-five open-ended text responses indicated a clear disagreement, another thirty-five indicated partial or strong agreement. Some respondents asserted that the mistrust or tension was long-standing, whereas others believed that the current state of the political-bureaucratic relationship was worse.

A 2011 report from the Public Service Commission of Canada has also asserted that tensions in the political–public service relationship are having negative institutional effects, in this case on the health of the federal public service. The commission argued that "some of the most significant risks to the non-partisanship of the public service stem from real and perceived tension regarding appropriate roles and responsibilities between the two [political and non-partisan] domains. This partly reflects the fact that the traditional relationship between elected officials and the public service has been deeply changed by the emergence of influential ministerial staff" (Barrados, Vennat, and Zussman 2011, 22).

In summary, though some empirical evidence suggests that the relationship between ministers' professional public service advisers and partisan political advisers is often constructive and healthy, there is also reason for concern. In the next section, we consider negative impacts on the institution of the public service by looking at measures of job satisfaction and confidence in senior management among individual federal public servants with different likelihoods of direct contact with ministers and their political staff.

Case Study

METHOD
We conducted a descriptive analysis of two surveys of federal public servants and reviewed qualitative findings from interviews with senior public

servants who served during the Harper government. Our quantitative analysis used data from two waves (2008 and 2014) of the Public Service Employee Survey, conducted by Statistics Canada on behalf of the Treasury Board Secretariat. The survey was sent to over 250,000 federal employees and had response rates of 65.9 percent in 2008 and 71.4 percent in 2014 (Office of the Chief Human Resources Officer 2009, 2015). We examined differences over time and between subgroups of employees with respect to job satisfaction and confidence in the senior managers of their departments or agencies. The surveys were cross-sectional, and the public data do not permit analysis of individual responses in which it would be possible to control for variables such as tenure and salary level.

We tested for significant differences between the responses of occupational groups of employees in the federal public service (PS) most likely to have direct professional interactions with political ministerial staff, including deputy ministers (DMs), members of the executive ranks (EXs), and the subset of executives in the Privy Council Office (EXs in PCO). Our analysis of the broad public service is limited to those who have a role as a supervisor. This limitation is both because of how public data are made available and to permit better comparisons with those in middle and senior management roles. We also tested for significant differences among public servants in the communications branches of federal departments (information services [IS]) because their work might be particularly affected by the permanent campaigning and political communications imperatives of ministers and their ministerial staff.[2] We present results for two waves of the survey that offer comparable data, in which all data collection took place during the tenure of the same Conservative government.[3] We tested for changes over time by comparing differences among these data points. The data did not, however, enable us to draw causal inferences about what is driving any observable change. The next wave of the same survey, scheduled for release in 2018, will provide data on the public service in the first two years of the Trudeau government.

Our quantitative results were complemented by qualitative analysis of semi-structured interviews, on the subject of political-bureaucratic relationships, with six current or former federal public service executives (three deputy ministers, two assistant deputy ministers, and one director) who held their positions during the later years of the Harper government. In order to assure anonymity, interview respondents are not named but identified only by their titles and, if needed, interview numbers, for example DM 1, ADM

2. Selection of the interview targets was based on convenience sampling. Interviews took place between February and October 2015, all prior to the general election that fall, and they provided important contextualization for the survey data. Interviewees were asked about their experiences and perceptions of interactions between senior public servants and political elites. Responses were not limited to their most recent government experiences.

Taken as a whole, our findings do not support the assertions of a poisoned relationship between the political and the public service sides of the government in Canada. It might be tempting to ascribe any evidence of tension to the particular style of the Harper government. Yet we found evidence of cooperation more often than conflict, with some notable exceptions among those involved in public communications on behalf of the government. Our results suggest that public servants working in communications have been less content and confident than other groups of public servants, including those who might have similar levels of interaction with political staff. According to some executives in the federal public service, communications work can present particular challenges in their relationships with political elites.

FINDINGS

Table 4.1 presents results of chi-square tests of independence for changes in satisfaction and confidence within each group. Table 4.2 uses the results for 2014 only and presents the results of multiple comparisons across groups. For simplicity, the table displays results only for subgroup comparisons using the general federal public service as the reference case. In the text, however, we do refer to additional paired comparisons (e.g., comparing deputy ministers and other executives), not shown in the table.

Between 2008 and 2014, measures of job satisfaction deteriorated in significant ways for the general federal public service population and public servants in communications roles (designated by the IS classification). Average declines in expressed satisfaction are between 4 percent and 6 percent in the time period. Confidence in management decision making actually increased significantly in the PS population, and among executives, but the magnitude is tiny (just 1 percent and 2 percent respectively). Otherwise, measures of satisfaction and confidence in senior management were not significantly changed. This is especially noteworthy given that our data cover a period that has been labelled by some observers as unprecedented for the

TABLE 4.1

Job satisfaction comparisons, Public Service Employee Survey, 2008 and 2014

	PS	DM	EX	EX in PCO	IS
"I get a sense of satisfaction from my work."					
2008	84	94	91	95	76
2014	80	100	90	95	74
Significance	**	–	–	–	**
"Overall, I like my job."					
2008	88	87	92	94	83
2014	83	100	89	95	78
Significance	**	–	*	–	**
"I have confidence in the senior management of my department or agency."					
2008	59	85	78	89	60
2014	59	100	80	92	59
Significance	–	–	–	–	–
"Senior management in my department or agency makes effective and timely decisions."					
2008	47	89	66	83	49
2014	48	96	68	85	49
Significance	**	–	**	–	–

NOTES: * $p < .05$, ** $p < .01$. Cell values are the percent who agree or strongly agree. Results for the IS (communications) group are highlighted for emphasis. Results for the public service (PS) are limited to those in supervisory positions.

degree of conflict between federal public servants and political elites (Griffith 2013; Jeffrey 2011).

Between-group comparisons on satisfaction (using the 2014 results only) demonstrated that communications employees (those in the IS classification) were, at the time of the survey, substantively and significantly less content in their work compared with all other groups in our analysis. Executives were substantively and significantly more satisfied than the PS population, and the effect was actually more pronounced for the subpopulation of executives in the PCO. Deputy ministers showed significantly different levels of satisfaction compared with the broader PS population of supervisors. Deputies and executives, particularly executives working in the PCO, were far more likely than the general population, and the IS population, to interact

TABLE 4.2

Job satisfaction comparisons, Public Service Employee Survey, 2014

	Less likely to agree	No difference	More likely to agree
	"I get a sense of satisfaction from my work."		
	IS**	–	DM EX** EX in PCO*
	"Overall, I like my job."		
In comparison to the general population of supervisors in the federal public service ...	IS**	–	DM EX** EX in PCO*
	"I have confidence in the senior management of my department or agency."		
	–	**IS**	DM* EX** EX in PCO**
	"Senior management in my department or agency makes effective and timely decisions."		
	–	–	DM** EX** EX in PCO** **IS**

NOTES: * $p < .05$, ** $p < .01$. The IS (communications) group is bolded for emphasis.

directly with ministers and their ministerial staff. If these interactions had any negative effect on employee satisfaction with their work, our results do not show it.

Interviews with senior officials suggest that relations with ministerial staffers can be positive, depending on the personalities involved. ADM 1 spoke about the importance of "individual relationships." He got on well with ministerial staff: "I think I was pretty clear with folks about my lack of hidden agendas. So I was able to build trust, and I think that helped." DM 3 expanded on the importance of personal interaction:

Personalities can play a big role. Generally, my experience was a happy one in that I met with very good, respectful relationships with people. It didn't mean we agreed on everything, by any means.

But we were all working to support the government and to advance its agenda. It doesn't mean there weren't challenges ... There's an inevitable tension there.

The deputy minister explained the importance of understanding the "swim lanes" in which the distinct kinds of advisers function, ideally with respect for and understanding of each other's responsibilities: "I've worked very closely with Conservative governments and Liberal governments, and it's pretty much the same in that respect. It's the nature of the system" (DM 3).

Yet the consistent difference in results for the IS population suggests that communications work can be more difficult and less satisfying. This might be partly because of the unrelenting pressures of 24/7 social media and permanent campaigning, which increase performance expectations for government communications staff. As DM 2 explained, "the need to be constantly vigilant about reputational risk" demands faster response times with no mistakes. ADM 2 explained how the pressure of modern communications for immediate response "leads to a kind of unpredictability in people's days, it upsets planning, [and] it crowds out some of the other work." It changes the "mood" in government offices: "There's a short termism and unpredictability in people's lives" and, at least in some parts of the system, "higher levels of stress." Not only do time pressures crowd out longer-term thinking, but also "the personality of the institution starts to shift so that even when it gets breaks from some of that pressure it may not be hardwired to do some of that longer-term analysis" (ADM 2).

A public service communications officer at the director level described how technological change, especially the wide distribution of smartphones, has increased demands on government communications: "The pace in which the communications staff in a minister's office carry out their business ... has changed dramatically. They're following what their political opponents are saying all the time and responding and occasionally asking the department to fact-check or provide ammunition, if you will." Furthermore, senior department officials are within reach all the time. In the past, he said, "you wouldn't have had that direct interaction on weekends with the minister's staff asking for something that must be delivered by Monday morning or even by that night, whether it's a correction or a 'detect and correct' of some news story that they don't quite like. These requests just come 24/7." Perhaps, in a bygone era, weekends provided a reprieve for public service communications officials and ministerial staffers alike before Monday morning's new task list arrived. This is now impossible since business is ongoing 24/7, and all staff are only a phone call or an instant message away from office demands and the expectation of an immediate response.

These stresses and intrusions outside regular working hours likely contribute to lower levels of job satisfaction within the public service communications community. But here again interpersonal relationships seem to matter. DM 1 described a varied experience: "I have seen some of the best in this government. I'd say my relationship with [name of ministerial chief of staff] was a very good and respectful, mature, professional relationship, ... and I've had one or two that haven't been that great." This respondent thought that relations under the Conservative government were "more strained" than had been the case with previous governments and attributed this in part to a perceived suspicion among some ministerial staffers of the public service and to the government's focus on issues management and minimizing reputational risks. These things together could sometimes create a "really corrosive culture" within some political communications units. "I've worked with some extremely professional [ministerial staffers], but some of them quite frankly are pretty young and inexperienced, and they throw their weight around a lot." This can make life difficult for departmental communications staff: "If public servants feel devalued or treated disrespectfully, then that can be very injurious. And I'm sure there are political staff who can feel the same way." These strains are undoubtedly increased by the political demand to combat, in real time 24/7, any criticism of the government as soon as it arises, whether in mainstream media or in social media. However, other factors – such as the overall culture of a government, or the cultures of specific ministers and departments, and even the personalities of individual staff members and public servants – can also contribute to tensions. From the outside, it is impossible to understand how these facets all relate, and we are reluctant to overinterpret the data available.

It is wrong to conceptualize the relationship between the public service and ministerial staff as universally or uniquely adversarial. There is, as our data show, much variation in the perceptions and experiences of different groups of public servants. Our findings do not support the contention, raised in some of the literature in Canada (and discussed earlier in this chapter), that the interface with ministerial staff presents significant risks to public service managers. In fact, senior public servants with whom ministerial staff most frequently have direct contact appear to show similar or higher levels of job satisfaction compared with the general PS population.

Further, the same senior public servants appear to have somewhat higher levels of confidence in one another when we compare executives and the broader population of public servants (see Table 4.2). These results suggest that interactions with ministerial staff are perhaps not as corrosive as is so often posited in the public administration literature.

Among communications staff, differences in satisfaction can be explained more by the nature of their work than by direct contact with ministerial staff. The nature of communications work, undoubtedly, is changing in ways that affect both professional work and quality of life for both political and bureaucratic communications staff. Public service executives in communications branches, in theory, could help to buffer the effects on their working-level staff and, arguably, ought to refuse requests that are overtly partisan or contravene managerial or ethical standards of the public service. However, public servants, in their relationships with political elites of the government, face opposing imperatives of responsiveness and accountability. Which imperative wins out might well be determined by the interpersonal relationships of those involved and the differences between communications roles and policy or administrative roles in the government. As ADM 2 observed in an interview, "comms is a hell of a lot trickier [than policy] in this regard. If there's anywhere where the challenge of the permanent campaign, [and] the increasing attention to political considerations in the context of the day-to-day business of government, have become more problematic, it's in the comms field."

Public servants support the elected government and recognize that ministers, often working through their political offices, have the democratic right to set the direction of government policy and communications. Public servants can give advice, but ultimately, as DM 1 put it, they are "takers," expected to be responsive to a government's direction. At the same time, they are required to observe a wide range of rules and measures intended to promote good governance and administration. These are measures for which public servants are individually and collectively held to account by Parliament, by oversight bodies, by media, and by internal discipline. Among these rules is a prohibition on engaging in partisan activity. On government communications tasks, in particular, under pressure and with severe time constraints, this balance between responsiveness and accountability can be particularly challenging to maintain. Websites that communicate government information but use colour schemes associated with party brands, departmental tweets that link to a minister's personal and partisan Twitter account, and even a minister's choice of attire at a departmental event can all blur the boundaries between government communications and partisan marketing.

Political Elites in Canada in the Digital Age

Since the coming into force of the Federal Accountability Act, ministerial staffers can no longer be described as "statutory orphans" (Benoit 2006) since they are now covered under the provisions of the Conflict of Interest Act and subject to enhanced post-employment restrictions under the Lobbying Act. Furthermore, in November 2015, the new Liberal government released for the first time a "Code of Conduct for Ministerial Exempt Staff," published as an annex to Prime Minister Justin Trudeau's guidance for ministers, *Open and Accountable Government* (PCO 2015). The code gathers together previously existing provisions for ministerial staffers, but it adds new ones and, importantly, is now explicitly part of the terms of employment for ministerial staffers, increasing their motivation to learn and abide by it. Ministers remain personally and directly accountable for the conduct of their staff members, as is consistent with the principle of ministerial accountability.

For their part, public servants have no shortage of measures and mechanisms aimed at holding them to account – or at least requiring that they report on performance, justify activities and expenditures, and observe myriad rules on day-to-day tasks. Some of these mechanisms are public (e.g., annual departmental reports), but many are internal to the systems of the public service itself (Jarvis 2014), not well understood by voters or even parliamentarians, and might be divorced from the priorities of the government in power. The traditional public service ethic of responding to the political direction of the government of the day can conflict at times with these accountability mechanisms, particularly in cases of public reporting or communications by individual public servants.

New forms of communication (particularly email but also internal systems to track documents or log media requests) are also creating records that can more easily be retrieved and used to hold both public servants and, increasingly, ministerial staffers to account for their behaviour in office. Written communications by ministerial staff with public servants have always been subject to access to information, though device-to-device instant messages, sent using BlackBerry personal identification numbers, are often not retained on departmental servers, and the information commissioner has called this an "unacceptable risk" to access to information in Canada (Legault 2013, 10). But ministerial staff can also expect their messages to political colleagues to be made public in cases of court-ordered disclosure or through investigations by police or officers of Parliament. For example, Conservative ministerial aide Sébastien Togneri found his exasperated emails to departmental staff reprinted in an information commissioner's report (Legault 2014), read into the record in the House of Commons, and reprinted in national media. In reviewing emails among PMO staff, the judge in Senator Mike Duffy's criminal trial marvelled that the documents provided an unprecedented look at the inner workings of the office (*R. v. Duffy*, 2016 ONCJ 220: 1029). Prime Minister Trudeau (2015) has mandated that the Access to Information Act be expanded "appropriately" to include offices of federal ministers and the prime minister. Even if the government backs away from this promise – legislation introduced in 2017 did not propose to add ministerial offices to the act (Stone 2017) – the clear trend is toward greater disclosure and publication. Although this trend might encourage sober second thought before ministerial staffers hit "send" on an ill-advised message, offline communication, in person or by phone, is likely to return as the default for interactions between political staffers and public servants. Although more face-to-face or phone contact might enhance working relationships by promoting more personable and professional conduct, it can also threaten to undo the written culture that began to emerge in ministerial offices (Craft 2016; Wilson 2016). Heightened disclosure requirements can also tempt ministers, political staffers, and public servants to use personal devices, or personal email accounts, in order to frustrate the release of documents. To the extent that these practices make such communications more difficult to verify or investigate, accountability will suffer.

Broadly, efforts to codify the conduct of staffers and enhance access to information, while laudable, amount to incremental attempts to remove bad apples from the ministerial staff barrel, and ultimately they are not a satisfactory substitute for skilled, professional staffers or a healthy, professional public service. The reality, however, is that ministerial staffers are not as experienced as their public service interlocutors, and studies consistently point to the need for better training (Benoit 2006, 243–44; Wilson 2015, 468). Undoubtedly, lack of understanding of and respect for the roles and limits of a non-partisan public service contribute to some of the tensions in the relationship. Although governments have made ad hoc attempts at staff training, doing so consistently is difficult given the short-term employment and high turnover of many staffers. Academic training in practical politics might provide over time a strong network of well-trained ministerial staffers who understand the importance and limits of partisan engagement. The Riddell Graduate Program in Political Management at Carleton University, Canada's only university program dedicated to building a professional foundation for political employment, is an example of such academic training. However, a more comprehensive solution is still desirable for political staff.

In contrast, federal public servants are formally encouraged to take professional training through dedicated annual learning plans, funding incentives, and mandatory courses required for advancement (TBS 2008). Yet it is not clear that this training equips public servants for their interactions with political elites. ADM 1 questioned whether both sides really are "fully cognizant" of how the interaction is supposed to work: "I'm not always convinced that everybody always shares a common understanding of that, let alone a depth of understanding around it." But he did not lay blame solely on ministerial staffers: "There may be, quite frankly, as much work on the public service side around that as there is on the political side ... We [public servants] have a much larger group of people to reach to get an understanding around that, and we probably don't do enough." Better training on roles and responsibilities, including practical skills as well as ethical guidance, is needed throughout the system.

Since ministers, with rare exceptions, are elected members of Parliament, they have a democratic mandate to represent voters. Public servants and ministerial staffers alike derive their legitimacy from serving these elected ministers. Public servants, as permanent and expert advisers, are expected to demonstrate "loyalty to the public interest as represented and interpreted by the democratically elected government and expressed in law and the Constitution" (Tait 1996, 54). They do so by providing frank advice to ministers and by loyally implementing the government's directions. Ministerial staff have no independent standing or authority but, for reasons of efficiency, can represent the minister in discussions with departmental officials. They interact frequently with public servants in order to gather information, discuss options, and encourage responsiveness; they contest public service advice by providing their own advice to ministers; and they represent ministers in dealings with other political offices. But there is a danger that staffers can go past their proper roles. For example, they should not, on their own authority, give direction to public servants, yet, according to survey data, almost 60 percent of ministerial policy staffers do just that, at least occasionally

(Wilson 2016). If the direction is about the optimal time to deliver a memorandum before the minister departs from the office, then perhaps this is less worrisome. If the direction is about the optimal recommendation that the memorandum should make, then this ought to be very worrisome. Although staffers do not believe that they hinder officials' access to ministers, or that they do not discourage free and frank advice on the full range of policy options (Wilson 2016), the risk of "funnelling" public service advice for political purposes remains (Eichbaum and Shaw 2007, 464).

Ministers receive input from both public servants and ministerial staffers on decisions regarding policy, strategy, and communications. Both sets of advisers can help their principals to fulfill multiple and sometimes competing roles, as ministers charged with fulfilling some aspect of crown responsibility, as members of the cabinet charged with arriving at whole-of-government decisions for which they are collectively responsible, as parliamentarians accountable to the House and Senate, as elected officials accountable to their constituents, and as senior representatives of their political parties, charged with responsibilities as partisan emissaries and spokespersons. Only the minister remains the decision maker in this triangle. This fact pertains, under our system of government, regardless of the ideology or style of the government in power.

In the Westminster tradition, the public service is expected to offer frank advice freely, based on the best available evidence and, ideally, taking into account a longer-term perspective. The public service will also present options to help ministers arrive at decisions. This process of research, analysis, and advice is most effective when public servants also have good information about the preferences and priorities of the minister whom they are supporting. In this respect, good working relationships with ministerial staff can play a crucial and positive role in the policy process.

Tensions, sometimes creative and sometimes not, are to be expected between public servants and political aides as they provide input into a minister's or prime minister's decision making. This is not only because of their distinct and sometimes competing functions and priorities but also because of important asymmetries in the relationship. Although political staff will have access to the department's advice provided to a minister, their own advice is not generally shared with their public service counterparts. Furthermore, though political staff enjoy a privileged direct, often personal, relationship with their minister, their jobs have short tenures. Public servants typically enjoy long careers in the government, building up a professional network of colleagues across the bureaucracy and a store of institutional memory from previous policy files and government decisions. Given these asymmetries in information and tenure, perhaps the surprise is not that conflicts sometimes arise between political staffers and public servants but that such conflicts are not more pervasive and that, even with heightened pressures from changing information technologies and permanent campaigning, tensions are not the norm. When political staffers and public servants conduct themselves with professionalism and mutual respect, the relationship can be productive and serve the public interest.

NOTES

1 We note that 14 percent of respondents to the IPAC survey were federal deputy ministers; the rest worked in provincial or municipal governments. Published data do not provide responses to individual questions tabulated by order of government.

2 For the purpose of this study, we used the Treasury Board Secretariat standard classification of "information services" as a subgroup that can be readily identified in the survey data.

3 A cycle of the same survey from 2011 is not included in this study because of analytical constraints. We focus instead on two cycles that came near the start and the end of the Harper government.

REFERENCES

Aucoin, Peter. 2010. "Canada." In *Partisan Appointees and Public Servants: An International Analysis of the Role of the Political Adviser,* edited by Chris Eichbaum and Richard Shaw, 64–93. Cheltenham, UK: Edward Elgar. https://doi.org/10.4337/9781 849803298.00008.

–. 2012. "New Political Governance in Westminster Systems: Impartial Public Administration and Management Performance at Risk." *Governance: An International Journal of Policy, Administration, and Institutions* 25, 2: 177–99. https://doi.org/10.1111/ j.1468-0491.2012.01569.x.

Barrados, Maria, Manon Vennat, and David Zussman. 2011. *Merit and Non-Partisanship under the Public Service Employment Act (2003): A Special Report to Parliament by the Public Service Commission of Canada.* Ottawa: Public Service Commission of Canada.

Benoit, Liane E. 2006. "Ministerial Staff: The Life and Times of Parliament's Statutory Orphans." In *Restoring Accountability: Research Studies. Vol. 1, Parliament, Ministers, and Deputy Ministers,* Commission of Inquiry into the Sponsorship Program and Advertising Activities, 145–252. Ottawa: Public Works and Government Services Canada.

Connaughton, Bernadette. 2010. "'Glorified Gofers, Policy Experts, or Good Generalists': A Classification of the Roles of the Irish Ministerial Adviser." *Irish Political Studies* 25, 3: 347–69. https://doi.org/10.1080/07907184.2010.497636.

Craft, Jonathan. 2016. *Backrooms and Beyond: Partisan Advisers and the Politics of Policy Work in Canada.* Toronto: University of Toronto Press.

Eichbaum, Chris, and Richard Shaw. 2007. "Ministerial Advisers and the Politics of Policy-Making: Bureaucratic Permanence and Popular Control." *Australian Journal of Public Administration* 66, 4: 453–67. https://doi.org/10.1111/j.1467-8500.2007.00556.x.

–. 2008. "Revisiting Politicization: Political Advisers and Public Servants in Westminster Systems." *Governance: An International Journal of Policy, Administration, and Institutions* 21, 3: 337–63. https://doi.org/10.1111/j.1468-0491.2008.00403.x.

Esselment, Anna, and R. Paul Wilson. 2017. "Campaigning from the Centre: Strategic Communications and Issues Management in the Prime Minister's Office." In *Permanent Campaigning in Canada,* edited by Alex Marland, Anna Esselment, and Thierry Giasson, 222–40. Vancouver: UBC Press.

Griffith, A. 2013. *Policy Arrogance or Innocent Bias: Resetting Citizenship and Multiculturalism.* Toronto: Anar Press.

Institute of Public Administration of Canada. 2012. "IPAC's 2011 Survey of Deputy Ministers and CAOs." Ottawa: IPAC.

Jarvis, Mark D. 2014. "The Black Box of Bureaucracy: Interrogating Accountability in the Public Service." *Australian Journal of Public Administration* 73, 4: 450–66. https://doi.org/10.1111/1467-8500.12109.

Jeffrey, Brooke. 2011. "Strained Relations: The Conflict between the Harper Conservatives and the Federal Bureaucracy." Paper presented at the Canadian Political Science Association Annual Conference, May 17, Waterloo, ON.

Kozolanka, Kirsten. 2012. "'Buyer' Beware: Pushing the Boundaries of Marketing Communications in Government." In *Political Marketing in Canada,* edited by Alex Marland, Thierry Giasson, and Jennifer Lees-Marshment, 107–22. Vancouver: UBC Press.

Legault, Suzanne. 2013. *Access to Information at Risk from Instant Messaging. Special Report to Parliament.* Ottawa: Information Commissioner of Canada.

–. 2014. *Interference with Access to Information: Part 2. A Special Report to Parliament.* Ottawa: Information Commissioner of Canada.

Maley, Maria. 2002. "Partisans at the Centre of Government: The Role of Ministerial Advisers in the Keating Government 1991–1996." PhD diss., Australian National University.

–. 2011. "Strategic Links in a Cut-Throat World: Rethinking the Role and Relationships of Australian Ministerial Staff." *Public Administration* 89, 4: 1469–88. https://doi.org/10.1111/j.1467-9299.2011.01928.x.

Marland, Alex. 2016. *Brand Command: Canadian Politics and Democracy in the Age of Message Control.* Vancouver: UBC Press.

Office of the Chief Human Resources Officer. 2009. *Public Servants on the Public Service of Canada: Summary of the Results of the 2008 Public Service Employee Survey.* Ottawa: Treasury Board of Canada Secretariat.

–. 2015. *2014 Public Service Employee Survey: Summary Report.* Ottawa: Treasury Board of Canada Secretariat.

Privy Council Office. 2015. *Open and Accountable Government.* Ottawa: Her Majesty the Queen in Right of Canada.

Public Service Commission of Canada. 2011. *History of Employment Equity in the Public Service and the Public Service Commission of Canada.* Ottawa: Her Majesty the Queen in Right of Canada.

Stone, Laura. 2017. "Liberal Government Tables Bill to Reform Access to Information." *Globe and Mail,* June 20, A7.

Tait, John C. 1996. *Report of the Task Force on Public Service Values and Ethics.* Ottawa: Canadian Centre for Management Development.

Thomas, Paul. 2013. "Communications and Prime Ministerial Power." In *Governing: Essays in Honour of Donald J. Savoie,* edited by James Bickerton and B. Guy Peters, 53–84. Montreal: McGill-Queen's University Press.

Tiernan, Anne. 2004. "Ministerial Staff under the Howard Government: Problem, Solution, or Black Hole?" PhD diss., Griffith University.

–. 2007. *Power without Responsibility: Ministerial Staffers in Australian Governments from Whitlam to Howard.* Sydney: University of New South Wales Press.

Treasury Board Secretariat. 2008. "Policy on Learning, Training, and Development." https://www.tbs-sct.gc.ca/pol/doc-eng.aspx?id=12405.

Trudeau, Justin. 2015. "Mandate Letter to the President of the Treasury Board." https://pm.gc.ca/eng/president-treasury-board-canada-mandate-letter.

Turnbull, Andrew. 2005. "Sir Andrew Turnbull's Speech: The Outgoing Cabinet Secretary's Valedictory Lecture before Handing Over to Sir Gus O'Donnell." *Guardian,* July 27. https://www.theguardian.com/politics/2005/jul/27/Whitehall.uk.

Wilson, R. Paul. 2015. "A Profile of Ministerial Policy Staff in the Government of Canada." *Canadian Journal of Political Science* 48, 2: 455–71. https://doi.org/10.1017/S0008423915000293.

–. 2016. "Trust but Verify: Ministerial Policy Advisors and Public Servants in the Government of Canada." *Canadian Public Administration* 59, 3: 337–56. https://doi.org/10.1111/capa.12175.

Yong, Ben, and Robert Hazell. 2014. *Special Advisers: Who They Are, What They Do, and Why They Matter.* Oxford: Hart Publishing.

5

Gender, Tone, and Content of Premiers' News Coverage: A Matched Comparison

Melanee Thomas, Allison Harell, and Tania Gosselin

The news media are crucial to our understanding of elites in Canada. We know that most citizens receive their information about politics and elites from the news media (Zaller 1996); we also know that the media themselves have changed considerably with the advent of the internet and social media (Tewksbury and Rittenburg 2012). Certainly, with the rise of social media, there are more opportunities for citizens to access information from political elites directly, and there are fewer opportunities for editors and mainstream news media outlets to frame, order, or restrict what citizens might learn about politics or politicians than was the case in the past (Tewksbury and Rittenburg 2012).[1] That said, research shows that very few explicitly use social media for political purposes (Small et al. 2014). Thus, many, if not most, Canadians rely on the media to gather their information about elites, and citizens, elites, and the media alike are actively engaging with and changing their practices to accommodate the digital media environment. These reactions are all the more important because voters' evaluations of some political elites – such as party leaders, prime ministers, or provincial premiers – are vital for vote choices. Evaluations of leaders are about as important as partisanship and more important than issues for the vote (Bittner 2010; see also Johnston 2002).

Perhaps most important for our purposes, media presentations of political elites vary systematically based on who those leaders are (Goodyear-Grant 2013), and these variations have been preserved or even amplified in the digital media environment (Burke and Mazzarella 2008; Conroy et al. 2015). The media are embedded in broader society, so they reflect the norms and barriers present in society. Society remains a gendered place, and politics is a social context that remains deeply gendered. For example, women continue to be dramatically underrepresented in Canada relative to their demographic weight; after the 2015 federal election, women still comprise a mere

26 percent of all elected members of Parliament (Interparliamentary Union 2016). They comprise between 9 percent and 37 percent of provincial and territorial Legislative Assemblies (calculated from Parliament of Canada 2016). And, until recently, the most powerful elite political offices in Canada – that of prime minister and premier – appeared to be closed to women.

Kim Campbell remains Canada's only woman prime minister, and she failed to secure election in 1993. To date, no woman has been selected as prime minister through a general election. And, prior to 2010, the same could have been said about premiers. The first woman premier was Rita Johnston, appointed premier in British Columbia in 1991. Of the eight women who have served as premiers in Canada as of 2016, six have been selected since 2010. In comparison, fifty-seven men have served as premiers since 1991, making men seven times more likely than women to hold this position. And, despite the pithy "because it's 2015" rationale that Prime Minister Justin Trudeau offered for why he appointed a parity cabinet, the idea that gender is an appropriate, let alone meritorious, category for political representation in Canada remains controversial (Franceschet, Beckwith, and Annesley 2015).

Research shows that media coverage of political elites is gendered. Politics is stereotyped as a masculine field, and this is (re)created and (re)enforced in how the media present politics and politicians to the public (Gidengil and Everitt 2003a, 2003b). Earlier studies showed that the media "symbolically annihilated" women by omitting them from coverage or by trivializing and/or condemning them when they were covered (Tuchman 1978). This suggests that media coverage of political elites who are women can vary from that of political elites who are men in three ways: volume, content, and tone. As discussed below, research consistently shows that women in elite positions can receive less coverage, less serious coverage in terms of subject and content, and more negative coverage than men in elite positions. Although this has changed considerably since Tuchman's early studies, there is still evidence to suggest that media coverage of Canada's political elites is gendered in the following three ways.

First, the volume of coverage that women elites in politics receive has changed significantly over time. As recently as the 2000 Republican primary in the United States, the second-place candidate and first serious woman contender for a party's presidential nomination in the United States, Elizabeth Dole, was simply not covered as such. She withdrew, in part because the volume of coverage that she received was far lower than expected for a candidate in second place in the polls (Heldman, Carroll, and Olson 2005). That said, by 2008, Hillary Clinton received significantly more coverage than any of her competitors (Miller, Peake, and Boulton 2010). In Canada, women who compete for the leadership of some federal parties do not appear to receive less media attention than their competitive positions warrant (Trimble 2007). Since the 2000 federal election, few gender differences in visibility can be found in television or print coverage of party leaders and candidates (Goodyear-Grant 2013). That said, during this period, very few of these political elites were contending for the top job of premier or prime minister.

Second, because politics is a masculine-stereotyped field in which women remain grossly underrepresented, the process to bring the public news about politicians uses "ostensibly gender-neutral news frames that are, in fact, masculine in nature" (Goodyear-Grant 2013, 5). For example, it is common to use metaphors that relate to sports or battles to describe political debates or events, and these metaphors are at odds with how society sees women and their acceptable roles. Thus, though it is no longer socially acceptable to show explicit gender bias in media toward politicians, the content generated about women in politics remains different from that presented about men in politics. A seemingly neutral frame for a politician who is a man can cue that politics is unnatural, or an odd fit, for his peer who is a woman.

Coverage of women party leaders at the federal level in Canada is disproportionately focused on "soft" issues such as health care and education.[2] Furthermore, women leaders are rarely associated with images of power, whereas their male peers are more likely to be presented with symbols of power such as Parliament or the flag (Goodyear-Grant 2013). These differences are attributable, in part, to the lower levels of electoral viability of women-led parties at the federal level as well as strategic decisions that these parties make in their press releases. Still, coverage of women candidates in Canada and elsewhere focuses far more on their appearance, personal relationships and marital status, and parental status than does that of their male peers (Goodyear-Grant 2013; see also Heldman, Carroll, and Olson 2005; Miller, Peake, and Boulton 2010; Trimble 2007; and Trimble et al. 2013). This coverage leads women in politics to make strategic decisions about how to present themselves that vary considerably from those of men. Men can often present their families as strategic or branding cues (see Thomas and Lambert 2017 for an overview); although women elites sometimes choose to cue their parental or marital status, the strategies and results are typically very different from those seen among their male peers. This reality leads many women political elites to be discreet, if not entirely closed, about their private lives in public (Everitt and Camp 2009; Goodyear-Grant 2013; Thomas and Lambert 2017; van Zoonen 1998, 2006).

Third, women political elites receive considerably more negative press than do their male peers. For example, Hillary Clinton did not receive the same kind of treatment from the media as Barack Obama. Research shows that Clinton only received positive media coverage, comparable to that of Obama, when she was polling ahead of him by about ten points in any given media market (Miller, Peake, and Boulton 2010). Furthermore, the majority of negative coverage that Clinton received was directed at her character, whereas the majority of negative coverage that Obama received questioned his credentials (Miller, Peake, and Boulton 2010). Similarly, after Canadian federal leaders' debates, women leaders have been presented in media coverage as more aggressive and adversarial than their male peers, even though objective analyses effectively debunk this presentation. In fact, it is not uncommon for women party leaders in Canadian debates to be the least aggressive and adversarial, yet coverage presents them as behaving in a more hostile manner than their male peers (Gidengil and Everitt 2003a, 2003b; Goodyear-Grant 2013). This is reflected even for parliamentary candidates; although the majority of coverage of all candidates is neutral, women are still more likely than men to receive negative coverage (Goodyear-Grant 2013).

The media's gendered approach to tone matters for a number of reasons. Media reports are not neutral in that they mediate and frame how the audience is to interpret or understand the subject of a story. Thus, when women in politics receive more negative coverage than men, or coverage that suggests they are more hostile, aggressive, or cold, the frame suggests that the audience should think of these political elites in the same way. This framing can have effects on vote choice, and research shows that voters' assessments of political elites' character matter significantly more for their vote choices than do their assessments of their competence (Bittner 2010; Johnston 2002).

Our study builds on this research by investigating how the media cover political elites in office. As noted above, very few women have served as prime minister or premier in Canada; thus, much of what we know about how the media cover women political elites is based on party leadership candidates or leaders of electorally uncompetitive political parties. Therefore, the sudden increase of women in the premier's office since 2010 provides us with an opportunity to study how political elites are gendered in the media in two unique ways: by examining them while they are in office and by examining them at the provincial rather than federal level. Doing so fills a major gap in the literature since this marks the first chance to study how the media gender women who lead governments in Canada.

Using the framework set out above, we investigate how media coverage varies for women in the premier's office compared with that for men in the premier's office in terms of volume, content and tone. Our case study is based on three hypotheses:

1. Women premiers will be less prominently covered than their peers who are men (volume).
2. The coverage of women premiers will vary systematically from that of premiers who are men by subject and policy area, with women tied more often to "soft" issues (content).
3. The tone of coverage of women premiers will be more negative than the tone of coverage about premiers who are men (tone).

In each case, the null hypothesis – that there is no relationship between the gender of the premier and the media coverage – is compelling. Although evidence shows that women political elites used to receive less coverage than men, more recent studies show that this is often no longer the case (Goodyear-Grant 2013; Miller, Peake, and Boulton 2010). Notably, there is no plausible reason to believe that this would be the case for sitting premiers outside of, perhaps, their gender. Furthermore, the provinces are constitutionally responsible for most "soft" policy areas that Canadians care deeply about, such as health care and education. Thus, though evidence shows that women's political coverage focuses more on these soft issues than does men's, it would be difficult for media coverage of men in the premier's office to avoid these subjects. And it might be surprising to find systematic gender differences in the tone of the coverage that premiers receive, in part because research shows that most political news stories are neutral in tone (Goodyear-Grant 2013) and in part because government popularity can change considerably over time. Thus, premiers could have a substantial number of both positive and negative stories published about them. Given these things, evidence confirming the three hypotheses outlined above speaks powerfully to the continued gendered nature of political news. Conversely, their rejection would also tell us something about gender and political elites, and more specifically political leaders, in a country where women in leadership positions have become more common.[3]

Case Study

Our case studies investigated all of the online media coverage of the first year of government for two premiers in each of three of Canada's largest provinces: Progressive Conservative Jim Prentice and New Democrat Rachel Notley in Alberta; Liberals Dalton McGuinty and Kathleen Wynne in Ontario; and Liberals Gordon Campbell and Christy Clark in British Columbia. The selection of these six cases follows a matched comparison strategy. In each of the three provinces under study, we selected one premier who was a woman and one premier who was a man during a relatively short time period from 2010 to 2016. This time period is important since women were almost entirely excluded from executive office at the provincial level between the early 1990s and 2010. Doing so allowed us to compare the three women leaders to their male counterparts with a measure of control for differences across provinces as well as differences among the major news sources that we chose in each one. These pairs allowed us to assess if the first year of coverage for a premier varied by their selection mechanism. Notley is the only woman premier selected to that office *first* by a general election; every other woman premier was first selected through an intraparty process while her party held the government. In contrast, most men were selected as premier via a general election; Prentice was one of the few in a powerful province who was not.[4] Notably, both Notley and Clark are the second women premiers in their respective provinces. Approximately twenty years passed between the selection of the first and second women premiers in British Columbia, but a much shorter time lag existed between the first woman premier in Alberta and Notley's selection (approximately fourteen months).

METHOD

The first step in our analysis was to gather all of the potentially relevant news articles. Using Canadian Newsstand Complete, we gathered every news story that contained each premier's name during the first twelve months in office, starting from the day that each was sworn into office, published online in the

Globe and Mail, the *National Post,* and the newspaper with the largest daily circulation in that premier's province.[5] We selected this time period deliberately since we expected that variations in the context faced by each premier should moderate over the course of a year in office, increasing the generalizability of the findings across provincial contexts. Importantly, each of these papers also has considerable online reach: each of the largest dailies not only has the largest conventional circulation but also the most followers on Facebook or Twitter compared with other print-based publications and television outlets such as CTV, CBC, and Global. In addition, evidence suggests that each publication reflects the hybrid media environment since the online coverage of these premiers includes, at least at times, reports about how they or their actions have been viewed on social media (see Gerson 2015).[6] In Alberta, the largest daily is the *Calgary Herald;* in Ontario, the largest daily is the *Toronto Star;* and in British Columbia, the largest daily is the *Vancouver Sun* (see Newspapers Canada 2014).[7] Our search yielded a total of 11,579 news articles, all from the digital media environment.[8] Articles were coded for date of publication, outlet, and first, second, and third mention of a person. Along with the number of overall articles, we used the first-mention variable to assess the prominence of each premier in articles.

We then used a quantitative dictionary-based content analysis tool, *Lexicoder 3.0* (Daku, Soroka, and Young 2015) with two separate dictionaries for *tone* (Young and Soroka 2012) and *topic* (Albaugh, Sevenans, and Soroka 2013). Net tone is a composite score that captures the proportion of positive words less the proportion of negative words. This gives us an index that runs from −1 (all negative words) to 1 (all positive words) and should be interpreted as the ratio of positive to negative words.[9] Scores closer to zero reflect coverage neutral in tone. Topic is a count of words related to nineteen policy domains, such as health, education, environment, and social welfare, inspired by the Policy Agendas Project (http://www.comparativeagendas.net/).

FINDINGS

Our first hypothesis focuses on the prominence of coverage of provincial political elites as measured by the quantity of coverage of premiers. Table 5.1 presents the average number of news articles that premiers received during their first year in office. Prentice received, on average, the most coverage online, followed by McGuinty, then by Notley.[10] If we consider our matched pairs, then we can see that in each province the men premiers received significantly more articles on average than the women premiers ($p < .001$). Notley received the most coverage among the women, though it was less than that of fellow Alberta premier Prentice.

In terms of overall levels, then, there is some evidence that women premiers receive less digital coverage, though only when we consider it within a provincial context. These differences are largely reproduced across sources of publication. In each provincial newspaper, the woman premier consistently received fewer daily articles online than her male counterpart. The same was true in one of the national papers, the *National Post*. The only exception was the *Globe and Mail*, in which the two women premiers received average daily counts of digital coverage not statistically distinguishable from those of their male provincial counterparts. Only Wynne received significantly less than McGuinty in the *Globe and Mail*, reproducing her overall low level of online coverage in contrast to that of McGuinty across news sources. This is noteworthy since Wynne is the first out sexual minority selected as a premier in Canada. This gap was by far the largest of any pair: Wynne's coverage varied from 3.4 to 6.3 fewer average articles a day compared with McGuinty's coverage. Gaps for the other two pairs were smaller in their local papers and the *National Post*, ranging from 1.3 to 3.0 articles per day.

Prominence can be measured by more than simply the quantity of articles published online. We can also look at the amount of coverage that leaders received over time during the first year of their mandate. As might be expected, there are peaks and declines in coverage corresponding to events that bring a premier into online news. The two most dramatic spikes were for Notley and Prentice, each of whom received a large amount of online coverage at the beginning and end of the first year in office. The spike for Notley at the beginning of her mandate can also be observed, though to a lesser extent, for Campbell and McGuinty. Prentice's late spike corresponded to Notley's win and his announcement of his resignation as party leader and reflected the large media interest in the change of power in Alberta after more than forty years of Progressive Conservative governance.

We can further test prominence with two other indicators: article length and placement of the leader's name in the article (e.g., whether the premier is mentioned first). Table 5.1 provides this information. When we considered word count, no clear gender pattern emerged. Overall word count was similar between the men and women premiers, and differences between the matched pairs were not in a consistent direction. Consistent with our expectations, Wynne was covered in significantly fewer words than McGuinty

TABLE 5.1

Prominence and tone of news coverage by premier and gender

Average N of stories daily			
Men premiers	10.1	8.0	Women premiers
Campbell (BC)	7.1	5.8	Clark (BC)
Prentice (AB)	11.6	10.0	Notley (AB)
McGuinty (ON)	10.8	7.1	Wynne (ON)
Average word count			
Men premiers	714	708	Women premiers +
Campbell (BC)	774	745	Clark (BC)+
Prentice (AB)	653	711	Notley (AB)
McGuinty (ON)	721	678	Wynne (ON)
% first mention			
Men premiers	76	81	Women premiers
Campbell (BC)	76	74	Clark (BC)
Prentice (AB)	84	83	Notley (AB)
McGuinty (ON)	71	85	Wynne (ON)
Net tone			
Men premiers	0.06	0.10	Women premiers
Campbell (BC)	0.06	0.16	Clark (BC)
Prentice (AB)	0.06	0.12	Notley (AB)
McGuinty (ON)	0.05	0.03	Wynne (ON)

NOTE: All pairs of premiers are statistically significant from each other at the 99.9 percent level unless indicated with +.

despite her having inherited several difficult files from his government; Notley was covered in significantly more words than Prentice, consistent with expectations grounded in her electoral victory. In terms of first mentions, women premiers seem to have had a slight advantage since they received 81 percent of first mentions compared with 76 percent among male premiers. However, this difference broke down among the matched pairs. The Ontario pair largely drove the difference: McGuinty received the fewest first mentions (71 percent), and Wynne received the most (85 percent) of all premiers. This pattern was largely reproduced if we consider the pairs by news source.

Overall, then, it appears that men premiers received more articles in the digital media environment but were not necessarily covered in more depth or placed more prominently within articles than women premiers. Furthermore, men's advantage in terms of numbers of articles held only within a provincial context. This means that the conventional expectation that women in politics receive less attention or coverage than men does not hold for women in executive office in Canada, at least with respect to the content that these media outlets were publishing online. Instead, when women are heads of governments, they are covered as such, at least in terms of volume. This mirrors results found in other contexts, notably coverage of Hillary Clinton's front-running candidacy in the 2008 Democratic primary (Miller, Peake, and Boulton 2010).

If men received somewhat more digital coverage, then it is useful to consider whether this coverage was also more positive. Table 5.1 also provides the net tone for each premier in our study. Overall, this online coverage tended to be relatively neutral (i.e., close to zero), though it appears that women's overall coverage was almost twice as positive. Men's coverage, on average, contained about 6 percent more positive words than negative words, whereas women's coverage was almost 10 percent more positive than negative ($p < .001$). If we consider the matched comparisons, then this also holds for two of the three cases. Prentice received about 6 percent more positive words, whereas Notley received over 12 percent. The difference in British Columbia was even greater, with Campbell just shy of 6 percent and Clark at almost 16 percent.

The case that does not hold is Ontario, where McGuinty (.051) received online coverage almost twice as positive as that of Wynne (.028). She presents an interesting case for our analysis as the first openly lesbian premier in Canada. Our argument about the potential "normalization" of women in politics should be less likely to hold for Wynne given her "first" status as well as how leaders' gender can intersect with their sexual orientation. In the previous subsection, we noted that in this digital media environment Wynne was the least-covered woman premier and the fifth least covered overall. Although she was the most likely to be mentioned first in the article, she tended to receive considerably fewer words and fewer articles. Her difference from the other two women premiers, as well as from the men premiers, was even more obvious with respect to tone, for she received the most neutral coverage by far. A number of factors might explain this beyond Wynne's sexual orientation, including the length of time that the Liberal government had been in office; arguably, though, many of these factors should also have applied to Clark. More research (and more LGBTQ politicians) are required before we can fully assess how sexual orientation affects the coverage that women and men in politics receive.

The relatively positive coverage of the two heterosexual women premiers runs counter to the general hypothesis in the literature. This coverage might have been driven initially by highlighting the novelty or importance of the premiers' gender early in their mandates. Figure 5.1 provides the net tone over the first year in office of each premier.

For four of the six premiers, their online news coverage became more negative over the course of their first year in office. Recall that the literature predicts that women premiers should be covered more negatively. Our findings do not clearly support this prediction. Only one premier, Wynne, fit this prediction: she received the most negative coverage of all the premiers, and this trend of negative coverage was steady over time. Four of the other premiers – two women and two men – saw their coverage become steadily more negative over time, though on average their coverage remained positive or neutral at the end of their first year in office. McGuinty was the only premier who saw his online news coverage become more positive over time.

Tone, then, fails to conform to our hypothesis for two of the three women premiers. Interestingly, the hypothesis does conform for Wynne; although we cannot confirm this with these data, it is noteworthy that she is the only woman premier who is also a sexual minority.

Our final analysis considers the policy domains most often linked to each premier. As indicated, past gender and politics research suggests that women candidates are most often linked to so-called soft issues such as health care and education. The extent to which this holds for women in elected offices in general, and in executive positions in particular, is less clear. When we further consider the provinces, largely responsible for such issues (and without jurisdiction over many "hard" issues such as foreign policy), we can expect coverage of every premier to be skewed toward soft issues regardless of gender.

Table 5.2 provides the average policy mentions per digital article for each premier, organized by province to facilitate our matched comparisons. Not surprisingly, local and provincial politics topped the list as the policy area most often mentioned in each article, with macroeconomics following at a close second. Articles about women premiers were also more likely to focus on these two topics than was the news coverage of their male peers. Larger

FIGURE 5.1

Net tone of news coverage during a premier's first year of office

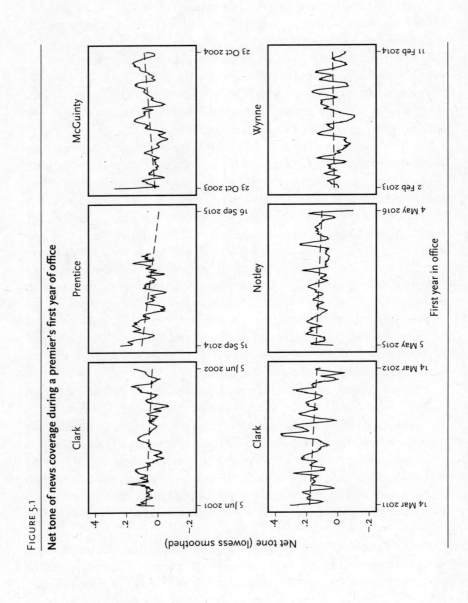

TABLE 5.2

Top policy news coverage, by premier, British Columbia, Alberta, Ontario

	British Columbia		Alberta		Ontario		Overall	
	Campbell	Clark	Prentice	Notley	McGuinty	Wynne	Men	Women
Local and provincial politics	5.3	6.3	5.4	5.5	5.8	6.0	5.5	5.9
Macroeconomics	5.2	6.3	5.8	6.8	5.4	4.6	5.5	5.8
Health care	3.8	1.2	1.6	0.8	4.1	1.0	3.3	1.0
Education	2.4	2.0	2.3	1.4	2.5	2.2	2.4	1.8
Labour	3.1	1.7	1.4	1.7	1.4	2.6	1.8	2.1
Finance	1.7	1.5	1.5	2.3	1.6	1.2	1.6	1.7
Energy	0.8	1.4	2.1	4.0	1.1	1.1	1.3	2.2
Crime	1.7	2.5	0.6	0.5	1.3	1.0	1.2	1.2
Transportation	1.1	1.2	0.6	0.7	1.3	1.6	1.0	1.2
Environment	0.6	0.9	1.1	3.0	0.5	0.3	0.7	1.4

gender differences appeared for policy domains most often associated with women in politics, education, and health care. Contrary to expectations, these topics were much less likely to be mentioned in online news in association with women premiers. The difference was particularly stark for health care, with articles on average containing one mention for women and over three mentions for men. In contrast, masculine domains such as energy, and to a lesser extent labour and transportation, were more often associated with women premiers. The only other notable difference was with the environment, about twice as many mentions for women premiers (especially for Notley) than for men.

What do these differences tell us? They suggest that women in the highest positions of power do not conform to expectations that they are more often covered in terms of social or "soft" policy areas. This might be partly because premiers are responsible for a host of policy areas, and candidates can either choose or be selected to specialize in certain policy domains that reflect their gender. Yet the differences that do emerge in coverage also suggest that women in power might be more hesitant to put traditionally women-centred policy domains – such as health care – on the media agenda. Or women premiers might not get the credit for policy innovations in more stereotypically feminine policy domains precisely because they are expected to be more competent with these policies than their male peers. Another explanation rests with governance decisions that women in executive offices make that their male peers do not. Alberta is a good example. Prentice might have been covered more in terms of health care and education precisely because his government proposed cuts to these social programs to deal with a budgetary deficit. Notley's government, in contrast, chose not to cut these programs, and that decision might have led the media to deem these topics less newsworthy. That said, whether these differences result from choices by the leader about what to focus on or choices by the media about what to cover (or both) cannot be assessed with our data. Future research could probe all of these potential explanations to determine which one has the most support.

Political Elites in Canada in the Digital Age

What has this chapter told us about the coverage of women premiers in Canada, and what can we learn about gender and the digital media environment from these results? After all, most of what we know about media and women candidates and party leaders focuses on the federal level in the 1990s and early 2000s, predating both the digital media environment and the increase in women political elites at the provincial level. Our chapter thus provides a test of this literature at the provincial level in a time period when women in political leadership roles have become more common, though still far from equal with men.

We find that men in the premier's office receive more coverage than their women peers, but this is the case only when we draw intraprovincial comparisons. That said, there does not appear to be a national trend showing that, across the three large provinces discussed here, men are systematically covered more frequently than women. Similarly, there is no evidence to show that women premiers are disadvantaged in terms of length or prominence of coverage. Thus, our results run contrary to some observations but confirm others generated from women who seek executive offices elsewhere (see Miller, Peake, and Boulton 2010).

Contrary to expectations, women premiers are covered more positively by the media during their first year in office than are men. It is not clear why, though perhaps the three women premiers in question here have garnered advantageous coverage because of their novelty. After all, though Clark and Notley were both the second women to head governments in their respective provinces, Clark was the first to do so in British Columbia in decades, and Notley's government was the first to defeat a long-standing political dynasty in Alberta. However, Wynne's coverage does not fit this narrative. Wynne certainly fits the "first" frame that dominates much of the coverage of women in political media, for she is both the first woman and the first sexual minority to lead the government in Ontario. Yet her coverage is less positive than that of any of her peers. This study is limited; although we can identify this pattern, it remains unclear why it exists. Perhaps Wynne's more negative coverage reflects her party's long tenure in government, for the Liberals have governed in Ontario since 2003. If that is the case, then it raises the question of why Clark's online coverage did not show a comparable pattern, for the Liberals have governed in British Columbia since 2001.

Gender differences, or the lack thereof, in the topics associated with men and women in the premier's office also run contrary to expectations. Women are no more likely than men to be associated with "soft" issues such as health care and education. This is not surprising perhaps given the constitutional roles that provincial governments play in Canada. That said, our results suggest that a government leader's agency adds a dimension to the literature on gender and media political coverage that might not have been considered much before.[11] Because women in Canada are so rarely premiers or prime ministers, research to date has not needed to address how their governance choices have affected their media coverage. Perhaps one reason why women premiers are less likely than their male peers to be mentioned in reports about health care or education is that women are less likely to cut these programs when they lead these governments. This analysis does not permit us to explicitly test this assertion, and this is an avenue for future research.

This study is limited in a number of other ways. Not all news stories published online are created equal, and the measures and methods used here are blunt. Certainly, gender bias would have to be strong to show up so consistently in the volume, tone, and topics covered in news reports about premiers in their first year of office. Indeed, as noted above, each of the three null hypotheses is arguably as compelling as the research hypotheses posed above. Because these measures are so blunt, they are likely to miss more subtle forms of gendered coverage that we know persist for women in politics in Canada and elsewhere. A comparable quantitative analysis of ostensibly gender-neutral concepts such as competence, cooperation, and competition might find gender differences that our analysis does not, and a more nuanced analysis is required to elucidate how each provincial context shapes the coverage of women and men in the premier's office.

Similarly, it is not surprising that blatant sexism is not obviously included in online news reports, for social forces in society and journalism alike have already rendered that unacceptable (Goodyear-Grant 2013). This suggests that more established news norms – specifically, the norm established in *The Canadian Press Stylebook* that journalists review content to ensure that the words and frames used to describe women are the same as those used to describe men – have been integrated into online news (see Chadwick 2013). It remains unclear, though, how much of the difference in this news coverage of women premiers now is a result of the changing media environment rather than changes in society, particularly with respect to women in the political executive, since Canada had so few women in these positions prior to 2010. And we cannot know from this study how sexism in online news percolates through reader comments posted with the article online or on social media or if negative coverage that women in politics or the premier's office receive is structured, at least in part, by potential hostility from new areas such as social media. We cannot know from these data how women political elites use social media to strategically disseminate information, especially photos and videos of events, nor can we know how the media choose to use this information, especially if they are constrained in terms of time and resources. Similarly, we cannot know how voters integrate this unfiltered information from elites into evaluations of leaders crucial to vote choices.

We also cannot know from this analysis how women political elites deal with gender bias and sexism that occur in social media or comments on online news stories. Anecdotally, it is known that social media are more hostile for women elites than for male elites. Notley had to take to Facebook to ask that people stop using pornographic language in their posts on her page. It is plausible that women political elites spend considerable resources and staff hours moderating their social media pages, not unlike how the *Guardian* (Gardiner et al. 2016) reports having had to moderate its comments section. The implication is twofold. First, it means that women political elites need to dedicate resources to moderating online spaces that their male peers can use on other things, such as constituency service, campaigns, or outreach. Second, if political elites have to moderate their online spaces, then they might be deleting comments that contain, or blocking users who engage in, profanity, violence, sexism, or other personal attacks. Does this constitute censorship, or do political elites have the right to moderate their own online spaces?

Clearly, more research is required. Yet we can conclude, based on these results, that as political leaders women premiers are not symbolically annihilated now as women in politics were in the past. Instead, they face new challenges in the digital media environment, the full extent of which is not yet known.

NOTES

1 When we refer to "the media" in this chapter, we typically mean "mainstream news media outlets" unless otherwise noted.

2 In contrast, typical "hard" issues include the economy and taxes, though some of this difference is arguably the result of the issues that leaders choose to emphasize in their campaigns (Goodyear-Grant 2013).

3 Little in the existing literature leads us to predict that the digital media environment would create differently gendered patterns in media coverage. Given that, and the fact that analyses of women in the premier's office are new because of the small number of women premiers, we hold with hypotheses derived from the literature on more conventional media coverage.

4 These factors justify the inclusion of Prentice in the study even though he did not serve a full year in office as premier of Alberta (September 2014 to May 2015).

5 Canadian Newsstand Complete provides full-text articles published by the newspapers that we use here. For more information, see https://library.ucalgary.ca/404?destination=search-collections/newspapers/canadian-newspapers.

6 A more detailed analysis of how online news coverage approaches social media representations of premiers is beyond the scope of this study. However, we argue that our exclusive use of all online articles from these newspapers should provide a good lens through which to view how premiers are presented in a hybrid media environment (see Chadwick 2013).

7 To do this, we created a program that would download (in a .txt file) every article found for each premier during the first year in office for each publication from Canadian Newsstand Complete. We would like to thank Dylan Dobbyn for his assistance with the program code.

8 Note that a small number of articles not clearly related to politics were eliminated from the total sample (e.g., condolences in an obituary).

9 This is the same formula used by Soroka (http://www.snsoroka.com/observatory-methodology.html).

10 This is remarkable given that Prentice did not serve a full year in office (see note 4).

11 For an exception, see Goodyear-Grant's (2013) discussion of party press releases.

REFERENCES

Albaugh, Quinn, Julie Sevenans, and Stuart Soroka. 2013. *Lexicoder Topic Dictionaries, June 2013 Versions*. Montreal: McGill University.

Bittner, Amanda. 2010. "Personality Matters: The Evaluation of Party Leaders in Canadian Elections." In *Voting Behaviour in Canada*, edited by Cameron D. Anderson and Laura B. Stephenson, 183–210. Vancouver: UBC Press.

Burke, Cindy, and Sharon R. Mazzarella. 2008. "'A Slightly New Shade of Lipstick': Gendered Mediation in Internet News Stories." *Women's Studies in Communication* 31, 3: 395–418. https://doi.org/10.1080/07491409.2008.10162548.

Chadwick, Andrew. 2013. *The Hybrid Media System: Politics and Power*. Oxford: Oxford University Press. https://doi.org/10.1093/acprof:oso/9780199759477.001.0001.

Conroy, Meredith, Sarah Oliver, Ian Breckenridge-Jackson, and Caroline Heldman. 2015. "From Ferraro to Palin: Sexism and Coverage of Vice Presidential Candidates in Old and New Media." *Politics, Groups, and Identities* 3, 4: 573–91. https://doi.org/10.1080/21565503.2015.1050412.

Daku, Mark, Stuart Soroka, and Lori Young. 2015. *Lexicoder*. Version 3.0. http://www.lexicoder.com.

Everitt, Joanna, and Michael Camp. 2009. "Changing the Game Changes the Frame: The Media's Use of Lesbian Stereotypes in Leadership versus Election Campaigns." *Canadian Political Science Review* 3, 3: 24–39.

Franceschet, Susan, Karen Beckwith, and Claire Annesley. 2015. "Why Are We Still Debating Diversity versus Merit in 2015?" *Federation for the Humanities and Social Sciences*, November 10. http://www.ideas-idees.ca/blog/why-are-we-still-debating-diversity-versus-merit-2015.

Gerson, Jen. 2015. "Alberta Election Debate 'Math' Remark Could Subtract Voters for PC's Jim Prentice." *National Post*, April 24. http://nationalpost.com/news/canada/canadian-politics/math-remark-during-debate-could-subtract-voters-for-alberta-pcs-jim-prentice/.

Gidengil, Elisabeth, and Joanna Everitt. 2003a. "Conventional Coverage/Unconventional Politicians: Gender and Media Coverage of Canadian Leaders' Debates, 1993, 1997, 2000." *Canadian Journal of Political Science* 36, 3: 559–77. https://doi.org/10.1017/S0008423903778767.

–. 2003b. "Talking Tough: Gender and Reported Speech in Campaign News Coverage." *Political Communication* 20, 3: 209–32. https://doi.org/10.1080/10584600390218869.

Goodyear-Grant, Elizabeth. 2013. *Gendered News: Media Coverage and Electoral Politics.* Vancouver: UBC Press.

Gardiner, Becky, Mahana Mansfield, Ian Anderson, Josh Holder, Daan Louter, and Monica Ulmanu. 2016. "The Dark Side of *Guardian* Comments." *Guardian,* April 12. https://www.theguardian.com/technology/2016/apr/12/the-dark-side-of-guardian-comments.

Heldman, Caroline, Susan J. Carroll, and Stephanie Olson. 2005. "'She Brought Only a Skirt': Print Media Coverage of Elizabeth Dole's Bid for the Republican Presidential Nomination." *Political Communication* 22, 3: 315–35. https://doi.org/10.1080/10584600591006564.

Interparliamentary Union. 2016. "Women in National Parliaments: Situation as of 1st April 2016." https://www.ipu.org/wmn-e/classif.htm.

Johnston, Richard. 2002. "Prime Ministerial Contenders in Canada." In *Leaders' Personalities and the Outcomes of Democratic Elections,* edited by Anthony King. Oxford: Oxford University Press. https://doi.org/10.1093/0199253137.003.0006.

Miller, Melissa K., Jeffrey S. Peake, and Brittany Anne Boulton. 2010. "Testing the *Saturday Night Live* Hypothesis: Fairness and Bias in Newspaper Coverage of Hillary Clinton's Presidential Campaign." *Politics and Gender* 6, 2: 169–98. https://doi.org/10.1017/S1743923X10000036.

Newspapers Canada. 2014. "Circulation Report: Daily Newspapers." http://www.newspaperscanada.ca/hScRP/sites/default/files/2014_Circulation_Report-Daily_Newspapers_in_Canada_FINAL_20150603_0.pdf.

Parliament of Canada. 2016. "Women in the Provincial and Territorial Legislatures." https://lop.parl.ca/ParlInfo/compilations/provinceterritory/Women.aspx?Province=edad4077-a735-48ad-982e-1dcad72f51b6&Current=True.

Small, Tamara A., Harold Jansen, Frédérick Bastien, Thierry Giasson, and Royce Koop. 2014. "Online Political Activity in Canada: The Hype and the Facts." *Canadian Parliamentary Review* 37, 4: 9–16.

Tewksbury, David, and Jason Rittenburg. 2012. *News on the Internet: Information and Citizenship in the 21st Century.* Don Mills, ON: Oxford University Press.

Thomas, Melanee, and L.A. Lambert. 2017. "Private Mom versus Political Dad? Communications of Parental Status in the 41st Canadian Parliament." In *Mothers and Others: The Impact of Parenthood on Politics,* edited by Melanee Thomas and Amanda Bittner, 135–54. Vancouver: UBC Press.

Trimble, Linda. 2007. "Gender, Political Leadership, and Media Visibility: *Globe and Mail* Coverage of Conservative Party of Canada Leadership Contests." *Canadian Journal of Political Science* 40, 4: 969–93.

Trimble, Linda, Angelina Warner, Shannon Sampert, Daisy Raphael, and Bailey Gerrits. 2013. "Is It Personal? Gendered Mediation in Newspaper Coverage of Canadian

National Party Leadership Contests." *International Journal of Press/Politics* 18, 4: 462–81. https://doi.org/10.1177/1940161213495455.

Tuchman, Gaye. 1978. *Making News: A Study in the Construction of Reality*. New York: Free Press.

van Zoonen, Liesbet. 1998. "'Finally, I Have My Mother Back': Politicians and Their Families in Popular Culture." *International Journal of Press/Politics* 3, 1: 48–64. https://doi.org/10.1177/1081180X98003001005.

–. 2006. "The Personal, the Political, and the Popular: A Woman's Guide to Celebrity Politics." *European Journal of Cultural Studies* 9, 3: 287–301. https://doi.org/10.1177/1367549406066074.

Young, Lori, and Stuart Soroka. 2012. "Affective News: The Automated Coding of Sentiment in Political Texts." *Political Communication* 29, 2: 205–31. https://doi.org/10.1080/10584609.2012.671234.

Zaller, John. 1996. "The Myth of Massive Media Impact Revived: New Support for a Discredited Idea." In *Political Persuasion and Attitude Change,* edited by Diana C. Mutz, Richard A. Brody, and Paul M. Sniderman, 17–78. Ann Arbor: University of Michigan Press.

6

From Elitism to Idealization: The Representation of Premiers in Social Media Videos

J.P. Lewis and Stéphanie Yates

Provincial premiers are powerful actors; their position allows them to dominate cabinet and caucus. Indeed, though premiers have a constitutional standing within their jurisdiction similar to that of prime ministers, the scale of the politics related to their position presents even more opportunity to centralize power (Dunn 1995; White 2005; Young and Morley 1983). Still, the threat of the autocratic premier is often overshadowed by the attention paid to centralizing forces at the federal level in the Prime Minister's Office (Aucoin 2012; Savoie 1999; Smith 1970). Regardless of where the academic and media attention has settled, the power of a premier is indisputable. Although this power gives premiers the ability to implement their policy agendas, the optics can be politically damaging. One way to combat perceptions of autocratic tendencies is through public image management, a function that has grown in importance since the advent of television (Delacourt 2013; Marland 2016). Through branding, premiers can try to convey an image of openness with and proximity to their constituents. Twenty-first-century technology allows them to do so in ways unimaginable only a few decades ago. A technological advance that stands out is video, which can be done at low cost and easily shared through social media. It gives premiers a direct route to influencing public opinion on policies and programs.

The use of social media videos by premiers began in about 2007 with one of the first premier videos posted on social media: a speech from Alberta Premier Ed Stelmach. At the time, a member of Stelmach's staff observed that it was a mechanism for communicating directly with people (Johnsrude 2007). Five years later Saskatchewan Premier Brad Wall's staff uploaded a video of humorous outtakes from his election campaign commercials. The clip quickly went viral, reaching 7,000 views in an afternoon. Wall's staff presented that initiative as a way to provide a window to a politician's personality (Couture 2012). The release of videos by Canadian politicians on social media such as Facebook, YouTube, and Twitter is now common. Prime Minister Stephen Harper formalized this practice in January 2014 with the launch of a new in-house-produced social media video series called *24 Seven* (Lalancette and Tourigny-Koné 2017). While previous PMOs shared photographs and videos of the prime minister, this new initiative, with finely honed episodic videos documenting the prime minister's week, attempted to give a behind-the-scenes glance. At the time, a PMO spokesperson promoted the new video series by stating that "Canadians are looking for their news and information online, especially video content. [*24 Seven*] is just one more tool the government is using to keep Canadians informed of its activities, events and announcements" (quoted in Vincent 2014).

These examples show that social media videos are seen as one more tool to keep Canadians informed, as a way to bypass the media filter, to frame a politician's personality, or to communicate directly with citizens, providing an intensification of instantaneous political communications for political elites. If such objectives are legitimate, then they tend to narrow the possibilities offered by the use of videos by politicians on social media. In an era marked by the so-called crisis of representation (Bougnoux 2006; Rosanvallon 2015), the release of videos on social media by elected representatives could help to restore confidence in political elites by somehow reversing their autocratic image, showing that they remain connected to the citizens whom they represent and that they care about their demands and concerns. Furthermore, taking into account the growing pressure to open up elites' decision-making processes by involving lay citizens and the groups that represent them (Blondiaux and Fourniau 2011; Fung 2015), digital videos could be used as a means of showing that the process is indeed more participative than it used to be. As we have observed, this method could be particularly relevant for premiers given the centralization of power associated with them. Finally, videos posted on social media could be used as a tool for accountability, another trend shaping the current political context (Bovens 2010; Savoie 2008; Thompson 2014). For instance, premiers could see them as an opportunity to reassess previous commitments or to show how things have evolved in relation to those commitments.

These possibilities are in line with the hopes that accompanied the early development of information and communications technologies (ICTs) in the 1990s and early 2000s. At that time, ICTs were seen as platforms that could help to foster new relationships between citizens and the state (Chadwick 2006). The internet introduced novel approaches to older styles of political communication. These approaches included e-government and digital democracy, the former defined as government communications and service delivery through electronic means, the latter defined as the online expansion of public participation and deliberation (Budd and Harris 2009, 5). Optimists saw the internet as a democratizing platform that could transform communications between citizens and their political representatives (Dahlgren 2005).

However, not long after the initial enthusiasm, skeptics argued that expectations of ICTs had not been met (Hindman 2009). The two-way engagement promise of social media for political participation and democratic deliberation remained largely unfulfilled. Indeed, early work on political communications and the internet identified broadcast approaches on campaign websites (Hill and Hughes 1998), and studies found that websites were not interactive and acted as static campaign flyers or brochures (Quiring 2009). Today, the dominant approach to digital communications by political elites in Western democracies supports the normalization thesis (Park and Perry 2008). It suggests that, instead of engaging citizens, politicians' use of the internet follows traditional patterns of one-way political communications.

This can be partly explained by the multiple challenges posed to political actors by the use of social media. First, staying current in the constantly evolving world of social media applications takes effort, with technology aging quickly.

Second, digital platforms provide new opportunities that change the practice of politics. Although many see these opportunities as positive, they also involve profound changes in the relations between citizens and political elites. This is particularly true when it comes to planning and implementing political campaigns. Several new digital instruments provide a better understanding of the electorate and help to mobilize online voters. This has led to the hybridization of political communications (Giasson et al. 2014a; Karlsen 2009; Kreiss 2012), according to which online party activists and supporters are called on to play paramount roles in a campaign by generating electoral communications, comments, questions, or reactions that become part of the campaign itself. This grassroots activity "has compromised the traditional top-down communication style" of parties (Bor 2014, 6), which political elites can perceive as destabilizing. This feeds a certain mistrust of social media.

Third, political elites have tended to consider the use of social media as a risky business that has to be carried out rather than a true opportunity to do politics differently. Several examples have fed this impression. For instance, the role of YouTube in politics gained widespread attention in 2006 after a video of American Republican Senator George Allen calling a college student of Indian descent a "macaca" went viral and contributed to Allen's election defeat (Gueorguieva 2008). In Canada, an example of YouTube embarrassing a politician occurred with a video posted by the federal Liberal Party titled "Stephen Harper Copies Australian Prime Minister John Howard" (Small 2010). The video was an attempt to catch Harper plagiarizing a Howard speech and an example of YouTube as a catchment for political gaffes more than a venue for positive branding and image management. The rise of personal recording devices on phones has increased the perceived risk since anyone can now post politically embarrassing content (Gueorguieva 2008).

Even a planned and controlled initiative such as the *24 Seven* series saw mixed results. Although the series gained media attention, there was no evidence that it was going viral, and it was difficult to foresee the troubles that the communications strategy would face (Lalancette and Tourigny-Koné 2017). Indeed, after complaints from the media and a few high-profile blunders, Harper's foray into YouTube made headlines for all the wrong reasons. What could have been celebrated as a novel and tech-savvy political communications approach left a legacy of complaints and criticisms. They included blocking media from events that would end up on *24 Seven* episodes (Ryckewaert 2014); leaving the videos on the PMO website despite the official beginning of the election campaign (Naumetz 2015); violating national security by showing compromising clips of Canadian special forces in Iraq (Berthiaume 2015); and bringing negative attention to the labour force that the production required – up to four public servants of the Privy Council Office worked on publication of the videos (McGregor 2014). In the end, the video series would set more of a precedent for the precarious nature of government advertising – notably through social media – rather than being a true game changer in terms of how political elites communicate in Canada.

Nevertheless, positive new social media strategies have also emerged along with political actors' growing understanding of the possible uses of the internet for political communications. Hence, despite the threat that they can pose, social media are increasingly understood to represent a powerful tool to reach targeted audiences by bypassing traditional media. This approach can be described as "disintermediation," a term first used in the banking business half a century ago that refers to the act of "dumping the middleman" (Von Drehle 2016, 37). Without the media as the intermediary, political elites can adopt their own controlled message approaches and promote certain images or brands (Marland 2012; Small 2010), with social media acting as digital information subsidies (Marland 2014). These subsidies can even be personalized, as is the case with "narrowcasting" – as opposed to the wider reach of broadcasting – an electioneering term describing messages designed for and directed at targeted audiences (Panagopoulos 2009). ICTs facilitate the implementation of these specific approaches and present new opportunities for the expanded exercise of power. Narrowcasting, also known as targeting, has a major impact in terms of outreach, fundraising, volunteering, and political marketing. This is because the message specifically formulated for niche segments of the electorate has more chance to be heard, understood, integrated, and thus acted on.

Tight control of the message leads to tight control of the image. Since research has found that a candidate's image has significant effects on voters' evaluations (Mattes et al. 2010), image management has become an essential part of any modern politician's interaction with the public. In fact, image has taken on such an importance that it is now entwined with the presentation of policies, ideas, or parties' programs. In this context, modern political parties have turned to a "TV-conscious approach based on presentation, personality and image-politics" (Sparrow and Turner 2001, 984). Successful image management can lead to what Aeron Davis (2010, 86) described as a "personalized form of media capital" that accumulates with presentation to and connection with an audience. The internet offers a dynamic venue for political actors to shape and manage their images. Indeed, the low cost and high accessibility of social media provide a potentially unlimited space for politicians to do so.

Disintermediation, targeting, and the will to present a controlled image are three trends that first and foremost respond to strategic political considerations. They do not echo the demands for elites to present greater accountability, more openness in decision making, and greater attentiveness to the different interests in a given community. In fact, as highlighted earlier, previous research seems to indicate that the normalized approach to political communications through social media prevails, an approach in which content posted on social media platforms is mainly unidirectional and controlled by political and partisan image makers and gatekeepers (Macnamara and Kenning 2011). Hence, faith in social media as a way to enhance political engagement and foster transactional relations between political elites and their constituents is often deemed simplistic (Dumitrica 2016, 36). Such faith fails to apprehend traditional power relationships and to acknowledge the sometimes weak will among political elites to genuinely move toward participatory engagement.

Although the adoption of social media by Canadian politicians is almost universal, it has received limited attention by academics (for notable exceptions, see Giasson et al. 2014b; Lalancette and Tourigny-Koné 2017; and Small 2014). This chapter seeks to examine a part of the phenomenon by investigating Canadian premiers' use of videos posted on social media. Although no premier has adopted an episodic series similar to Prime Minister Harper's approach with *24 Seven,* most of them have used at least one platform to share videos highlighting some of their political and personal actions. We examine to what extent these videos highlight premiers' role as representative of the diverse interests within their province, take into account the demand for a more open decision-making process, and improve accountability. In doing so, videos posted on social media could contribute to tempering, even lightly, the perception of centralization of power in premiers' hands and eventually partly restore confidence in political elites.

Case Study

METHOD

Our data set comprises 362 videos posted on Facebook, YouTube, Twitter, and/or the premier's official government website. The videos were uploaded by premiers' offices between January 1 and October 1, 2016. We chose this period in order to include videos posted during both legislative sessions and breaks, since we wanted to include all types of videos, including those with lighter content that are more frequent during the summer months. In addition, the length of the period (nine months) allowed us to include a sufficient number of cases to identify clear patterns of communication. Table 6.1 lists the number of videos in our data set for each premier.

Table 6.1 also displays the breakdown in videos collected from Facebook versus YouTube. Tracking platforms for videos was difficult for premiers who actively used both social media sites to post videos since there was no consistency in approach. Although the focus of this chapter is on the content of videos, the view counts still tell a story. As the table clearly shows, Facebook videos are seen much more frequently, almost seventy times more, with averages of 19,309 views on Facebook and 289 views on YouTube. The

TABLE 6.1

Number of online videos for premiers, first nine months of 2016

Province	Name of premier	Political party	Number of videos**	Average views**
British Columbia	Christy Clark	Liberal	58**	259**
Alberta	Rachel Notley	New Democratic Party	13*	38,044*
Saskatchewan	Brad Wall	Saskatchewan Party	17*	87,214*
Manitoba	Greg Selinger (January 1–May 3)	New Democratic Party	1** (Selinger)	51**
	Brian Pallister (May 3– October 1)	Progressive Conservative	7* (Pallister)	4,432*
Ontario	Kathleen Wynne	Liberal	68*	8,391*
			54**	136**
Quebec	Philippe Couillard	Liberal	59*	5,891*
New Brunswick	Brian Gallant	Liberal	9**	375**
Nova Scotia	Stephen McNeil	Liberal	2**	1,379**
Prince Edward Island	Wade MacLauchlan	Liberal	66**	284**
Newfoundland and Labrador	Dwight Ball	Liberal	8**	860**
Total Facebook			164*	19,309*
Total YouTube			198**	289**

NOTE: Views as of March 1, 2017; *n* = 362; * Facebook; ** YouTube.

top-ten viewed videos were all on Facebook, and all came from Saskatchewan, Ontario, and Alberta. The most-viewed video by far was Brad Wall's Facebook video of a speech on carbon emissions from June 2016 (865,476 views). The second-most-viewed video was Kathleen Wynne's Facebook video of greetings for Ramadan from June 2016 (243,992 views). We can speculate on why these videos went viral: Wall's position on natural resources in opposition to that of Prime Minister Justin Trudeau was national news, and Wynne's greetings to certain ethnic groups (Vaisakhi greetings, Eid-al-Adha greetings) tend to create negative reactions from xenophobic individuals who post racist comments and draw attention to the videos. Nevertheless, as with all data presented in this chapter, the number of views does not necessarily reflect the reach and impact of digital messages.

After the data were collected, the videos were coded to analyze content and presentation. The coding framework included dichotomous and objective variables conceived as indicators of the three main dimensions that we wanted to analyze: representation of interests, decision making, and accountability. A series of questions corresponded to each dimension. First, we tried to determine if the premiers were using the videos posted on social media to promote their role as elected representatives of the constituents in their provincial jurisdictions. Accordingly, the questions included in this series were aimed at determining if the videos were a tool to reflect this role, portraying the presence of interest or citizen groups and conveying the idea that the premier was collaborating with these groups or showing coordinated actions with them. We also indicated whether the videos were providing responses to certain demands from these groups. Finally, we highlighted whether the videos addressed economic, social, institutional, or partisan issues.

Second, we wanted to examine what types of political decision makers were depicted in the videos. Were the videos a means to show premiers' collegial style, or did they communicate a quasi-authoritarian approach? The fact that the premiers were sharing their voices with other actors, being shown with other members of their teams, or being depicted as social and economic actors was considered an indicator of a more open decision-making style. The visual presence of elites and non-elites was also taken into account when trying to determine if the decision-making approach depicted in the videos was somewhat inclusive of individuals from outside the premier's circle. Our objective was to assess the type of decision-making approach portrayed in the videos, knowing that it does not necessarily reflect how decisions are made in reality.

Third, we wanted to appraise whether the videos posted on social media were used as an accountability mechanism. To do so, we paid attention to the premiers' recorded comments in order to determine if explicit references to previous commitments were made. We also noted whether the premiers were shown taking questions from audiences, which we considered another form of accountability. Finally, we included references to specific government legislation or funding since these elements, once officially stated, become concrete indicators to evaluate premiers' accountability.

In order to assess the validity of our empirical study, we completed an intercoder reliability test. A second coder analyzed 20 percent of the sample; there was coder agreement in 85 percent of the cases, which is considered above the standard level of acceptability (following Cronbach's alpha reliability test).

FINDINGS

Our findings show a great disparity between premiers in their use of social media videos during the period of our study. Some of them used this communication mechanism on a regular basis – this was the case with Ontario Premier Kathleen Wynne, BC Premier Christy Clark, PEI Premier Wade MacLauchlan, and Quebec Premier Philippe Couillard – whereas others used it occasionally. Greg Selinger from Manitoba and Stephen McNeil from Nova Scotia stand out since they respectively posted only one and two videos during the study period. Even though Selinger's time in office was truncated, his successor, Brian Pallister, was not a heavy user of digital videos either, suggesting that there is an institutional political culture at work in Manitoba. The lengths of the videos included in our data set also vary greatly, from fifteen seconds to fifty-nine minutes.

Taken together, almost half of the videos (42 percent) reassert the premiers' role as elected representatives of their constituents. The premiers are depicted as cooperating with several interest and citizen groups as well as other politicians. In a third of the cases (33 percent), the videos display a targeted message, a policy directed at either a distinct constituency or a distinct demographic. For instance, Premier Clark's videos highlight her government's support for British Columbia's music sector and a landmark agreement signed with First Nations. Premier Notley's videos underline her presence at and commitment to the unexpected and catastrophic wildfire in Fort McMurray. Some of Premier Wynne's videos showcase a free-tuition initiative for low- and middle-income college students as well as an investment in the Ontario music fund, while two of Premier Couillard's videos announce support for film production and funding in aerospace technology.

About two-thirds of the videos (67 percent) are targeted at all provincial residents. For example, some of Clark's videos call attention to an anti-bullying campaign and the province's house-"flipping" epidemic; some of Notley's messages focus on investments in health care and education; one of Couillard's videos features railway safety. A video from New Brunswick Premier Brian Gallant underlines the province's innovation week, and one from Dwight Ball in Newfoundland and Labrador addresses that province's fiscal situation.

Looking at the policy messages in the videos reveals a consistent pattern of attention to both economic (government budgeting, tax policy, economic development) and social (health, education, environment, immigration) issues. More than half of the videos (60 percent) relate to economic policy, and close to half (46 percent) display social policy. Some videos simultaneously cover both areas. Interestingly, a tiny portion of the videos (2 percent) highlights partisan content, a sign of a clear distinction between the premiers' role and their duty as party leaders. Videos presenting institutional content (e.g., electoral or legislative reform) are also not frequent (4 percent), which again confirms the tendency to present tangible and easily consumable content for constituents. This is sometimes described as "kitchen table" politics.

Turning to the type of decision maker depicted in the video, we examined whether the premiers were presented as having a collegial or an authoritative approach. To do so, we first tracked if the premiers appeared as the only speaker in the video. This was the case in just under half of the data set (49 percent). We then noticed the presence (speaking or not speaking) of elites and non-elites and found that both are present in the majority of videos (60 percent and 59 percent respectively). This can be interpreted as an attempt to display a collegial approach according to which collaboration and teamwork are privileged.

Finally, to appraise behaviour and imagery that reflect accountability, we examined whether the premiers are shown taking questions, invoking commitments, mentioning legislation or policies, and announcing funding. We found that premiers do mention funding in about one-third of the videos (35 percent). However, they seldom refer to previous commitments (22 percent of the videos), mention specific policies and regulations (17 percent of the videos), or answer questions from an audience, including the media (only 11 percent of the videos). Therefore, it seems that videos are seldom used as tools to foster stronger accountability.

The types of videos posted by premiers' offices can also be considered as indicators of the styles that they want to publicly portray. Thus, videos can be classified in five main categories. In "message" videos, premiers directly address the camera with a greeting or an announcement. The "speech" videos are footage of the premier delivering a speech or edited segments of a speech; the premiers are usually behind a podium, speaking from notes or a script. The "press" videos present a portion or the entirety of a press conference given by the premier; these videos frequently include other individuals on camera, such as cabinet ministers or economic and social leaders. The "news stories," in line with the *24 Seven* series video style created by the Harper PMO, consist of videos that display premiers interacting with constituents or social or economic actors in a natural setting, such as a community facility, a business, a school, or an urban environment. This style features a journalistic approach. The premier is shown making comments to someone off camera rather than directly to an interviewer, and the videos usually include footage of the event, program, or related content with the premier speaking over the visuals. Finally, the "outreach" videos are characterized by the premier having a conversation with a provincial resident, without evidence of production or editing.

Our findings indicate a strong tendency toward the adoption of the *24 Seven* video approach. As shown in Table 6.2, half of the videos in our data set correspond to the news story style (50 percent). In contrast, speech, message, and press styles represent a small portion of the data set (from 8 percent to 13 percent). Finally, though the outreach style was found in close to one-fifth of the cases (17 percent), these cases are all associated with Premier MacLauchlan in Prince Edward Island.

The styles vary greatly among the premiers. Some of them rely almost exclusively on more traditional approaches such as press or message videos, whereas others adopt more innovative modes. This is why it is particularly relevant to examine the results obtained per premier, even if, in some cases, the small number of videos in the data set limits the generalizations

Table 6.2

Video styles adopted by premiers

Premier	Message	Speech	Press	News story	Outreach	Total
Clark (BC)	2	0	0	56	0	58
Notley (AB)	4	0	0	9	0	13
Wall (SK)	0	15	2	0	0	17
Selinger/Pallister (MB)*	0	1	1	5	0	7
Wynne (ON)	17	2	38	65	0	122
Couillard (QC)	13	7	0	39	0	59
Gallant (NB)	2	1	0	6	0	9
McNeil (NS)	1	1	0	0	0	2
MacLauchlan (PEI)	0	1	2	1	62	66
Ball (NL)	3	0	5	0	0	8
Total	42	28	48	181	62	361

NOTE: * One news story is prior to the term of Pallister.

that we can make for them. Still, the analysis of video style, combined with the results on representation, decision-making approach, and accountability, allow us to distinguish two different patterns regarding the use of videos by premiers.

On one side of the spectrum, premiers use social media videos in ways that reassert their power and authority as well as their position as representatives of the political elite. On the other side, premiers post videos that emphasize an open, collegial, and dynamic approach, thus renewing the traditional, quasi-authoritarian image associated with premiers in the Westminster system.

The videos of Premiers Ball, McNeil, and Wall clearly belong to the first category. The Newfoundland and Labrador premier's videos, featuring message and press components, carry the image of an authoritative and powerful premier embodying his role in a purely traditional manner, where interest groups and constituents are virtually absent. The same can be said about his Saskatchewan counterpart's videos. They almost exclusively consist of speech videos, a good portion of them in the legislature. They portray the premier alone, in charge, and as the only speaker. The only exception is an interview on CTV News in which we can see the newscaster asking Wall questions.

Interestingly, his videos are the only ones in the data set in which we found partisan content, which can be explained by the electoral campaign going on in Saskatchewan during the period studied. The partisan videos consist of declarations in the Legislative Assembly, either about the New Democratic Party's position on energy or about broader issues such as the province's budget or the throne speech. By depicting a combative and sometimes aggressive premier, these videos reaffirm the traditional image of his function. Regarding the Nova Scotia premier, the two videos posted depict McNeil in his official role, providing a message or giving a speech, such as in the "State of the Province" address, a thirty-minute video.

The Quebec premier's videos are also close to this authoritative side of the spectrum. Although Couillard is mostly shown in news stories and shares his voice with other actors, these actors are mainly part of the elite, such as cabinet ministers, representatives of different industries, or local entrepreneurs. Non-elites are present in less than one-third of the videos, which is few compared with the aggregated results. Furthermore, even when they are present, non-elite actors are rarely shown interacting with Couillard.

The videos of Premiers Clark, Notley, Gallant, and Pallister can be classified in the middle of the spectrum, communicating the image of dynamic premiers close to their constituents, even if the approach remains conventional and low risk, with very few elements of accountability. The videos of the premier of British Columbia are almost exclusively news stories. Clark is shown collaborating and working with interest or citizen groups in two-thirds of the cases as well as addressing specific demands from different segments of the electorate more than half of the time. Next door in Alberta, Notley's style is similar, with most videos adopting the news story approach in which the premier is depicted as someone close to her constituents. Furthermore, the majority of her videos address specific demands from citizen or interest groups. The same can be said about the New Brunswick premier's videos, with a majority of news stories characterized by footage of Gallant interacting with different types of groups, including the media. All of these videos reveal a dynamic and human image of the premiers. For instance, Clark makes an announcement on new regulations to protect pets while sharing the stage with golden retrievers; Notley is shown learning how to take professional photographs; and Gallant is portrayed meeting with Syrian refugees. Despite the small size of the sample, the videos of Manitoba Premier Pallister also emphasize the human part. This emphasis includes a news story video of his reaction to a surprise party and another in which he accepts a "challenge" to raise awareness of prostate cancer.

Just two premiers seem to use social media videos as a means to emphasize an open, collegial, and accessible style, and are willing to take some risks in doing so, which place them at the other end of the spectrum. Wynne's office not only posts the largest number of videos in our sample but also uses them as a mechanism for accountability. Hence, the Ontario premier takes questions from an audience in more than a quarter of her videos, refers to specific government commitments in a third of them, addresses government legislation and policies in more than a quarter of them, and announces government funding in half of them. This emphasis on accountability is notable when compared with the aggregated results. Although Wynne's videos correspond for the most part to the news story style, about a third of them are associated with the press style. These videos often present complete press conferences, including the portion when the premier answers questions from the media. Finally, as mentioned, PEI Premier MacLauchlan has introduced a unique style of videos that we identified as outreach videos. They picture "ordinary" citizens conversing in an interview style with the premier, who leads the conversation. Thus, these videos give the image of an accessible and open premier, far from the authoritative portrait of premiers at the other end of the video style spectrum. Wynne's and MacLauchlan's videos introduce elements of interaction with constituents and thus mark a willingness to move away from tight image control, leaving room for spontaneity and authenticity.

Political Elites in Canada in the Digital Age

Overall, our findings show that the use of social media videos by premiers is still evolving. Premiers such as Kathleen Wynne, Wade MacLauchlan, and to a certain extent Christy Clark seem to have adopted this vehicle of communications as a means to create a transformed image of the traditional premier. Their use of digital videos steers away from the autocratic and elitist style associated with the position in Westminster systems, becoming what we call the "accessible premier." Other premiers seem to lean in that direction, too, especially Rachel Notley, Brian Gallant, and Brian Pallister. Some of their videos also display clear elements of openness in decision making by depicting them as individuals capable of working with others, elites and non-elites alike. These videos emphasize the human, accessible nature of premiers.

Our findings point to a diverse collection of policies and target audiences. Through these broad strokes of political activity and policy focus, the idealized accessible premier style presents provincial leaders as leaders of all the people, not as political actors solely focused on their office or partisanship. In addition, reflective of the trend of permanent campaigning (Marland, Giasson, and Esselment 2017), these videos often include mentions of deliverables, especially of specific funding schemes and investments that place tangible figures on policy objectives and accomplishments.

Nevertheless, it seems that several premiers have some difficulties in adapting their communication styles to the new opportunities offered by social media. They post videos that reflect a bluntly elitist and power-centric approach, as is the case with Dwight Ball, Brad Wall, Stephen McNeil, and, to a certain extent, Philippe Couillard. These results are in sync with the findings of Julie Killin and Tamara Small presented in Chapter 12 of this volume. Their examination of the use of Twitter by local candidates in the 2015 federal election showed that safe social media approaches were favoured. If local candidates were more engaged with followers than party leaders, they still used the platform predominantly for broadcasting official party messages. Hence, pragmatic communication approaches emerge regardless of audience, platform, or level of government.

In fact, with the notable exception of Wynne, premiers do not use their social media videos as accountability mechanisms. Few videos mention previous governments or party commitments, and they seldom include references to new policies. Furthermore, videos rarely show premiers answering questions when the audio can be heard. Hence, the videos studied reflect a low-risk, cautious, clearly planned approach to government communications and public relations. In our study, premiers appear in the best light possible, promoting government policies, presenting program achievements, or sharing greetings with citizens. Footage is often staged and scripted. These findings could merely be reflections of the characters of the men and women holding the position of premier rather than evidence of their poor capacities to take advantage of these new media. Whatever the conclusion, these results tend to confirm that image building and control remain the main objective of the use of social media videos by Canadian politicians. Therefore, our data indicate that videos are mostly used as another form of broadcasting to serve strategic communication objectives and image-building considerations while influencing the public policy process. This confirms the "normalization" thesis.

And yet, we believe that social media videos represent an opportunity for politicians to expand past the simple promotion of image to foster genuine accountability. They can become a part of the communications ecosystem, bypassing traditional media and hence allowing dialogue between elites and citizens. Moreover, given the low cost of modern video technology and the ease of production and distribution, leaders of smaller provinces could invest in this type of communication knowing that they can have a significant reach in a less crowded media market. This should hold true even in smaller jurisdictions with fewer resources and staff available.

In the long term, communications activities focused not only on projecting the accessible, collegial, and human image of politicians but also on their accountability to their constituents could help to restore public confidence in political elites. From a pragmatic point of view, we can put forward that citizens' expectations of engagement and dialogue with these elites through social media will continue to increase, pressing elites to further explore and adapt to technological innovations to improve not only their visibility but also their public accountability.

REFERENCES

Aucoin, Peter. 2012. "New Political Governance in Westminster Systems: Impartial Public Administration and Management Performance at Risk." *Governance: An International Journal of Policy, Administration, and Institutions* 25, 2: 177–99. https://doi.org/10.1111/j.1468-0491.2012.01569.x.

Berthiaume, Lee. 2015. "Harper's *24 Seven* Videos Move from Prime Minister's Website to Archives." *National Post,* November 4, A4.

Blondiaux, Loïc, and Jean-Michel Fourniau. 2011. "Un bilan des recherches sur la participation du public en démocratie: Beaucoup de bruit pour rien?" *Participation* 1, 1: 8–35. https://doi.org/10.3917/parti.001.0008.

Bor, Stephanie. 2014. "Using Social Networking Sites to Improve Communication between Political Campaigns and Citizens in the 2012 Election." *American Behavioral Scientist* 58, 9: 1195–1213. https://doi.org/10.1177/0002764213490698.

Bougnoux, Daniel. 2006. *La crise de la représentation.* Paris: La Découverte.

Bovens, Mark. 2010. "Two Concepts of Accountability: Accountability as a Virtue and as a Mechanism." *West European Politics* 33, 5: 946–67. https://doi.org/10.1080/01402382.2010.486119.

Budd, Leslie, and Lisa Harris. 2009. "Introduction." In *E-governance: Managing or Governing?,* edited by Leslie Budd and Lisa Harris, 1–25. New York: Routledge.

Chadwick, Andrew. 2006. *Internet Politics: States, Citizens, and New Communication Technologies.* Oxford: Oxford University Press.

Couture, Joe. 2012. "Saskatchewan Premier Takes Blooper Reel to YouTube." *Leader-Post* [Regina], January 10, A2.

Dahlgren, Peter. 2005. "The Internet, Public Spheres, and Political Communication: Dispersion and Deliberation." *Political Communication* 22, 2: 147–62. https://doi.org/10.1080/10584600590933160.

Davis, Aeron. 2010. *Political Communication and Social Theory.* London: Routledge.

Delacourt, Susan. 2013. *Shopping for Votes: How Politicians Choose Us and We Choose Them.* Toronto: Douglas and McIntyre.

Dumitrica, Delia. 2016. "Imagining Engagement: Youth, Social Media, and Electoral Processes." *Convergence: The International Journal of Resarch into New Media Technologies* 22, 1: 35–53. https://doi.org/10.1177/1354856514553899.

Dunn, Christopher. 1995. *The Institutionalized Cabinet: Governing the Western Provinces.* Kingston: Institute of Public Administration of Canada.

Fung, Archon. 2015. "Putting the Public Back into Governance: The Challenges of Citizen Participation and Its Future." *Public Administration Review* 75, 4: 513–22. https://doi.org/10.1111/puar.12361.

Giasson, Thierry, Frédérick Bastien, Mireille Lalancette, and Gildas Le Bars. 2014a. "Is Social Media Transforming Canadian Electioneering? Hybridity and Online Partisan Strategies in the 2012 Quebec Election." Paper presented at the annual meeting of the Canadian Political Science Association, Brock University, St. Catharines, ON, May 27–29.

Giasson, Thierry, Gildas Le Bars, Frédérick Bastien, and Mélanie Verville. 2014b. "#Qc2012": L'utilisation de Twitter par les partis. In *Les Québécois aux urnes: Les partis, les médias, et les citoyens en campagne,* edited by F. Bastien, É. Bélanger, and F. Gélineau, 135–48. Montréal: Les Presses de l'Université de Montréal.

Gueorguieva, Vassia. 2008. "Voters, MySpace, and YouTube: The Impact of Alternative Communications Channels on the 2006 Election Cycle and Beyond." *Social Science Computer Review* 26, 3: 288–300. https://doi.org/10.1177/0894439307305636.

Hill, Kevin, and John Hughes. 1998. *Cyberpolitics: Citizen Activities in the Age of the Internet.* Lanham, MD: Rowman and Littlefield.

Hindman, Matthew. 2009. *The Myth of Digital Democracy.* New York: Lexington Books.

Johnsrude, Larry. 2007. "Stelmach May Be a Regular on YouTube." *Edmonton Journal,* May 8, A6.

Karlsen, Rune. 2009. "Campaign Communication and the Internet: Party Strategy in the 2005 Norwegian Election Campaign." *Journal of Elections, Public Opinion, and Parties* 19, 2: 183–202. https://doi.org/10.1080/17457280902799030.

Kreiss, Daniel. 2012. *Taking Our Country Back: The Crafting of Networked Politics from Howard Dean to Barack Obama.* Oxford: Oxford University Press. https://doi.org/10.1093/acprof:oso/9780199782536.001.0001.

Lalancette, Mireille, and Sofia Tourigny-Koné. 2017. "*24 Seven* Videostyle: Blurring the Lines and Building Strong Leadership." In *Permanent Campaigning in Canada,* edited by Alex Marland, Thierry Giasson, and Anna Esselment, 259–77. Vancouver: UBC Press.

Macnamara, Jim, and Gail Kenning. 2011. "E-Electioneering 2010: Trends in Social Media Use in Australian Political Communication." *Media International Australia* 139, 1: 7–22. https://doi.org/10.1177/1329878X1113900104.

Marland, Alex. 2012. "Political Photography, Journalism, and Framing in the Digital Age: The Management of Visual Media by the Prime Minister of Canada." *International Journal of Press/Politics* 17, 2: 214–33. https://doi.org/10.1177/1940161211433838.

–. 2014. "The Branding of a Prime Minister: Digital Information Subsidies and the Image Management of Stephen Harper." In *Political Communication in Canada: Meet the Press and Tweet the Rest,* edited by Alex Marland, Thierry Giasson, and Tamara Small, 55–73. Vancouver: UBC Press.

–. 2016. *Brand Command: Canadian Politics and Democracy in the Age of Message Control.* Vancouver: UBC Press.

Marland, Alex, Thierry Giasson, and Anna Esselment, eds. 2017. *Permanent Campaigning in Canada.* Vancouver: UBC Press.

Mattes, Kyle, Michael L. Spezio, Hackjin Kim, Alexander Todorov, Ralph Adolphs, and R. Michael Alvarez. 2010. "Predicting Election Outcomes from Positive and Negative Trait Assessments of Candidate Images." *Political Psychology* 31, 1: 41–58. https://doi.org/10.1111/j.1467-9221.2009.00745.x.

McGregor, Glen. 2014. "Four Staff Work on Widely-Unwatched PM Promo Videos." *Ottawa Citizen,* March 25. http://ottawacitizen.com/uncategorized/four-staff-work-on-widely-unwatched-pm-promo-videos.

Naumetz, Tim. 2015. "Harper's Last *24/7* Video Violates Spirit of 'Caretaker' Government Rules during Election." *Hill Times,* September 10. http://www.hilltimes.com/2015/09/10/harpers-last-247-video-violates-spirit-of-caretaker-government-rules-during-election-critics/33334/feed#!

Panagopoulos, Costas, ed. 2009. *Politicking Online: The Transformation of Election Campaign Communications.* New Brunswick, NJ: Rutgers University Press.

Park, Hun Myoung, and James Perry. 2008. "Does Internet Use Really Facilitate Civic Engagement? Empirical Evidence from the American National Election Studies." In *Civic Engagement in a Network Society,* edited by Kaifeng Yang and Erik Bergrud, 237–69. Charlotte, NC: Information Age Publishing.

Quiring, Oliver. 2009. "What Do Users Associate with 'Interactivity'? A Qualitative Study on User Schemata." *New Media and Society* 11, 6: 899–920. https://doi.org/10.1177/1461444809336511.

Rosanvallon, Pierre. 2015. *Le bon gouvernement.* Paris: Seuil.

Ryckewaert, Laura. 2014. "Press Gallery Should Take Collective Action to Counter Government Control: Critics." *Hill Times,* March 31, 1.

Savoie, Donald. 1999. *Governing from the Centre: The Concentration of Power in Canadian Politics.* Toronto: University of Toronto Press.

–. 2008. *Court Government and the Collapse of Accountability in Canada and the United Kingdom.* Toronto: University of Toronto Press.

Small, Tamara. 2010. "Still Waiting for an Internet Prime Minister: Online Campaigning by Canadian Political Parties." In *Election,* edited by Heather MacIvor, 173–98. Toronto: Emond Montgomery Publications.

–. 2014. "The Not-So Social Network: The Use of Twitter by Canada's Party Leaders." In *Political Communication in Canada: Meet the Press and Tweet the Rest,* edited by Alex Marland, Thierry Giasson, and Tamara Small, 92–110. Vancouver: UBC Press.

Smith, Denis. 1970. "President and Parliament: The Transformation of Parliamentary Government in Canada." In *Apex of Power: The Prime Minister and Political Leadership in Canada,* edited by Thomas Hockin, 224–41. Toronto: Prentice-Hall.

Sparrow, Nick, and John Turner. 2001. "The Permanent Campaign: The Integration of Market Research Techniques in Developing Strategies in a More Uncertain Political Climate." *European Journal of Marketing* 35, 9–10: 984–1002. https://doi.org/10.1108/03090560110400605.

Thompson, Dennis F. 2014. "Responsibility for Failures of Government: The Problem of Many Hands." *American Review of Public Administration* 44, 3: 259–73. https://doi.org/10.1177/0275074014524013.

Vincent, Donovan. 2014. "Keeping Up with the Harpers? New Video Series to Keep Public 'Informed' on Prime Minister's Activities." *Toronto Star,* January 14, A6.

Von Drehle, David. 2016. "Donald Trump's Art of the Steal." *Time,* January 7, 32–39.

White, Graham. 2005. *Cabinets and First Ministers.* Vancouver: UBC Press.

Young, Walter, and Terence Morley. 1983. "The Premier and the Cabinet." In *The Reins of Power: Governing British Columbia,* edited by J. Terence Morley, Norman J. Ruff, Neil A. Swainson, R. Jeremy Wilson, and Walter D. Young, 45–82. Vancouver: Douglas and McIntyre.

7

Supreme Court Judges: Traditional Elite Roles in a Digital Age

Erin Crandall

Judges of the Supreme Court of Canada occupy a central position in today's political landscape. This has not always been the case. Although the Supreme Court was created in 1875, it was actually the Judicial Committee of the Privy Council in the United Kingdom that served as Canada's apex court until 1949. Because of its second-tier status, the Supreme Court did not have the final say in many of Canada's highest-profile public law decisions and sometimes struggled to attract well-qualified jurists to its bench (Snell and Vaughan 1985). Moreover, even after 1949, the political impact of the Supreme Court has not always been evident. Because of comparatively strong intergovernmental cooperation into the 1970s, it heard relatively few major cases, casting its judges as minor players in the nation's constitutional politics (Simeon 1972, 29–30).

The status of the Supreme Court changed dramatically with the introduction of the Canadian Charter of Rights and Freedoms in 1982. The court went from a body concerned primarily with resolving private disputes between individuals and businesses to a body tasked with deciding the constitutionality of matters of enormous public importance (Manfredi 2001; Songer 2008). When we look at high-rofile decisions made by the court in the past five years – from striking down government policies on doctor-assisted death, the legality of prostitution, mandatory minimum sentences in the Criminal Code, Senate reform, and even the status and composition of the court itself – there is little question that today's Supreme Court judges exercise significant influence and decision-making power over the work of the government.

Supreme Court judges can thus be understood as political elites within both the judicial branch and the government as a whole. As the apex judges in Canada, their rulings are the final word, setting binding precedents for all lower courts. Furthermore, as members of a court that exercises strong-form judicial review, Supreme Court judges hold significant policy-making authority by deciding which laws are constitutional. With strong-form judicial review, courts have the general authority to determine the meaning of the constitution, which is then considered authoritative for and binding on the other branches of the government, at least in the short to medium term (Tushnet 2003, 2784). In fact, the Supreme Court's ability to strike down government legislation arguably makes its judges the only substantive formal checks on political executives. This development in the court's power is consistent with general trends in courts elsewhere in the world, in which scholars have noted an increase in rights awareness and entrenched bills of rights (Epp 1998; Hirschl 2004). This, in turn, has prompted vigorous academic debate in Canada concerning the democratic legitimacy of rights review in which unelected judges can overturn laws passed by elected legislators, and whether this power has made Supreme Court judges too politically powerful (Baker 2010; Hogg, Bushell Thornton, and Wright 2007; Manfredi 2001).

However, though the Supreme Court has transformed in important ways over the past few decades, the changing media landscape does not appear to be one of the determinants of this transformation. Considering the unique role that the judicial branch is asked to play, this is arguably not surprising. The Supreme Court is charged with acting as an impartial mediator and independent arbiter, and though both of these concepts are essentially contested they are generally understood to refer respectively to (a) an absence of bias, actual or perceived, in a judge's decision making and (b) the objective institutional relations between courts and other actors that facilitate such impartiality (Hausegger, Riddell, and Hennigar 2008, 174–75). These principles place a strong limit on which interactions between the Supreme Court and other government branches are considered proper. Given the court's role as a third-party arbiter, impartiality and independence are critical to its institutional integrity, making respectful relations between the judiciary and other branches essential. Historically, there has been a strong tradition within the Anglo-American legal system discouraging politicians from publicly criticizing judges for their rulings. Although this tradition appears to have faded somewhat, it is still salient. In turn, though judges are not asked to take a vow of political silence, there is a strong expectation that they refrain from commenting publicly on current and controversial political matters (Hausegger, Riddell, and Hennigar 2008, 174–205). Where this line is drawn for politicians and judges, however, is far from clear. For example, Chief Justice Beverley McLachlin's public statement in 2015 that Canada engaged in "cultural genocide" against Indigenous peoples was criticized by some for crossing this line (Fine 2015a).

Importantly, the need to maintain judicial independence and impartiality limits the types of communication that the Supreme Court has with the public and other political elites. The primary vehicle by which judges communicate about their work is through their judgments, which outline the evidence and reasoning behind their decision making. Although the Supreme Court's decisions are publicly available, this mode of communication undoubtedly creates distance between the court and the public, with most people learning about its work through the media. This means that the Supreme Court has a strong incentive to ensure that the media accurately report its decisions. This is apparent in changes that the court has implemented over the past few decades to facilitate interactions with the media. In 2004, for example, the court was the first in the world to introduce media lockups for high-profile decisions. As in budget lockups, the media are briefed on the court's judgment prior to its official release in order to decrease the likelihood of inaccurate reporting (Macfarlane 2009). The most important development for the court in this regard was creation of the executive legal officer (ELO) in 1985. Functioning as a kind of executive assistant to the chief justice, the ELO is to act as the liaison between the court and the media, providing briefings and information to reporters covering the court. Creation of the ELO has been a particularly significant development given that few journalists who cover the court have legal training (Sauvageau, Schneiderman, and Taras 2006, 200), a gap that has undoubtedly been compounded by media consolidation in Canada. In this respect, the ELO has arguably acted to increase the media's reliance on the court's institutional resources.

The limits to the Supreme Court's public engagement are also apparent in its use of other forms of communication. Like other government actors, the court has begun using digital technologies to widen public access but not in ways that fundamentally change its interactions with the public. Since 2009, the court has offered live webcasts of its hearings on its website, and in 2014 it opened Twitter accounts in both French and English. However, this is hardly a move by the court toward interactive online communications. In its notice on social media engagement, the court makes it clear that these Twitter accounts are used as "an alternative method of sharing the content posted on our website and the Judgments of the Supreme Court of Canada"

(Supreme Court of Canada 2016). In other words, the court's Twitter accounts essentially function as notice boards for press releases and case decisions, directing followers toward more conventional forms of communication. This approach is similar to research findings on political parties in which one-way communication is the norm (Small 2014).

The potential controversy that digital communications technologies can bring to an institution built on independence and impartiality was recently demonstrated with the appointment of Justice Russell Brown to the Supreme Court in August 2015. Prior to being appointed to the Court of Queen's Bench of Alberta in 2013, Justice Brown was a member of the Faculty of Law at the University of Alberta and an active contributor to the faculty's law blog. On his appointment to the Supreme Court, these blog posts were heavily scrutinized, and Justice Brown was criticized in the media for a perceived conservative bias. In reporting on his appointment, the *Globe and Mail*'s justice writer, Sean Fine, detailed the contents of Brown's blog as "describing Justin Trudeau as 'unspeakably awful' and deriding the Canadian Bar Association as a left-wing, anti-Conservative group" (Fine 2015c). Because of the Supreme Court's centralized appointment process, such media criticism never put Justice Brown's elevation to the court at real risk; however, it does demonstrate how even the semblance of partisan political opinion prior to a judicial career can raise questions about the propriety of a judge's appointment. It is this type of controversy that non-partisan political officials seek to avoid, creating strong incentives to limit public engagement not just during one's judicial career but even prior to it.

The potential influence of social media over Supreme Court judges was made even more apparent in August 2017 when the court initially rejected the application of four LGBTQ groups to intervene in an upcoming case dealing with Trinity Western University in British Columbia, which requires students to sign a code of conduct limiting sexual intimacy to heterosexual marriage. A flurry of criticism on social media directed at the Supreme Court quickly appeared, with lawyers and LGBTQ advocates criticizing the exclusion of these groups (Gallant 2017). Only a few days after this initial order was released by Justice Richard Wagner, Chief Justice McLachlin made the unprecedented move of modifying his order by granting intervenor status to all applicants who had applied, including the four LGBTQ groups. Although no explanation for the change accompanied the modified order, in an interview with the *Globe and Mail* two days later Justice Wagner acknowledged that criticism of the initial order observed on social media had prompted the court to make the change (Fine 2017). Thus, though the Supreme Court's interactions with the public and other political actors continue to be heavily controlled, there is no question that its judges are sensitive to public opinion and that the speed of and access to public views provided by social media have affected how the court operates.

Concerns about the power exercised by the Supreme Court have also manifested themselves in debates about institutional reform, most frequently in regard to how justices are appointed (for further details, see Crandall 2015). Although formally it is the governor in council who makes appointments to the court, in practice it is the prime minister, in consultation with the minister of justice, who exercises this power. Concerns about the appointment process have focused not just on the prime minister but also on Supreme Court nominees. Since Supreme Court judges hold significant political power and lifetime appointments until the mandatory retirement age of seventy-five, concerns have been raised about how little we know about them at the time of appointment. Ultimately, many of these objections appear to be rooted in a concern that the power of the prime minister to select Supreme Court judges will produce a court sympathetic to the governing party's political ideologies, though studies of judicial decision making have found limited evidence that this is the case (Macfarlane 2013; Ostberg and Wetstein 2007).

Since 2004, both Liberal and Conservative governments have responded to these concerns by introducing informal reforms to the appointment process. These reforms have included an advisory committee charged with evaluating and creating a shortlist of candidates and an ad hoc parliamentary review process whereby MPs can interview Supreme Court candidates prior to appointment (for further details, see Dodek 2014). The parliamentary review process, in particular, received considerable attention when it was introduced in 2006, with Prime Minister Stephen Harper praising it as an "unprecedented step towards the more open and accountable approach to nominations that Canadians deserve" (quoted in Curry 2006, A1). In practice, however, these processes have added little substantive information on those about to serve on the court and largely have acted as window dressing for an appointment process that remains executive driven (Dodek 2014; Lawlor and Crandall 2015).

Not only were the Conservatives' changes notably modest, but they were also temporary. Following the unsuccessful appointment of Judge Marc

Nadon to the Supreme Court in 2014, the Conservative government abandoned its own process of parliamentary review. This event is discussed in greater detail below, but it is worth noting here that this choice appeared to be in reaction to the partisan rancour surrounding the Nadon appointment and a story in the *Globe and Mail* that detailed the behind-the-scenes politicking (Fine 2014b). Consequently, Harper's final three appointments to the court followed the original, relatively opaque, path toward the bench. The Liberal government of Justin Trudeau announced that its appointments to the court would follow a revised process that included an independent nominating committee designed to limit partisan influence (Trudeau 2016). This process led to the appointments of Justice Malcolm Rowe in October 2016 and Justice Sheilah Martin in December 2017, though it is too early to say if this new process differs significantly from that followed by the Harper Conservatives.

Although efforts to reform the Supreme Court's appointment system show that it is not immune to criticism, because of its unique position within the government, the court operates largely outside the messiness of partisan politics. This fact relies, however, on the goodwill of other political actors. Although perhaps not obvious at first glance, these self-imposed restrictions can place Supreme Court judges in a more vulnerable position compared with other political elites in the event of political criticism. There is a strong expectation that the court, barring extraordinary circumstances, will not be criticized by other branches of the government for its conduct, but this is not a guarantee. Although public criticism is routine for politicians, who are typically ready to respond in kind, how can Supreme Court judges do likewise given the constraints on their public communications prerogatives, particularly as expectations for "real time" communications are on the rise? This is an important question for the court since its legitimacy relies in large part on public support and the appearance of judicial impartiality.

Given how few interactions outside this norm have occurred in Canada, it is not surprising that existing research has not addressed this question directly. However, as we shall see, the comparatively tumultuous relationship between the Conservative government of Prime Minister Harper (2006–15) and the Supreme Court (see Macfarlane 2018) provides the opportunity to analyze such an outlier case to see how the Supreme Court can communicate in a transformed media environment when it is publicly rebuked.

Case Study

The public confrontation between the government and the chief justice analyzed here pivots around an extraordinary legal event, namely the Supreme Court's nullification of Prime Minister Harper's appointment of Justice Marc Nadon to the Supreme Court (*Reference re Supreme Court Act, ss. 5 and 6,* [2014]). A timeline of relevant events is presented in Table 7.1. In October 2013, Harper announced that Nadon was the government's choice to replace retiring Justice Morris Fish, who occupied one of three seats on the court reserved for Quebec. Because Nadon was a judge of the Federal Court of Appeal, whose membership in the Quebec bar had lapsed some twenty years earlier, questions quickly arose about whether Nadon was technically eligible to replace Fish as a Quebec judge. The appointment was soon challenged, and within a few weeks the Conservative government chose to refer the issue of his eligibility to the Supreme Court. In March 2014, the court issued its ruling, finding that Nadon did not meet the requirements to serve as a Quebec judge as set out in the Supreme Court Act. His appointment was accordingly void.

Although ultimately Nadon's disqualification was rooted in law, the politics of the government's loss were well on display. None of the challengers of the appointment, including the government of Quebec, could be considered an ally of the Conservative government, and many suspected that the appointment was an effort by Harper to bring a more conservative ideology to the bench (Fine 2015b). Although the court's ruling was a significant political blow, the prime minister quickly confirmed that his government would accept both the letter and the spirit of the ruling (Fine and Chase 2014). However, about a month later, and only a week after the government lost another major case before the Supreme Court on Senate reform (*Reference re Senate Reform* [2014]), the *National Post* broke a story that "senior levels of government" were "frustrated" with the court (Ivison 2014). On the same day, the Prime Minister's Office issued an unusual statement suggesting that the chief justice had attempted, inappropriately, to contact both the prime minister and the minister of justice during the process of selecting Justice Nadon. The press release noted that "neither the Prime Minister nor the Minister of Justice would ever call a sitting judge on a matter that is or may be before their court," seeming to imply that Chief Justice McLachlin had tried to interfere in the Nadon appointment while the issue was before the Supreme Court (Kennedy 2014).

TABLE 7.1

Timeline of dispute between Conservative government and chief justice of Supreme Court

Date	Event
2013	
April 22	Chief justice (CJ) meets with prime minister (PM) to present retirement letter of Justice Morris Fish.
July 29	CJ attends judicial selection consultation session held by parliamentary committee.
July 31	CJ calls office of minister of justice and PM's chief of staff to provide information about eligibility requirements for judges.
October 3	Justice Nadon appointed to Supreme Court of Canada.
October 7	Justice Nadon officially sworn in as SCC judge.
October 22	In response to legal challenges to Justice Nadon's appointment, government introduces amendments to Supreme Court Act to clarify eligibility requirements for SCC judges. Government also refers questions to SCC regarding constitutionality of these amendments and Justice Nadon's appointment.
2014	
March 21	SCC issues opinion in Reference re *Supreme Court Act, ss. 5 and 6*, [2014], that Justice Nadon is not eligible to serve as a Quebec justice on SCC.
April 25	SCC issues opinion in *Reference re Senate Reform*, 2014 SCC 32, in which major components of government's Senate reform proposal are found to require constitutional amendment to implement.
May 1	*National Post* reports "frustration from senior levels of government" concerning SCC (Ivison 2014). PM's Office releases statement noting CJ had initiated inappropriate call to minister of justice during judicial appointment process (Kennedy 2014).
May 2	SCC issues press release through its executive legal officer in response to media controversy denying any wrongdoing by CJ (Executive Legal Officer of the Supreme Court of Canada 2014).
May 4	Canadian Bar Association calls on PM to acknowledge CJ has not acted inappropriately (Canadian Press 2014).
May 5	Minister of justice repeats criticisms of CJ and SCC (Bryden 2014).
May 6	Eleven former presidents of Canadian Bar Association publicly state government's allegations show disrespect toward judicial branch and CJ (CBA Presidents 2014).

2014	
May 9	Group of Canadian law professors submit complaint to International Commission of Jurists (ICJ) concerning actions of Harper government.
July 23	ICJ issues its report, finding PM's criticisms "not well-founded" and amounting to "encroachment upon the independence of the judiciary and integrity of the Chief Justice" (Tayler 2014, 7).

The following day the Office of the Chief Justice of Canada responded by issuing a news release outlining the timeline of the chief justice's interactions with the government during the process of selecting Justice Nadon. Per his role, the executive legal officer acted as the media point of contact. This timeline made clear that the chief justice had not attempted to contact the prime minister or minister of justice after the appointment had been made. Although consultations had occurred prior to Justice Nadon's selection, the release went on to state that it is "customary for Chief Justices to be consulted during the appointment process and there is nothing inappropriate in raising a potential issue affecting a future appointment" (Executive Legal Officer of the Supreme Court of Canada 2014). In other words, nothing in the chief justice's actions should have been construed as unusual or inappropriate. This was the only public statement issued by the chief justice during this dispute. At the time of her retirement from the court in December 2017, however, McLachlin offered a few reflections on this series of events, including her decision to issue the public statement: "Judges can't get into fights with politicians. We have to just be quiet if we are accused normally. But I do believe the public is entitled to the facts" (quoted in Harris and Barton 2017).

A few days later the minister of justice repeated similar criticisms directed at the chief justice. Both the Conservative government's remarks and the public responses by the Supreme Court were unprecedented in Canadian executive-judicial relations. Notably, the key remarks by both government and SCC officials were made and reported on in a twenty-four-hour cycle, a quick succession of declarations and reactions enhanced by a fast-paced digital media environment.

Other members of the legal and political communities quickly responded to the exchange and appeared overwhelmingly to side with the chief justice. In an article published in the *Globe and Mail*, eleven former presidents of the Canadian Bar Association expressed their concerns about the incident, explaining that the "Prime Minister's statements may intimidate or harm the ability of the Supreme Court of Canada to render justice objectively and fairly" (CBA Presidents 2014). The Canadian Council of Law Deans echoed similar concerns (Fine 2014a). Just over a week after the initial comments from the Prime Minister's Office, a group of Canadian law professors submitted a complaint about the government's actions to the International Commission of Jurists, an NGO mandated to advance the independence of the judiciary and legal profession. The ensuing report by the commission found that the prime minister's criticism "was not well-founded and amounted to an encroachment upon the independence of the judiciary and integrity of the Chief Justice" (Tayler 2014, 7). Not surprisingly, the Conservative government did not acknowledge these findings.

Beyond its unprecedented nature in executive-judicial relations, this event highlights differences in how the government and the Supreme Court communicate publicly when dealing with a politically contentious issue. In particular, whereas the ELO, on behalf of the chief justice, issued a single press release that did not criticize but merely disputed the facts of the government's claims, a significant number of legal elites (law associations, professors, lawyers, etc.) responded to the Conservative government's criticisms in a more critical manner. Thus, whereas the Supreme Court maintained limited and controlled communications with the public, consistent with traditional expectations of its position, other legal elites appeared to fill the gap, compensating for what otherwise could have been an institutional vulnerability of the court. Through an analysis of both legacy news media and Twitter coverage of this dispute, we can better understand which actors publicly responded, to what ends, and whether these responses differed between traditional and social media.

Method

The goals of this media analysis are listed below.

1. To identify who engaged in media commentary on this dispute between the Conservative government and the chief justice.
2. To determine which actors were critical/supportive of the Conservative government and/or the chief justice.
3. To identify the reasoning of actors' criticism or support, including considerations of fact (i.e., the facts of the dispute suggest that one side acted rightly or wrongly), principle (i.e., the actions of one side were

138

appropriate/inappropriate given the understood relations that should exist between the court and the government), and/or politics (i.e., the actions of one side constituted good/bad political strategy).

4. To determine whether legal and political elites who engaged in legacy news media also commented on this dispute using Twitter.

The data for the legacy news media analysis were derived from four English-language daily newspapers (*National Post, Globe and Mail, Ottawa Citizen,* and *Toronto Star*) as well as the Canadian Press. A total of eighty-eight full-text articles were retrieved using the Dow Jones Factiva for a one-month period, beginning with the day that the *National Post* broke the story of the government's criticisms (May 1–31, 2014).[1] Duplicate stories retrieved using these search parameters were counted and coded only once. These articles were manually coded by the author using a predefined coding scheme. The codebook was designed to probe various aspects of the coverage of this political controversy, including the different speakers commenting on the issue (a list of these groups is presented in Table 7.2), whether they were supportive or critical of the actions of the chief justice and/or the government, and the reasoning behind their positions. A speaker could be the author of an article (e.g., written by the president of the Canadian Bar Association or an op-ed columnist) or quoted in an article. Consequently, a single article could have multiple actors defending/criticizing the chief justice and/or the government. The total number of coded mentions ($n = 143$) is consequently more than the eighty-eight stories reviewed. The length of speech among the identified speakers was not differentiated. A second coder reviewed a set of randomly assigned articles that constituted 10 percent of the database. Krippendorff's alpha was used to measure intercoder agreement; this measure was 0.93 for position (criticize/support) and 0.72 for reasoning. The data for speakers' positions can thus be used with considerable confidence, whereas the data for speakers' reasoning should be interpreted with some caution.

The limitations of this media analysis should be acknowledged. These newspapers do not capture regional and local variance in coverage. In particular, the absence of community newspapers and Alberta-based outlets, which tended to be more favourable to Conservative causes, and French newspapers, which tended to be more critical of them, are gaps. The latter point seems to be especially relevant given that the Supreme Court appointment at the root of this controversy came from Quebec. The findings

TABLE 7.2

Criticism/defence of Conservative government and chief justice in newspaper coverage

	CJ criticized/ government defended		CJ defended/ government criticized		No position	
	N	(%)	N	(%)	N	(%)
CPC government	18	(100)	0	(0)	0	(0)
Supreme Court of Canada	0	(0)	9	(100)	0	(0)
Legal elites	3	(9)	28	(88)	1	(3)
Public	6	(23)	20	(77)	0	(0)
Journalists	2	(5)	26	(65)	12	(30)
Other political elites	1	(6)	16	(94)	0	(0)
Total coverage	30	(21)	99	(70)	13	(9)

NOTES: Original coding distinguishes among (1) criticism, (2) defence, and (3) criticism and defence. These categories have been collapsed here, but I can provide data on request. One media mention in which the CJ and the government were both criticized and defended has been excluded from this analysis. Coding of the Conservative government includes (1) prime minister, (2) minister of justice, and (3) Conservative MPs. Coding of the SCC includes (1) SCC spokesperson and (2) chief justice. Coding of legal elites includes (1) law associations (regional bar associations, Criminal Lawyers' Association, Canadian Council of Law School Deans), (2) law professors and other legal academics, (3) retired judges, and (4) lawyers. Coding of the public includes individuals who did not provide any identifiable affiliation. Coding of journalists includes op-eds and columns in which the opinion of the writer is shared. Coding of other political elites includes (1) opposition MPs, (2) political staffers, (3) former politicians, and (4) former deputy minister of justice.

presented here should therefore not be considered representative of the overall news media coverage of this event. However, this selection of newspapers does provide a comprehensive sample of English-language national newspaper coverage – useful given the national scope of the event – and adequate source material to identify key actors who engaged in the media on this issue, a primary objective of this study.

The Twitter analysis examined tweets during the same time period through a selection of the speakers identified by their mentions in the eighty-eight originally reviewed stories, including members of the Conservative government, opposition MPs, legal academics, legal associations, and the media. Forty-six individuals or groups were identified, of which thirty-six had Twitter accounts during the period of analysis. This data set excluded some speakers identified in the print media coverage because they were either anonymously quoted (Conservative MPs) or could not be identified on Twitter (members of the public, retired judges, and lawyers). The SCC did not have a Twitter account during this time period, and, because (former) Minister of Justice Peter MacKay had since deleted his ministerial Twitter account, only his personal Twitter account could be coded. The objective of this analysis was to establish whether those identified as having contributed commentary to English-language national newspapers also used Twitter to communicate on the same issue. This analysis did not compare whether the positioning and messaging of these elites were consistent across these two forms of communication; rather, it tried to determine whether some of these elites were more likely to use interactive online communications such as Twitter. Tweets by these actors were analyzed and coded according to the following categories: (1) original content (directed at specific Twitter users or a general audience); (2) link to a traditional media source; (3) link to a social media source (e.g., blog or podcast). The second and third categories were also coded when the account users linked to a source that they had authored or in which they were mentioned. The total number of tweets reviewed was 331.

FINDINGS

Looking at the media coverage of the Supreme Court and the government over this one-month period illustrates a news event that quickly turned against the government. The first two days during which this event was covered (May 1 and 2) saw a majority of articles ($n = 6$) focused on criticism of the Supreme Court or defence of the government. However, after the Supreme Court issued its news release on May 2, criticism of the chief justice dropped precipitously, never reaching higher than 20 percent of daily coverage after day three. Meanwhile, criticism of the government increased over time, making up nearly 60 percent of the coverage over the course of the month. Table 7.2 provides an overview of who commented on this dispute and the positions that they took. Again we see that media coverage was overwhelmingly in defence of the chief justice and critical of the government. In fact, with the exception of the government itself, all groups overwhelmingly spoke in defence of the chief justice and criticized the government.

Looking at the different views expressed by these groups also reveals interesting patterns. Although the government focused its commentary on criticizing the chief justice, it also defended its own actions. In comparison, all media coverage of the Supreme Court's position came from its press release of May 2, which served to defend the chief justice's actions and offered no criticism of the government, an approach consistent with the traditional relationship maintained between the two branches. Although a handful of legal elites (primarily political scientists with a specialization in law) were critical of the chief justice and defended the government, 88 percent of the commentary from this group was either defence of the chief justice or criticism of the government. Overwhelming support of the chief justice by legal elites is not especially surprising given the adversarial relationship that a significant portion of the academic community had with the Conservative government. Yet it is notable given the sizable portion of media coverage that this group received, and it suggests that legal elites were able to mobilize effectively in defence of the chief justice and the Supreme Court. Although commentary from the public comes a close third in terms of total coverage, it is worth noting that the majority of public comments were in the form of letters to editors, and as such they were not as prominently featured as other news stories on the topic. Among journalists, views were overwhelmingly supportive (65 percent) of the chief justice and critical of the government, though a significant number of these pieces displayed no discernible position (30 percent) and were largely focused on descriptions of the unfolding events. Whereas comments from the government and the Supreme Court came mostly in the initial days after the story broke, mentions from journalists on this issue, especially in op-ed columns, continued throughout the month, explaining their high coverage compared with other groups of actors. In this later coverage, the conflict between the chief justice and the government was frequently not the primary focus but part of a larger critique of the Conservative government.

Were the actors identified in print media also active on this issue on Twitter? Although those coded for Twitter do not constitute all of the speakers identified in the newspaper analysis, the distribution of opinions on Twitter is nonetheless revealing (Table 7.3). Legal elites made up 22 percent of the coverage in the analyzed print media, but they were responsible for 64 percent ($n = 212$) of the tweets commenting on the dispute. Within this group, legal academics stood out as the most prolific tweeters, making up all but six of these tweets. Twenty-eight percent of these tweets by legal academics shared links to additional coverage of the dispute, of which 93 percent ($n = 53$) linked to legacy news media stories. However, the vast majority of tweets produced by this group (72 percent) were original content, which frequently included the actors' evolving views as events unfolded in real

TABLE 7.3

Distribution of tweets by type during chief justice dispute

	Original tweets		Shares, traditional media		Shares, social media		Mean no. of tweets (# accounts)	
	N	(%)	N	(%)	N	(%)	N	(%)
PM/justice minister	0	(0)	0	(0)	0	(0)	0	(2)
Legal associations	0	(0)	6	(100)	0	(0)	6	(1)
Legal academics	149	(72)	53	(26)	4	(2)	26	(8)
Journalists	58	(65)	30	(34)	1	(1)	4	(21)
Opposition MPs	7	(23)	14	(46)	9	(31)	7.5	(4)
Total	214	(65)	103	(31)	14	(4)	9	(36)

NOTE: A complete list of the reviewed Twitter accounts is available at https://docs.google.com/spreadsheets/d/1p_8zSr_TElLviVEjXy2MTo63a4d5eq9NHnPFsbCfJIA/pubhtml.

time. Political elites, in comparison, were much less likely to share their views using Twitter. The prime minister made no tweets regarding the dispute, and opposition MPs were responsible for only 9 percent ($n = 30$) of the total number of tweets. Unsurprisingly, journalists were also frequent distributors of legacy news media stories, making up 29 percent of the tweets of this type ($n = 30$). Of these tweets, 40 percent linked to stories for which the account user was also the author. However, even here, journalists were significantly outpaced by legal academics, who distributed 51 percent of the tweets that shared traditional news stories. Journalists were similar to legal academics in regard to original content, with a majority of tweets from each group made up of this type, suggesting that both felt comfortable engaging on this issue in real time. Altogether, we see that legal elites, in particular legal academics, played a visible role on Twitter, whereas other elites (prime minister and Supreme Court) did not engage in the debate and were left out of the fold. The prominence of legal academics on Twitter is especially notable given that they were focused not simply on sharing legacy media stories but also on producing original content.

Finally, it is worth considering the specific arguments deployed by these various speakers in the newspapers analyzed here. Their reasoning is of special interest given the specific parameters in which interactions between the Supreme Court and the government are traditionally expected to unfold. Figure 7.1 illustrates the breakdown of these arguments according to five categories: (1) fact-based (i.e., the facts of the dispute suggest that one side acted rightly or wrongly); (2) principle-based (i.e., the actions of either the government or the chief justice, based on expectations of their behaviour, were in principle correct/incorrect); (3) political (i.e., the actions of one side constituted good/bad political strategy); (4) combined (i.e., the actions of either the government or the chief justice were assessed based upon the interests of politics in addition to facts and/or principles); and (5) unclear.

Although these findings should be interpreted cautiously, here again we see interesting differences among the groups of speakers. The press release issued by the Supreme Court set out points of both fact and principle in defending the actions of the chief justice, yet the court's timeline of events (presenting a fact-based argument) was the primary focus of media coverage. In comparison, nearly 60 percent of the statements documented by members of the Conservative government were based on issues of principle: that is, it was inappropriate for the chief justice to speak to a member of the government on an issue before the court. Although a majority of the reasons offered by legal elites were also based on points of principle (53 percent), in most of these cases they were part of a position critical of the government: that is, the government's criticisms of the chief justice impugned the integrity and independence of the Supreme Court. In contrast,

FIGURE 7.1

Reasoning for support or criticism by type of speaker, chief justice dispute

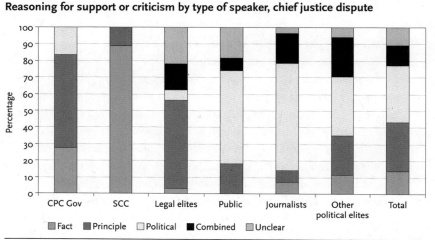

NOTE: Coding for these groups is described on page 139.

the reasoning offered by the public and journalists was significantly different, with the majority grounding their arguments in terms of strategic politics. For example, some mentioned the prime minister's long-standing dislike of the Supreme Court, and the recent series of legal defeats, as motivations for his criticisms of the chief justice. Notably, journalists' political framing of this event was consistent with other research on the media's approach to the Supreme Court, which has found that "coverage begins and ends with politics" (Sauvageau, Schneiderman, and Taras 2006, 227). The positions among other political elites were more diverse, but here again we see that more than 50 percent of the media coverage included a political argument.

Political Elites in Canada in the Digital Age

The focus of this chapter is on whether the traditional and limited methods of communication used by the Supreme Court mean that it is more vulnerable to political criticism than other political elites in the digital age. A focus on the court's unique institutional position is not meant to imply that judges should be immune from political criticism. After all, the days (if they ever existed) when judges could be characterized as non-political legal specialists are long past. In a post-Charter era, when the Supreme Court is frequently tasked with deciding politically divisive questions that can frustrate a government's policy ambitions, criticism should be seen as both an inevitable and an acceptable by-product of democratic governance. This tension was especially apparent in the relationship that developed between the Supreme Court and the Harper Conservative government, which culminated in the 2014 criticisms of the chief justice considered here.

In contrast to many of the contributions to this volume, this chapter reveals a Supreme Court that continues to operate within its traditional parameters of communication. Even under the extraordinary circumstances of the case study considered here, the court did not directly criticize the federal government and limited itself to a single press release on the matter. In contrast, media engagement by the government most frequently came in the form of direct criticism of the conduct of the chief justice. The question of who countered this criticism is an especially interesting one. Whereas national newspaper coverage was overwhelmingly supportive of the chief justice and critical of the Harper government, legal and political elites, as well as members of the public, offered direct criticisms of the government in a manner that the Supreme Court could not. The reasoning behind these positions is also notable. Legal elites, in particular, tended to focus on issues of principle and the unique relationship between the executive and judicial branches of the government, directly countering many of the arguments put forward by the government. This added an important and nuanced perspective on the issue that otherwise would have been largely absent from national newspaper coverage. Returning to one of the original concerns raised by this chapter, whether the Supreme Court is politically vulnerable because of its unique institutional features, the findings presented here suggest that the court has a well of other elites prepared to act in its defence when required. The ability of these actors to mobilize and have their views expressed in legacy and social media alike means that, in practice, SCC judges do not appear to be as politically vulnerable as might otherwise be expected.

The prominence of legal academics was especially apparent on Twitter. This group, first identified by their engagement in legacy news media, became active in sharing original content via social media. This resulted in a notable difference between the legacy news media and the social media analyzed here. Thus, whereas both the Conservative government and the Supreme Court followed traditional approaches to communication during this dispute, the use of Twitter by legal academics suggests that it has become an alternative forum for discussion, debate, and information on the Supreme Court. The importance of this forum is corroborated by the recent acknowledgment by the court that it modified the list of intervenors permitted to participate in an upcoming case in response to social media criticism. Thus, though the Supreme Court is not embracing interactive online communications, this chapter shows that its judges are nonetheless affected by the digital age. The online footprints of judges, old and new, are now scrutinized, and judges themselves appear to be paying attention to what is said on social media. The speed at which the news story analyzed here unfolded illustrates some of the ways that Canadian judges must now navigate this digital communications landscape.

NOTE

1 The search terms used were (McLachlin OR "Chief Justice") AND (Harper OR "Prime Minister" OR "MacKay" OR "Justice Minister").

REFERENCES

Baker, Dennis. 2010. *Not Quite Supreme: The Courts and Coordinate Constitutional Interpretation*. Montreal: McGill-Queen's University Press.

Bryden, Joan. 2014. "Peter MacKay Escalates Feud with Supreme Court, Suggesting Top Court Overstepped on Nadon." *National Post,* May 6. http://nationalpost.com/news/canada/canadian-politics/peter-mackay-escalates-feud-with-supreme-court-suggesting-top-court-overstepped-on-nadon/.

Canadian Press. 2014. "Lawyers' Association Calls on Stephen Harper to Acknowledge Chief Justice Did Nothing Wrong." *Toronto Star, Thestar.com,* May 4. https://www.thestar.com/news/canada/2014/05/04/lawyers_association_calls_on_stephen_harper_to_acknowledge_chief_justice_did_nothing_wrong.html.

CBA Presidents. 2014. "Harper's Disrespect for the Supreme Court Harms the Workings of Government." *Globe and Mail,* May 6. https://www.theglobeandmail.com/opinion/harpers-disrespect-for-the-supreme-court-harms-the-workings-of-government/article18478269/.

Crandall, Erin. 2015. "Defeat and Ambiguity: The Pursuit of Judicial Selection Reform for the Supreme Court of Canada." *Queen's Law Journal* 41, 1: 73–103.

Curry, Bill. 2006. "Top-Court Pick Praised, Review Process Panned." *Globe and Mail,* February 24, A1.

Dodek, Adam M. 2014. "Reforming the Supreme Court Appointment Process, 2004–2014: A Ten Year Democratic Audit." University of Ottawa Faculty of Law Working Paper Series 2014-07. https://doi.org/10.2139/ssrn.2439336.

Epp, Charles R. 1998. *The Rights Revolution: Lawyers, Activists, and Supreme Courts in Comparative Perspective.* Chicago: University of Chicago Press.

Executive Legal Officer of the Supreme Court of Canada. 2014. News release. https://scc-csc.lexum.com/scc-csc/news/en/item/4602/index.do.

Fine, Sean. 2014a. "Law-School Deans Join Critics of Harper's Attack on Top Judge." *Globe and Mail,* May 7. https://www.theglobeandmail.com/news/national/law-school-deans-join-critics-of-harpers-attack-on-top-judge/article18510787/.

–. 2014b. "The Secret Short List that Provoked the Rift between Chief Justice and PMO." *Globe and Mail,* May 23. https://www.theglobeandmail.com/news/politics/the-secret-short-list-that-caused-a-rift-between-chief-justice-and-pmo/article18823392/.

–. 2015a. "Chief Justice Ignites Debate over Canada's Treatment of Aboriginals." *Globe and Mail,* May 29. https://www.theglobeandmail.com/news/national/chief-justice-ignites-debate-over-canadas-treatment-of-aboriginals/article24710491/.

–. 2015b. "Stephen Harper's Courts: How the Judiciary Has Been Remade." *Globe and Mail,* July 24. https://www.theglobeandmail.com/news/politics/stephen-harpers-courts-how-the-judiciary-has-been-remade/article25661306/.

–. 2015c. "Law School Blog Sheds Light on Supreme Court's Newest Judge." *Globe and Mail,* July 31. https://www.theglobeandmail.com/news/national/law-school-blog-sheds-light-on-supreme-courts-newest-judge/article25803859/.

–. 2017. "Supreme Court Justice Offers Explanation for LGBTQ Decision." *Globe and Mail,* August 2. https://beta.theglobeandmail.com/news/national/supreme-court-justice-offers-explanation-for-lgbtq-decision/article35870614/.

Fine, Sean, and Steven Chase. 2014. "Harper Backs Off Nadon Appointment: Prime Minister Says He Will Accept Ruling that the Federal Appeal Court Justice Is Ineligible for the Country's Top Court." *Globe and Mail,* March 26, A4.

Gallant, Jacques. 2017. "Supreme Court Reversal Allows LGBTQ Groups to Take Part in Case Involving B.C. Christian University. *Toronto Star,* August 1. https://www.thestar.com/news/gta/2017/08/01/supreme-court-reversal-allows-lgbtq-groups-to-take-part-in-case-involving-bc-christian-university.html.

Harris, Kathleen, and Rosemary Barton. 2017. "'Shocked': Retiring Chief Justice Was Blindsided by Stephen Harper's Public Attack." http://www.cbc.ca/news/politics/mclachlin-supreme-court-harper-battle-1.4433283.

Hausegger, Lori, Troy Q. Riddell, and Matthew A. Hennigar. 2008. *Canadian Courts: Law, Politics, and Process.* Don Mills, ON: Oxford University Press.

Hirschl, Ran. 2004. *Towards Juristocracy: The Origins and Consequences of the New Constitutionalism.* Cambridge, MA: Harvard University Press.

Hogg, Peter M., Allison A. Bushell Thornton, and Wade K. Wright. 2007. "Charter Dialogue Revisited – Or Much Ado about Metaphors." *Osgoode Hall Law Journal* 45, 1: 1–65.

Ivison, John. 2014. "Tories Incensed with Supreme Court as Some Allege Chief Justice Lobbied against Marc Nadon Appointment." *National Post,* May 1. http://nationalpost.com/news/canada/canadian-politics/tories-incensed-with-supreme-court-as-some-allege-chief-justice-lobbied-against-marc-nadon-appointment.

Kennedy, Mark. 2014. "Harper Refused 'Inappropriate' Call from Chief Justice of Supreme Court on Nadon Appointment, PMO Says." *National Post,* May 1. http://nationalpost.com/news/canada/canadian-politics/harper-refused-inappropriate-call-from-chief-justice-of-supreme-court-on-nadon-appointment-pmo-says.

Lawlor, Andrea, and Erin Crandall. 2015. "Questioning Judges with a Questionable Process: An Analysis of Committee Appearances by Canadian Supreme Court Candidates." *Canadian Journal of Political Science* 48, 4: 863–83. https://doi.org/10.1017/S0008423915000530.

Macfarlane, Emmett. 2009. "Administration at the Supreme Court of Canada: Challenges and Change in the Charter Era." *Canadian Public Administration* 52, 1: 1–21. https://doi.org/10.1111/j.1754-7121.2009.00057.x.

–. 2013. *Governing from the Bench: The Supreme Court of Canada and the Judicial Role.* Law and Society Series. Vancouver: UBC Press.

–. 2018. "'You Can't Always Get What You Want': Regime Politics, the Supreme Court of Canada, and the Harper Government." *Canadian Journal of Political Science* 51, 1: 1–21.

Manfredi, Christopher P. 2001. *Judicial Power and the Charter: Canada and the Paradox of Liberal Constitutionalism.* Don Mills, ON: Oxford University Press.

Ostberg, C.L., and E. Matthew Wetstein. 2007. *Attitudinal Decision Making in the Supreme Court of Canada.* Law and Society Series. Vancouver: UBC Press.

Reference re Senate Reform, 2014 SCC 32.

Reference re Supreme Court Act, ss. 5 and 6, 2014 SCC 21, [2014] 1 S.C.R. 433.

Sauvageau, Florian, David Schneiderman, and David Taras. 2006. *The Last Word: Media Coverage of the Supreme Court of Canada.* Vancouver: UBC Press.

Simeon, Richard. 1972. *Federal-Provincial Diplomacy: The Making of Recent Policy in Canada.* Toronto: University of Toronto Press.

Small, Tamara A. 2014. "The Not-So Social Network: The Use of Twitter by Canada's Party Leaders." In *Political Communication in Canada: Meet the Press and Tweet the Rest,* edited by Alex Marland, Thierry Giasson, and Tamara A. Small, 92–110. Vancouver: UBC Press.

Snell, James G., and Frederick Vaughan. 1985. *The Supreme Court of Canada: History of the Institution.* Toronto: University of Toronto Press.

Songer, Donald R. 2008. *The Transformation of the Supreme Court of Canada: An Empirical Examination.* Toronto: University of Toronto Press.

Supreme Court of Canada. 2016. "Supreme Court of Canada – Terms and Conditions." http://www.scc-csc.ca/terms-avis/notice-enonce-eng.aspx#sm-ms.

Tayler, Wilder. 2014. "Letter from International Commission of Jurists." July 23. http://voices-voix.ca/sites/voices-voix.ca/files/letter_canada_230714_2_tayler_to_heckman.pdf.

Trudeau, Justin. 2016. "Why Canada Has a New Way to Choose Supreme Court Judges." *Globe and Mail,* August 2. https://www.theglobeandmail.com/opinion/why-canada-has-a-new-way-to-choose-supreme-court-judges/article31220275/.

Tushnet, Mark. 2003. "Alternative Forms of Judicial Review." *Michigan Law Review* 101, 8: 2781–802. https://doi.org/10.2307/3595395.

PART 3

Non-governmental Political Elites · · · · · · · · · · · ·

8

Communications as the Workhorse of Governmental Politics: The Liberal Party Leader and the Liberal Caucus

Cristine de Clercy

Canada's political parties provide a pathway to join the ranks of the elite through their institutional structures and organizational processes. Each party is supported by a group of formal members, of which a subset is deeply involved in shaping party policy, administering its processes, and waging election campaigns. Party members who secure the opportunity to stand as candidates in an election join a select cohort within the organization. And those members who go on to win seats then form an elite group: the party caucus. Members of the House of Commons and, historically, the Senate who belong to the same party are collectively designated that party's parliamentary caucus. Canada's system of responsible government rests on the ability of the governing party to secure the confidence of the House of Commons mainly through the support of its caucus members (O'Brien and Bosc 2009, Chapter 1). Given that a single party can form and control the cabinet, and through it the timing of the legislative agenda, ensuring cohesive party behaviour is indeed the "central strategic problem of Westminster government[s]" (Kam 2009, 6). Working together as a team, caucus members represent partisan interests, contribute to decision making in the public sphere, communicate the group's views to the leadership, and are held accountable for their activities and decisions.

Although the party caucus serves key roles in representing partisan interests and executing legislative agendas, its roles are often misunderstood. The behaviour of the caucus regularly puzzles citizens when it appears to unflinchingly support the leader on key issues. Because of their dual roles as party caucus members and constituency representatives, elected politicians face complexity in representing their public and partisan constituencies, making decisions, and demonstrating accountability. The mysterious politics of caucus behaviour is exacerbated by the small amount of academic attention paid to political elites in general and the caucus in particular.

Compared with the large canon of work on American political leaders, there is little about Canadian political leaders. Perhaps no more than two dozen scholars in political science, sociology, and economics currently devote some attention to the subject of Canadian political leadership beyond conducting biographical analyses. Fashionable in the 1970s and 1980s, the study of leadership became somewhat dormant in the 1990s. In the past decade or so, there has been a revival of interest in the subject. Some analysts examine leaders explicitly (e.g., Bittner 2012; Cross and Blais 2012; de Clercy 2007), whereas others discuss leadership as a function of studying party politics (e.g., Carty 2015).

Although the extant literature on leadership is shallow, we know even less about how Canadian party caucuses operate. In part, this lacuna reflects the scholarly habit of considering political parties as operating beyond the legislative sphere of influence. Although certain aspects of their operation have slowly become subject to some regulation (e.g., leadership contest spending), largely they remain private associations. As well, the practice of keeping caucus discussions confidential, and the personal nature of caucus interactions, present large challenges for academic study. However, since Martin Westmacott's 1983 study of party discipline, several authors have explored the team cohesion and independence that mark modern parties (e.g., Blidook 2012; Kam 2009; Malloy 2003; Wilson 2015). As well, there is an emerging political marketing literature that probes the role of social media in politics and its implications for party messaging (e.g., Marland 2016). In summary, though there is a discernible literature on party leaders and the parliamentary caucus, it is a small body of work. Despite its centrality to Westminster governments, there is a tendency to overlook the role of the party caucus, and this is surprising particularly given the modern concerns to ameliorate excessive party discipline and reinvent members' roles.

There is merit in viewing the party, the leader, and the members removed from the current political context. For this task, positive political theory can be helpful, for it isolates the cardinal features and functions of key institutions. The observation by Anthony Downs that "parties formulate policies in order to win elections, rather than win elections in order to formulate policies," is popular because it reminds us that it is the competition for power that motivates party behaviour (quoted in Mueller 2003, 278). Yet it does not reveal why individuals choose to unite under the umbrella of a party or why elected representatives follow their leaders. In short, rational individuals play the party game because it is beneficial to do so, but they play it insofar as it benefits them. There are significant information and resource costs to individual politicians when entering a political market, so joining a party allows them to access many resources and much information at much less cost.

On the hustings, party labels allow voters to make informed judgments about how a politician whom they support ought to behave if elected and facilitate partisan accountability. In the legislative chamber, party members act cohesively to protect their "brand name" and to maximize their chances of winning legislative battles (Müller 2000, 313). However, as John Aldrich (1995, 24) notes, "politicians turn to their political party, that is, use its power, resources and institutional forms, when they believe doing so increases their prospects for winning desired outcomes, and they turn from it if it does not." The tension between an individual's self-interest and the group's interest generates the need for the party to solve the collective action problem: that is, to curb the propensity for individuals to "free-ride" on group goods.

Party organizations overcome the collective action problem in part by monitoring members to ensure contributions to the common good. Leaders are key to the execution of this task. Using their offices as leaders and the different sorts of resources available to them, they reward compliance and punish defection. As Albert Hirschman (1970, 120–21) observes in his study of organizational decline, the members of any group who experience a decline in their satisfaction can choose to remain loyal to the group, elect to voice their concerns to the leadership, or simply decide to leave the group. Particularly in democratic contexts, wise leaders cultivate followers' loyalty and listen to their concerns to curb the exit option. Because parties are hierarchically organized, and because leaders stand at the head of the party structure, they are amply enabled to police party members and elicit their support. And, for the good of the party organization, leaders must ensure that their elected members work together as a team. "Disunity costs votes," writes Christopher Kam (2009, 27), "and left unchecked it can lose elections." The ability to communicate with citizens, and the clear prerogative to speak for (and thus represent) their parties, are central ways in which leaders can shape the team and unify the group. The party leader's role as the primary communicator facilitates the group's mission, and this role has been expanded and reaffirmed as the communications revolution of the past century has unfolded and as modern digital technologies have been pressed into political service (e.g., Courtney 1995, Chapter 5; Marland, Giasson, and Lees-Marshment 2012).

Case Study

METHOD

This theoretical perspective provokes consideration of how, in the real world, leader-follower relationships are created and reified. Specifically, how exactly are party elites, such as the leader and the caucus, formally empowered, established as representatives, and held accountable to members? How does each caucus establish cohesion in the wake of fresh elections that send new cohorts of MPs to Parliament Hill? Has the rise of social media in the digital age checked, or augmented, leaders' responsibility to exercise leadership and ensure party cohesion? These three core questions are explored below in a case study of the Liberals under Justin Trudeau. The focus here is explicitly on the party leader and the party caucus inside Parliament and beyond its walls. Because of space constraints, consideration of other sorts of elites who exert influence (e.g., PMO personnel, campaign organizers, local constituency managers) lies beyond this analysis.

To address how political elites are formally empowered as representatives and held accountable to members, I analyzed the 2012 constitution of the Liberal Party of Canada. Party constitutions are often overlooked in the academic literature, and this is unfortunate because their provisions structure power, which in turn establishes political elites and delimits their responsibilities. So this analysis contributes original insights into the formal constitutional foundations underlying modern leader-caucus relations. To understand how team cohesion is established within a new caucus, I then turn to a consideration of the early political interactions that connect the Liberal Party leader to the group of candidate recruits. These interactions are important in demonstrating how unity is built up over time and as a consequence of iterated leader-follower interactions. Drawing on salient data gathered from secondary sources, such as news reports, I traced the chronological pattern of leader-follower relations from Trudeau's election as leader to the establishment of his government. Finally, to address the third question, concerning the effects of social media, I conducted a semi-structured interview with the Liberal caucus chair and further grounded the analysis with a few key examples drawn from secondary sources. It is worth remembering that the strictures on confidentiality traditionally governing caucus proceedings mean that there are few public sources of credible knowledge about the modern party caucus in the digital age.

FINDINGS

Regarding the first question guiding this study – how are the leader and the party caucus formally empowered, established as representatives, and held accountable to their members? – all political parties set out the roles and responsibilities of members and leaders in constitutional documents. The 2012 constitution of the Liberal Party of Canada (LPC) provides excellent insights into exactly how its political elites are defined, empowered, and held to account. Moreover, the constitution articulates rules in effect when Trudeau became leader in 2013, and they governed the party until a new version of the constitution was adopted three years later. Given these facts, the 2012 version of the constitution, rather than later ones, is the correct one to examine for the purposes of this study.

It is striking how extensively the party leader is authorized to control many aspects of the organization and to represent its members in almost all policy areas. This is common among Canadian party constitutions. Yet the provisions formally empowering the party leader provide a vivid example of how leaders are granted much capacity to bend party organizations to their will. Chapter 12 of the document asserts that "the Leader is entitled to exercise all authority of a leader under the Canada Elections Act and is elected by the members of the Party" (LPC 2012, 40). In the next section, the leader is authorized, among other things, to speak for the party concerning any political issue; to appoint the national campaign co-chairs, in consultation with the national president; and to designate the caucus accountability officer, who reports on the implementation of party policies by the caucus. The leader alone is empowered, in Chapter 6, to refuse to certify an electoral district association if it fails to meet certain criteria and unilaterally to call a meeting of the council of presidents. Along with the national president and the board of directors, the leader appoints key party officers and automatically is a member of every committee established by the board of directors (LPC 2012, 20–22).

In terms of ensuring accountability to the party, constitutional provisions establish that the membership meeting in convention is the highest authority of the party, and the leader must report to every convention (LPC 2012, 50). There is a method for ensuring the leader's responsiveness to members in the case of a poor electoral performance. In the event that a Liberal leader fails to assume the Prime Minister's Office in the wake of an election, party support must be measured through the mechanism of a leadership endorsement ballot. This is a secret, direct vote of all members eligible to vote in delegate selection meetings in every federal riding in the country. Leaders are not endorsed if they secure less than half of the available electoral district points (LPC 2012, 54–55). Note that this accountability mechanism operates only when a leader fails to assume power after a general election is held. An electorally successful party leader who goes on to form the government is freed from such strictures.

In this version of the Liberal constitution, the caucus is also defined and empowered. The caucus comprises party members who are members of the House of Commons or Senate. The constitution empowers the party caucus to appoint people to key party committees, such as the leadership vote committee, and caucus members can serve as delegates or alternates to any convention or general meeting. Interestingly, one section establishes that the LPC does not view the caucus as a constituent body, and the caucus is not subject to the jurisdiction of its internal governance groups (LPC 2012, 41–42). So the caucus is recognized as a type of political office, and granted some representational capacities, in addition to those available to ordinary party members. However, the party edifice exerts no authority over the caucus. Rather, caucus accountability is implicitly linked to the leader rather than directly and explicitly to the party. This is rather interesting insofar as it can be considered as enhancing the caucus's linkage to (and dependence on) the leader while severing its attachment to (and representation of) the party members.

There are a few important specifications of the Liberal leader's relationship with the caucus. One key sanction that the leader exerts concerns rejecting nominees for election to the House of Commons. Chapter 13(2) of the constitution declares that the leader, or the national campaign committee, has absolute discretion over the approval of candidates for election to the House of Commons, and decisions to decline a nomination are not appealable (LPC 2012, 41). The power to control the candidate pool is noted regularly in academic explanations of how party leaders discipline their followers (Kam 2009). At the same time, the leader's constitutional pre-eminence in communications is an often-overlooked empowerment that directly influences caucus coherence. In Chapter 12 of the constitution, the Liberal leader alone is authorized to speak for the party on any political issue (LPC 2012, 40). A subtle but sweeping provision, it means that the message that the leader communicates on any issue is the party's position. Certainly, this proviso places the leader in a pre-eminent position among the caucus members.

This provision raises questions about representation and accountability. For example, if the leader publicly communicates one position but some caucus members publicly take up a different position, whom are the caucus members representing? Does a difference in messaging constitute a breach of caucus loyalty? And, if so, does it merit sanction? These issues are not resolved in the document; in no place is the caucus formally directed to follow the leader or advised about what constitutes disloyalty. The 2012 LPC constitution, in sum, establishes the authority of the party leader clearly. The leader is unambiguously empowered as the chief representative and spokesperson of the party. The Liberal caucus is defined within the document and extended some representational rights and opportunities within the party structure. However, constitutionally, it is exempted from the jurisdiction of the party organization, with the exception of the leader's office. Although several key constitutional provisions ensure that the leader is held accountable to the party membership in various areas, clearly the caucus is accountable only to the leader.

This discussion clarifies how the party leader and caucus are formally established at the apex of power, but sterile laws of party organization do not explain how leaders lead or why followers follow: that is, the realpolitik of leadership. The exercise of leadership is at the heart of the second question guiding this study: how is team cohesion established within a new caucus group? The focus here is on the initial decisions and political interactions that work to bind the caucus to the leader. These interactions are important in demonstrating how group unity is built over time, and as a consequence of iterated leader-follower relations, in which the leader leads and the followers support him or her. Drawing on data gathered from secondary sources, I traced the pattern of leader-follower relations from Justin Trudeau's assumption of the leadership through the first year of his government.

Trudeau was first elected to represent the Papineau riding in 2008 and contested the leadership after the 2011 general election campaign produced the worst results in party history. He was elected leader early in 2013, and at this point his party caucus of thirty-six members of Parliament was a minor opposition party. Indeed, this was the only time in its extensive history that this party was not serving either as the governing party or as the official opposition. The new Liberal leader regularly aimed to portray himself as being committed to democratizing his party and diminishing excessive party discipline. In support of these objectives, he initiated some major changes. For example, in the context of controversy over senatorial spending and accountability, early in 2014 he announced that senators were no longer members of the Liberal caucus. Furthermore, he declared that as prime minister he would appoint only independent senators after employing an open and transparent process, with public input, for nominating worthy candidates. This decision was made rapidly and communicated without much warning to party insiders. As a consequence, it shocked many people, in no small part because it violated extant LPC constitutional provisions concerning caucus membership, as described earlier in this chapter.[1] In light of this problem, the Liberal leader responded that he would seek to amend the party's constitution at the next available opportunity (Bryden 2014).

Because of this decision, many Liberal senators obliged Trudeau and moved to sit as independent members of the Senate. Senator Nick Sibbeston, of the Northwest Territories, released a statement welcoming his new status as an "independent senator" (Wingrove 2014). Other senators, however, declared that they intended to meet as the "Senate Liberal Caucus" *sans* Trudeau and the House of Commons members. Trudeau then wrote to the speaker of the Senate and explained that, because the senators in question were no longer members of his caucus, they were therefore independents. Speaker of the Senate Noël Kinsella, a Conservative, ruled that they could be called Liberal senators in the Red Chamber as long as there were at least five members and they belonged to a party recognized by Elections Canada, as per the chamber's rules.

This incident reveals much about the caucus as it functions within and beyond Parliament. It is clear that the Liberal leader, and at least some of the caucus members, believe that heads of parties ought to have paramount control over who can use their brands in the legislature (Wingrove 2014). Yet legislative rules can offer party members the opportunity to constitute themselves as political entities beyond the leader's reach. The issue was finally resolved when the Liberal senators designated themselves as "the Senate Liberals," created a new website, and employed new public outreach methods to represent Canadians (Senate Liberals 2016). It is noteworthy that Trudeau's decision making proceeded without the formal support of his party, consulted much later (Wingrove 2014).

A few months later Trudeau embarked on another initiative that required his followers to support him unconditionally in public. He set out an unequivocal position – new for the Liberals – on the abortion issue, stating that he had made it clear that future candidates would be expected to vote pro-choice on any bill (Proussalidis 2014). Moreover, future candidates would have to pass checks on their values. Trudeau said that he would check with candidates and ask them a number of questions, such as how they felt about the Charter of Rights and Freedoms or same-sex marriage. He promised that new candidates who stepped forward would be consistent with the Liberal Party "as it is now" (quoted in Proussalidis 2014). The new vetting parameters came into force the following spring as campaigning began for the pending election, and they were generally accepted.

The Liberal leader recruited and approved 338 candidates and, aside from the handful of veterans, created a largely new team. This was the most significant test yet of his capacity to bring together the candidate team and party members. Compared with previous elections, social media played a heightened role, and for all of the parties social media communications generated some controversy (Canadian Press 2015a). In fact, several candidates stepped down over controversial communications. The Liberal candidate in Calgary Nose Hill, for example, resigned voluntarily after offensive tweets that she had posted years before, as a teenager, began circulating on Twitter (Canadian Press 2015b). In most instances, candidates resigned voluntarily. However, in the case of the candidate in the Alberta riding of Sturgeon River–Parkland, the Liberal Party (but not the leader) issued a statement that he was no longer its representative there after controversial Facebook comments surfaced (CBC News 2015). Naturally, it is open to speculation whether the party took responsibility for rejecting this candidate in order to deflect any criticism that might arise if the leader personally rejected him.

Since the purpose of this analysis is to probe how the cohesion of the party caucus was built over time, in the examples of some key early decisions and political interactions recounted above, one clear pattern occurs: the leader simply announced a new policy, without much prior consultation with the affected groups and members, and the caucus members then responded with their support for it. These examples are important in demonstrating how group unity is built over time and as a consequence of iterated leader-follower relations: the leader selects a policy path to pursue, and the followers choose to express their support for it. In the examples of Senate caucus reform and endorsement of pro-choice candidates only, Trudeau made decisions that promised significant changes in the composition of the party caucus without consulting the members. Employing his constitutionally entrenched and unrestricted prerogative to speak for the Liberal organization, he then simply announced these initiatives as new party policies. In each case, the new policy was largely unanticipated, and the Liberal leader did not later ameliorate his position. Clearly, he expected the caucus and the party to line up in support of his position, and this in fact occurred. Therefore, securing public cohesion of the caucus in these examples rested on the leader acting in his role as the party's chief representative and primary communicator, a role bestowed by the party's basic law.

The unity of the caucus can also be secured by removing problematic members from it. In the examples of party candidates who ran into controversy over their social media postings, interestingly, Trudeau did not overtly exercise his constitutionally rooted prerogative to reject them. Most of these candidates resigned voluntarily, with the exception of one person, whom the party organization rejected. It is reasonable to assume that these candidates were encouraged to step aside voluntarily for the good of the party. If so, then this strategy might be explained through Trudeau's commitment to move away from the sort of strict discipline associated with Conservative leader Stephen Harper.

In sum, the leader-follower relationship between Trudeau and the candidates who would ultimately go on to constitute the caucus was established early. After taking office in 2013, the Liberal leader moved to establish his control of the party agenda, unilaterally choosing to adopt new policies that reflected his political views and that directly affected caucus organization and interest representation. Trudeau recruited a new candidate team, vetted them, and led them in the campaign that resulted in a majority victory. Once he was in the leader's office, he quickly established his dominance over the field of candidates, the legislative caucus members, the party elite, and the general members. These groups, in turn, accepted his leadership and responded to it by supporting his decisions. The main point here is that, long before Trudeau sat to the right of the speaker as the prime minister, he had successfully exercised leadership and fashioned a cohesive and disciplined party team.

Before considering the final question under study here, it is worth examining briefly caucus unity within the context of the forty-second Parliament. As the theoretical perspective guiding this study holds, leaders must ensure that their party teams act cohesively in the legislature and speak with one voice in public discourse. At the same time, the Liberals campaigned on specific promises to open up the government, mitigate excessive party discipline, and increase the efficacy and transparency of the House of Commons, reforms that could undermine caucus cohesion. As well, it is worth keeping in mind that the preceding Parliament had featured much concern among its members about excessive party discipline, and several bills to address this problem had been introduced. How did the cohesion of the Liberal caucus fare once it was in government?

One answer to this query is found by considering the reforms brought about by Conservative MP Michael Chong that took effect with the new Parliament. Chong proposed provisions that would shift power away from party leaders and toward caucus members. These proposals were presented in 2014 in the form of Bill C-586, which sought to change the process by which candidates were endorsed by their parties, add a leadership review process to the Parliament of Canada Act, establish a process for the admission and expulsion of caucus members, and set up the means to select a caucus chair (Barnes 2015, 1). When the Reform Act was presented to the House of Commons in the spring of 2015, Trudeau chose not to direct how his caucus members voted on it. Revised substantially, Chong's bill provided party caucuses, and the substantially larger contingent of Liberal MPs, with the choice to adopt the new rules and therefore increase their independence. In the first fall caucus meeting of the newly elected governing party, Liberal MPs chose unanimously to defer a decision on the new rules pending consultation with party members in convention (Bryden 2015). It is not known why Trudeau's caucus made this choice because of the confidential nature of its discussions. And in the future the caucus might decide to access the new provisions. What is clear, however, is that the initial decision of the Liberal caucus was to eschew the new opportunities for more independence and continue to work under the traditional strictures.

The analysis above finds that the Liberal leader has relied heavily on his role as primary communicator to assume control of his party and unify his caucus in support of his leadership. This leads to the third question under consideration: if communication is key to the group's unity, then what are the effects – if any – of social media on leadership and caucus cohesion? In other words, has caucus leadership changed in the digital age? To answer this third question, I ground the analysis in an interview with the Liberal caucus chair, along with a few key examples drawn from secondary sources. Given the confidential nature of caucus proceedings, the interview data supply rare, authoritative insights into how the modern caucus functions.

Given the popular and institutional pressures to reform party caucuses, the extent to which the modern Liberal caucus operates in the traditional mode is striking. In the new Parliament, the basic structure and function of the Liberal caucus continued much as they had in the preceding Parliament.

The new group was constituted under chair Francis Scarpaleggia, MP for Lac-Saint-Louis, at its first meeting in December 2015. He had served as the caucus chair in the previous Parliament and was re-elected to this post (Scarpaleggia 2015). With more than a decade of experience as an MP, Scarpaleggia explained in an interview the distinctive aspects of the modern caucus and the role of the chair: "The role of the Liberal Caucus Chair [LCC] is quite different than the house leader's role. It is more managerial." He referred to the Liberal caucus as a team and emphasized that its chair "is elected by the caucus members, not appointed by the party leader, as are the house leader and the party whip." Within the broad team are sub-caucuses with specific representative interests, organized along regional lines, thematic lines, and issue lines. He observed that caucus members generally want to support the party's agenda, but gathering and optimizing such support relies on excellent organization and communication skills. In terms of organization, Scarpaleggia emphasized that he devotes much energy to managing the weekly, two-hour-long meeting that can be busy given the large caucus. As well, there are major summer and winter retreat-style meetings every year, along with other significant events such as the annual December party for several thousand people. In his comments, he emphasized that these opportunities for caucus members to meet, network, and communicate are critical to maintaining a healthy, functioning group.

In terms of how caucus communications are generally managed, the chair commented that transparency is important, along with ensuring that members are heard by leaders. Communication flows are not only one way from the leaders down to the members; the caucus has an important role to play in providing a respectful, effective forum for members to represent their views to the leader. Scarpaleggia emphasized that ensuring that this communication channel is viable is a personal responsibility of the caucus chair: "I make sure those who want to get their point across" can do so (Scarpaleggia 2016). In addition to ensuring that members are heard, the chair can disseminate advice, particularly to new MPs. His office serves as one source of institutional information for new politicians in search of guidance. Scarpaleggia noted, however, that the overarching principle of caucus confidentiality affects how communications occur. Because "the caucus very much is an inner sanctum," most conversations occur in person, within a group context (Scarpaleggia 2016). The effect of modern communications technology is limited. For example, he observed that the use of email is largely limited to transmitting information such as the times and locations of meetings, which can also by relayed by telephone.

Concerning the uses and effects of social media on caucus communications, Liberal caucus members – before forming the government – were free to carry cellphones and other wireless devices into the weekly national caucus meeting. However, after they won office, the Liberals followed in the footsteps of the Harper Conservative government, which in 2006 became the first party caucus to ban electronic communication devices from its confidential meetings. The Liberals claimed that the rule change was necessary to preserve the candid nature of caucus conversations, along with the need to reduce opportunities for distraction presented by electronic devices (Rana 2015, 1).

Certainly, the quick dissemination of breaking news stories and pending headlines via modes such as Twitter helps party members to monitor the news cycle and keep up to date on their leader's and party's positions. When queried whether social media are employed to communicate among caucus members, Scarpaleggia replied that social media were not used within the caucus. He explained this with reference to the long-standing confidentiality convention: "It would be a real breach [of this principle] to start tweeting caucus conversations" (Scarpaleggia 2016). Considering the best uses of social media for modern politicians, the Liberal caucus chair commented that social media are mainly useful for communications within the riding. For example, he observed that using social media channels such as Facebook nicely enables MPs to publicly signal their support for a particular community group, local activity, or charity. Also, social media are invaluable tools for letting citizens know which daily activities their representative has sponsored or attended in the riding. These comments are helpful and supported in the study by Julie Killin and Tamara Small in this volume. They explore local candidates' use of Twitter during the 2015 election and report that over 38 percent of all tweets under study were "broadcast" in nature. That is, a significant portion of these social media communications simply disseminated "one-sided" information from the local candidate to the constituents. Moreover, Killin and Small report that many candidates used "status" updates to communicate their whereabouts in the riding and their attendance at specific organizations and community events.

Under Trudeau's initial years as leader, then, the basic role of the party's caucus in connecting Liberal MPs to the leader and to one another continued on much as it had before. In the months since the Trudeau Liberals first assumed office, the party caucus has been highly cohesive and following its leader. Along with this support, key functions of the party caucus remain ensuring opportunities for its members to consult with one another and representing views and interests personally and confidentially to the leadership. The Liberal caucus chair's comments underscore the large contributions of caucus meetings to ensuring that the political team works together, providing an effective forum for interest expression, and supplying important feedback from members to leaders. Interestingly, but unsurprisingly, the use of social media for communications literally stops at the caucus meeting door. In the digital age, communications within this group of political elites occur in private, as a meeting of peers, without the intrusion of social media technology. Despite the spread of modern communications options, private, face-to-face conversations among politicians within the caucus environment remain a workhorse of governmental politics.

Political Elites in Canada in the Digital Age

In line with this volume's focus on how political elites represent interests, make decisions, and are held accountable in the digital age, three questions helped to guide the analysis in this chapter. The first asked how party elites, such as the leader and the caucus, are formally empowered, established as representatives, and held accountable to their members. The second concerned how, in the real world, caucus cohesion is created and reified in the wake of fresh elections returning new cohorts of MPs. And the third asked whether the rise of social media in the digital age has checked, or augmented, leaders' responsibility to exercise leadership and ensure party cohesion.

The three questions were addressed in a case study of the Liberals under Justin Trudeau. The first question was engaged through an analysis of the party constitution that endowed the Liberal leader and his caucus with power. The relationship between the party leader and the caucus is established within the context of the party; it is the primary relationship that underlies all others. The constitutional provisions articulate the sweeping powers formally granted to the party leader. As well, the rules set out the party members as the highest authority and establish the means by which the leader is held accountable to those members. The document establishes the party caucus, identifies its members, and enables some degree of organizational participation. Yet the caucus is not held accountable to the party.

Rather, it is allocated to the jurisdiction of the party leader, empowered to represent the caucus and the entire organization because of his exclusive prerogative to speak for the party. The party leader's role as the primary communicator is a central resource for the exercise of leadership.

The answer to the second question was pursued through an examination of the pattern of early leader-follower interactions. As noted above, leadership is realized when self-interested politicians join a party and support their leader in exchange for certain benefits. Successful leaders work sincerely to elicit loyalty and build group cohesion given the possibility that caucus members might choose to leave the group and join another. Exploring how the leader-follower relationship was constructed and reified, the analysis revealed that, by using his constitutionally entrenched and unrestricted prerogative to speak for the Liberal organization, Trudeau set several new policy objectives early in his term. In each case, a common pattern appeared: the new policy was largely unanticipated, the leader clearly expected the caucus and the party to line up in support of his position, and this support occurred. Through the iterated process of articulating an objective, and then securing support for it, Trudeau built a new, unified team. Importantly, this exercise of leadership was grounded in the leader's role as the party's chief representative and primary communicator. The cohesion among members that Trudeau achieved initially, and fostered during the 2015 election, has continued to mark his caucus in government.

With respect to whether the rise of social media in the digital age has checked or augmented leaders' responsibility to ensure party cohesion, the analysis uncovered little evidence that contemporary leaders are unduly constrained. Particularly with regard to information dissemination and decision making in the inner sanctum of the party caucus, the analysis found that the traditionally opaque nature of elite communications remains untouched by social media. At the same time, the discussion above clearly pointed to several ways in which politicians today employ social media tools to pursue their goals. So the results of this case study of the Liberals under Justin Trudeau underscore that much of the contemporary leader's power is rooted in a long-standing, constitutionally entrenched prerogative to speak for the party, and the exercise of this power binds the caucus members together. Given the centrality of communications to the exercise of leadership, going forward one might well expect the rise of social media technology to augment the role and reach of party leaders.

NOTES

ACKNOWLEDGMENT: I thank Francis Scarpaleggia for his generous help.

1 Note that at its annual general meeting in the spring of 2016 the Liberal Party of Canada amended its constitution. Although the 2016 version retains key elements of the leader's role and authority as found in the 2012 version discussed here, the sections defining the party caucus were deleted (LPC 2016).

REFERENCES

Aldrich, John. 1995. *Why Parties?* Chicago: University of Chicago Press. https://doi.org/10.7208/chicago/9780226012773.001.0001.

Barnes, Andre. 2015. *Bill C-586: An Act to Amend the Canada Elections Act and the Parliament of Canada Act (Candidacy and Caucus Reforms).* Ottawa: Library of Parliament.

Bittner, Amanda. 2012. *Platform or Personality? The Role of Party Leaders in Elections.* New York: Oxford University Press.

Blidook, Kelly. 2012. *Constituency Influence in Parliament: Countering the Centre.* Vancouver: UBC Press.

Bryden, Joan. 2014. "Trudeau Boots Senators from Liberal Caucus in Bid to Restore Senate Independence." *Maclean's,* January 29. http://www.macleans.ca/politics/trudeau-boots-senators-from-liberal-caucus-in-bid-to-restore-senate-independence/.

–. 2015. "Liberal MPs Ask Party to Decide on Adoption of Reform Act Rules." *iPolitics,* November 5. http://ipolitics.ca/2015/11/05/trudeau-addresses-first-caucus-as-pm/

The Canadian Press. 2015a. "Social Media Can Be Achilles Heel for Politicians, Aides." *CBC News,* September 9. http://www.cbc.ca/news/politics/canada-election-2015-social-media-1.3220589.

–. 2015b. "Liberal Ala Buzreba Apologizes, Steps Down after Offensive Tweets Found." *CBC News,* September 29. http://www.cbc.ca/news/politics/canada-election-2015-ala-buzreba-tweets-1.3195193.

Carty, R. Kenneth. 2015. *Big Tent Politics: The Liberal Party's Long Mastery of Canada's Public Life.* Vancouver: UBC Press.

CBC News. 2015. "Chris Austin, Liberal Candidate, Pulled for Views 'Irreconcilable' with Party Values." *CBC News,* September 16. http://www.cbc.ca/news/politics/canada-election-2015-chris-austin-sturgeon-river-parkland-nomination-1.3230350.

Courtney, John C. 1995. *Do Conventions Matter? Choosing National Party Leaders in Canada.* Montreal: McGill-Queen's University Press.

Cross, William, and André Blais. 2012. *Politics at the Centre: The Selection and Removal of Party Leaders in the Anglo Parliamentary Democracies.* New York: Oxford University Press. https://doi.org/10.1093/acprof:oso/9780199596720.001.0001.

de Clercy, Cristine. 2007. "Declining Political Survival among Parliamentary Party Leaders, 1867–2005." In *Political Leadership and Representation in Canada: Essays in Honour of John C. Courtney,* edited by Hans J. Michelmann, Donald C. Story, and Jeffrey S. Steeves, 60–80. Toronto: University of Toronto Press. https://doi.org/10.3138/9781442684706-006.

Hirschman, Albert O. 1970. *Exit, Voice, and Loyalty: Responses to Decline in Firms, Organizations, and States.* Cambridge, MA: Harvard University Press.

Kam, Christopher. 2009. *Party Discipline and Parliamentary Politics.* Cambridge, UK: Cambridge University Press. https://doi.org/10.1017/CBO9780511576614.

Liberal Party of Canada. 2012. *Constitution.* https://www.liberal.ca/wp-content/uploads/2012/04/Liberal-Party-of-Canada-2012-Constitution-English.pdf.

–. 2016. *Constitution.* https://www.liberal.ca/wp-content/uploads/2016/07/constitution-en.pdf.

Malloy, Jonathan. 2003. "High Discipline, Low Cohesion: The Uncertain Patterns of Canadian Parliamentary Party Groups." *Journal of Legislative Studies* 9, 4: 116–29. https://doi.org/10.1080/1357233042000306290.

Marland, Alex. 2016. *Brand Command: Canadian Politics and Democracy in the Age of Message Control.* Vancouver: UBC Press.

Marland, Alex, Thierry Giasson, and Jennifer Lees-Marshment. 2012. *Political Marketing in Canada.* Vancouver: UBC Press.

Mueller, Dennis C. 2003. *Public Choice III.* Cambridge, UK: Cambridge University Press. https://doi.org/10.1017/CBO9780511813771.

Müller, Wolfgang C. 2000. "Political Parties in Parliamentary Democracies: Making Delegation and Accountability Work." *European Journal of Political Research* 37, 3: 309–33. https://doi.org/10.1111/1475-6765.00515.

O'Brien, Audrey, and Marc Bosc. 2009. *House of Commons Procedure and Practice.* 2nd ed. Cowansville, QC: Éditions Yvon Blais. http://www.ourcommons.ca/procedure-book-livre/Document.aspx?sbdid=7C730F1D-E10B-4DFC-863A-83E7E1A6940E.

Proussalidis, Daniel. 2014. "Liberal Candidates Must Be Pro-Choice: Justin Trudeau." *Toronto Sun,* May 7. http://torontosun.com/2014/05/07/liberal-candidates-must-be-pro-choice-justin-trudeau.

Rana, Abbas. 2015. "Cellphones Barred from Liberal Caucus Meetings, Goodale Says Grits Don't Want Any Distractions." *Hill Times,* December 14, 1–2.

Scarpaleggia, Francis. 2015. "Release: Francis Scarpaleggia Re-Elected Chair of National Liberal Caucus." December 3. http://www.scarpaleggia.ca/.

–. 2016. Interview by the author via telephone. June 23.

The Senate Liberals. 2016. *Liberal Senate Forum.* http://liberalsenateforum.ca/.

Westmacott, Martin W. 1983. "Whips and Party Cohesion." *Canadian Parliamentary Review* 6, 3: 14–19.

Wilson, R. Paul. 2015. "Minister's Caucus Advisory Committees under the Harper Government." *Canadian Public Administration* 58, 2: 227–48. https://doi.org/10.1111/capa.12112.

Wingrove, Josh. 2014. "Trudeau's Shakeup Sows Confusion in the Senate over Who Owns the Liberal Brand." *Globe and Mail,* January 30. https://www.theglobeandmail.com/news/politics/liberals-independents-and-the-independent-independents-whats-in-a-senators-name/article16602890/.

9
Political Strategists in Canada

Jamie Gillies and David Coletto

The idea of a political mastermind or architect behind a major election victory is a compelling concept and one on which the media like to focus, particularly when explaining an election outcome. In 2015, for example, media stories focused on Justin Trudeau's campaign architects, Katie Telford and Gerald Butts, as Canada's equivalents to Americans such as David Axelrod, Karl Rove, and James Carville. These American masterminds are often thought of as political consultants, defined as "a person who is paid, or whose firm is paid, to provide services for one national or more than one sub-national campaign per election cycle for more than one such cycle, not including those whose salary is paid exclusively by a party committee or interest group" (Medvic 2003, 124). The key to this definition is that the individual is not an employee of a political party, is paid to advise a campaign, and works on many campaigns in different jurisdictions. Much of what the Canadian public understands about these campaign professionals comes from the narrative of American consultants in presidential elections. To differentiate between the American-style consultant and the less-formal approach taken in Canada, we use the term "political strategist" to refer to Canadian campaign professionals because they differ fundamentally from consultants. Canadian strategists tend to work directly for the political party and are not highly paid service-selling consultants.

Going back to the 1950s, individuals such as Dalton Camp, Norman Atkins, Keith Davey, Martin Goldfarb, Allan Gregg, Hugh Segal, Rick Anderson, Warren Kinsella, David Herle, Patrick Muttart, Brad Lavigne, and in 2015, Jenni Byrne, Anne McGrath, and the team of Katie Telford and Gerald Butts helped to define how the public would view their parties, their leaders, and ultimately the themes of each election. Therefore, the concept of a political consultant – like the professional political consultants in the United

States and elsewhere who rightfully get credit for election victories – should apply to Canada.

But the reality is that there is no political consulting industry in Canada. There are no American-style political and election consultant professionals called into action to manage campaigns for candidates or parties or to develop campaign plans. Instead, there are those who work directly for a political party or an elected official, pollsters and digital strategists hired to provide public opinion–based advice or technological expertise, or those who volunteer their time working on campaigns as organizers because they believe in the cause. For a variety of reasons, the Canadian political party system has not Americanized much despite adapting to the same technological changes that have occurred in campaigns south of the border. This is somewhat inconsistent with studies conducted that suggest an Americanization of the election campaign process across Western Europe (Farrell, Kolodny, and Medvic 2001). In Canada, we contend, there exists a media myth of hired gun, American-style political consultants who mastermind campaigns, but in reality we have an insular, party-oriented, and small political strategist industry.

The term "political strategists" incorporates three types of key political professionals:

1. outside strategists hired to work with the political party or candidate for an election campaign or on branding or rebranding of the party itself;
2. party insider strategists who work from the ground up within the party, rise through the grassroots and staff ranks, become the key political advisers in a campaign, and then often take up key inner-circle positions if their party/candidate wins the election, often in the role of prime minister's or premier's chief of staff, party president, or some other plum position in the government to reward party loyalty; and
3. party-oriented operatives at a lower level in the campaign who join the government as paid staffers, leave the party after electoral success and set up consulting firms, or become lobbyists not involved in the day-to-day running of either the government or the party.

It is our contention, from data collected in interviews with leading campaign and political strategists, that Canada has not developed a professional political consulting class like that in the United States. Even in comparison with other British parliamentary systems, there is a uniquely insular group of political strategists in Canada and no consulting core at all.

The literature on political consultants in the United States describes a professional class that, beginning as early as the 1940s on a widespread basis but going back to contentious elections in the 1800s, operated outside the political parties themselves and expanded as more money and resources were spent on capturing the White House and control of Congress. Joe McGinniss's (1969) seminal look at the dynamics of the 1968 presidential election described how strategists had changed American campaigns. Building on his study, practitioners and academics described in detail the continuing evolution into the social media age as the consulting class became fully integrated into modern campaigning and essential to elites who grasped for power (Dulio 2004; Issenberg 2012; Johnson 2007). By the 2010s, these sophisticated operations employed not just wizard-like strategists but also polling firms, data collection, vote microtargeting analytics, digital media firms, and traditional political and media consultants.

Although the 2010 US Supreme Court decision in *Citizens United* opened the floodgates to unlimited campaign contributions to political action committees, creating new markets and funding for America's political consultants, Canada's strict campaign spending and lobbying rules are problematic for political strategists. These accountability rules, especially in terms of lobbyist influence, have developed in a piecemeal fashion over time. But the 2003 party finance reforms implemented by the Liberal government in Bill C-24, and tightened by the Conservative government in 2006, have changed the flow of money to political parties. Furthermore, the Federal Accountability Act (2006), the Fair Elections Act (2014), and recent changes to how senators are appointed have made it more difficult for parties to retain loyal campaign strategists by reducing the funds available to pay for them. The new rules governing lobbying make it difficult for campaign staff to enter the government relations sector and then offer themselves to campaigns when an election approaches. Not only do the rules prohibit lobbyists from volunteering their time on political campaigns, but also parties are sensitive to the perception that lobbyists advise on campaign strategies or tactics. In effect, and rather ironically given the desire for more transparency and accountability of the government, these stricter ethics rules might ultimately affect the ability of seasoned political strategists to contribute to government decision making. This is of particular concern in terms of successful campaign strategists who enter the government and then are replaced with less seasoned strategists.

Placing this political consultant myth in Canadian historical context is helpful. In 1952, Dalton Camp organized the first message-focused election campaign by working with the politicians, the party brass, and the media, including television, to help the New Brunswick Progressive Conservatives win the provincial election. That victory cemented his reputation as an election wunderkind, and Camp would go on to a career as a key Conservative insider. He also recognized that by the 1970s party pollsters and strategists had adapted those early public relations techniques and used the full arsenal of communication techniques to win election campaigns. As Camp (1979, 43–44) wrote, "elections are henceforth to be preordained, issues determined and strategy decided, out of the tabulations of [pollsters]. This would be the new cleared ground on which the wars of politics would be contested. Nothing need any more be left to chance or to wait for inspiration." His facetiousness aside, Camp understood that modern technological-based polling, image making, and focus group testing were the new standards in Canadian party politics. But he was not like American political consultants either. He was a party insider, a particular kind of Canadian political adviser, and he became the mould for today's Canadian political strategist.

Insider accounts of the operation of the Progressive Conservative and Liberal Parties from the John Diefenbaker and Lester Pearson eras through to Pierre Trudeau and Brian Mulroney demonstrate that the key consulting work was actually done by party insiders, often unpaid volunteers who had risen in party circles over time but had other lucrative careers (Camp 1970, 1979; Davey 1986). In this era, the only consulting work provided was by major national party pollsters, who had their own market research companies, could drum up enough consistent private sector business to make a decent living, and did political polling for the publicity (Hoy 1989).

As campaigns changed in the 1990s, the more technical aspects of campaigning and the marketing of leaders were addressed. The role of the campaign manager now included the need to employ pollsters, build a strategy for the campaign based on accurate polling research, build a motivated organization around the campaign strategists, use advertising effectively when needed, keep within a campaign spending limit with enough in reserve for the final election push, and have an effective fundraising operation throughout each election effort (Laschinger and Stevens 1992, 53). Lead strategists also worked to build political teams effectively, looking at the interaction between policy and communications and the need to get messaging right before building an election organization. The lead strategist helped to make the party's election goals clear for everyone on the campaign team and to set the stage for an efficient election campaign (Goldenberg 2006).

By the 2000s, lead campaign strategists also had to focus on the power of the internet and on social media as a populist mobilization tool (Flanagan 2014, 95–108; Kinsella 2007, 269–76). Adapting and integrating new technologies more speedily than one's opponents became an essential part of a successful campaign. Using advertising and communications to jam up opposition parties' communications and disrupt their election operations (Flanagan 2009, 285) became an effective strategy in an era of negative campaigning that began with Stephen Harper's leadership of the Conservative Party of Canada.

Today strategists play an increasing role in new and evolving campaign tasks as the demand for digital political information and technology increases (Howard 2005). This has created new kinds of digital strategists involved in election campaigns with specialties in social media marketing, voter identification software, and automated phone- and robo-call contracting. For example, even five years ago, a campaign manager did not hire someone who could build conversion funnels to identify voters through party websites and social media. The digital strategists, in terms of both data collection and creative content, are becoming as important as the campaign managers.

In Canada, party insider memoirs and accounts of campaigns have dominated the small literature on political strategists. These autobiographies and analyses of elections provide important insights into how political strategy has moved from party boss backrooms to a highly sophisticated world of campaign strategy. A small body of academic research has focused on the role of consultants in policy making (Craft 2016; Howlett and Migone 2013; Saint-Martin 2000; Speers 2007) and a growing understanding of what Kimberly Speers has termed the "private service." There has also been consideration of the political consultant role in greater detail, especially with regard to the increasing centrality of political market research to the task of election preparation (Lees-Marshment and Marland 2012; Marland 2012). Yet there has been minimal qualitative research on professional strategists involved in campaigns in Canada (Giasson 2006). This chapter helps to fill that gap.

Case Study

In this chapter, we attempt to build more granularity into the consulting and strategist folkways and explore how and why political elites, especially party leaders, rely so heavily on their advice and counsel. Using interviews with many of Canada's leading political strategists, we suggest that Canada's professional political class is unique even compared with those of other Anglo-American democracies and, for particular reasons, has not become like the American consulting class. The central research questions that we aim to answer are why there is no sustained political consulting class in Canada, what is unique about these Canadian elites, how parties and leaders utilize campaign strategists, and how these strategists are adapting, especially in terms of accountability, to new rules about transparency.

METHOD

The primary data for this project were in-depth interviews with Canadian practitioners who played formal roles in recent federal or provincial election campaigns. Our objective was to collect data on political strategists in Canada from the perspectives of those who have been directly involved in election campaigns.

To develop the respondent pool, we created a multi-partisan list of party strategists, pollsters, and former staffers. This list was composed of high-ranking strategists who were either the senior strategists in at least one federal or provincial campaign or the lead strategists in one particular aspect of a campaign, such as party pollster or digital communications coordinator. Fifteen women and men were invited to participate in the interviews, including strategists of varying age and experience. We completed interviews with nine respondents from April 20 to May 19, 2016. The average length of each interview was forty-five minutes. Six interviews were recorded over the phone and recoded with the consent of the respondents, and three were conducted in person. The interviews were semi-structured.

The respondents included three pollsters, two digital campaign staffers, and four general strategists directly involved in election campaigns with the Conservative Party, the Liberal Party, and the New Democratic Party. Many of the respondents had also advised provincial parties, including the Wildrose Party of Alberta; the Progressive Conservative Parties of Alberta, Manitoba, Nova Scotia, and Prince Edward Island; and the Liberal Parties of British Columbia, Ontario, Nova Scotia, New Brunswick, and Newfoundland

and Labrador. The three pollsters are still active and manage their own research firms. The other six respondents work in private firms in government relations, communications, or digital marketing.

The interview guide included questions about their histories in politics, their roles in different campaigns and for different parties, and their perspectives on how campaigning and the roles of political professionals have changed in Canada. Questions also explored their perspectives on political strategists in Canada and the effects of the Federal Accountability Act and the Fair Elections Act on political professionals and party involvement. The interviews also provided opportunities for respondents to offer insights that went beyond the formal questions in the interview guide. Random identifiers have been assigned in non-chronological order to the respondents (e.g., R1, R2) to indicate the source of information yet protect respondent confidentiality.

FINDINGS

Based on our analysis, our first observation is that insider strategists dominate in the management of Canadian election campaigns. Despite rapid changes in how campaigns are organized and the increased role that digital technology plays, outside political consultants are not becoming the central players in Canadian election campaigns. The focus on branding, market intelligence, and big data has not produced the rise of a professional political consulting class in Canada. In other words, the first type of strategist (as mentioned above), the outsider strategist, is the exception to the rule. Furthermore, the third type of strategist, the lower-level operative, does help with campaigns but rarely plays a role in formulating campaign strategy. This group often volunteers for the political cause, sometimes moving from provincial to federal campaigns. These volunteers usually do this work with the hope of landing a paid position with a government or working directly with a politician. Campaigns are run by paid party staff and supported by the staff of elected officials in the party leader's office or the Prime Minister's Office. That said, some of those whom we interviewed see potential for movement toward a consulting class given the rapid pace of digital technological change in campaigns and the many skills that a campaign strategist needs to advise a modern campaign.

Canada has seen more of the second type, insider strategists, play major roles in campaigns. The party insider strategist – whether election strategist, policy strategist, pollster, image specialist, or digital strategist – is paramount in Canadian politics. The other types are rare, called on in particular occasions or to do specific tasks, but often they are after-thoughts and not central to election and political party planning. Within the past decade, as a result of party finance reforms and the adoption of much tougher rules for transparency and lobbying, government relations and public affairs professionals who might have played formal roles in campaigns in the past are prohibited from playing formal roles in follow-up campaigns and discouraged from any informal participation. All respondents agreed that there is not enough money or election frequency in the system as a whole to sustain a consulting class. As with Giasson's (2006) research on the election of 2000, these interviews confirm the importance of in-house or ideologically coherent professionals to Canadian parties. Almost everyone involved in political strategy is either selling a service to a political party, such as polling research or voter identification software and analysis, or a party loyalist who has worked on campaigns and in the government as a volunteer or staffer and has matured to the level of strategist. As one respondent described it, "there are no domestic political consultants in Canada because the cycles aren't frequent enough, and there isn't enough capital in them to allow for that level of professionalization" (R6).

More frequent elections and larger campaign budgets secure a place for professional political consultants in the United States. There are elections every year, at every level of government, that command enough resources to provide work for thousands. In Canada, even though provincial campaigns provide another ten campaigns every five years, provincial campaign budgets rarely have enough resources to advertise extensively, let alone pay for outside political consultants. As one respondent said, "no provincial campaign could afford to pay my professional rate. And if they could I would suggest that spending that money on advertising is a better use of resources than spending [it] for my advice" (R8).

This became even more apparent when respondents spoke about the personal cost and overhead of setting up a business. American political parties "have a perpetual election cycle from the municipal level on up. We have fewer jurisdictions, doing fewer elections, with fewer dollars. It is just about impossible to sustain yourself as a sole prime campaign operative" (R1). On this point, all of those interviewed agreed that the motivation for working on campaigns, or volunteering, or giving their expertise at extremely reduced rates was about their own political or personal convictions, "a partisan passion ... or some sort of ideological drive to see the party go in the right direction or to change things or to kind of run the show perhaps, or some sort of personal loyalty to the person running. Few people go into it as an investment" (R6).

This is in sharp contrast to a for-profit American consulting class with professional political mercenaries. In reality, a Canadian political party's campaign funds are spent not on professional political strategists but on the few ads that a party might be able to afford, on campaign materials, on communication devices such as smartphones, on research, and on campaign operatives and staffers given very little in salaries. When the Liberal and Conservative Parties, both of which have campaign war chests, use "hired gun" consultants for advice prior to or during an election campaign, it is for a short time. They simply cannot afford their full-time services to manage or run campaigns.

A number of Canadian political strategists have honed their skills for the international consulting market. John Laschinger is one of the few who turned a specialization into a consulting career. As one respondent suggested, "Canadians are very good generalists, so they are in demand internationally" (R8). Others have worked on Canadian campaigns and then gravitated to steadier career-based American and European election campaign work because they enjoy that kind of employment or believe in the ideals of various political causes. A few, such as Nick Kouvalis, are still based in Canada and offer full political service consulting, but it is usually for local and provincial campaigns. These strategists are almost non-existent at the federal election level.

Our second observation is that Canadian political party culture has played a strong role in determining why there has not been a political consulting profession in Canada. In the United States, campaign resources are much larger than in other political systems, political parties tend to be weak and decentralized organizations, and candidate-centred rather than party-centred campaigns dominate national, state, and local contests. Frequent elections allow a good number of people with diverse skills to become involved with party politics. Canadian parties have tended to be more insular and less evangelical in their messages to supporters to join them. They remain parties operating in an electoral-professional environment reliant on volunteers, low-paid staff, and a contingent of strategists often close to the party leader or senior staff.

Respondents suggested that the kind of political strategist whom every party was looking for is a combination of committed loyalist and campaign specialist, with experience and expertise in polling, branding, advertising, digital campaigning, or political strategy. As one expert suggested, "the pollsters and the advertisers have always been people with real external expertise" (R2). Even with the rise of big data – going from party contact lists, to phone banks, to internet databases, to social media microtargeting – Canadian parties rarely seek independent consulting firms to run their campaigns. They might hire outside consultants in a non-election year or have campaign veterans discuss some strategies, but no campaign has turned over its operation to these consultants. Parties still value loyalty to the party and work for the party over time as more important. This is perhaps because most campaigns really do not have much money given the long-standing and comparatively transparent party finance system. Because of this and the strict rules for financing campaigns, senior campaign leaders tend to be unpaid or on very small salaries:

> They are majority volunteer[s] every time. They are people who might have careers that allow them time to give that level of contribution, they might in some cases be vendors, [or] they might in some cases be staffers, otherwise paid with public dollars to support people who are in office. But you don't see a cadre of mercenaries that those people bring in to run their team. (R6)

The top strategists of the major federal parties for each election campaign were almost uniformly individuals who were either volunteers or paid low salaries and then went on to either inner-circle roles with the party or the leader or left politics after the campaign. Not a single strategist would be considered a political consultant during those elections. Instead, they were campaign managers, national party campaign chairs, or pollsters.

Our third observation is that, because of the limited amount of money in the system as a whole, there is only a small pool of talent in these top strategist positions. Each major party, at the provincial and federal levels, circulates the same party insider strategists and lower-level, third type of strategist operatives in campaigns. Since political management work is poorly paid, there is a smaller supply of talent. Only a few people are willing to work long hours for pay far less than that from private sector clients, so only a small number end up developing the skill and experience that campaign management requires. Even in Canada's relatively small market, demand outstrips supply, but the finance rules and small budgets of the parties mean that fees for services do not necessarily get adjusted accordingly. Candidates, even leaders of the major three national political parties, rely on a small group of strategists who can bring expertise and experience to a campaign. In fact, all of those whom we interviewed had worked on at least one federal campaign and one provincial campaign. Although federal and provincial party organizations are not formally linked, many of the elite-level strategists and campaign operatives are connected.

Historically, however, these political elites do not make the move for leadership of a party and then win an election without having in place a campaign manager or strategist who does have specialized skills. Since the time of Pierre Trudeau, key campaign strategists have usually been on board, or acquainted with the leaders, before they won leadership races and then were often the architects of the initial election campaigns that propelled the leaders to power.

Where parties and leaders should be concerned about the state of political advice is that, after election breakthroughs, when a party wins an election or a new leader takes over and is given a mandate, as occurred in the 2006 and 2015 elections, institutional memory can quickly dissipate. For most of these strategists, especially after a campaign success such as a new majority government, even the possibility of relatively well-paid government positions as a reward for their efforts often pales in comparison to what they could earn in the private sector. The outcome is that political parties have a particular type of person who manages these campaigns and then moves on to a paid position in the government. Those who remain, however, can burn out quickly because of the pressure cooker work environment. As one respondent put it,

> they [strategists] leave politics, and they go on, and they end up earning two or three or four times as much as they earned on the Hill, and then they have the added pain in the ass of somebody in the *Globe and Mail* ... insinuating they are a criminal, and they just say "to hell with it, I don't need the loss in income, I don't need the hassle and the impact on my reputation, so I'll donate a cheque to someone, but that's the extent of my involvement." So you lose good people and people of experience. (R1)

This can lead to an institutional memory deficit that greatly affects the quality and predictability of a party's long-term election agenda: "The big strategists on campaigns usually have to come in and take a public sector job or take a party job as a salary ... or be volunteers and donate their time because they work in a profession that's going to allow them to do that" (R3). After the government is formed, poor decision making can occur when campaign staff leave and are replaced with neophytes without high-level political experience.

Consider the Conservative Party's disastrous 2015 campaign, and how the work done to build a winning 2011 coalition was likely not used, given the lack of veterans of previous campaigns in command. As one respondent suggested, "if you look at the 2015 Conservative campaign, ... it is evident that they were relying on the judgment of some people who didn't know a lot about running national campaigns, ... and it was not as effective a campaign" (R1). The Conservative messaging fell apart around the optics of the niqab debate. Myopic thinking about strategy in Quebec hurt the party deeply in terms of a national narrative that it needed to change during the campaign. Instead, it was the decisive moment at which point centrist voters chose the Liberals. This example demonstrates that Ottawa is susceptible to periods when there is a lack of political strategy gleaned from years of institutional memory or periods when political strategy might not be accessible to political leaders as a result of the disincentives for strategists to remain active in the government for long periods of time.

The exception to this narrative is perhaps the NDP, whose strategists are unionized, and there tends to be a more formalized bidding process for key positions within the federal campaign. The party's culture is different in that the strategists and managers often come from union and activist community backgrounds, and they get loaned to campaigns and then go back to and continue to work in those NDP "grassroots" base communities. Like other party strategists, though, they are subject to party finance and accountability laws.

Our fourth observation was the increasing importance of digital strategists. The increased amounts of money spent largely on advertising and branding (Marland 2016) in the lead-up to the 2011 and 2015 elections, as well as greater media focus on the strategists running campaigns, suggest that an American-style political consulting class could become a reality in campaigns in Canada. Patrick Muttart, for example, was lauded for his professionalization of vote targeting with the Conservative Party. Coverage of the targeting and branding work done by Muttart and others demonstrated that all parties invested in these kinds of microtargeting analytics (Delacourt 2013; Marland 2016). The past two federal elections, however, appear to indicate that we are entering a new era of political consulting. Campaign managers and party organizers in place for decades, from the governments of Pierre Trudeau through to Stephen Harper, were largely absent. The techniques used in 2011 and 2015, especially vote targeting employed by the Conservatives in 2011 and social media and digital technology used by the Liberals in 2015, were engineered and managed by a new team of campaign professionals. Although national campaign chairs were still parts of the elections, more complex strategic decisions included technologically savvy strategists. Contrary to media narratives that they were highly paid consultants, we suggest that strategists such as Muttart are in fact a variation of the traditional Canadian, Dalton Camp–style insider or expert service provider, with new technologies, different campaign needs, but the same roles as an underpaid party insider. As one respondent suggested with reference to the 2015 election, it is the "same evolution that has happened in every other sector of the economy. It is just that the thing campaigns need to achieve, identifying voters, is cheaper and easier to do at scale online as it is offline" (R2). The work that needs to be done in campaigns has changed in the digital era, but it is the same type of volunteer or underpaid party insider doing the work.

Political Elites in Canada in the Digital Age

Although Canada does not have "political consultants" in the American sense of the term, Canadian political parties rely on strategists directly employed by the parties or elected officials to help them run election campaigns. As our interviews with a cross-section of leading Canadian political strategists demonstrate, these individuals are not hired guns but party loyalists who contribute their time and expertise to support their chosen party or leader. Despite increasing desire among the public for more accountability and transparency, changes to the Federal Accountability Act have made a new era of political consulting even less likely. Increasing the money available to hire more political strategists will likely not occur because of party and campaign finance laws. So much scrutiny is focused on how politicians and parties spend both their campaign war chests and the public funds associated with elections that committed loyalists are the only strategists who remain from one election to the next. In terms of accountability, mechanisms are in place both legally and institutionally to keep money out of politics.

Although laws might actually have strengthened the role of political parties by removing the influence of lobbyists and government relations professionals in campaigns, they might also have pushed the role of political strategists further into the shadows. The work of campaigning has never been an open or transparent process. As advisers to elected officials or those seeking elected office, political strategists are accountable to the party, not to the public. In some cases, this is positive because those involved in campaigns are likely direct employees of the political parties. But it can also limit outside voices and perspectives in the process of campaigning and conducting elections – the ultimate form of representation in our democratic system.

The lack of institutional memory is problematic as well. Although the Federal Accountability Act is consistent with a perceived public desire for more transparency, and necessary to eliminate backroom deal making and advising, that backroom work has long served a useful purpose in providing internal guidance and advice. But it is difficult to keep strategists on for more than one election. Even having these strategists and party insiders in the upper chamber is no longer an option with changes to the appointment process that Justin Trudeau has adopted. Successful party leaders will often hire their campaign managers and key strategists for inner-circle positions following elections. As a result of the close relationship that has developed between political elites and strategists, they can move to advisory capacities if they are hired on and work for the government, or the opposition, following an election in key decision-making roles. However, if these strategists work for a campaign and then leave politics, they must step away for an extended period of time and are often not eligible to work in the next election. The result is that strategists who become senior staffers can burn out in the pressure cooker environment at the centre of power.

New digital tasks for strategists are allowing younger and motivated partisans to become involved in party politics. This is an evolution in campaigns that might create a more specialized election professional. But it is likely that digital-savvy loyalists will volunteer their time to work on campaigns. So, for political leaders in Canada to run successful campaigns and then follow them up with successful parliamentary agendas, they need to rely on effective political strategists. This is where strategists can represent the interests of their leaders and parties and utilize their formal insider positions to advance electoral agendas. A competent strategy team allows leaders to represent the needs and attitudes of all factions of their parties, reach out broadly to party bases, and appeal to large cross-sections of independent voters in Canada. Strategists make all of this happen not only through a combination of traditional campaign management techniques but also by acting as the links to bring together the different strands of a political party during a campaign. It would be very difficult for a major political party to win federally in Canada without these key people. However, unlike in the United States, a Canadian consulting "class" does not actually exist.

REFERENCES

Camp, Dalton. 1970. *Gentlemen, Players, and Politicians*. Toronto: McClelland and Stewart.

–. 1979. *Points of Departure*. Ottawa: Deneau and Greenberg.

Craft, Jonathan. 2016. *Backrooms and Beyond: Partisan Advisers and the Politics of Policy Work in Canada*. Toronto: University of Toronto Press.

Davey, Keith. 1986. *Rainmaker: A Passion for Politics*. Toronto: Stoddart.

Delacourt, Susan. 2013. *Shopping for Votes: How Politicians Choose Us and We Choose Them*. Toronto: Douglas and McIntyre.

Dulio, David A. 2004. *For Better or Worse? How Political Consultants Are Changing Elections in the United States*. Albany: SUNY Press.

Farrell, David M., Robin Kolodny, and Stephen Medvic. 2001. "Parties and Campaign Professionals in a Digital Age: Political Consultants in the United States and Their Counterparts Overseas." *Harvard International Journal of Press/Politics* 6, 4: 11–30. https://doi.org/10.1177/108118001129172314.

Flanagan, Tom. 2009. *Harper's Team: Behind the Scenes in the Conservative Rise to Power*. 2nd ed. Montreal: McGill-Queen's University Press.

–. 2014. *Winning Power: Canadian Campaigning in the 21st Century*. Montreal: McGill-Queen's University Press.

Giasson, Thierry. 2006. "La préparation de la réprésentation visuelle des leaders poli-tiques: Le cas du débat télévisé francophone de l'élection parlementaire fédérale canadienne." *Questions de communication* 9: 357–82.

Goldenberg, Eddie. 2006. *The Way It Works: Inside Ottawa*. Toronto: Douglas Gibson.

Howard, Philip N. 2005. "Deep Democracy, Thin Citizenship: The Impact of Digital Media in Political Campaign Strategy." *Annals of the American Academy of Political and Social Science* 597, 1: 153–70. https://doi.org/10.1177/0002716204270139.

Howlett, Michael, and Andrea Migone. 2013. "Searching for Substance: Externalization, Politicization, and the Work of Canadian Policy Consultants 2006–2013." *Central European Journal of Public Policy* 7, 1: 112–33.

Hoy, Claire. 1989. *Margin of Error: Pollsters and the Manipulation of Canadian Politics*. Toronto: Key Porter Books.

Issenberg, Sasha. 2012. *The Victory Lab: The Secret Science of Winning Campaigns*. New York: Crown.

Johnson, Dennis W. 2007. *No Place for Amateurs: How Political Consultants Are Reshaping American Democracy.* 2nd ed. New York: Routledge.

Kinsella, Warren. 2007. *The War Room: Political Strategies for Business, NGOs, and Anyone Who Wants to Win.* Toronto: Dundurn.

Laschinger, John, and Geoffrey Stevens. 1992. *Leaders and Lesser Mortals: Backroom Politics in Canada.* Toronto: Key Porter Books.

Lees-Marshment, Jennifer, and Alex Marland. 2012. "Canadian Political Consultants' Perspectives about Political Marketing." *Canadian Journal of Communication* 37, 2: 333–43. https://doi.org/10.22230/cjc.2012v37n2a2472.

Marland, Alex. 2012. "Amateurs vs. Professionals: The 1993 and 2006 Canadian Federal Elections." In *Political Marketing in Canada,* edited by Alex Marland, Thierry Giasson, and Jennifer Lees-Marshment, 59–75. Vancouver: UBC Press.

–. 2016. *Brand Command: Canadian Politics and Democracy in the Age of Message Control.* Vancouver: UBC Press.

McGinniss, Joe. 1969. *The Selling of the President, 1968.* New York: Trident Press.

Medvic, Stephen. 2003. "Professional Political Consultants: An Operational Definition." *Politics* 23, 2: 119–27. https://doi.org/10.1111/1467-9256.00187.

Saint-Martin, Denis. 2000. *Building the New Managerialist State: Consultants and the Politics of Public Sector Reform in Comparative Perspective.* New York: Oxford University Press.

Speers, Kimberly. 2007. "The Invisible Private Service: Consultants and Public Policy in Canada." In *Policy Analysis in Canada: The State of the Art,* edited by Laurent Dobuzinskis, Michael Howlett, and David Laycock, 399–421. Toronto: University of Toronto Press. https://doi.org/10.3138/9781442685529-018.

10

Hybridity and Mobility: Media Elite Status on Political Twitter Hashtags

Geneviève Chacon, Andrea Lawlor, and Thierry Giasson

Citizens are influenced by opinion leaders. In classical political communications theory, such as Elihu Katz and Paul Lazarsfeld's (1955) seminal work on the two-step flow of communications or David White's (1950) account of journalistic gatekeeping practices, influence was the reserved domain of opinion leaders such as politicians, clergy, union or business leaders, editors, and leading reporters of news organizations. Similarly, in the literature on communications and journalism, political news is traditionally described as the result of negotiations within small groups of elite actors, comprising mainly political journalists, politicians, officials, and political staff (Charron 1994; Ericson, Baranek, and Chan 1989). Political information is then provided to the public by a closed group of professionals who distinguish themselves from others by their access to and influence over political authorities. This group of elite journalists criticize those in positions of power while asserting their own authority as providers of news about political actors, events, and institutions (Nielsen and Kuhn 2014).

However, following major technological changes in the media environment, the construction of political news now tends to integrate new practices and new actors. Therefore, the concept of the media elite, as it has generally been understood in Canada, is in transition. With the rise of online access and digital technologies among a large proportion of the population, more actors now have opportunities to be involved in the negotiation of political news. Gradually, internet users have gotten into the habit of sharing knowledge, verifying information, and disseminating first-hand accounts and visuals of events that they witnessed (Glaser 2010). This public endeavour of ordinary citizens observing, diffusing, and interpreting information is facilitated by the availability of technical devices that enable them to capture and instantly share digital content – communicative functions that, historically, have been the reserved domain of the media industry (Hermida

2012). The popularity of integrated online platforms, such as Twitter, lowers the cost of entry to the public sphere, levelling the playing field for discussions between elite and non-elite actors (Broersma, den Herder, and Schohaus 2013). Furthermore, the immediacy of communications flow on news websites and social media helps to make visible the negotiation process over political information that used to take place behind closed doors (Broersma and Graham 2016; Karlsson 2011). In sum, the networked media environment enables a greater variety of actors from various locations to follow and engage in political events and debates (Revers 2015). Equally, it increases the volume of news available to citizens across platforms.

From the perspective of politicians, social media tools have become an essential part of daily routines, incorporated into public relations activities and broader campaign strategies (Elmer 2013; Gainous and Wagner 2014; Giasson and Small 2017; Serazio 2015). Because of its instantaneous nature, Twitter has also become a key platform to intervene in the political arena in a timely manner. In some circumstances, social media posts allow politicians to grab the attention of professional journalists. In others, posts allow elected officials and political candidates to increase their control of the public agenda or issue framing by communicating directly with voters, bypassing journalists' filters.

The presence of politicians on social media sites, especially Twitter, has made these platforms central to political journalists' work. Twitter was quickly embraced in newsrooms for monitoring information, breaking news, and conveying information in real time (Chacon, Giasson, and Brin 2015; Hermida 2010). It allows journalists to engage with users, to broaden their networks, to brand their personal or organizational images, and to promote their own contents (Molyneux and Holton 2015; Rogstad 2014). The microblogging platform also facilitates access to non-elite information sources by supplying journalists with real-time news content coming from online users across various locations.

Thus, the networked logic of social media sites, which have become a part of both politicians' and political journalists' daily routines, challenges the role of information gatekeeper traditionally assumed by professional journalists. It also weakens the information monopoly of media elites. Traditional media elites might benefit from the authority that they acquired offline, either in Parliament or through mass media institutions. However, their power might also become dependent on their capacity to convert their authority to the networked environment by attracting attention and creating interactivity.

Just as professional journalists have gradually incorporated digital media logics into their routines, amateurs and semi-professional bloggers have increasingly adopted the rules for defining, selecting, and presenting information used by professional journalists (Bruns and Highfield 2012; Chadwick, Dennis, and Smith 2016). The result is a hybrid media system in which the mass media logic and the networked digital media logic interact (Chadwick 2013). In this system, actors from each side of the political communications triangle – politicians, journalists, and citizens – can create, share, or modify political information in order to meet their specific goals. This dynamic has led to a re-envisioning of the newsmaking process as a "political information cycle" (Chadwick 2013). This concept reflects not only the accelerating rhythm of news production but also a more complex structure "composed of multiple, loosely coupled individuals, groups, sites, and temporal instances of interaction involving diverse yet highly interdependent news creators that plug and unplug themselves from the newsmaking process" (Chadwick 2013, 64). This process enhances the capacity of the audience to generate and frame information online and subtly alters the balance of power, giving active citizens a more important role in the production of political news.

Nevertheless, Chadwick's proposal raises some questions. According to Jay Blumler and Stephen Coleman (2013), these transformations in political communications have been empirically studied only in a few specific cases. Also, once we acknowledge the composite and transitional character of the contemporary media system, it is unclear which forms hybridity takes in different settings and why. Empirically, these questions remain largely unanswered, especially in non-US contexts. More specifically, this novel hybrid media system and the resources that it provides to ordinary citizens to generate and broadcast content raise questions regarding elite status and influence in political information and communications processes.

Influence refers to an individual's ability to be "exceptionally persuasive in spreading ideas to others" (Cha et al. 2010, 11) or to convince someone else "to change his or her opinion/attitudes, and/or behaviour" (Dubois and Gaffney 2014, 1261). Influential members of the media drive trends that affect their followers. They shape the message of the day, and their influence can sway public opinion or guide political behaviour. With the advent of online technologies and social media platforms, influence can be redistributed among a broader range of content producers and disseminators, including regular citizens. Although we do not delve into the question of how these individuals garner their followings, we speculate that to some degree they use elements of online networking, such as consistently posting new content, linking to outside news sources, tagging prominent personalities in their commentaries to generate interest, and potentially framing their contents in a way that drives interest (e.g., by using sensational and/or thought-provoking descriptions). Thus, qualitative and quantitative studies to explore these new patterns of power relations at work in the negotiation of political information are necessary. Monitoring how various political communications actors interact in key digital environments, such as Twitter hashtags, which gather messages from various users around specific key-words and topics, appears to be a relevant first step in the investigation.

Measuring influence in the political Twittersphere has become a central question of empirical work (Albaugh and Waddell 2014; Cha et al. 2010; Chu and Fletcher 2014; Dang-Xuan et al. 2013; Dubois and Gaffney 2014). Different metrics have been used to highlight the potential influence of elite and non-elite microblogging users. Influence implies the capacity of a message producer or sender to achieve certain effects on the audience. For example, Quinn Albaugh and Christopher Waddell (2014) measured par-ticipation in discussions on Canadian politics by identifying and classifying the most prolific users. However, as they acknowledge, this kind of measure does not tell us much about the degree of attention received by these top producers. According to Linh Dang-Xuan and his collaborators (2013, 797–98), attention effects can be persuasive in nature (change or reinforce prior attitudes and opinions), affect knowledge (agenda-setting or cultivation ef-fects), and modify behaviour (voting, information consumption). In other words, different metrics of influence measure different types of effects.

The literature seems to agree on three types of measures of influence on Twitter. The first refers to in-degree influence or followership influence and is related to an individual user's (or node's) number of followers. It is a strong metric to evaluate a node's popularity on the network, but it has not always been associated with a high degree of persuasion, knowledge, or effect on behaviour in past research (see, e.g., Cha et al. 2010). The second measure deals with content dissemination influence, or retweet influence, and meas-ures a Twitter user's ability to generate content that has a strong "pass-along value" (Dang-Xuan et al. 2013, 799) and is therefore shared through a high number of retweets. The third metric refers to a user's capacity to influence the conversational agenda on Twitter through the number of personal men-tions in tweets generated by other users (Chu and Fletcher 2014). Some scholars consider the last two measures indicators of expertise/elite status within the network (Dubois and Gaffney 2014, 1263). Finally, research has pointed out the role of Twitter hashtags as devices that contribute to the creation of online discussions on given topics among users who do not necessarily follow one another on the network (Albaugh and Waddell 2014; Bruns and Burgess 2012; Small 2011). In tracking an online political community for a period of time, we can assess, using these metrics, who has digital influence in leading and disseminating political information and who makes the most robust contributions to the broader political debate. We can do exactly this through an analysis of the #cdnpoli and #elxn42 hashtags.

The hashtag #cdnpoli is the most frequently used for Canadian political affairs, whereas #elxn42 was used to mark commentary related to Canada's forty-second general election. These hashtags aggregate political debates from all quarters, including traditional elites (e.g., politicians, journalists, public figures, entertainers), societal elites (e.g., advocacy group leaders), as well as citizens. As such, they represent an ongoing discussion (a) between elites and (b) between elites and citizens. In many ways, Twitter breaks down the barriers that previously guarded elite communications and widely exposes their expressed agendas, even letting non-elites participate in political discussions. Compared with other types of political communications, such as press releases or speeches, the content of tweets is generally less constrained or carefully considered. The following is a case study of what role journalists, pundits, politicians, and citizens played in the diffusion of Canadian political news on these two hashtags in the months preceding and following the federal election of October 19, 2015.

Case Study

Method

Twitter data were collected using ASPIRA, a proprietary database tool developed at Université Laval that queries Twitter for all historical tweets either by user name or by hashtag. Using "#cdnpoli" and "#elxn42" as our key search terms, we obtained all tweets posted from August 1 to December 31, 2015. This time period captures both the official campaign period (August 4–October 19) and the first months of the governing period (October 20–December 31) of the newly elected Trudeau Liberals. Note that this period also captures a segment when the House of Commons was in session (fifty business days) and not in session (fifty-four business days, excluding statutory holidays, summer holidays, and weekends). It also captures "non-routine" business, including campaign dynamics, formation of the government (October 20–November 3), and the holiday season, when politicians are not necessarily communicating on government business but still conveying season's greetings to citizens. Our query of #cdnpoli resulted in a total of 700,803 tweets from 41,341 users, whereas #elxn42 resulted in 480,485 tweets from 57,563 users, for a total of 1,180,960 tweets over 152 calendar days.[1] Although these hashtags attract both English-language and French-language content, we limited our analysis to English tweets.

Our research looked at a combination of metrics of influence to investigate how traditional media and political elites interacted with other users on Twitter during and after the 2015 election campaign. Thus, we had three goals.

1. We wanted to track the overall trends that comprise #cdnpoli and #elxn42 during this time period among all individuals (elites or otherwise) who used these hashtags as parts of their communications.
2. We wanted to determine the composition of political/media elites in the social media debate and sketch the broad landscape of Canadian political discussion on Twitter.
3. We wanted to identify the top communicating elites and top communications (tweets) in terms of Twitter activity and gauge their influence by measuring how often their messages were recirculated (retweeted).

Findings

Although Twitter activity does not necessarily need to be driven by current events, it is likely that topical coverage will feature prominently in the tweets of political elites and non-elites alike. The time period under investigation contained a number of events that featured prominently in both Canadian and international news – and therefore were also covered on social media. Internationally, the Syrian military and refugee crisis continued to dominate news broadcasts, with a specific focus on the humanitarian aspect of the crisis, which included the picture of young drowning victim Alan Kurdi being carried ashore by a law enforcement official on September 4. Domestically, events such as the trial of Senator Mike Duffy focusing on his expenses, the negotiation of the Trans-Pacific Partnership, and the formation of the new Liberal government with a cabinet comprising 50 percent women were among the many issues that episodically governed the news and captured public interest.

FIGURE 10.1

Overall number of tweets on #cdnpoli and #elxn42, last five months of 2015

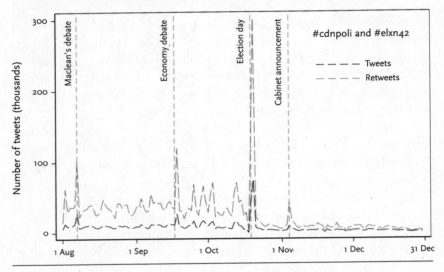

Looking at the overall landscape of activity on the two hashtags in question, Figure 10.1 illustrates the volume of tweets and retweets using #cdnpoli and #elxn42 (aggregated) from August 1 to December 31, 2015. A few trends are immediately noticeable. First, individuals use Twitter to share or redistribute information (i.e., retweet) more than they use it to produce original content (i.e., tweet). In other words, there is less of what Manuel Castells (2007) refers to as "mass self-communication" than there is redistribution of information. Second, activity on these hashtags is variable throughout the period under investigation. The largest volume of coverage is on election day and the days immediately preceding and following it. There are similar but not nearly as pronounced peaks around the announcement of the campaign in early August and around September 18, which corresponded with the federal leaders' debate on the economy (and likely represented the "real" start to the campaign – a month from election day). Although there is also a small peak in coverage in early November, when the new cabinet was announced and sworn in at Rideau Hall, the post-campaign level of coverage remains much lower than that of the campaign period (about one-fifth the rate of the campaign period coverage). In part, this decline in activity stems from retirement of the #elxn42 hashtag in the weeks following the election, but it also signals a return to the norm once the campaign period is over and governance returns to its regular schedule.

Yet broad trends in coverage do not reveal anything about the composition or activity of media elites on social media. Table 10.1 illustrates the top ten Twitter users on the specified hashtags, their profiles, and the number of tweets and retweets that they posted during the five months under investigation. The most obvious and perhaps surprising trend is that, of the top ten most frequent users of the #cdnpoli and #elxn42 hashtags, none is a mainstream journalist or news source, a politician, or a group that we might typically associate with the traditional "media elite." Indeed, most individuals or groups are private citizens or undisclosed bodies. Only @CanadaNewsHunt, a news aggregator that typically combines stories manually retrieved by individuals with the results of automated searches by "bots," has "semi-formal" media status. Two others have outwardly partisan motivations. Both @MapleLeaks and @BeenHarperized are self-proclaimed anti–Stephen Harper sources (both of which fell dormant after the Liberal victory).

TABLE 10.1

Most frequent Twitter users on #cdnpoli and #elxn42, last five months of 2015

Screen name	Profile	Tweets (N)	Retweets (N)
@MapleLeaks	Undisclosed/anti-Harper news feed	16,755	2,570
@Bergg69	Private citizen (Toronto)	15,159	58,103*
@DavidMorrison17	Private citizen (Whitby, ON)	11,720	6,086
@deepgreendesign	Private citizen (Toronto)	10,411	13,807
@hashtag_cdnpoli	Undisclosed	9,227	1,121
@WorldwideHerald	Undisclosed	6,376	1,904
@BeenHarperized	Anti-Harper news feed (Washington, DC)	6,352	2,259
@CanadaNewsHunt	News aggregator	6,226	3,360
@MuskokaMoneybag	Private citizen (Ottawa)	6,032	29,903*
@billhillier	Private citizen (location not specified)	5,693	16,637

NOTE: * Among the top fifteen retweeted users during this time period on #cdnpoli and #elxn42.

Figure 10.2

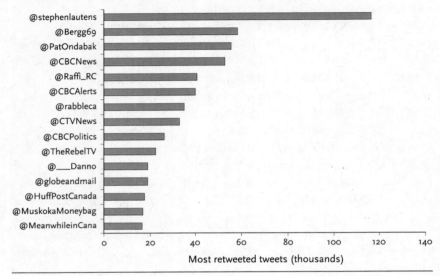

Most retweeted on #cdnpoli and #elxn42, last five months of 2015

At the top ten most common Twitter users on these hashtags are not part of the mainstream media elite is telling. It suggests that, though mainstream media might seek to participate in the social media conversation about Canadian politics, by no means do they intend – or have the required combination of drive, resources, and savvy – to lead it. Furthermore, the absence of politicians, pundits, and members of political industries (e.g., polling, advertising firms) suggests that other traditional political elites are not the chief sources of political content.

Nevertheless, a high volume of tweets is not tantamount to being a part of the media elite. Users can put messages out into the Twittersphere but receive no attention in return. Of the top fifteen retweeted users who employed the #cdnpoli and #elxn42 hashtags during the final five months of 2015, suggesting the greatest amount of message proliferation, we see far more variety in the composition of Twitter users among average citizens and the mainstream press (see Figure 10.2). Of the top fifteen retweeted users, six are mainstream online or print news sources (e.g., the CBC, *Globe and Mail*, *Huffington Post*), two are niche online news sources (i.e., rabble.ca and *The Rebel*), and seven are ordinary citizens or "non-elites" (e.g., Meanwhile in Canada).

Although mainstream news sources can play a far larger role in the proliferation of information than in the generation of content on social media, it is interesting to note that they fail to break into the top three retweeted users on #cdnpoli and #elxn42. The most retweeted mainstream source (@CBCNews) ranks fourth on the list with 52,829 retweets, less than half the number of retweets for the top retweeted user (@stephenlautens), suggesting that commentary might be of greater interest on social media than the day-to-day transmission of news.

Interestingly, only two Twitter users on the list of most frequent tweeters appear to be equally as active in terms of their volume of retweets. Users who go by the handles @Bergg69 and @MuskokaMoneybag appear to have both volume of activity ($n = 15,159$ and $n = 6,032$, respectively) and community support (retweets: $n = 58,103$ and $n = 29,903$, respectively). It could be argued that these two users elevated their role of "non-elite" to part of the social media elite because of the volume of their activity and its proliferation to the wider community, thereby illustrating the potential of digital media to expand the number and type of media elites to whom the public is exposed. These cases are rare but valuable; they suggest a mobility among the digital elite previously unattainable in the mainstream media or limited to the infrequent use of more constraining methods of participating in the media such as letters to the editor, calling in to talk radio shows, or writing guest pieces for newspapers and magazines.

Looking at the messages that had the most impact on the #cdnpoli and #elxn42 hashtags also provides some insight into which individuals and/or organizations have the most clout online. Table 10.2 illustrates the most retweeted or "high-impact" individual tweets as well as the user who authored the particular tweet and the number of retweets that it received. In part, the number of tweets and retweets might be considered comparatively small in a country such as Canada with only 36 million citizens. Coverage of Canadian politics tends to be localized to Canada, and therefore we might not expect a global proliferation of these hashtags. Perhaps it is only fitting that Justin Trudeau's tweet, at the time of his party's victory in the forty-second general election, can be considered the tweet with the highest impact at over 5,000 retweets. This post published during election night includes two pictures of Trudeau and his wife, Sophie Grégoire Trudeau, one greeting their supporters and the other sitting among family members. This timely glimpse of their personal lives shows how political elites create parasocial or unidirectional relationships between themselves and the public, generating engagement by opening up the more personal aspects of their lives in a way similar to that of a celebrity (Colliander and Dahlén 2011). A distant second and third are tweets from mainstream media sources, Global News and CBC, referencing matters related to the election and its outcome. Farther down the list, the most popular tweets are a mix of mainstream news sources, such as CTV News and CP24, and political entertainment (*This Hour Has 22 Minutes*), likely maintained by teams rather than individuals, and some more colourful tweets by private citizens.

Once again a traditional understanding of media elites fails to fully explain the trends evident in Table 10.2. Certainly, some members of the "old" elite, including politicians and mainstream media sources, appear to have transitioned well to digital social media platforms such as Twitter. That PM-designate Trudeau topped the list of most retweeted messages during this time suggests that Twitter users still have a strong appetite for communications by traditional elites. Similarly, the rather formulaic or standard content of news tweets from mainstream media sources, such as @globalnews (disseminating a link to a full story) and @CTVNews (announcing its election results call), suggests an adherence to the status quo in terms of the content of news reporting if not the medium. Nonetheless, such tweets are intermingled with tweets by non-elites that managed to "crack the ceiling" of high-impact messages, either because of the robustness of their personal social media networks or because of the sensationalist or catchy nature of their communications.

We can observe the number of followers that a user has on Twitter as one final measure to help triangulate who constitutes the social media elite. Figure 10.3 depicts the Twitter users with the largest number of followers who tweeted using the hashtags #cdnpoli and #elxn42 from August to December of 2015 (bars), overlaid with the number of times that they tweeted during the period under review (line). Users who fell into this category were omitted if they did not tweet using the #cdnpoli or #elxn42 hashtag more than five times. Although five tweets might appear to be a seemingly arbitrary number, it signifies that the users tweeted (on average) once a month during the time period studied. In sum, this figure discerns whose messages will inevitably have high impacts on users because their messages will pop up in their followers' news feed, coupled with how often they exercised this privilege of being high impact on the #cdnpoli and #elxn42 hashtags. The five most-followed individuals/organizations on Twitter fall into

Table 10.2

Most retweeted/high-impact tweets, last five months of 2015

Tweet	User name	Retweets
Ready. #elxn42	@JustinTrudeau	5,273
BC woman's Facebook letter to Stephen Harper goes viral.	@globalnews	2,052
CBC News projects a #Liberal government. #elxn42	@CBCAlerts	2,043
My hope that Canada might one day become a fully weaponized, drunk on oil, earth-fucking-anger-dildo are officially over. #Elxn42	@VanCityReynolds	1,961
BREAKING: #CTVElection desk projects a Liberal win in #Elxn42	@CTVNews	1,912
New polls show 100% of Canadians will have to live with the choice made by the ones who actually get out and vote. #elxn42	@22_Minutes	1,768
#BREAKING: CP24 declares a Liberal majority government in #elxn42 #cdnpoli	@CP24	1,704
Watch Flaherty's reaction when #Harper says Nigel Wright didn't tell Ray Novak about #Duffy bribe!	@Tony_Tracy	1,500
Today Canada decides who it wants to be Prime Minister: Young Mandy Patinkin or Old Mandy Patinkin. #22votes #Elxn42	@TheAdamChristie	1,429
When Harper wakes up tomorrow, Nenshi will be his mayor, Notley will be his Premier, and Trudeau will be his Prime Minister. #elxn42 #yyc	@west_ender	1,383

the category of established elites – though not necessarily mainstream media. The lead organization is @CBCNews with 1.1 million followers. CBC is followed by @rickmercer (a political entertainer, also with 1.1 million followers), @JustinTrudeau (the incoming prime minister in 2015), @CP24 (mainstream news media), @NatureNews (specialized but still mainstream media), and a mix of domestic and international news sources.

Although the list of most-followed users is largely dominated by mainstream news sources – some of which, such as @CBCNews, @globeandmail,

Figure 10.3

Users on #cdnpoli and #elxn42 with most followers, last five months of 2015

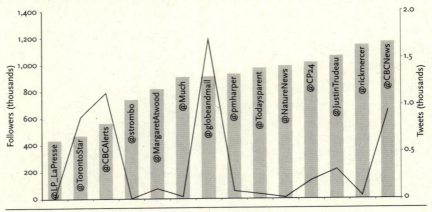

NOTE: The black line represents the number of tweets per user from August 1 to December 31, 2015.

@CBCAlerts, and @TorontoStar tweeted with great frequency – a number of political and entertainment elites, such as @strombo (television personality George Stroumboulopoulos) and @MargaretAtwood (author and activist), also make the list. This cross-population of entertainers on an otherwise political list is telling; it suggests that individuals who have gained notoriety in other aspects of public life can leverage their authority and celebrity to effectively weigh in on political debates. Similarly, the presence of non-political news sources, such as *Today's Parent,* suggests that individuals or groups with a particular constituency (such as middle-class parents) can forward their agenda using social media. In this case, the publication authored contributions (forty-nine tweets during the election campaign) geared to its over 900,000 followers about the family-friendliness of each party's policies. Thus, we can see that, even when the most-followed users are not necessarily the most prolific, in terms of number of tweets, their impacts can be considerable nonetheless, driven as much by personality, clout, or fame as by actual online activity.

An inductive look into the Twitterverse shows a mix of mainstream media elites and non-mainstream media sources as well as private citizens. But the emphasis on mainstream media across all metrics evaluating social media impacts suggests that we should more deeply investigate how the traditional

TABLE 10.3

Mainstream media Twitter activity, last five months of 2015

	Profile	Tweets (N)	Retweets (N)	Ratio
Globe and Mail	@globeandmail	1,697	32,396	1:19
	@globepolitics	1,803	11,396	1:6
	@garymasonglobe	10	76	1:7
National Post	@nationalpost	51	813	1:15
	@acoyne	22	551	1:25
Toronto Star	@TorontoStar	870	20,065	1:23
	@SusanDelacourt	800	22,433	1:28
	@ChantalHbert	1	151	1:15
Ottawa Citizen	@ottawacitizen	1,537	10,169	1:6
	@kady	175	3,092	1:17
Canadian Press	@CdnPress	292	2,259	1:7
	@jenditchburn	188	6,152	1:32
	@ellekane	52	199	1:3
Maclean's	@MacleansMag	1,450	17,302	1:12
	@InklessPW	10	199	
	@MartinPatriquin	75	593	1:8
Global News	@globalnews	502	17,645	1:35
CTV News	@CTVNews	1,471	33,029	1:22
CBC News	@CBCNews	944	52,829	1:55
	@rosiebarton	492	9,890	1:20

media elite engages on Twitter. Furthermore, given the exposure of Canadians to social media, what is said about traditional political elites on this platform? Table 10.3 looks at nine of the top-circulating mainstream Canadian print, broadcast, and wire news sources – *Globe and Mail, National Post, Toronto Star, Ottawa Citizen*, Canadian Press, *Maclean's*, Global News, CTV News, and CBC News – and considers how often they, and their most active journalists, engage on social media using the #cdnpoli and #elxn42 hashtags.

The top-tweeting English-language mainstream news sources from August to December of 2015 were the *Globe and Mail* (1,697 tweets from its core,

@globeandmail, and 1,803 tweets from @globepolitics), CTV News (1,471 tweets), the *Ottawa Citizen* (1,415 tweets), and *Maclean's* (1,450 tweets). Others, such as CBC News, Global News, and the *Toronto Star* tweeted roughly half as much. The *National Post* appears to be the least active on the studied hashtags during this time with only fifty-one tweets from its @nationalpost handle. Some prominent journalists associated with particular news outlets are also included in the table, but only a handful – Susan Delacourt of the *Toronto Star*, Kady O'Malley of the *Ottawa Citizen*, Jennifer Ditchburn of the Canadian Press, and Rosemary Barton of CBC News – actively used the #cdnpoli and #elxn42 hashtags.

To further establish the impact of the social media activities of mainstream media, we report the ratio of tweets to retweets, which functions as a metric of message proliferation. The higher the ratio, the more impact any given tweet by the author would have had on the Twitter audience. The highest tweet to retweet ratios belong to @CBCNews, @globalnews, @jenditchburn, and @SusanDelacourt, suggesting that these organizations and journalists received the most exposure on a tweet-by-tweet basis. In the aggregate, these findings are important if we consider that the media sources themselves – not their journalists – are leading the mainstream media's political presence on the #cdnpoli and #elxn42 hashtags. This can be explained in part by the fact that institutional accounts tend to be operated by a team of hired professional social media managers exclusively dedicated to managing the operation's online presence (and therefore more likely to systematically include hashtags to increase message views), whereas journalists are more likely to tweet on an ad hoc basis while performing their primary duty, namely reporting (though these things are not mutually exclusive).

The combination of these metrics – number of tweets, retweets, and followers and ratio of tweets to retweets – indicates a way to evaluate a large volume of social media data and identify meaningful trends in an otherwise noisy set of data. The utility of taking this approach in evaluating elites is that it considers who, among the traditional media influencers, has successfully transitioned to manage their presence across multiple platforms. Equally, by using this type of inductive approach to spot trends in a data set, which covers the population of political commentary, for a set of prominent (though ultimately subject-specific) hashtags such as #cdnpoli and #elxn42, we can identify and examine the behaviour of individuals or groups who would typically have been excluded from previous conversations about the media elite. As such, the conversation about media opinion leaders and how previously "ordinary" citizens can access this level of prestige has been fundamentally changed by the rise of social media.

Political Elites in Canada in the Digital Age

This chapter has investigated how, in a hybrid media environment, influence and elite status play out among journalists, pundits, politicians, and citizens on Twitter. Through a quantitative analysis of the #cdnpoli and #elxn42 Twitter hashtags, we looked at the patterns of conversation between old and new media elites in Canada. A few general conclusions can be drawn from the data that we collected and analyzed. First, the most frequent users of these hashtags were not mainstream media journalists or politicians but mostly private citizens, aggregators, or undisclosed bodies. Second, we observed diversity among the users who received the highest number of retweets, including ordinary citizens, niche media, and mainstream media. Third, looking at the number of followers for each user and the messages with the greatest impacts, we noticed that mainstream media elites, as well as top politicians (the former and current prime ministers), were still central actors in the Canadian political Twittersphere. Nevertheless, when considering the most-retweeted messages, a strong metric of content influence on Twitter, original posts by ordinary citizens were noted to have substantial traction. Fourth, with few exceptions, mainstream media institutional accounts were far more active on the two studied hashtags than the accounts led by their star journalists. We also observed a large discrepancy among mainstream media organizations' levels of engagement on the hashtags, but our analysis did not allow us to understand this diversity of uses. However, these differences among organizations indicate that norms and standards of production on Twitter are far from homogeneous across the board.

Our study focused on political discussion regarding a single country and used data from two English-language hashtags on a specific platform, Twitter, in a certain time period. Thus, it is not possible to know if the results are generalizable to other countries, hashtags (e.g., #polcan), or platforms. Also, it is important to keep in mind that less than 20 percent of Canadians have accounts on Twitter according to a 2014 survey on digital citizenship (Small et al. 2014), and many of them might have had limited exposure to the two hashtags studied here. In addition, our study did not explore how social media followings develop, nor did it allow us to assess the impacts of online political discussions on the public agenda, the political agenda, or the overall election campaign. We acknowledge that these are important questions, each of which would require different sets of methodological tools and data, and should be addressed in further research. However, taking into account the large number of posts included in our analysis and the number of users who were active on the hashtags during the months preceding and following the federal election, we believe that our study represents an important step in assessing how elite status and influence express themselves among traditional actors (mainstream media, politicians, parties) and non-traditional actors (citizens, grassroots organizations, niche media) in Canadian political conversations on social networking sites.

Finally, by combining different metrics of influence, our results suggest that, if traditional elites – mainstream media and politicians – appear to be influential actors in the social media conversation on Canadian politics, some private citizens also seized opportunities to be heard. From a normative point of view, these findings are encouraging, especially in the light of recent research showing that political engagement on social media might foster other forms of political engagement (Vaccari and Valeriani 2016). In fact, not only did citizens actively participate in the political conversation on Twitter, but also some of them garnered substantial degrees of attention in the Twittersphere. In contrast, traditional elites, including mainstream media organizations, benefited from their authority acquired offline. Despite this, other types of users managed to convey information efficiently on the network. These cases demonstrate interesting potential for mobility among the contemporary digital media elite. They also indicate a disruption of the traditional one-sided information flow in which mainstream media act as gatekeepers. Instead, we observed two-way mediatization (Casero-Ripollés, Feenstra, and Tormey 2016) or even a multidirectional process in which information circulates along the different axes of the political communications triangle. Obviously, mainstream media continue to act as important intermediaries for accessing political knowledge. However, political parties and their leaders also communicate their messages across the network directly to citizens, bypassing the traditional media elites' filter and interpretation. Thus, we believe that these findings can transform how we conceptualize political mediatization, gradually moving away from a mainstream media-centric model.

NOTE

1 Because of a change in the Twitter application program interface (API) that took place just before the forty-second Canadian general election, ASPIRA was unable to harvest a full set of tweets between October 14 and 19. Therefore, our results for this time period should not be considered a complete analysis of the political debate that ensued using the #cdnpoli and #elxn42 hashtags. The database does not include tweets deleted by the user. Note that users might have tweeted using both #cdnpoli and #elxn42 during the same time frame – even within the same tweet – resulting in a total of 75,339 users, also explaining why the total number of tweets is less than the sum of the individual tweets per hashtag.

REFERENCES

Albaugh, Quinn, and Christopher Waddell. 2014. "Social Media and Political Inequality." In *Canadian Democracy from the Ground Up: Perceptions and Performance,* edited by Elisabeth Gidengil and Heather Bastedo, 102–19. Vancouver: UBC Press.

Blumler, Jay G., and Stephen Coleman. 2013. "Paradigms of Civic Communication: Buddy, What's My Paradigm?" *International Journal of Communication* 7: 173–87.

Broersma, Marcel, Bas den Herder, and Birte Schohaus. 2013. "A Question of Power: The Changing Dynamics between Journalists and Sources." *Journalism Practice* 7, 4: 388–95. https://doi.org/10.1080/17512786.2013.802474.

Broersma, Marcel, and Todd Graham. 2016. "Tipping the Balance of Power: Social Media and the Transformation of Political Journalism." In *The Routledge Companion to Social Media and Politics,* edited by Axel Bruns, Gunn Enli, Eli Skogerbo, Anders Olof Larsson, and Christian Christensen, 89–103. New York: Routledge.

Bruns, Axel, and Jean Burgess. 2012. "Researching News Discussion on Twitter: New Methodologies." *Journalism Studies* 13, 5–6: 801–14. https://doi.org/10.1080/14616 70X.2012.664428.

Bruns, Axel, and Tim Highfield. 2012. "Blogs, Twitter, and Breaking News: The Production of Citizen Journalism." In *Producing Theory in a Digital World: The Intersection of Audiences and Production in Contemporary Theory,* edited by Rebecca Ann Lind, 15–32. New York: Peter Lang.

Casero-Ripollés, Andreu, Ramon A. Feenstra, and Simon Tormey. 2016. "Old and New Media Logics in an Electoral Campaign: The Case of Podemos and the Two-Way Street Mediatization of Politics." *International Journal of Press/Politics* 21, 3: 378–97. https://doi.org/10.1177/1940161216645340.

Castells, Manuel. 2007. "Communication, Power, and Counter-Power in the Network Society." *International Journal of Communication* 1, 1: 238–66.

Cha, Meeyoung, et al. 2010. "Measuring User Influence in Twitter: The Million Follower Fallacy." *Proceedings of the Fourth International AAAI Conference on Weblogs and Social Media* 10: 10–17. Washington, DC, May 23–26.

Chacon, Geneviève, Thierry Giasson, and Colette Brin. 2015. "Le journalisme politique en 140 caractères: Le cas du Québec." *Sur le journalisme, About Journalism, Sobre jornalismo* 4, 1: 34–49.

Chadwick, Andrew. 2013. *The Hybrid Media System: Politics and Power.* New York: Oxford University Press. https://doi.org/10.1093/acprof:oso/9780199759477.001.0001.

Chadwick, Andrew, James Dennis, and Amy P. Smith. 2016. "Politics in the Age of Hybrid Media: Power, Systems, and Media Logics." In *The Routledge Companion to Social Media and Politics,* edited by Axel Bruns et al., 7–22. New York: Routledge.

Charron, Jean. 1994. *La production de l'actualité: Une analyse stratégique des relations entre la presse parlementaire et les autorités politiques.* Montréal: Boréal.

Chu, Wayne, and Fred Fletcher. 2014. "Social Media and Agenda Setting." In *Canadian Democracy from the Ground Up: Perceptions and Performance,* edited by Elisabeth Gidengil and Heather Bastedo, 148–70. Vancouver: UBC Press.

Colliander, Jonas, and Micael Dahlén. 2011. "Following the Fashionable Friend: The Power of Social Media." *Journal of Advertising Research* 51, 1: 313–20. https://doi.org/10.2501/JAR-51-1-313-320.

Dang-Xuan, Linh, Stefan Stieglitz, Jennifer Wladarsch, and Christoph Neuberger. 2013. "An Investigation of Influentials and the Role of Sentiment in Political Communication on Twitter during Election Periods." *Information Communication and Society* 16, 5: 795–825. https://doi.org/10.1080/1369118X.2013.783608.

Dubois, Elizabeth, and Devin Gaffney. 2014. "The Multiple Facets of Influence: Identifying Influentials and Opinion Leaders on Twitter." *American Behavioral Scientist* 58, 10: 1260–77. https://doi.org/10.1177/0002764214527088.

Elmer, Greg. 2013. "Live Research: Twittering an Election Debate." *New Media and Society* 15, 1: 18–30. https://doi.org/10.1177/1461444812457328.

Ericson, Richard V., Patricia M. Baranek, and Janet B.L. Chan. 1989. *Negotiating Control: A Study of News Sources.* Toronto: University of Toronto Press.

Gainous, Jason, and Kevin M. Wagner. 2014. *Tweeting to Power: The Social Media Revolution in American Politics.* New York: Oxford University Press.

Giasson, Thierry, and Tamara A. Small. 2017. "Online All the Time: The Strategic Objectives of Canadian Opposition Parties." In *Permanent Campaigning in Canada,* edited by Alex Marland, Thierry Giasson, and Anna Lennox Esselment, 109–26. Vancouver: UBC Press.

Glaser, Mark. 2010. "Citizen Journalism: Widening World Views, Extending Democracy." In *The Routledge Companion to News and Journalism,* edited by Stuart Allan, 578–90. New York: Routledge.

Hermida, Alfred. 2010. "Twittering the News." *Journalism Practice* 4, 3: 297–308. https://doi.org/10.1080/17512781003640703.

–. 2012. "Tweets and Truth: Journalism as a Discipline of Collaborative Verification." *Journalism Practice* 6, 5–6: 659–68. https://doi.org/10.1080/17512786.2012.667269.

Karlsson, Michael. 2011. "The Immediacy of Online News, the Visibility of Journalistic Processes, and a Restructuring of Journalistic Authority." *Journalism* 12, 3: 279–95. https://doi.org/10.1177/1464884910388223.

Katz, Elihu, and Paul F. Lazarsfeld. 1955. *Personal Influence: The Part Played by People in the Flow of Mass Communications.* Piscataway, NJ: Transaction Publishers.

Molyneux, Logan, and Avery Holton. 2015. "Branding (Health) Journalism: Perceptions, Practices, and Emerging Norms." *Digital Journalism* 3, 2: 225–42. https://doi.org/10.1080/21670811.2014.906927.

Nielsen, Rasmus Kleis, and Raymond Kuhn. 2014. "Political Journalism in Western Europe: Change and Continuity." In *Political Journalism in Transition: Western Europe in a Comparative Perspective,* edited by Raymond Kuhn and Rasmus Kleis Nielsen, 1–23. London: I.B. Tauris.

Revers, Matthias. 2015. "The Augmented Newsbeat: Spatial Structuring in a Twitterized News Ecosystem." *Media, Culture, and Society* 37, 1: 3–18. https://doi.org/10.1177/0163443714549085.

Rogstad, Ingrid Dahlen. 2014. "Political News Journalists in Social Media." *Journalism Practice* 8, 6: 688–703. https://doi.org/10.1080/17512786.2013.865965.

Serazio, Michael. 2015. "Managing the Digital News Cyclone: Power, Participation, and Political Production Strategies." *International Journal of Communication* 9: 1907–25.

Small, Tamara A. 2011. "What the Hashtag? A Content Analysis of Canadian Politics on Twitter." *Information Communication and Society* 14, 6: 872–95. https://doi.org/10.1080/1369118X.2011.554572.

Small, Tamara A., Harold Jansen, Frédérick Bastien, Thierry Giasson, and Royce Koop. 2014. "Online Political Activity in Canada: The Hype and the Facts." *Canadian Parliamentary Review* 37, 4: 9–16.

Vaccari, Christian, and Augusto Valeriani. 2016. "Party Campaigners or Citizen Campaigners? How Social Media Deepen and Broaden Party-Related Engagement." *International Journal of Press/Politics* 21, 3: 294–312. https://doi.org/10.1177/1940161216642152.

White, David M. 1950. "The 'Gate Keeper': A Case Study in the Selection of News." *Journalism Quarterly* 27: 383–91.

11
Scandals and Screenshots: Social Media Elites in Canadian Politics

Fenwick McKelvey, Marianne Côté, and Vincent Raynauld

As the next federal election looms, it is helpful to draw insights from some of the more unconventional political actors who have been influential in past contests. In 2015, Prime Minister Stephen Harper faced a difficult campaign for re-election. His opposition included traditional political and media elites but also what this chapter calls social media elites. In the days leading up to the dropping of the writ, the online hacker collective Anonymous vowed to scandalize the Harper government. As members of Anonymous mobilized their campaign, known as #OpAnonDown, an established political blogger and Indigenous critic, Robert Jago, also decided to target the Conservative Party of Canada for its lack of action on electoral reform. In other years, Jago and members of Anonymous would have been seen as largely peripheral players in the formal political arena, but in 2015 their distinct set of skills coupled with the influence of social media on the Canadian political information cycle positioned them as elite digital influencers. This chapter takes an interest in these types of new political elites, likely to become increasingly prominent in years to come as social media continue to develop and gain more traction among all segments of Canadian society.

We consider social media elites to be non-professional expert users of digital platforms as well as partisans. They are the people who fill our newsfeeds with expertly crafted stories, photos, and commentaries. We qualify them as "non-professional" social media elites to distinguish them from online traditional elites who have professional status or affiliation. Whereas online elites include journalists, politicians, publicists, and corporate leaders, social media elites remain mostly outside professional politics and are active through less formal – and sometimes illegal – participants in political affairs. They can be citizen journalists, bloggers, ideologues, microcelebrities, pranksters, or hackers. We also stress that social media elites are political without necessarily being members of political parties. As partisans, social media elites might be used by parties, or their activities might help them, but they are often kept at a distance from central decision making (for a more detailed discussion, see Elmer, Langlois, and McKelvey 2012, 9–12).

Social media elites are attractive to parties because of their technological acumen and, by extension, their influence online. When 61 percent of Canadians check Facebook daily, and 51 percent of Canadians get their news online first, that influence is tangible (Blevis and Coletto 2017). Whereas journalists are experts in writing articles for newspapers, social media elites excel at creating content to circulate through digital platforms and ensuring that content spreads to as wide an audience as possible (Jenkins, Ford, and Green 2013). They are experts at crafting tactical messages with the appropriate styles and genres for social media platforms (Kreiss, McGregor, and Lawrence 2017). As social media become increasingly heterogeneous, expertise differs greatly by platform (van Dijck 2013). For example, social media elites might be experts in using Twitter to amplify messages or YouTube to make videos go viral. More often they are well versed in multiple platforms. Social media elites are also skilled at leveraging content dispersion and social interaction capabilities of digital platforms. To some, their expertise makes them media manipulators, a new kind of rogue spin doctor. This expertise is difficult to come by as these media channels evolve constantly, in terms of both their structural and functional properties and their audience pool. A short history of social media in politics helps to situate and understand the changing influence of their elite users.

The term "social media" refers to "Internet-based channels that allow users to opportunistically interact and selectively self-present, either in real-time or asynchronously, with both broad and narrow audiences who derive value from user-generated content and the perception of interaction with others" (Carr and Hayes 2015, 51). The term was developed as an attempt to categorize the popularity of blogging in the early 2000s. Starting in 1998, blogs have served as important outlets for political reporting, commentary, and public debate internationally, such as when the news blog Drudge Report published the first details of the Monica Lewinsky scandal in the United States. In Canada, bloggers used their online publishing expertise to bypass mainstream media and engage in journalism independently, a practice commonly known as citizen journalism. Their audiences tended to be like-minded partisans. By 2006, the Canadian blogosphere had self-organized into three blogrolls for Conservatives, Liberals, and New Democrats. These blogrolls had clear opinion leaders and were forums for sharing political information, often related to scandals and infighting, as well as deliberation, debate, and fundraising (Hindman 2009; Koop and Jansen 2009). That year marked the point that bloggers were sufficiently prominent that they joined the ranks of political elites. Political parties began treating bloggers as allies in their campaigns, but relations between the two actors varied. The federal Conservative Party turned to bloggers to test and seed messages, as they seemingly could say publicly what the campaign could not, and used them as a new venue for testing opposition research (Flanagan 2007, 232). Conversely, the NDP avoided enlisting or mentioning its own partisan bloggers even though their blogs actively covered the campaign. Brian Topp, then the national campaign director, claimed that there was little value in researching these online actors (McLean 2012, 119–22). Although long-form blogging has since been eclipsed by other social media formats, the political blogger remains a paradigmatic social media elite: a mixture of citizen journalist, activist, and unofficial digital strategist working for the benefit of the party.

Social media elites adapted and expanded with the arrival of Facebook in 2004, YouTube in 2005, Twitter in 2006, Instagram in 2010, and Snapchat in 2012. Each new platform arrived amid speculation (and often hype) that it would disrupt politics (Muñoz and Towner 2017; Taras and Waddell 2012, 104). Although they have not been as disruptive as foretold by their initial coverage, 46 percent of Canadians use Facebook to get their news, 17 percent use YouTube, and 12 percent turn to Twitter (Brin 2016). Whereas blogging removed gatekeepers in political reporting, these latter social media introduced new communicative affordances to be perfected by elites (Nagy and Neff 2015). Facebook, for example, simplified political organization, allowing political movements with ad hoc leadership structures and focused interests to spring up online (Glenn 2014; Haggart 2013; Karpf 2012). Over time, new elite users of these platforms joined bloggers as informal political operatives. Many of these elites evolved into a new generation of political advocacy groups (Karpf 2016).

One of our cases, Robert Jago, fits into this narrative of the evolving nature of political bloggers, whereas our other case, Anonymous, requires us to discuss another lineage, politically motivated hacking or "hacktivism" (Coleman 2015). Groups such as Anonymous, Telecomix, WikiLeaks, and Phineas Fisher, as well as whistleblowers such as Edward Snowden and Chelsea Manning, have used their technical prowess to obtain and release confidential information to tremendous effect. Although the relationship can be tense, individual hackers and hacktivist groups have partnered, on occasion, with mainstream media outlets to leak valuable information. These collaborations have been seen as a new mixture of investigative journalism and political activism affecting media and political processes (Beyer 2014). Beyond leaking sensitive information, hacktivist groups and individual hackers have engaged in a wide range of digital actions with political intentions (Sauter 2014; Wray 1998). In Canada, these actions have included lone hacks, such as road signs being reprogrammed to display antigovernment messages (Rosencrance 2006), coordinated attacks shutting down government websites as a form of protest (McGuire 2014), and sophisticated attacks, such as when hackers hijacked the Conservative Party website to spread a fake news story that Prime Minister Harper had choked on a hash brown (Taber 2011).

For all of the attention paid to social media, there is a significant gap in the scholarly literature on the nature and influence of social media elites in the Canadian political landscape. In what follows, we consider different theories to possibly measure the influence of these elites. A big test for social media elites is whether they can affect voting or not. Changing voters' behaviours is perhaps the strongest measure of political influence (Verba, Schlozman, and Brady 1995). Social media and other digital media outlets have not been seen to have major effects on political participation in Canada, in contrast to an international review determining that social media had a net positive impact (Boulianne 2015; Small et al. 2014). The lack of impact does not imply a lack of effort. Social media elites actively support and campaign for parties, as seen in the highly partisan nature of the Canadian blogosphere. Digital advocacy groups have also been active in extending the tradition of strategic voting in Canada (Leadnow 2015). Preliminary analysis indicates that Leadnow's 2015 campaign had a marginal impact on its targeted ridings but perhaps contributed to an increased youth turnout (Breguet 2015).

Beyond voting, online influence can be measured through effects on the "political information cycle." Andrew Chadwick (2013) introduces that term to replace the more conventional term "traditional news cycle." Political information cycles include traditional broadcasters and newspapers interacting with and adapting to social media alongside new entrants made possible by emerging platforms. This dynamic is reshaping the power structure in the media environment and how news is constructed and circulated, especially in a political context. As much as the cycle might have changed, traditional elites such as newspaper journalists endure alongside social media elites, creating what Chadwick calls a "hybrid media system." The success of elites new and old can be evaluated through their ability to "prime" news reception, increase the accessibility of certain stories, and set the agenda of the information cycle (Cacciatore, Scheufele, and Iyengar 2016). Priming refers to how "news content suggests to news audiences that they ought to use specific issues as benchmarks for evaluating the performance of leaders and governments" (Scheufele and Tewksbury 2007, 11), whereas agenda setting can be defined as the way in which elites influence the accessibility of information. Since online audiences tend to select and rely on information sources corresponding to their beliefs (Bennett and Iyengar 2008; Bennett and Manheim 2006), social media elites increase the accessibility of information by passing on, commenting on, or echoing certain stories to their sympathetic followers. A social media elite's ability to amplify certain stories has been compared to traditional gatekeeping, and collaborations among elites to highlight stories have been called collaborative gatewatching or networked gatekeeping (Barzilai-Nahon 2008; Bruns 2005). Often in tandem with these agenda-setting and gatekeeping practices, social media elites prime their followers in favour of specific perceptions and interpretations of news, actions, or events by adding comments or opinions when linking to stories. There is a healthy debate about the influence of social media elites on the political information cycle (especially after the alleged "meme magic" of the "alt-right" in the 2016 US presidential election). Worries about elite manipulation of information cycles appear to be out of sync with the "limited" effects tradition in communications studies. Measured studies of media manipulation and computational propaganda demonstrate that social media elites do influence information salience and propagation but not enough to usher in a new paradigm of direct effects (Marwick and Lewis 2017; Woolley and Howard 2016).

Social media elites also play an important role in mobilizing more conventional forms of political action, including offline protests, petitions, boycotts, and letter-writing campaigns (Earl and Kimport 2011). For some time, they have helped campaigns and movements to raise awareness and funds as well as mobilize and cultivate support for important issues. In large part, the success of political mobilization depends on social media elites' capacity for connective action, which refers to the logic at work in building and sustaining decentralized sociopolitical networks (Bennett and Segerberg 2013). Fundraising and protests might then be seen as outcomes of sustained connective action to create networks capable of mass mobilization.

Connective action also provides a mode to interpret the often emotional activity on social media. These platforms, particularly Twitter, foster what Zizi Papacharissi (2015, 29) describes as networked structures of feeling that, in contrast to rational evaluations of online activity, "can drive powerful disruption, help accumulate intensity and tension, or simply sustain infinite loops of activity and inactivity." Social media content often promotes the kinds of shared feelings that strengthen network ties, generating "affective publics" that support other forms of political mobilization. These different measures of influence provide a way for us to deduce how social media elites attempt to influence elections.

Case Study

To study social media elites' influence in Canada, we chose a period of heightened political activity: the 2015 Canadian federal election. Two actors during the election caught our eye as indicative of the recent evolution of social media elites in the Canadian political landscape: the blogger Robert Jago and Operation Anon Down ("OpAnonDown" on Twitter), part of the global hacktivist movement Anonymous. At first glance, both cases resembled citizen journalism in their overall online activities. They created their own news content about un- or under-reported stories, amplified their stories on social media, and tried to push them into the mainstream political information cycle.

Jago describes himself as a former member of the Conservative Party. He is a long-standing participant in the Canadian political blogosphere and today is a staple of the Canadian media space. His blog, named *Some Random Political Blog,* has been active since 2008, and his posts were highly cited by bloggers during the federal election that year (CBC News 2008). He joined Twitter in August 2008 and remained an infrequent user until the 2015 election. From 2008 to 2014, he averaged twelve tweets a month. In contrast, he was much more active during the 2015 election campaign, tweeting 61 times in August, 317 times in September, and 35 times in October. Even if the increase in the volume of tweeting is not extraordinary, Jago's influence on the campaign was noteworthy.

Our other case, Anonymous, has been active in the Canadian political landscape since at least 2008, in some cases affecting the dynamics of policy making and governing. In 2011, Anonymous played a pivotal role in reopening the investigation into the events that led to the death of Rehtaeh Parsons by the Halifax Police Department. By threatening to release the names of the individuals responsible for cyberbullying Parsons, they forced the municipal police to pursue the investigation and ultimately lay charges (CBC News 2015b). More recently, OpAnonDown – a subgroup of Anonymous likely including a few different people sharing the same account (this cannot be verified independently) – emerged online in protest of the RCMP shooting of James Daniel McIntyre in Dawson Creek, British Columbia, on July 17, 2016. That day Anonymous-associated Twitter account @YourAnonNews described McIntyre as a comrade and called for justice (CBC News 2015a). They threatened a mix of offline protests and online cyber-protests against the RCMP (Chase 2015). Soon thereafter they released uncensored copies of Treasury Board of Canada documents under the hashtag #CCLeaks. Just before the writ dropped, OpAnonDown promised to target Conservative and Liberal candidates as part of their ongoing campaign against government surveillance and to bring attention to McIntyre's death. The federal election resulted in an intensification of their activities on Twitter. They tweeted 150 times in July, 309 times in August, 597 times in September, and eighty-four times in October.

Method

Our study took an in-depth look at the online activities of Robert Jago (username @rjjago on Twitter) and OpAnonDown (username @OpAnonDown on Twitter) during the 2015 federal election campaign. Since both used Twitter, we focused on that platform as their main record of activity. Specifically, we collected tweets because they acted as a clearing house for Jago's and Anonymous's other activities online, such as blog posts and YouTube videos. We archived 972 tweets from OpAnonDown's public feed and 399 tweets from Jago's public feed posted between August 2 and October 20, 2015.[1] Interestingly, their total number of tweets are significantly lower than those of the most active accounts during a similar period. Twitter served as an important outlet for information dispersion and social interaction related to the 2015 federal election. Over 770,000 election-related tweets were shared on Twitter's public timeline on election day, and Canadians tweeted more than 3.4 million times with the #elxn42 hashtag during the campaign (Bogart 2015).

We used a deductive approach to code tweets, drawing on our prior definition of political influence. We designed nine codes corresponding with different repertoires of influence. The codes are the following: (1) direct comments about parties or politicians meant to influence voter behaviour;

(2) amplification of a news story through retweeting (a form of agenda setting); (3) original tweets or retweets functioning as a form of citizen journalism; (4) original tweets linking to news stories that include commentary meant to influence its interpretation by followers (a form of agenda setting and priming); (5) original tweets or retweets encouraging a form of online mobilization (e.g., calls to donate, invitations to sign a petition, a call for a boycott); (6) original tweets or retweets fostering networked structures of feeling through hashtags, memes, or other public interactions; (7) original tweets checking in online or general commentary about life; (8) quasi-public interactions or replies; and (9) unknown, other, or unrelated tweets.[2] Two coders read and classified, independently and manually, each tweet in the sample for the dominant intent of influence. Tweets were analyzed chronologically so that coders would be aware of their contexts and dynamics of interaction, if tweets served a social interaction function. Following an intercoder reliability test at 76 percent (Krippendorff's alpha of 0.68), tweets were consensus-coded to remove any disagreements, an approach used in recent studies with a similar methodological approach (Humphreys, Krishnamurthy, and Newbury 2013).[3]

In addition, we measured the influence of Jago and OpAnonDown through an analysis of a mixture of press coverage, social media indicators, and party reactions. Methods of data collection varied for each. First, we relied on Twitter's own metrics of influence, counting the number of retweets that our cases received. Retweets are an important measure of a user's influence since they demonstrate an ability to produce content worth sharing (Cha et al. 2010). Second, we measured press coverage by searching for stories about Jago, OpAnonDown, and the candidates whom they mentioned in major Canadian newspapers, specifically the Canadian Press, *Financial Post*, *Globe and Mail*, *National Post*, *La Presse*, *Toronto Star*, and *Winnipeg Free Press*. Our manual review of tweets also revealed mentions of emergent and online outlets such as news aggregator National Newswatch and the now-defunct political bureau of BuzzFeed Canada. When appropriate, we refer to this coverage in our discussion.[4]

FINDINGS

Analysis of the Twitter data set collected for this study shows clear patterns within these social media elites' tweeting (see Table 11.1). On the one hand, 85 percent of Jago's tweets were related to either citizen journalism (23 percent of his tweets) – most of them featuring links to posts on his blog – or

Table 11.1

Tactics of influence in tweets by social media elites during the 2015 Canadian federal election

Tactics of influence in tweets	@rjjago Tweets (N)	@rjjago Tweets (%)	@OpAnonDown Tweets (N)	@OpAnonDown Tweets (%)
Direct comments about parties or politicians meant to influence voter behaviour	18	5	90	9
Amplification of a news story through retweeting	11	3	132	14
Original tweets or retweets functioning as forms of citizen journalism	92	23	259	27
Original tweets linking to news stories that include commentaries meant to influence their interpretations by followers	3	1	13	1
Original tweets or retweets encouraging a form of online mobilization	0	0	24	2
Original tweets or retweets meant to foster networked structures of feeling through hashtags, memes, or other public interactions	15	4	121	12
Original tweets checking in online or general commentary about life	11	3	33	3
Quasi-public interactions or replies	246	62	262	27
Unknown, other, or unrelated tweets	3	1	38	4
Total	399	100	972	100

NOTE: Might not total 100 percent because of rounding.

interactions with other Twitter users (62 percent of his tweets). Many of his tweets that we deemed to serve a social interaction function involved conversations and debates with journalists and news organizations, including Holly Nicholas from the *The Rebel* (9.3 percent of social interaction tweets), Kady O'Malley from the *Ottawa Citizen* (2.4 percent of his social interaction tweets), as well as National Newswatch (2.8 percent of his social interaction tweets). No other type of tweet made up more than 5 percent of his total activity in the Twitterverse.

On the other hand, OpAnonDown's tweeting was far more diversified and had as much to do with supporting the larger Anonymous movement as influencing the election (see Table 11.1). Accordingly, 14 percent of their tweets and retweets amplified stories and news, many of them generated by Anonymous-affiliated accounts. Also, 27 percent of their tweets served a social interaction function, many of them with Anonymous accounts such as @Anon_GovWatchCA (10 percent of social interaction tweets) and @Anonymous (9.5 percent of social interaction tweets). Finally, OpAnon-Down engaged in much more affective tweeting (12 percent of all tweets) than Jago (4 percent of all tweets), using hashtags such as #Anonymous, #VoteAnonymous, and #OpDeathEaters to try to foster networked structures of feeling among their followers. Their inclusion in an established network helps to explain why OpAnonDown received a significantly larger volume of retweets than Jago. This fact allowed them to gain access to followers and allies willing to share and amplify their messages. Therefore, the more they tweeted, the more chances they had to connect with supporters willing to share their messages.

A closer look at the data shows that references to leaks and scandals were frequent in our cases' public Twitter feeds. Both users were active when it came to generating or promoting their own stories about candidates' embarrassing behaviour, in the case of Jago, or leaking private – or classified – government information, in the case of OpAnonDown. Approximately a quarter of all posts on both accounts referenced or promoted news stories, as seen in Table 11.1. Promotion of their stories accounts for much of their interactions as well. For example, on the busiest day for OpAnonDown (September 15), they sent forty-eight tweets coded as citizen journalism and fifty tweets coded as interactions.

Jago's tweets largely focused on opposition research against the Conservative Party's candidates. Jago worked on finding stories, scandalous screenshots, and inappropriate posts to embarrass the party. His stated objective was to affect vote choice by moving "a few thousand votes in the GTA and the 905, and a few thousand votes in the Lower Mainland [around Vancouver]" (Hutchins 2015). This suggests a certain strategy in his research targeting, though our data show that he maintained a relatively broad scope: he included candidates running for elections in six of the ten provinces.

Was Jago successful in achieving his stated goal of influencing coverage of the Conservative Party? Our research found that he had a receptive partner in the mainstream media (see Table 11.2). *Maclean's* called him "the most dangerous blogger in Canada" since his political blog appeared to be a source of influence on campaign coverage (Hutchins 2015). In addition,

Table 11.2

Media coverage of social media elites during the 2015 Canadian federal election

	@rjjago	@OpAnonDown
Retweet	1,358	6,076
Press coverage about them	14	7
Press coverage about the candidates targeted	31	1
Candidate/party reactions	3 candidates	Unclear

popular news aggregator National Newswatch shared ten of his posts. The CBC included four stories about his opposition research, and his stories appeared on various online news sources, such as BuzzFeed and Vice News. Coverage included both stories about his opposition research and uptake of stories first posted on his blog. These latter posts led to the most press coverage, even though *Maclean's*, CBC's *As It Happens*, and the podcast *CANADALAND* published feature interviews with him. This dynamic can be explained by several factors, including his propensity to interact through Twitter with journalists and news organizations, such as National Newswatch.

Moreover, Jago's online activities adversely affected the Conservative Party's candidate slate. As indicated in Table 11.2, Jago appears to have prompted at least three candidates to resign or be dropped by the party. Tim Dutaud, the Conservative pick for Toronto–Danforth, was the most notable of the three. Jago unearthed Dutaud's YouTube videos on September 4, 2016. These controversial videos record Dutaud sexually harassing a woman customer service representative and mocking people living with mental disabilities. This discovery came only a few hours after hidden-camera footage of the Conservative candidate for Scarborough–Rouge Park, Jerry Bance, urinating in a mug when on a call as a service technician was released publicly. The Conservative Party dropped both candidates that day.

Jago is also credited by journalists with at least two other Conservative candidate withdrawals. He publicized the scandalous comments that Gilles Guibord, the candidate for Rosemont–La-Petite-Patrie in Quebec, made on various websites, including in the comment section of *Le Journal de Montréal*. After Jago exposed these comments, the *Toronto Star* reported that "Guibord's exit as a Tory candidate follows the publication Thursday of screenshots of comments attributed to him regarding women, aboriginal people and religion" (Kestler-D'Amours 2015). Later in the campaign, Jago targeted Blair Dale, the candidate for Bonavista–Burin–Trinity in New-foundland and Labrador, finding that he had made scandalous comments on race, abortion, and drug use on his Google+ account and OkCupid profile. Later the *Toronto Star* credited Jago with Dale's resignation. Its article states that "news that Dale was no longer contesting the riding came just hours after Jago revealed his alleged on-line postings" (Campion-Smith 2015).

OpAnonDown also focused primarily on citizen journalism during the election (27 percent of all tweets) but with much less success than Jago. They had some press attention going into the election after their Treasury Board leak. Our qualitative review of their tweeting revealed that they kept a playful tone in early August, making promises to leak information related to John Baird, the minister of foreign affairs from 2011 to 2015, before deciding to leak another document supposedly connected to a court case between Nathan Jacobson, an alleged Tory supporter, and the attorney general and CSIS on August 6, 2015. This leak received no mainstream press attention, but did result in a feature interview on the podcast *CANADALAND*. This pattern repeated itself throughout the campaign. Subsequent attempts at citizen journalism on September 15 and 21 failed to attract mainstream attention.

OpAnonDown developed a more antagonistic relationship with the press than Jago. Paul McLeod of BuzzFeed and Justin Ling of Vice News – then two new journalistic outlets in Canada – both criticized OpAnonDown for circulating unsubstantiated claims. McLeod and OpAnonDown had a long debate on Twitter, hence his frequent mentions (5.79 percent of total social interaction tweets). Here we can observe an interesting dynamic at work in the conflict between the attempts by Anonymous to act as unofficial citizen journalists and the efforts of emergent journalist outlets such as BuzzFeed and Vice News to be considered legitimate. McLeod and Ling represented journalism's evolving practices in an era of change. Comparable studies of hacktivist-press relations found that new journalist outlets such as BuzzFeed "use new technologies to transform the way in which investigative work is produced and distributed," but ultimately "they are firmly committed to traditional journalistic values and see themselves as preserving an industry at least as much as reshaping it" (Lynch 2010, 317). In other circumstances, McLeod and Ling used their interactions with OpAnonDown to reiterate their journalistic values and to venerate their upstart organizations as important gatekeepers in the political information cycle. OpAnonDown had to pitch their stories elsewhere.

Political Elites in Canada in the Digital Age

Scandals and screenshots proved to be a recipe for success for social media elites in the 2015 Canadian federal election – a finding with implications for the role of social media in politics more broadly. Scandals occur "where private acts that disgrace or offend the idealized, dominant morality of a social community are made public and narrativized by the media" (Lull and Hinerman 1998, 3). Today scandals circulate as screenshots, photos, or other "proofs" of transgression. By finding these digital objects, social media elites successfully influence the political information cycle. Their work functions as an information subsidy for a press looking for politainment and celebrity-like gossip. These stories disrupt communications strategists and interrupt the daily agenda enough to be worth it for social media elites to find these stories (see Marland 2016, 82–98).

The popularity of social media among Canadians can amplify the influence of social media elites and their scandalous finds. Members of the public might desire the convenience of scandals and pseudo-scandals when expected to be updating their status constantly. Scandals give people a chance to "participate" by sharing their emotional reactions, feelings of moral outrage and shame, to the spectacle of "tire fires" in modern politics (Jenkins, Ford, and Green 2013; Nahon and Hemsley 2013). The government of Justin Trudeau – which came to power in November 2015 – seemed to have learned a similar lesson. The memetic prime minister saturates the political information cycle with photos of himself happily hugging pandas or explaining quantum theory in front of chalkboards – discrete objects meant to nourish the Liberal's youthful brand or what Trudeau called "Sunny Ways" as people happily share them.

Scandals threaten modern political parties devoted to maintaining their brands as well as politicians who avoid controversy and debate on social media in favour of status updates and the appearance of accessibility. For example, Jago's stories – nineteen by our count – created a broader narrative of a scandal-prone party meant to tarnish the Conservative brand. Jago explained, in an interview with *Maclean's*, that he sought to expose the "norm of what is believed within the Conservative party" (Hutchins 2015). Certainly, his posts about racist, sexist, and off-colour comments clashed with the Conservative Party's branding. None of those disgraced candidates ran in ridings that the Conservative Party expected to win. The loss of these candidates hurt the brand far beyond these "no hope" ridings by drawing attention away from more positive or brand-sanctioned stories. This dynamic illustrates the growing influence of social media elites and the possibility that a single individual with technological know-how and a knack for finding the right image can destabilize a large political operation.

Social media elites, however, compete and collaborate with other elites to set the information cycle and frame political coverage. Decisions about coverage are brokered between elites, particularly journalists and social media elites. This phenomenon diminishes the hypothesis that social media elites are master manipulators who solely control the news from the shadows. Far from setting the agenda, our cases followed traditional journalism's emphasis on scandal. Although elite logics of Canadian journalism are beyond the scope of our chapter (see Chapter 10 by Chacon, Lawlor, and Giasson in this volume), social media elites accommodated mainstream media interests. A symbiotic relationship developed between Robert Jago and journalists. He fulfilled a demand from political journalists for stories designed for easy outrage, especially as the number of scandals became a story in itself. In return, Jago used his profile to try to raise issues such as electoral reform and pervasive racism against Indigenous peoples in Canada. OpAnonDown, in contrast, struggled to create an easy-to-spread outrageous screenshot to discredit the Harper government and suffered as a result. Journalist demands then constrain the influence of social media elites. In an interview with *Maclean's*, Jago admitted that "I'm bored to tears with jerk-off candidates. People think I'm getting some joy about finding this stuff. I don't. But it's a project I'm going to finish" (Hutchins 2015). He continued to find stories that tarnished the Conservatives, but his narrow influence did not sway the mainstream media focus on scandals (certainly not in comparison to his more recent media actions that have convincingly changed coverage of Indigenous issues in Canada).

The uneven uptake of stories also sheds light on the political economy and professional practice of Canadian journalism. Jago produced a few good stories for free that could easily be transferred into content for news cycles. Conversely, Anonymous did not produce a "smoking gun," but it did produce information that required further verification. In other words, they called for investigations into their stories, a process taking time and money – both of which are in short supply in the mainstream media during an election. OpAnonDown seemed to be more circumscribed by media expectations. As one member commented in an interview published in the *National Post*, "we know that we've got an audience that wants us to do certain things – especially hack and leak" (Humphreys 2015). Indeed, they were rewarded with coverage when they leaked documents. Their tactics – which can be perceived as illegal – made it easy for journalists to frame their activities as a threat to security rather than the work of citizen journalists concerned about government surveillance.

Finally, the ephemeral nature of both OpAnonDown and Robert Jago raises questions about whether social media elites represent a crisis of public accountability or a mechanism to ensure it. Both of the social media elites studied in this chapter mobilized in response to their political beliefs and drew on their different levels of technical sophistication. They also believed in the system, hoping to influence rather than undermine the election. Canada has no guarantee that the next generation of social media elites will leverage these talents with such public interest. The 2016 US presidential election illustrated how social media elites can use their skills cynically to undermine democracy. Media coverage focused on the influence of "fake news" about Democratic presidential nominee Hillary Clinton (Higgins, McIntire, and Dance 2016) and social media manipulation by supposed Kremlin agents. Numerous reports profiled the cottage industry of former bloggers and social media elites who realized the profitability of their skills. Attempts by Facebook and Google to suppress the industry served as a reminder that other elites, such as mainstream journalists, have to hold social media elites in check. In that way, social media elites constitute both a challenge and a solution to public accountability during and long after a campaign.

NOTES

1 We used Tweet Dumper to extract data from Twitter; see https://gist.github.com/yanofsky/5436496.

2 Examples of tweets from the different categories are available on request.

3 Although discouraged by Krippendorff (2004), we consensus-coded all disagreements to have complete agreement. Our disagreements often related to debates distinguishing OpAnonDown's citizen journalist tweets (code 3) from their participation in the Anonymous movement (codes 1, 2, and 6). These differences in interpretation are arguably baked into Twitter with its 140-character limit and necessitate consensus coding.

4 The search patterns and databases that we used are available on request.

REFERENCES

Barzilai-Nahon, Karine. 2008. "Toward a Theory of Network Gatekeeping: A Framework for Exploring Information Control." *Journal of the American Society for Information Science and Technology* 59, 9: 1493–1512. https://doi.org/10.1002/asi.20857.

Bennett, W. Lance, and Shanto Iyengar. 2008. "A New Era of Minimal Effects? The Changing Foundations of Political Communication." *Journal of Communication* 58, 4: 707–31. https://doi.org/10.1111/j.1460-2466.2008.00410.x.

Bennett, W. Lance, and Jarol B. Manheim. 2006. "The One-Step Flow of Communication." *Annals of the American Academy of Political and Social Science* 608, 1: 213–32. https://doi.org/10.1177/0002716206292266.

Bennett, W. Lance, and Alexandra Segerberg. 2013. *The Logic of Connective Action: Digital Media and the Personalization of Contentious Politics.* Cambridge, UK: Cambridge University Press. https://doi.org/10.1017/CBO9781139198752.

Beyer, Jessica L. 2014. "The Emergence of a Freedom of Information Movement: Anonymous, WikiLeaks, the Pirate Party, and Iceland." *Journal of Computer-Mediated Communication* 19, 2: 141–54. https://doi.org/10.1111/jcc4.12050.

Blevis, Mark, and David Coletto. 2017. "Matters of Opinion 2017: 8 Things We Learned about Politics, the News, and the Internet," *Abacus Data,* February 7. http://abacus data.ca/matters-of-opinion-2017-8-things-we-learned-about-politics-the-news -and-the-internet/#sthash.9aUsDjL3.dpuf.

Bogart, Nicole. 2015. "By the Numbers: How the 2015 Federal Election Played Out on Social Media." *Global News,* October 20. https://globalnews.ca/news/2287969/ by-the-numbers-how-the-2015-federal-election-played-out-on-social-media/.

Boulianne, Shelley. 2015. "Social Media Use and Participation: A Meta-Analysis of Current Research." *Information Communication and Society* 18, 5: 524–38. https://doi. org/10.1080/1369118X.2015.1008542.

Breguet, Bryan. 2015. "Canada Election 2015: Did Strategic Voting Work?" *Huffington Post,* November 11. http://www.huffingtonpost.ca/2015/11/02/canada-election-2015 -strategic-voting-lead-now_n_8452212.html.

Brin, Colette. 2016. *Digital News Report 2016.* Oxford: Reuters Institute for the Study of Journalism. http://www.digitalnewsreport.org/survey/2016/canada-2016/.

Bruns, Axel. 2005. *Gatewatching: Collaborative Online News Production.* New York: Peter Lang.

Cacciatore, Michael A., Dietram A. Scheufele, and Shanto Iyengar. 2016. "The End of Framing as We Know It ... and the Future of Media Effects." *Mass Communication and Society* 19, 1: 7–23. https://doi.org/10.1080/15205436.2015.1068811.

Campion-Smith, Bruce. 2015. "Tory Candidate Dumped after Social Media Comments on Race, Drug Use." *Toronto Star,* September, 15. https://www.thestar.com/news/ federal-election/2015/09/15/tory-candidate-dumped-after-social-media-comments -on-race-drug-use.html.

Carr, Caleb T., and Rebecca A. Hayes. 2015. "Social Media: Defining, Developing, and Divining." *Atlantic Journal of Communication* 23, 1: 46–65. https://doi.org/10.1080/ 15456870.2015.972282.

CBC News. 2008. "Blog Buzz Top 5 Posts – Sept. 8/08." *CBC News – Canada Votes 2008,* September 8. http://www.cbc.ca/news2/canadavotes/campaign2/ormiston/2008/09/ blog_buzz_top_5_posts.html.

–. 2015a. "Anonymous Vows to Avenge RCMP Dawson Creek Shooting." *CBC News,* July 18. http://www.cbc.ca/news/canada/british-columbia/activist-group-anonymous -vows-to-avenge-dawson-creek-shooting-1.3159093.

–. 2015b. "Rehtaeh Parsons's Father Credits Anonymous for Reopening Investigation." *CBC News*, August 3. http://www.cbc.ca/news/canada/nova-scotia/rehtaeh-parsons -s-father-credits-anonymous-for-reopening-investigation-1.3177605.

Cha, Meeyoung, et al. 2010. "Measuring User Influence in Twitter: The Million Follower Fallacy." In *ICWSM 2010: Proceedings of the 4th International AAAI Conference on Weblogs and Social Media*, 10–17. Menlo Park, CA: AAAI Press. http://hdl.handle. net/11858/00-001M-0000-0028-8BAB-9.

Chadwick, Andrew. 2013. *The Hybrid Media System: Politics and Power*. New York: Oxford University Press. https://doi.org/10.1093/acprof:oso/9780199759477.001.0001.

Chase, Steven. 2015. "Cyberattack Deals Crippling Blow to Canadian Government Websites." *Globe and Mail*, June 17. https://www.theglobeandmail.com/news/national/ canadian-government-websites-appear-to-have-been-attacked/article24997399/.

Coleman, E. Gabriella. 2015. *Hacker, Hoaxer, Whistleblower, Spy: The Many Faces of Anonymous*. New York: Verso.

Earl, Jennifer, and Katrina Kimport. 2011. *Digitally Enabled Social Change: Activism in the Internet Age*. Cambridge, MA: MIT Press. https://doi.org/10.7551/mitpress/ 9780262015103.001.0001.

Elmer, Greg, Ganaele Langlois, and Fenwick McKelvey. 2012. *The Permanent Campaign: New Media, New Politics*. New York: Peter Lang.

Flanagan, Tom. 2007. *Harper's Team: Behind the Scenes in the Conservative Rise to Power*. Montreal: McGill-Queen's University Press.

Glenn, Ted. 2014. *Professional Communications in the Public Sector: A Practical Guide*. Toronto: Canadian Scholars' Press.

Haggart, Blayne. 2013. "Fair Copyright for Canada: Lessons for Online Social Movements from the First Canadian Facebook Uprising." *Canadian Journal of Political Science* 46, 4: 841–61. https://doi.org/10.1017/S0008423913000838.

Higgins, Andrew, Mike McIntire, and Gabriel J.X. Dance. 2016. "Inside a Fake News Sausage Factory: 'This Is All about Income.'" *New York Times*, November 25. https:// www.nytimes.com/2016/11/25/world/europe/fake-news-donald-trump-hillary -clinton-georgia.html.

Hindman, Matthew. 2009. *The Myth of Digital Democracy*. Princeton, NJ: Princeton University Press.

Humphreys, A. 2015. "The Face of Operation Anon Down." *National Post*, July 30. http:// nationalpost.com/features/the-face-of-operation-anon-down.

Humphreys, Lee, Phillipa Gill, Balachander Krishnamurthy, and Elizabeth Newbury. 2013. "Historicizing New Media: A Content Analysis of Twitter." *Journal of Communication* 63, 3: 413–31. https://doi.org/10.1111/jcom.12030.

Hutchins, Aaron. 2015. "Robert Jago: The Most Dangerous Blogger in Canada." *Macleans. ca*, September 16. http://www.macleans.ca/politics/ottawa/robert-jago-the-most -dangerous-blogger-in-canada/.

Jenkins, Henry, Sam Ford, and Joshua Green. 2013. *Spreadable Media: Creating Value and Meaning in a Networked Culture*. New York: New York University Press.

Karpf, David. 2012. *The MoveOn Effect: The Unexpected Transformation of American Political Advocacy*. New York: Oxford University Press. https://doi.org/10.1093/ acprof:oso/9780199898367.001.0001.

–. 2016. *Analytic Activism: Digital Listening and the New Political Strategy*. Oxford Studies in Digital Politics. New York: Oxford University Press.

Kestler-D'Amours, Jillian. 2015. "Tories Drop Outspoken Quebec Candidate." *Toronto Star*, August 21. https://www.thestar.com/news/canada/2015/08/21/tories-drop -quebec-candidate.html.

Koop, R., and H.J. Jansen. 2009. "Political Blogs and Blogrolls in Canada: Forums for Democratic Deliberation?" *Social Science Computer Review* 27, 2: 155–73. https:// doi.org/10.1177/0894439308326297.

Kreiss, D., S. McGregor, and R. Lawrence. 2017. "Audience, Genres, Affordances, and Timing: A Framework for Analyzing Campaign Communications across Social Media Platforms." *Political Communication*. Advance online publication. https:// doi.org/10.1080/10584609.2017.1334727.

Krippendorff, Klaus. 2004. "Reliability in Content Analysis: Some Common Mis-conceptions and Recommendations." *Human Communication Research* 30, 3: 411– 33. https://doi.org/10.1111/j.1468-2958.2004.tb00738.x.

Leadnow. 2015. "Defeating Harper: Reflections on the Vote Together Campaign." *Lead-now*. http://www.votetogether.ca/report.

Lull, James, and Stephen Hinerman. 1998. "The Search for the Scandal." In *Media Scandals*, edited by James Lull and Stephen Hinerman, 1–33. New York: Columbia University Press.

Lynch, Lisa. 2010. "'WE'RE GOING TO CRACK THE WORLD OPEN': Wikileaks and the Future of Investigative Reporting." *Journalism Practice* 4, 3: 309–18. https:// doi.org/10.1080/17512781003640752.

Marland, Alex. 2016. *Brand Command: Canadian Politics and Democracy in the Age of Message Control*. Vancouver: UBC Press.

Marwick, Alice, and Rebecca Lewis. 2017. "Media Manipulation and Disinformation On-line." *Data and Society*, May 15. https://datasociety.net/output/media-manipulation -and-disinfo-online/.

McGuire, Patrick. 2014. "A Hacking Group Is Attacking Canadian Government Websites to Exonerate an Alleged Teen Swatter." *VICE News*, November 24. https://www. vice.com/en_ca/read/this-hacker-is-attacking-canadian-government-websites-to -exonerate-an-alleged-teen-swatter-555.

McLean, James S. 2012. *Inside the NDP War Room: Competing for Credibility in a Federal Election*. Montreal: McGill-Queen's University Press.

Muñoz, C.L., and T.L. Towner. 2017. "The Image Is the Message: Instagram Marketing and the 2016 Presidential Primary Season." *Journal of Political Marketing* 16, 3–4: 290–318. https://doi.org/10.1080/15377857.2017.1334254.

Nagy, P., and G. Neff. 2015. "Imagined Affordances: Reconstructing a Keyword for Communication Theory." *Social Media and Society* 1, 2: 1–9. https://doi.org/10.1177/ 2056305115603385.

Nahon, Karine, and Jeff Hemsley. 2013. *Going Viral*. Cambridge, UK: Polity Press.

Papacharissi, Zizi. 2015. *Affective Publics: Sentiment, Technology, and Politics*. Oxford Studies in Digital Politics. New York: Oxford University Press.

Rosencrance, Linda. 2006. "Hacker Hits Toronto Transit Message System, Jabs Prime Minister." *Computerworld*, May 5. https://www.computerworld.com/article/2555194/

cybercrime-hacking/hacker-hits-toronto-transit-message-system-jabs-prime
-minister.html.

Sauter, Molly. 2014. *The Coming Swarm: DDOS Actions, Hacktivism, and Civil Disobedience on the Internet.* New York: Bloomsbury Academic.

Scheufele, Dietram A., and David Tewksbury. 2007. "Framing, Agenda Setting, and
Priming: The Evolution of Three Media Effects Models." *Journal of Communication* 57, 1: 9–20. https://doi.org/10.1111/j.0021-9916.2007.00326.x.

Small, Tamara A., Harold Jansen, Frédérick Bastien, Thierry Giasson, and Royce Koop.
2014. "Online Political Activity in Canada: The Hype and the Facts." *Canadian
Parliamentary Review* 37, 4: 9–16.

Taber, Jane. 2011. "Hackers Cause Stir with Harper Choking-on-Hash-Brown Hoax."
Globe and Mail, June 7. https://www.theglobeandmail.com/news/politics/ottawa-
notebook/hackers-cause-stir-with-harper-choking-on-hash-brown-hoax/article
2050044/.

Taras, David, and Christopher Robb Waddell. 2012. "The 2011 Federal Election and the
Transformation of Canadian Media and Politics." In *How Canadians Communicate
IV: Media and Politics,* edited by David Taras and Christopher Robb Waddell, 71–
107. Edmonton: Athabasca University Press.

van Dijck, José. 2013. *The Culture of Connectivity: A Critical History of Social Media.* Oxford: Oxford University Press. https://doi.org/10.1093/acprof:oso/9780199970773.
001.0001.

Verba, Sidney, Kay Lehman Schlozman, and Henry E. Brady. 1995. *Voice and Equality:
Civic Voluntarism in American Politics.* Cambridge, MA: Harvard University Press.

Woolley, S., and P.N. Howard. 2016. "Political Communication, Computational Propaganda, and Autonomous Agents: Introduction." *International Journal of Communication* 10: 4882–90.

Wray, Stefan. 1998. "Electronic Civil Disobedience and the World Wide Web of Hacktivism: A Mapping of Extraparliamentarian Direct Action Net Politics." *Switch* 4, 2.
http://switch.sjsu.edu/web/v4n2/stefan/.

12

The National Message, the Local Tour: Candidates' Use of Twitter during the 2015 Canadian Election

•••• *Julie Killin and Tamara A. Small*

This chapter looks at the use of Twitter by local candidates in the 2015 federal election. Twitter is a social medium that allows people to "tweet" short messages to their followers in general and to send directed messages to particular users. Twitter is relatively popular in Canada. It is used by an estimated 40 percent of Canadian internet users (Pellegrini 2016), and it was used by all major party leaders as well as most local candidates in the 2015 campaign. Its use for election and political purposes has been studied in a variety of contexts across many Western nations and levels of government. Studies have focused on its use as a reflection of the offline campaign and for the purpose of prediction (Murthy and Petto 2015; Tumasjan et al. 2010); the types of people who use it for political purposes (Bekafigo and McBride 2013; Hosch-Dayican et al. 2016); and whether it has fundamentally changed the nature of campaigning and citizen interaction with political elites (Cross et al. 2015; Effing, van Hillegersberg, and Huibers 2011; Small 2014).

Local candidates are an important group of political elites in Canada because they serve both as local spokespersons for citizens and as liaisons between citizens and political parties. In this chapter, we seek to understand how local candidates use Twitter within the context of Canadian political campaigns, focusing on whether this type of digital technology is improving the democratic relationship between citizens and one group of political elites – local candidates.

Since the 1970s, the literature on local candidates in Canada has suggested that the importance of local campaigns and candidates pales in comparison to that of the national campaign and party leaders when it comes to voters making their decisions at voting booths. However, though their importance in vote choice is low, local candidates can still make a difference, for not all candidates are equal, and some are better able than others to cultivate a personal vote (Black and Erickson 2000; Blais et al. 2003; Flanagan

2014). We see Twitter as allowing for the cultivation of a personal vote in two ways: (1) by allowing for direct interactions with supporters; (2) by providing local candidates with a space to promote their local campaigns and to communicate local information to citizens, as opposed to the national campaign and national information.

One of the dominant debates in the literature on the political use of Twitter concerns investigating whether political elites are using it as a communications tool to engage and interact with citizens. Twitter, like other social media, is designed in a way to facilitate participation from the audience. Social media have the potential to fundamentally change election campaigns and political dialogues between citizens and political elites because they offer low-cost ways to communicate, which assist candidates who lack the financial resources to develop personal campaigns (Ward, Gibson, and Nixon 2003). Social media can also appeal to younger citizens who tend toward political participation apathy, and they carry the ability for everyday citizens to involve themselves in the political dialogues of their communities (Tapscott 2009). Theoretically, social media can enhance the democratic nature of campaigns because these digital technologies allow candidates to have greater connections with their voters (Towner 2012). Online communications allow candidates to reach and directly communicate with their constituents without the financial costs of transportation and meeting venues and without the perhaps more important limitation during a campaign: the expense of time.

There is evidence that political campaigns can and have taken advantage of social media technologies, with Barack Obama's 2008 presidential campaign being the most prominent example (Stromer-Galley 2014). During that campaign, the Obama team solicited online donations, engaged with voters via Twitter, and benefited from the networking capacity of online technologies, as people shared and discussed information with their friends, resulting in increased levels of support at his campaign events and at the polls. More recently, there has been less optimism regarding the changing nature of citizen engagement via social media. Canadian studies have shown that many political users of social media technologies are not taking advantage of all that Twitter and Facebook have to offer and instead are using these technologies to simply disseminate information. Much of this literature has focused on national-level politics (Francoli, Greenberg, and Waddell 2012; Small 2010) or provincial campaigns (Cross et al. 2015; Giasson et al. 2013; Small and Giasson 2014), with relatively little known about how

Twitter has affected local political campaigns. So we will explore the extent to which local candidates attempt to engage directly with citizens using Twitter in an attempt to cultivate personal votes.

In addition, we consider whether Canadian local candidates use Twitter as a tool to promote their own campaigns and local issues. Indeed, some see that by definition it is a personalized medium (Kruikemeier 2014). The literature on candidate personalization is helpful here. In the personalization of politics, the individual politicians become the "main anchor[s] of interpretation and evaluation" (Adam and Maier 2010, 213). Although the personalization literature tends to focus on the growing importance of party leaders within politics, we are concerned with a second type of personalization that focuses on local candidates. This type of personalization considers whether individual candidates focus their campaigns around themselves (their personalities and local issues) as opposed to mimicking the national campaign that focuses on the party leader, main platform issues, and central party organization in general (Cross and Young 2015). The Canadian literature on candidate personalization is somewhat mixed. Some studies have found that, for most local races, the focus is on the national campaign with a specific focus on party leaders (Cross et al. 2015), whereas others have noted that there is a large degree of variance, depending on candidate, party, and constituency factors. In particular, R. Kenneth Carty and Munroe Eagles (2005) argue that, on the whole, local actors are not passive, and they can anchor their party campaigns in local communities. Similarly, others have found that there is a "significant degree of personalization" (Cross and Young 2015, 307) and that quality and so-called star candidates, as well as those able to spend more money on their local campaigns, do better than their similarly situated counterparts (Carty and Eagles 2005; Coletto 2010; Sayers 1999). We see local candidates' tweets as an excellent tool to assess local campaign personalization by exploring whether candidates in the sample engage in a personal-local campaign or a party-national one.

As mentioned, relative to studies on party leaders and higher offices, there is a dearth of literature on local candidates' use of social media in Canada, let alone the use of Twitter specifically. One of the few studies conducted looked at municipal campaigns in Niagara, Ontario, and found a low level of social media interaction between candidates and voters, but it noted that there was a positive correlation between electoral success and the number of likes and posts for challengers on Facebook. Interestingly, for incumbents, there was a negative correlation between electoral success and the use of social media (Hagar 2014). A study of tweets during municipal elections in Ontario found that the focus was primarily on candidate campaign updates and messages of support from voters as opposed to discussions about political issues. Despite the perceived shallowness of these interactions, it was found that the use of Twitter did have a positive impact on electoral performance (Hagar 2015). Outside Canada, it has been found that Dutch candidates who use Twitter are more likely to be elected and are most likely to tweet about their private personas (Kruikemeier 2014). Regarding electoral success, a British study found a positive correlation between the response rate for incoming tweets and candidates' elections (Gaber 2016). Although local candidates might not come to mind when we speak of political elites in Canada, they remain important political actors. As such, it is important to understand how they communicate with voters and whether that relationship is shifting because of digital media such as Twitter.

Case Study

This chapter has three objectives. First, we seek to assess if local candidates use Twitter as part of their local campaigns. Second, we want to assess the extent to which candidates use it to interact with voters. Third, we wish to explore whether local candidates use it as a personal medium or to "toe the party line." Overall, we argue that local candidates use Twitter as a regular component of their political campaigns and that this medium of communication can strengthen democracy in Canada as candidates employ social media to interact with their constituents and share local features of their campaigns.

METHOD

Our case study looked at the Twitter accounts of a sample of local candidates who contested the 2015 federal election. Drawing on the approach of Anthony Sayers (1999) to selecting representative ridings, we chose ten ridings from Canadian regions representing a variance of conditions that we thought were important, such as the gender composition of an election race; whether or not the race was competitive; whether or not the riding was urban, suburban, or rural; and whether or not there was an incumbent running. We included two ridings from each of British Columbia, Alberta, Manitoba, and Ontario and one each from Newfoundland and Nova Scotia. We selected two ridings from the bigger provinces to reflect their distinct sizes and geographies. Quebec was excluded from our analysis because the

Bloc Québécois, historically a competitive party, does not run candidates outside the province, and we expected to find variations in our results based on party affiliation. We followed candidates in these ridings from the four major national parties, the Conservative Party of Canada (CPC), the Liberal Party of Canada (LPC), the New Democratic Party (NDP), and the Green Party (GP). In total, we looked at the Twitter feeds of thirty-six candidates.[1]

To obtain the Twitter feeds of these candidates, we used the services of Tweet Archivist, a data analytics company that scraped each of the selected candidates' accounts once per hour for the month prior to and including election day 2015. The parameters of the scrapes included the candidates' tweets and any tweets directed at the candidates via the use of their @usernames.

Our main unit of analysis was the individual tweet. As noted, though tweets are only 140 characters, considerable information can be conveyed through hashtags or website hyperlinks (Parmelee and Bichard 2011). Only those tweets authored by the candidate's Twitter account and of a relevant political nature were included in the analysis. They included general tweets such as those commenting on where the candidate would be canvassing for the day; tweets directed toward a specific user or account, such as thanking a volunteer for assistance; and retweets, when a candidate posted a message authored by another user. Overall, the database included 7,694 tweets by thirty-six candidates across four parties.

To analyze the candidates' tweets, a single coder followed Tamara Small's (2010) coding scheme, with some variation to account for the local nature of our data. Small recognized two main categories of data: social tweets and broadcast tweets. Social tweets are either @replies or retweets. Replies and retweets are often used in the literature as indicators of political interaction on Twitter between politicians and citizens (Giasson et al. 2013; Parmelee and Bichard 2011). Replies are interactive because they consist of a dialogue among users, and a retweet is considered a social form of communication because it implies that the candidates are critically engaged as they read the tweet before further disseminating it (Grant et al. 2010, 594). Retweets and @replies directed toward a candidate's party leader or official party account were not included as social tweets because they were meant not to engage local constituents but to publicize official information. Whereas social tweets characterize the social media model of participation between the politician and the citizen, broadcast tweets move in one direction from the politician to the citizen. We coded broadcast tweets according to whether they were

FIGURE 12.1

Coding criteria for local and national messages contained within broadcast tweets

National Campaign	Messages related to political issues that are not specifically local, such as references to party policy and the leader, general information about voting, requests to vote for the party, social communications between the candidate and party leader or party account, and negative attacks directed toward a party leader or party in general.
Local Campaign	Messages related to either the local campaign or the candidate. These include messages about local political events, local political issues, status updates, information about the local campaign such as volunteer recognition and endorsements, requests to vote for the candidate specifically, localized election day information and negative attacks on local opponents. Messages about the candidate include information such as family-life details, work experience, hobbies or where they grew up.

related to the national campaign or to the local campaign. Details are provided in Figure 12.1.

One important note regarding our analysis of broadcast tweets is that some tweets contained messages both national and local in nature. The following is an example of such a tweet: "Kent Hehr: Get out your popcorn, the debate has begun! Come watch with us at the Blind Monk, or online http://t.co/mEMaVrDfQM." This tweet contains a local message to join Kent Hehr (LPC, Calgary Centre) as well as a national message about the leaders' debate. When we assessed the degree to which broadcast tweets are localized, we analyzed the messages contained within the tweets. Thus, the number of messages (3,038) was greater than the number of broadcast tweets (2,944).

In addition to the coded tweets, we collected data on how many tweets were made by each candidate, the number of followers that the candidate had as of election day, and basic demographic information such as party affiliation; incumbent or challenger status; gender; region; urban, suburban, or rural residency; and electoral success.

FINDINGS

Our analysis suggests that Twitter has indeed become a normal component of local candidates' campaigns. Almost all of the candidates in our selected ridings had Twitter accounts that we could follow, and most candidates tweeted several times per day. Table 12.1 lists information about the candidates along with their numbers of followers, their Twitter activities, and the social or broadcast nature of their tweets.

However, the audiences that our candidates reached varied considerably (see Table 12.2). The average number of followers whom our candidates had as of election day was 3,346, but incumbents were significantly more likely to have many followers. The average number of followers for incumbents was 6,241, while this figure was only 2,520 for challengers. Like local campaigns in general, not all campaigns in the Twitterverse are equal in at least two respects. The first respect is the sheer number of followers that the candidates had. At the low end, Tanya MacPherson (NDP, Foothills) had only eighty followers, while Chrystia Freeland, the Liberal incumbent for Toronto Centre running in the new riding of University–Rosedale, had 32,569 followers. Freeland appears to have been an outlier; most candidates had a smaller number of followers. Almost half (seventeen) of the thirty-six candidates had fewer than 500 followers, five had between 500 and 1,000, seven had between 1,000 and 5,000, three had between 5,000 and 10,000, and only four had more than 10,000. Although many of the candidates with the greatest number of followers were incumbents, "star" challengers (see Sayers 1999) were included in our sample, and they clearly garnered larger followings than their less popular colleagues. For example, Kent Hehr, the popular provincial Liberal MLA from Calgary, had 11,000 followers, former television personality Jennifer Hollett (NDP, University–Rosedale) had 10,162 followers, and Conservative Party Director Fred DeLorey (Central Nova) had 3,560 followers. The wide variance in the number of followers suggests that quasi-celebrity status matters and that at least some of the candidates in our study were successfully using their Twitter accounts to garner attention to their personal campaigns.

The second respect in which Twitter campaigns differed greatly concerns the number of tweets that the candidates authored during the last month of the election campaign. Overall, candidates tweeted an average of seven times per day (median = 4). However, this figure varied as well. Five of the thirty-six candidates were what we call "heavy users," tweeting over 500 times during the time frame of our analysis. This translated into tweeting an average of eighteen times per day for Hehr (LPC, Calgary Centre) and up to thirty-five times per day for Hollett. When these five candidates are excluded, the candidates tweeted an average of four times per day. Some users

TABLE 12.1

Candidates, Twitter activity, and tweet content, last month of 2015 federal campaign

Candidate information		Twitter activity			Type of tweet			Broadcast messages	
Candidate	Party	Followers	Total tweets	Tweets per day	Social (%)	Broadcast (%)	Total messages	National messages (%)	Local messages (%)
Bonavista–Burin–Trinity (Newfoundland)									
Jenn Brown	NDP	676	114	4	73	27	36	81	19
Judy Foote	LPC	378	284	9	45	55	167	75	25
Bruce–Grey–Owen Sound (Ontario)									
David McLaren	NDP	246	124	4	23	77	101	49	51
Chris Albinati	GP	345	154	5	54	46	71	69	31
Kimberley Love	LPC	827	244	8	45	55	138	65	35
Larry Miller	CPC	2,879	1,024	34	87	13	131	21	79
Calgary Centre (Alberta)									
Jillian Ratti	NDP	533	257	9	58	42	117	58	42
Joan Crockett	CPC	6,803	73	2	42	58	44	32	68
Kent Hehr	LPC	11,000	533	18	64	36	199	26	74
Thana Boolert	GP	248	66	2	65	35	23	35	65
Central Nova (Nova Scotia)									
Fred DeLorey	CPC	3,560	16	1	6	94	15	33	67
Sean Fraser	LPC	490	160	5	46	54	90	37	63
David Hachey	GP	230	94	3	34	66	68	69	31
Ross Landry	NDP	196	107	4	44	56	63	41	59
Charleswood–St. James–Assiniboia–Headingley (Manitoba)									
Doug Eyolfson	LPC	381	101	3	58	42	42	40	60
Kevin Nichols	GP	110	675	23	74	26	177	92	8
Steven Fletcher	CPC	5,960	16	1	81	19	3	33	67

Fleetwood–Port Kells (British Columbia)

Gary Begg	NDP	252	16	1	44	56	9	0	100
Ken Hardie	LPC	2,827	139	5	37	63	90	64	36
Nina Grewal	CPC	20,793	38	1	0	100	38	66	34
Richard Hosein	GP	751	190	6	55	45	86	85	15

Foothills (Alberta)

Alison Thompson	NDP	1,091	204	7	17	83	177	34	66
John Barlow	CPC	2,329	6	0	33	67	4	0	100
Tanya McPherson	LPC	80	36	1	44	56	20	65	35
Romy Tittel	GP	880	101	3	11	89	92	52	48

New Westminster–Burnaby (British Columbia)

Chloe Ellis	CPC	206	30	1	30	70	21	52	48
Kyle Routledge	GP	105	113	4	65	35	39	74	26
Peter Julian	NDP	9,638	283	9	77	23	66	92	8
Sasha Ramnarine	LPC	341	57	2	25	75	46	41	59

University–Rosedale (Ontario)

Chrystia Freeland	LPC	32,569	992	33	71	29	303	23	77
Jennifer Hollett	NDP	10,162	1,063	35	72	29	315	22	78
Karim Jivraj	CPC	676	144	5	69	31	48	6	94

Winnipeg South Centre (Manitoba)

Andrew Park	GP	135	9	0	11	89	8	63	37
Jim Carr	LPC	1,163	178	6	19	81	145	50	50
Joyce Bateman	CPC	1,145	24	1	8	92	22	64	36
Matt Henderson	NDP	466	29	1	28	72	24	21	79
Total		120,471	7,694	–	–	–	3,038	1,730	1,870
Average		3,346	214	7	45	55	84	48	52

NOTE: Bold print indicates the winner; italics indicate the incumbent.

TABLE 12.2

Percentage of local election candidates by Twitter follower and tweet count, 2015

Followers			Tweets		
Follower count	Candidates (N)	(%)	Average tweets per day	Candidates (N)	(%)
80–499	17	(47)	< 1	2	(17)
500–1,000	5	(14)	1–3	14	(19)
1,000–5,000	7	(19)	4–5	8	(25)
5,000–10,000	3	(8)	6–15	7	(25)
10,000+	4	(11)	15+	5	(14)
Total candidates	36	(100)	Total candidates	36	(100)
Total followers	12,471		Total tweets	7,694	
Average	3,346		Average per day	7	

did not tweet often, and ten of the thirty-six candidates tweeted once or less per day. A closer inspection of the data suggests no relationship between the number of tweets and the number of followers. For example, Kevin Nichols (GP, Charleswood–St. James–Assiniboia–Headingley) tweeted almost 700 times but had only 110 followers. A clear trend was that, despite their relatively high number of followers, many Conservative Party incumbents did not tweet all that often. Joan Crockett (Calgary Centre), despite having 6,803 followers, tweeted on average just over twice a day; Nina Grewal (Fleetwood–Port Kells), who had 20,793 followers, tweeted on average just over once a day; and Stephen Fletcher (Charleswood–St. James–Assiniboia–Headingley) and Joyce Bateman (Winnipeg South Centre) tweeted on average less than once per day despite having 5,960 and 1,145 followers, respectively. This result was somewhat surprising since we expected incumbent MPs to be engaged with constituents. Perhaps these candidates were more likely to focus their energies in offline campaign activities. However, five of the ten winners were in the top nine in terms of the number of tweets. We are not suggesting that Twitter use was a prerequisite to winning the campaign (and John Barlow (CPC, Foothills) registered the fewest tweets of the candidates in our study and still won by an overwhelming majority), but perhaps a high number of tweets is a feature of more competitive campaigns. Clearly, at least as far as challengers are concerned, as their campaigns become more competitive, they communicate more. This supports the findings of previous studies on the association between Twitter use and electoral success among municipal candidates in Ontario (Hagar 2015) and candidates in the Netherlands (Kruikemeier 2014).

As discussed, one common debate in the literature is the extent to which political actors take advantage of the democratic potential presented by social media. When all tweets are considered, local candidates were more likely to be social (62 percent) than focused on one-way information dissemination. However, when we look at the average percentage of each candidate's tweets, we see that social tweets comprise only 45 percent of the tweets. That is, some "heavy users" such as Kevin Nichols (GP, Charleswood–St. James–Assiniboia–Headingley) and Peter Julian (NDP, New Westminster–Burnaby) are very social compared with other candidates, and as outliers they increased the number and proportion of social tweets for the sample.

Of the social tweets, candidates were far more likely to retweet than to have a directed conversation (@reply). Only 16 percent of all the social tweets were @replies, whereas 84 percent of these tweets were retweets. Nine of the thirty-six candidates had over half of their total number of tweets comprising retweets, but only three candidates had a quarter or more of their total tweets comprising @replies (Kyle Routledge: 40 percent; Ken Hardie: 25 percent; Gary Begg: 25 percent), though none of these candidates had more than 140 total tweets. These findings suggest that local candidates were indeed using Twitter in an interactive capacity at least some of the time. Moreover, they show that candidates were more likely to be engaged in listening than conversing on Twitter. This finding runs contrary to studies that focus on party leaders' use of Twitter (Small 2010, 2015), and perhaps the more local the campaign the more social Twitter campaigns become. This makes sense since a party leader has a much larger constituency than a local candidate, so locally there is more opportunity to engage socially, and directly, with constituents/followers.

Overall, 38 percent of all tweets were "broadcast" in nature. This includes retweets of party leaders and official party accounts. Although candidates engaged in the interactive capacities of Twitter, these results show that they also regularly used it as a forum to disseminate one-sided information.

The third objective of this chapter is to contribute to the broader discussion about candidate personalization. Candidates used Twitter to engage in both local and national campaigns. However, few of the candidates used this type of social media as a forum to introduce themselves on a personal level to the electorate. This is somewhat surprising since we assumed that

Twitter, being a free medium of communication, could provide a forum for all candidates to present their messages locally and personally. Less than 2 percent of all the messages in the tweets related to information such as introducing family members, mentioning locations where the candidates lived or grew up, and presenting past and present work experiences. Freeland (LPC, University–Rosedale) tweeted the largest number of personal messages, mostly introducing voters to various members of her family.

Although personalized messages were rare, just over half (53 percent) of all broadcast tweets were dedicated to the local campaign in some way. These tweets included status updates; information on events; information about the local campaign, such as acknowledging volunteers and supporters; personal information about the candidate; criticisms of local opponents; or appeals to vote for the candidate specifically. This finding differs from studies that look at local campaigns on the ground, which suggest that the national campaign is the focus of most local campaigns (Cross et al. 2015). Although the local Twitterverse campaigns did pay attention to national politics and party leaders, this medium of communication has clearly made it possible for candidates, "star" and non-"star" alike (Sayers 1999), to present a local focus in at least one element of their overall campaigns.

Of the local broadcast tweets, candidates were most likely to provide status updates. These updates generally referred to where the candidate was in the riding and often included an endorsement of a local business or organization. This type of update left a trail showing all of the specific neighbourhoods and towns that candidates had visited, allowing them to pay homage as well as to prove that they had visited different areas of the riding. A further outcome of this type of update was that, for many candidates, they posted either where they were going or where they were, which in theory would allow voters to come and meet them if they chose to do so. One trend especially prominent in University–Rosedale, the riding with the greatest amount of Twitter activity, was that these status updates included references to specific people whom the candidate had engaged with, often including details about the topics of conversation. This type of update adds an element of transparency to these campaigns since it not only informs voters where candidates are but also presumably indicates which issues the candidates and other voters deem important in the riding. It is unlikely that a candidate would announce having a conversation with a constituent about an overly contentious topic on which they have opposing views. It has long been common for political leaders to mention in speeches specific people to whom they have spoken, but linking such references to an actual user's account brings a new level of transparency and verification to candidates' communications.

Candidates also used Twitter to highlight the work of their campaign team. It was common for candidates to explicitly tag volunteers to provide thanks for helping with campaign activities such as canvassing or erecting signs. Kent Hehr (LPC, Calgary Centre) – even played a song game in which various volunteers selected a song for the day, and he would announce the song, and the volunteer, on his Twitter account. This type of public acknowledgment can increase political activity in the future since followers with an interest in politics receive information via acknowledgment tweets about the people who participate in campaigns and details about the type of work that they assist with. In addition, some candidates, such as Doug Eyolfson (LPC, Charleswood–St. James–Assiniboia–Headingley), regularly included logistical information, such as telephone numbers and meeting locations, which allowed interested followers to immediately participate in campaign activities. This type of request takes interaction to the next level since candidates are not only engaging followers to discuss political issues but also inviting them to participate in the campaigns. Accepting this invitation allows followers to meet the candidates and other campaign volunteers as well as other members of the electorate, depending on the activity.

Despite locally focused tweets, very few candidates emphasized local political issues. Rarely were important issues brought up that related, for instance, to economic regulation of a local industry. Rather, local messages were mainly geared to making status updates, announcing endorsements, and thanking volunteers. In addition, though it was relatively rare, when candidates engaged in negative critiques, they were likely to focus on other parties' policies or leaders rather than on local opponents. Thus, it appears that, in terms of the local campaign, the messages are kept light. This supports the finding of Douglas Hagar (2015), who also saw this type of information being tweeted in Ontario municipal campaigns. Although Hagar found these types of messages to be superficial, for local candidates at the federal level the conversations about deeper issues of election politics that could be discussed between candidates and party elites are not broadcast on such a transparent platform as Twitter. Nonetheless, these superficial messages do play an important role, for they inform the voter about where the candidate is and provide updates about activities taking place and ways that interested followers can become involved.

Although candidates use Twitter to promote their local activities, about half (47 percent) of all their broadcasting messages related to the national campaign and election. Unlike local tweets, these messages focused on opinions about other parties' policies, calls for changes in policy, and government operations, highlighting the party's position on a platform issue and retweeting the leader and official party communications. Green Party members often focused their tweets on political opinions about environmental issues, whereas Liberal Party and NDP candidates often retweeted their leaders' and parties' official Twitter accounts. The Conservative Party members were the least likely to post national campaign messages, perhaps because, as the incumbent governing party, they were in the position of having to defend policy.

Overall, our case study has shown that political candidates use Twitter as a regular component of their campaigns and that they regularly engage in an interactive, dialogic mode of communication when tweeting. As noted, though our findings are similar to studies conducted at the municipal level, they differ from studies of digital social media within national and provincial campaigns. Moreover, local candidates certainly use their Twitter accounts to promote their parties' national campaigns, but they are as likely to feature local elements, suggesting that, though Twitter is not necessarily being used to convey information about the local candidate's persona, it is being used to highlight the local campaign.

Political Elites in Canada in the Digital Age

When it comes to election campaigning, it is easy to forget that local candidates are indeed important political elites in Canada. This is because most Canadians experience election campaigns through the lens of the news media, largely focused on national coverage. As David Taras (1990) notes, when it comes to election news coverage, the media are heavily fixated on the national campaign and leaders. Unless there is a star candidate or a highly competitive race, local politics receive little media attention (Cross et al. 2015). Local media coverage focuses more on local candidates, but this coverage is not as in-depth and constant as the national coverage. This lack of attention is concerning since local candidates carry the messages of their party to their constituents and convey their constituents' opinions back to the party elite. Candidates also act as the local faces of the party, with many constituents identifying candidates as points of contact to get in touch with a political party and those who can provide both national and local political information.

Twitter, as our case study has shown, provides local candidates with a novel, unmediated way to communicate with their supporters. Indeed, almost all of the major party candidates in our sample had a Twitter account, and almost all of them tweeted daily. It certainly appears that maintaining a Twitter account has become a normal element of local political campaigns. Our study found that, though Twitter was a normal part of local campaigns, its use varied considerably. Furthermore, competitive status was not necessarily associated with the number of followers that one had on Twitter. However, this finding must be accompanied by an important caveat: many of the less competitive candidates in our sample did not garner large followings. Thus, though they were easily able to disseminate their messages via Twitter, it does not follow that these messages necessarily reached their desired audiences. The variance in Twitter use and number of followers likely also reflects the varying technical abilities of candidates and their levels of support since tweeting can be a time-consuming activity. This does not differ much from more traditional sources of communication, for candidates have differing abilities to deliver traditional materials and can never guarantee that their constituents will be captivated by a newspaper advertisement or look over a hand-delivered campaign brochure.

Local candidates use Twitter, at least some of the time, as a form of interactive communication. This finding differs from previous studies concluding that Canadian political actors at the national level, such as parties and party leaders, were more likely to use social media in a top-down, broadcasting capacity. This suggests that local candidates might have a special niche with voters since they can use digital technologies such as Twitter for meaningful communications with the smaller populations that they serve. Although national leaders can also engage directly with voters via their Twitter accounts, their follower counts are often in the millions, which makes contacting all of those who initiate dialogues with them difficult if not impossible. In addition, this type of public communication might not be their priority. This forum provides benefits to both candidates and their constituents since it is accessible, timely, and can be used to engage other users to increase political dialogue.

Two key findings emerged from our data regarding interactions with followers. Regarding social tweets, the candidates were far more likely to retweet than they were to engage in direct dialogue. This is important because our study excluded retweets from the candidate's party and leader from this category. Thus, for many of these retweets, candidates were likely giving their constituents a public forum via their Twitter accounts to voice their opinions. Because elected members are supposed to represent their local constituents, this enhances democracy since candidates can show their party, leader, and the public (rather than just make claims) how their constituents feel on a given issue and how they support that sentiment. We also found that candidates who dedicated more of their messages to directed dialogues were associated with winning campaigns. This suggests that, at the local level, at least for our sample, candidates who engage with their constituents are rewarded. This can spur local engagement, thereby increasing the quality of democracy in Canada, as candidates become more aware of this winning strategy.

The candidates in our study rarely used their Twitter accounts to publicize information about themselves. However, though the Twitter campaigns were not personalized in the sense of focusing on the candidates, they certainly were localized. Half of all the broadcast messages were local in nature, which sends a clear message that candidates were localizing their campaigns, at least in the Twitterverse, and not just highlighting their national party's message and leader. This finding contradicts previous literature suggesting that the national campaign is of utmost importance, even in local ridings. These localized messages tended to focus on the candidates' whereabouts and who was helping with their local efforts. At the least, this demonstrates to constituents where the candidate is, shows the character of the local campaign, and offers the opportunity for followers to participate in it. One note about these localized messages is that they are arguably superficial. Rarely did candidates use Twitter to discuss the needs of their specific localities, let alone highlight for their constituents how their party's platform would benefit their regional needs. Thus, though tweets were used to show that the local candidate was actively campaigning locally, at least for those in our sample, Twitter was not a forum in which to engage citizens on the deeper issues of decision making. This reinforces Cristine de Clercy's findings in Chapter 8 of this volume regarding the discipline that leaders impose. Once party policy is set, candidates broadcast it rather than seek citizen engagement on the details.

It is questionable whether the use of Twitter in local election campaigns has affected candidates' accountability, and their level of transparency, in regard to positions on political issues and their associations. Because of the public nature of Twitter, all tweets theoretically hold a candidate to account, yet we find this claim questionable. Follower numbers for most of the candidates were small. Moreover, our data show that few controversial exchanges emerged between candidates and followers. This is curious, and candidates likely deleted negative tweets addressed to them, either dealing with them privately through direct messaging or simply ignoring them. Thus, though Twitter is theoretically a technology that allows citizens to engage candidates in transparent dialogues, it is obvious that candidates have found ways to skirt the public nature of this technology. Two trends did emerge from our data that demonstrated how this social medium can enhance the transparency of local campaigns. First, the majority of all local messages were status updates. Thus, candidates were announcing where they were (and were not) visiting in their ridings. Since Canada's political representation is geographically based, this can be important as citizens can note who pays attention to their areas of residence. Second, many of the candidates communicated about whom they were speaking with, what they were speaking about, and who was supporting their campaigns. Doing so also adds an element of transparency, for one can infer levels of support and issues of importance from these tweets. Twitter is being used to increase democracy in Canada in that it presents an opportunity for everyday citizens to publicly declare their electoral support. Candidates often tagged regular citizens as being part of their campaign teams or those voting for them. Endorsements have traditionally been reserved for prominent members of society. Twitter offers a medium for this type of political activity to become available to the masses.

Our study has shown that local candidates, compared with party leaders, seem to be using Twitter a little differently since they regularly engaged with their followers. These candidates used Twitter to localize, but not personalize, their online campaigns. In terms of Twitter fostering democratic decision making, we did not find any evidence to suggest that candidates, even those with high profiles, used Twitter to engage constituents on issues of local importance. Our study suggests that local candidates use Twitter as a tool to advertise locally the campaign as preset at the national level.

NOTE

1 A few candidates are missing from our analysis either because they entered the race after we started to collect data or because we could not locate Twitter accounts for

them. These candidates included Tom Paulley (NDP) from Charleswood–St. James–Assiniboia–Headingley, Nick Wright (GP) from University–Rosedale, and Mike Windsor (CPC) and Tyler Colbourne (GP) from Bonavista–Burin–Trinity.

REFERENCES

Adam, Silke, and Michaela Maier. 2010. "Personalization of Politics: A Critical Review and Agenda for Research." In *Communication Yearbook 34,* edited by Charles Salmon, 213–57. London: Routledge. https://doi.org/10.1080/23808985.2010.11679101.

Bekafigo, Marija Anna, and Allan McBride. 2013. "Who Tweets about Politics? Political Participation of Twitter Users during the 2011 Gubernatorial Elections." *Social Science Computer Review* 31, 5: 625–43. https://doi.org/10.1177/0894439313490405.

Black, Jerome H., and Lynda Erickson. 2000. "Similarity, Compensation, or Difference? A Comparison of Female and Male Office-Seekers." *Women and Politics* 21, 4: 1–38. https://doi.org/10.1300/J014v21n04_01.

Blais, André, Elisabeth Gidengil, Agnieszka Dobrynska, Neal Nevitte, and Richard Nadeau. 2003. "Does the Local Candidate Matter? Candidate Effects in the Canadian Election of 2000." *Canadian Journal of Political Science* 36, 3: 657–64. https://doi.org/10.1017/S0008423903778810.

Carty, R. Kenneth, and Munroe Eagles. 2005. *Politics Is Local: National Politics at the Grassroots.* Toronto: Oxford University Press.

Coletto, David. 2010. "A Matter of Quality? Candidates in Canadian Constituency Elections." PhD diss., Department of Political Science, University of Calgary.

Cross, William, Jonathan Malloy, Tamara A. Small, and Laura B. Stephenson. 2015. *Fighting for Votes: Parties, the Media, and Voters in the 2011 Ontario Election.* Vancouver: UBC Press.

Cross, William, and Lisa Young. 2015. "Personalization of Campaigns in an SMP System: The Canadian Case." *Electoral Studies* 39: 306–15. https://doi.org/10.1016/j.electstud.2014.04.007.

Effing, Robin, Jos van Hillegersberg, and Theo Huibers. 2011. "Social Media and Political Participation: Are Facebook, Twitter, and YouTube Democratizing Our Political Systems?" In *Electronic Participation: Third IFIP WG 8.5 International Conference, ePart 2011,* edited by Efthimios Tambouris, Ann Macintosh, and Hans de Bruijn, 25–35. Berlin: Springer. https://doi.org/10.1007/978-3-642-23333-3_3.

Flanagan, Tom. 2014. *Winning Power: Canadian Campaigning in the 21st Century.* Montreal: McGill-Queen's University Press.

Francoli, Mary, Josh Greenberg, and Christopher Waddell. 2012. "The Campaign in the Digital Media." In *The Canadian Federal Election of 2011,* edited by Jon H. Pammett and Christopher Dornan, 219–46. Toronto: Dundurn Press.

Gaber, Ivor. 2016. "Twitter: A Useful Tool for Studying Elections?" *Convergence: The International Journal of Research into New Media Technologies* 26, 6: 603–26. http://journals.sagepub.com/doi/abs/10.1177/1354856516646544.

Giasson, Thierry, Gildas LeBars, Frédérick Bastien, and Mélanie Verville. 2013. "#Qc2012: L'utilisation de Twitter par les partis." In *Les Québécois aux urnes: Les partis, les médias, et les citoyens en campagne,* edited by Éric Bélanger, Frédérick Bastien, and François Gélineau, 133–46. Montréal: Les Presses de l'Université de Montréal.

Grant, Will J., Brenda Moon, and Janie Busby Grant. 2010. "Digital Dialogue? Australian Politicians' Use of the Social Network Tool Twitter." *Australian Journal of Political Science* 45, 4: 579–604. https://doi.org/10.1080/10361146.2010.517176.

Hagar, Douglas. 2014. "Campaigning Online: Social Media in the 2010 Niagara Municipal Elections." *Canadian Journal of Urban Research* 23: 74–98>.

–. 2015. "#vote4me: The Impact of Twitter on Municipal Campaign Success." In *Proceedings of the 2015 International Conference on Social Media and Society*, 1–7. New York: Association for Computing Machinery. https://doi.org/10.1145/2789187.2789190.

Hosch-Dayican, Bengü, Chintan Amrit, Kees Aarts, and Adrie Dassen. 2016. "How Do Online Citizens Persuade Fellow Voters? Using Twitter during the 2012 Dutch Parliamentary Election Campaign." *Social Science Computer Review* 34, 2: 135–52. https://doi.org/10.1177/0894439314558200.

Kruikemeier, Sanne. 2014. "How Political Candidates Use Twitter and the Impact on Votes." *Computers in Human Behavior* 34: 131–39. https://doi.org/10.1016/j.chb.2014.01.025.

Murthy, Dhiraj, and Laura R. Petto. 2015. "Comparing Print Coverage and Tweets in Elections: A Case Study of the 2011–2012 US Republican Primaries." *Social Science Computer Review* 33, 3: 298–314. https://doi.org/10.1177/0894439314541925.

Parmelee, John H., and Shannon L. Bichard. 2011. *Politics and the Twitter Revolution: How Tweets Influence the Relationship between Political Leaders and the Public*. Lanham, MD: Lexington Books.

Pellegrini, Christina. 2016. "Twitter's New Canadian Chief: 'We Have a Ton of Work to Do.'" *Financial Post*, February 18. http://business.financialpost.com/technology/twitters-new-canadian-chief-we-have-a-ton-of-work-to-do.

Sayers, Anthony. 1999. *Parties, Candidates, and Constituency Campaigns in Canadian Elections*. Vancouver: UBC Press.

Small, Tamara A. 2010. "Canadian Politics in 140 Characters: Party Politics in the Twitterverse." *Canadian Parliamentary Review* 33, 3: 39–45.

–. 2014. "The Not-So Social Network: The Use of Twitter by Canada's Party Leaders." In *Political Communication in Canada: Meet the Press and Tweet the Rest*, edited by Alex Marland, Thierry Giasson, and Tamara A. Small, 92–108. Vancouver: UBC Press.

Small, Tamara A., and Thierry Giasson. 2014. "#elections: The Use of Twitter by Provincial Political Parties in Canada." Paper presented at the meeting of the British Association of Canadian Studies, London, April 25–26.

Stromer-Galley, Jennifer. 2014. *Presidential Campaigning in the Internet Age*. New York: Oxford University Press. https://doi.org/10.1093/acprof:oso/9780199731930.001.0001.

Tapscott, Don. 2009. *Grown Up Digital: How the Net Generation Is Changing Your World*. New York: McGraw-Hill.

Taras, David. 1990. *The Newsmakers: The Media's Influence on Canadian Politics*. Scarborough, ON: Nelson Canada.

Towner, Terri L. 2012. "Campaigns and Elections in a Web 2.0 World: Uses, Effects, and Implications for Democracy." In *Web 2.0 Technologies and Democratic Governance: Political, Policy, and Management Implications*, edited by C.G. Reddick

and S.K. Aikins, 185–99. New York: Springer. https://doi.org/10.1007/978-1-4614
-1448-3_12.

Tumasjan, Andranik, Timm O. Sprenger, Philipp G. Sander, and Isabell M. Welpe. 2010.
"Predicting Elections with Twitter: What 140 Characters Reveal about Political
Sentiment." *ICWSM* 10: 178–85.

Ward, Stephen J., Rachel Kay Gibson, and Paul G. Nixon. 2003. "Parties and the Internet:
An Overview." In *Political Parties and the Internet: Net Gain?,* edited by Rachel Kay
Gibson, Paul G. Nixon, and Stephen J. Ward, 11–38. London: Routledge.

13

Going Digital: Non-Profit Organizations in a Transformed Media Environment

Rachel Laforest

The digital landscape in Canada has evolved exponentially over the past twenty years and has led to significant changes in every aspect of political life. The proliferation of internet use, the expansion of social sharing networks, the digitalization of information, and the greater reach of communications technologies are now defining characteristics of the contemporary era. Political communications scholar Manuel Castells (2015, 7) refers to this era as that of the network society in which "power is multidimensional and is organized around networks programmed in each domain of human activity according to the interests and values of empowered actors." In this new context, digital technologies provide the platforms that enable social actors to act autonomously and to challenge the institutions of society. There is an increasing perception in the field that traditional forms of participation are on the wane. New funding trends, aided by digital communications technologies, have encouraged organizations to shift to more informal, horizontal, and loose patterns of organized interests. Although Castells and others, such as Paolo Gerbaudo (2012), have written on how these trends have enabled individuals to effect changes through social movements, this chapter extends the analysis to non-profit organizations, understood here as social actors that exert an enormous influence on the political arena both through their advocacy work and through their service delivery function.

The study of non-profit organizations is crucial to the understanding of political elites in Canada. The non-profit sector in Canada is large, complex, and diverse, from foundations and charities to voluntary organizations and community groups. According to the 2003 National Survey of Nonprofit and Voluntary Organizations, there are over 170,000 non-profit organizations in Canada (Hall et al. 2004). The non-profit sector is a significant social, political, and economic force in Canada. It accounts for 8.5 percent of the gross domestic product (GDP), and has a full-time equivalent workforce of over

2 million, employing 12 percent of Canada's economically active population (Hall et al. 2004). More importantly, it brings value to all aspects of communities and has a direct impact on the quality of life of Canadians. It is important to remember as well that ten years ago the term "digital" was virtually unknown in the non-profit sector. Organizations were just beginning to focus on developing web presences. As a result, we know little about how non-profit organizations are coping with changes in digital media technology and how those changes are affecting their relationships with citizens and governments.

Non-profit organizations are political elites in the sense that they play an important role in public policy debates. Our political system is dependent on non-profits to aggregate the interests of the people whom they serve and to articulate those interests before the state. Since many social services have been contracted to non-profit providers, the relationship between the government and the sector has become increasingly intertwined. Influencing legislation, for example, is an important strategy that non-profit organizations use to advance their causes or the interests of their members. Not all advocacy strategies, however, are directed toward the state. Non-profit organizations also try to influence citizen opinions on policy matters and encourage citizens to contact legislators. So it is important to examine how digital technologies have revolutionized the communications space between the government and non-profits and between non-profits and the broader public.

Working from a neo-institutionalist theoretical perspective, this chapter focuses on the changing social, economic, political, and institutional conditions that have shaped, and been shaped by, the strategies that leaders in the non-profit sector adopt. The neo-institutionalist theoretical framework has deeply influenced non-profit scholarship and organizational thinking (Powell and DiMaggio 1991). Kathleen Thelen (1999, 395) notes that "rather than taking the interests of political actors as given ... authors step back to ask how groups originally got constituted in the particular ways they did, then to consider how this affects the group's understanding and pursuit of their interests." As this quotation illustrates, organizations embody rules and norms that influence how resources are allocated and how incentives are structured at a particular point in time.

Neo-institutionalists also view non-profits as constantly trying to carve out niches for themselves. Given that these organizations emerge to represent multiple interests, and work on issues that can be intangible to measure, non-profits constantly try to juggle competing demands and diffuse goals, all while trying to survive operationally and gain legitimacy. It follows that their understanding of legitimacy and their reading of the social and political environment really matter, for they will affect the strategies adopted (Meyer and Rowan 1977).

The contribution of this theory to understanding the impact of the digital era on non-profit strategies is important because it draws attention to the role of ideas. Although the adoption of new technologies and tools is on the rise, it is important to recognize that an emphasis on digital approaches to communication, program implementation, and evaluation can lead to cultural shifts within the sector. Theda Skocpol's seminal work (2003) illustrated how the use of direct mass-mailing fundraising and recruitment methods by national advocacy organizations was profoundly changing the face of civil society in America. This new tool allowed large organizations with resources to engage with a huge number of members through the mail. It led to greater professionalization and created a disconnect between members and the executive (management body) of the organization. Since members no longer engaged in the organization but sent cheques, they became "members" in name only. Organizational theorists, such as Connie Gersick (1991), describe times when organizations break structural and cultural inertia as revolutionary periods. They attribute these disruptions to two main causes: a misalignment of internal changes with the environment and environmental changes that threaten the ability of the organization to obtain resources. Indeed, financial considerations are paramount for organizational survival (Saidel 1991), and they help us to understand the behaviour of non-profit organizations as they respond to changes in their environments to secure resources and to differentiate themselves (Pfeffer and Salancik 1978).

When using a neo-institutional lens, the first observation to make is that funding pressures, as well as social and political dynamics, influence the ability of non-profits to adapt to the new digital era. Typically, non-profit organizations rely on three main sources of revenue: government funding, charitable donations, and earned income. Over the past decades, the federal government and the provincial governments have had to deal with serious budgetary constraints. Federal government expenditures, as a percentage of the GDP, decreased from 23.4 percent in 1992 to 14.6 percent in 2013.[1] The deficit reduction measures implemented in the late 1990s translated into a reduction in contributions from various levels of government, both provincial and municipal, to the non-profit sector. Paradoxically, this shift occurred at a time when many of the services formerly provided by the government were being reduced or transferred to non-profits, the assumption being that they would have the capacities and resources to take on this additional burden. What is more, new norms for advocacy have been embodied in drastic funding cuts to organizations deemed too political and in a progressive tightening of rules for charities' political activities (Laforest 2013; Levasseur 2012). The 2008 economic crisis also hit the sector hard; demand for services surged, charitable donations shrank, and foundations suspended grants to protect their endowments (Imagine Canada 2010). Almost half of organizations reported having difficulty fulfilling their missions, and more than one in five reported that their very existence was at risk, according to Imagine Canada, the national umbrella for the non-profit sector.

Moreover, because of the important role of non-profits in the public policy process and the influence that they can exert, the government has long regulated their activities. However, this space further constricted under the government of Stephen Harper, particularly for certain non-profits that opposed the government in the fields of the environment, human rights, and international development charities, when more than $13 million was dedicated to increased reporting and auditing of non-profit advocacy activities. It matters how such regulatory activities affect the non-profit sector's ability to represent its constituents before the government. Although the newly elected government of Justin Trudeau quickly put a stop to these audits, the advocacy chill had reverberated within the sector.

These uncertainties brought on by the political environment pose a number of challenges to non-profit organizations in Canada. Not surprisingly, Georgina Grosenick (2014, 184) observed that they have been slow to adapt to new digital technologies in this context of shrinking resources and advocacy "chill": "Non-profit organizations are abandoning or underutilizing social and new media forums and their potential to create and sustain media and public debate about their issues and to connect with external audiences."

Mario Levesque (2017) also noted these challenges, yet he found that digital communications is critical for non-profit organizations in the field of disability. Email blitzes, online communications for event planning, and online meetings were all tools that he identified as being used by non-profit organizations.

Although our understanding of how these new communications tools are affecting organizational strategies within the non-profit sector is limited, we do know that the use of digital technologies by citizens themselves has increased over this period of time. Citizens are increasingly engaging with non-profits through digital technologies. According to the latest General Social Survey (Statistics Canada 2015), a growing number of citizens – 44 percent in 2013 compared with 23 percent in 2003 – report using the internet to interact with organizations of which they are members. The forms of engagement that they reported using most frequently were emails, blogs, forums, and social networks (59 percent), knowledge and information sharing (58 percent), and activity organizing and scheduling (53 percent) (Statistics Canada 2015). There are certainly growing opportunities to engage with non-profits via the internet, yet Tamara Small and her colleagues (2014), who specifically researched patterns of online political activity in Canada, found little evidence to suggest that these opportunities were taken advantage of by large numbers of citizens.

What is more, there is no evidence that increased use of digital technologies has translated into more members for non-profit organizations. In 2015, nearly two in three Canadians were members of or participants in a group, organization, or association (65 percent), up only slightly from 2003 (61 percent). Some research suggests that the need for formal membership, as an organizational construct, has become outdated. Clay Shirky (2009) suggests that, as informal channels of influence expand, demands for formalized spaces of policy discussion decline because new technologies have made "organizing without organizations possible." Clearly, new digital communications tools can make significant impacts on the organizational front by redesigning the nature of the relationship between non-profit organizations and citizens. Hence, it is important to turn now to actual data to see how this relationship has unfolded in Canada.

Case Study

This chapter examines the use of digital technologies by non-profit organizations in Canada. The unit of analysis is the *organization* rather than individual citizen behaviour – a departure from the typical work on digital technologies, which has tended to focus on microlevel data. The focus is on the leadership, and organizations that have innovated by taking full advantage of digital technology, drawing out the challenges that have emerged on an organizational front. In a digital era, in which the organizational structure and tools used are very different, it is not enough to simply count how many people engage with non-profits on Twitter or Facebook. Rather, it is important to understand how these new channels are reshaping the relationship between them. This means examining the types of organizations that have flourished in the digital era and considering the impacts that these changes have had on Canadian democracy.

METHOD

One of the challenges of studying non-profit organizations in Canada is that the field of research is empirically weak. Partly because of the multidisciplinary nature of this field of study, it is challenging to delimit the object of study in order to precisely define the common characteristics of organizations. To this day, various names are used to describe the institutions and practices not within either the public domain or the private domain. The existing definitions speak of "interest groups," "civil society groups," "community organizations," "voluntary sector organizations," "non-profit organizations," and "social movements." In this chapter, the term "non-profit organization" is used in its broadest sense to refer to organizations in civil society whose purpose is something other than making a profit. If a non-profit organization makes a profit, it will use that profit to advance its mission for the benefit of the public. Moreover, there are relatively few quantitative data sets available because of measurement difficulties, for many organizational types (e.g., charities, foundations, voluntary organizations) fall under the umbrella of the non-profit sector. As a result, much of the research in the field adopts smaller-scale analyses, focusing on one specific policy area or decision. Large data sets on the non-profit sector are also expensive to gather given the size and scope of the sector. There are only a few institutionally financed data sets on political participation available in Canada through Statistics Canada surveys. The Canadian Survey of Giving, Volunteering, and Participating, conducted by Statistics Canada in 1997, 2000, 2004, and 2007, includes data on volunteer activities, charitable giving, and civic participation collected from over 13,000 respondents. Unfortunately, for the purposes of this chapter, these data sources provide no information on digital technologies because they are dated.

To overcome the lack of data, a two-pronged methodological approach was used. First, the grey literature was surveyed to find material and research on digital technologies produced by organizations within the non-profit sector. The term "grey literature" refers to publications and reports produced outside traditional academic and commercial publishing. It generally includes material produced by different levels of government, non-profit groups, think tanks, private companies, and consultants. Three research reports were identified: the *2015 Digital Outlook Report,* the *2014 State of the Canadian Web Nation Benchmark Report,* and website audits conducted by the non-profit organization Framework. The *2015 Digital Outlook Report* collected data from 473 non-profit leaders, 127 of which are based in Canada. The report provides data on digital strategies adopted by non-profits and isolates Canadian data on the matter. It was published by Care2, a privately held B-corporation that helps non-profits to develop online platforms and recruit donors. A B-corporation is a certification by the non-profit B Lab for for-profit companies that use their business activities to effect social changes within communities and that meet high standards of accountability and transparency in so doing. The *2014 State of the Canadian Web Nation Benchmark Report* was based on data from 516 charities across Canada. A charity is a charitable organization or public or private foundation that can issue tax receipts for the donations that it receives because it is registered with the Canada Revenue Agency. It is considered part of the non-profit sector. The report provides data on web platforms and organizational support for website strategies. It was published by Good Works, a fundraising consultant that specializes in website strategies and digital fundraising. In 2014, Framework conducted audits of the websites of over 500 non-profit organizations. These audits analyzed user experience, content, and level of online engagement. Framework received funding from the Canadian Internet Registration Authority, which manages the .ca domain name registry. It has a direct interest in how websites are being used by non-profit organizations because it is a key provider.

These data are arguably limited for three reasons. First, the sample size in each report is small. The precision of the data on the use of digital technologies in the non-profit sector might be somewhat unreliable given the size and complexity of the sector in Canada. Second, the data are cross-sectional at a particular time and therefore cannot help us to identify the magnitude of change brought about by digital technologies. Third, the producers of the data have commercial interests served by publication of the reports. For these reasons, I opted to combine all three data sets at least to validate the directions of the trends identified in the reports. Taken together they provide some much-needed light on often invisible digital practices. As such, they provide a good benchmark to assess the extent to which the sector is using digital technologies. I complemented that analysis with six open-ended interviews, of ninety minutes each, conducted with leaders in the Canadian non-profit sector whose mission is to advance digital innovation. They are obviously innovators in their adoption of digital technologies, but this research strategy enabled me to shed light on what might be the factors of innovation within the sector. All of the organizations contacted agreed to participate in the study. The purpose of these interviews was to examine which digital technologies were being used within the sector and to explore how these new communications tools were reshaping relationships with the government and the broader public. Organizations were first asked to describe the tools that they were using and then to discuss the impacts of these new tools within and beyond the organizations. Although the sample size was small, these in-depth cases provided insights into the extent of organizational changes taking place within the sector as a result of the digital revolution. The cases were selected from the review of the grey literature that enabled me to identify key players and areas of innovation in the sector. The interviews were conducted between June and August 2016. They were recorded, and interviewees were assured anonymity.

FINDINGS
Although political and institutional environments have had constraining effects on non-profit organizations, much has changed at an organizational level in the non-profit sector over the past decade and at a rapid pace. Today the vast majority of non-profits have websites, use email marketing, and accept online donations. According to the *2015 Digital Outlook Report,* 94 percent of Canadian non-profits interviewed use email marketing strategies, 88 percent use Facebook, and 79 percent use Twitter. These new technologies are less expensive and easy to manage, thereby lowering the cost of collective action and expanding the potential reach of the organizations. In a context of funding cuts, it is not surprising to see Canadian non-profit organizations trying to leverage technologies to expand their reach. The *2014 State of the Canadian Web Nation Benchmark Report* found that 60 percent of respondents use a content management system to manage website content, and another 49 percent use a third-party bulk email system, such as

MailChimp. These data echo the audits launched by Framework, which revealed that 63 percent of organizations use a content management system to maintain their websites and that 86 percent collect donations online.

Digital technologies enable non-profit organizations to mobilize, organize, and publicize their grievances more effectively and efficiently by directing citizens to sign petitions, write letters, and launch phone call campaigns to politicians. Innovative tools of engagement have emerged that did not exist ten years ago, such as pledging support for a cause on social media and Twitter chats. As respondent five indicated, "one of the things that has been shown to have an impact is pledging to your friends and voting. Making 80,000 people pledge on Facebook, that costs us no money, and it is a neat viral campaign." Similarly, respondent two noted that hers was one of the first organizations to be on Twitter and to use it on a regular basis to start discussions. Now with over 29,000 Twitter followers, it organizes Twitter chats every six weeks and brings people together to discuss five or six questions to foster interaction. It gauges interest in the issue and attention that it receives, whether the conversation is trending, the number of tweets, and the number of participants. Clearly, non-profits are using social media to track and shape policy debates to their advantage.

However, such technologies need to be managed and streamlined into current operations to be used to their full potential. On average, non-profit organizations can use over twenty different software applications at any one point in time. The systems often do not work well together, and the data cannot be integrated across platforms. As an indicator, the *2014 State of the Canadian Web Nation Benchmark Report* showed that only 30 percent of the non-profit organizations surveyed had seamlessly connected their websites to social media such as Facebook, Twitter, and LinkedIn. To seamlessly integrate all of these platforms and tools requires some resources and adaptations that might not be within the reach of all organizations. In fact, most non-profits do not have support staff dedicated to communications or digital strategies. According to the *2015 Digital Outlook Report,* only 35 percent of Canadian non-profits, compared with 54 percent of American non-profits, had a staff person dedicated to digital strategy. Staff size is in fact a determinant of digital capacity. Organizational capacity appears to correlate with digital capacity. Indeed, the larger the staff, the more likely an organization is to have a dedicated staff member for digital strategy. With 74 percent of non-profit organizations in Canada having fewer than ten employees, and

53 percent fewer than five, it is not surprising that many organizations struggle to establish structures that enable digital technologies to reach their full potential.

These data are corroborated by the *2014 State of the Canadian Web Nation Benchmark Report,* which probed specifically into organizational support for digital strategies. It reported that, in 48 percent of Canadian organizations surveyed, the marketing and communications departments have primary control over website content. Only 19 percent of organizations share regular reports on their websites' performance, including traffic, donations, and referrals, with their own fundraising departments. That might explain why just 12 percent report that cross-departmental collaboration works well. As respondent one argued, "you need someone on the team who is again really embracing some of these new forms of working or shared understanding of what measurable impact is or how well the tools come together." Through these cross-departmental conversations, respondent five noted, "people are starting to realize, instead of using it for sharing data across organizations, why wouldn't you want to use it internally as well? Because then your fundraising department can get better access to your project updates all of a sudden." In the absence of these cross-departmental conversations, innovation or even acceptance of the new digital realities can be challenging.

Because my selection of cases prioritized innovators, the non-profit organizations that we interviewed had slightly different profiles. What made them so successful? First, and this was not anticipated prior to the selection of cases, all of the non-profit organizations interviewed were uniquely positioned to invest in digital technologies because they had sought funding from foundations or corporate donors. Finding resources to support the development and implementation of a digital strategy is important. Respondent three noted that "we've been lucky that one of our corporate donors has given us unrestricted funds as well as our family foundation, because it enables us to build in a long-term way." Respondent one stated that "I have been able to access and our team has been able to access financing in ways that the non-profit sector just cannot." The availability of these funds certainly explains their capacity to innovate. Many of the contribution agreements that define funding relationships between non-profit organizations and governments do not allow for the recovery of reasonable administrative and infrastructure costs such as those discussed in this chapter. With the rise of project base funding and the move away from core operational funding, a digital strategy is a luxury that many non-profits cannot afford (Laforest 2011). This speaks to the ability of these organizations to use digital technologies to position themselves in relation to other elites and to stand out from the crowd. Foundations and corporate donors obviously see them as leaders in the field and want to support their initiatives.

Second, the organizations interviewed for this chapter have been successful at navigating digital technologies because they have dedicated staff for the development and implementation of digital strategies. All had a social media person on staff who managed the online presence of the organization. As respondent six stated, "that means trying to stay ahead of the trends and see where digital marketing, digital engagement is moving towards," whereas respondent one noted that "digital strategy and social media should be treated by the organization as [a] time investment worthy as other pillars of the organization. Not just an afterthought, a very important thought of your success." In addition, these organizations were also willing to take risks and to experiment with new technologies, communication techniques, and platforms. Respondent five explained that "our first idea we quickly threw out and since then gone on, and we were good at figuring out what worked and what didn't work. We have lots of young people, so we got some really killer wins of use of social media." This freedom to experiment and take risks is linked to the financial security from which these organizations benefit, given their relationships with foundations and corporate donors. Because non-profit organizations are mission driven, they face public scrutiny, and it is difficult to divert resources to invest in technology.

Third, these organizations have unique relationships with the public because of their use of digital technologies. The need for formal membership, as an organizational construct, has indeed become outdated, as the literature suggests. Of the six organizations that I interviewed, none had an official membership list. It is important to recognize that these are not purpose-driven organizations in the traditional sense of organizations representing particular constituencies and pressing governments for changes on behalf of particular interests. Without clearly defined memberships, these organizations are not democratically controlled by members who hold them to account. This is a significant shift in terms of how non-profits use their power to influence the policy process and shape political debates. Although their power in the political arena is intensifying with their ability to leverage their followers, without membership bases this influence is episodic and issue specific.

Understanding how non-profits nurture their followers is therefore important. Thanks to new technologies, once individuals participate in an event, or sign up for a newsletter, their email addresses become part of a database that the organization can activate at any time to communicate content. The person becomes a "member." This approach has been facilitated by the use of customer relationship management (CRM) software to track the activities of nominal members. According to the *2014 State of the Canadian Web Nation Benchmark Report,* 21 percent of non-profit organizations surveyed now use CRM. Some CRM software uses bots to track trends, curate content to foster trends and sway the public, and increase the number of followers. Bots are automated scripts that produce content thanks to algorithms. They enable organizations to tailor messages on social platforms such as Twitter and Facebook and on the web using A/B testing to offer more personalized content. They calculate exactly when, how, and how many times to solicit individuals for donations or signatures. A/B testing is when an organization sends two versions of a message to compare which one the public responds to better.

One of the organizations interviewed uses software called NationBuilder. It connects to its website, Twitter, and Facebook accounts, and it pulls information on all of the individuals and organizations that have been in contact with the organization in some form. This provides a database that the organization can use to understand the demographics of its supporters and with which aspects of the organization they engage. Respondent two detailed how it is used within the organization: "It is super helpful to be able to look at trends and how we are going to communicate to the issues, how we will approach our social media strategy. For example, more people follow us on Twitter and Facebook, but not the newsletter, so we address more of our attention to Facebook and Twitter." The respondent also underscored how challenging it is to change the organizational culture and adapt to the new CRM software: "We started in the last year, and we are still trying to figure it out." In addition, these non-profit organizations have integrated digital strategies into their core operations. Respondent four noted that "we spend a lot of time on strategy, ... user requirements that convert into a solution, working with them to determine what's best suited ... Other sectors have done well on anticipating skills and competencies to drive a digital workplace, and we are borrowing these things and asking 'what does that mean for a high-functioning philanthropic landscape?'"

Digital technologies also require new ways of thinking and acting in digital spaces. As respondent one argued, "change management is a key piece to technology planning, which often doesn't get talked about. There's talk about how you successfully project-manage, but there is often a lot of non-technical things that need to be addressed ... It is like learning a whole new language – it's both fun and exciting but terrifying at the same time." Many of the organizations that I interviewed were not hierarchical but operated more on a team-based approach. They had to reimagine their organizational structures to make them more fluid and horizontal. Some repurposed an existing job description, placing digital strategy at the core of operations. Others created horizontal teams from different units to take on the key components of being a digitally enabled group.

This organizational restructuring has enabled these organizations to plan new investments ahead of time. Nevertheless, from a strategic perspective, the organizations that I interviewed reported that it remains challenging to know where to invest because public expectations can change quickly. Respondent three noted that "we invested a lot of money and time making our blog look good, and after that we thought it was very good, and it will do what we want to do. When it was beautiful and functional, it still wasn't working. People are moving away from blogs, and newsletters are the hot new thing." Furthermore, ever-changing technologies mean that they can be surpassed relatively quickly. Respondent four mentioned that "a lot of the tools we see and recommend today didn't exist five years ago. And some of them are moving at paces that it's hard for us to keep up." Respondent one observed that, "just like many other industries, we've come into an era of incredible abundance, [and] it's paralyzing now how much choice is out there. So there's something in the new trends of today of how to read ... which tools are the right ones to pull together." As is clear from the interviews conducted, there remains a lack of adequate technical knowledge in the non-profit sector required to keep abreast of new developments. Even those who are digitally savvy struggle to keep up. In fact, the technical experts that corporate firms hire are often out of the price ranges of non-profits, and, though consultant companies can work specifically with non-profit organizations, little funding is currently available to non-profits for investing in infrastructure, let alone technological infrastructure. Because most Canadian non-profit organizations are too small to invest many resources in this type of long-term strategizing – particularly regarding digital communications – they are at a disadvantage compared with the sample group here.

Unfortunately, much of the integration of digital technologies in the work of non-profit organizations at large has occurred without much strategic reflection or direction. The biggest barriers to full utilization of digital strategies, according to organizations surveyed in the *2015 Digital Outlook Report,* were staff shortages (74 percent) and budget restraints (63 percent). Similarly, the *2014 State of the Canadian Web Nation Benchmark Report* identified capital investment and cultural buy-in as the two main challenges facing organizations. Respondent three stated that "it's not easy, especially for a civil society organization. You can't take the same risk as a big organization."

Leadership also appears to be an important factor in an organization's successful adoption of digital technologies. Recent studies of management and the diffusion of management knowledge have emphasized the importance of organizational leaders in spreading new ideas and being carriers of innovation (Sahlin-Andersson and Engwall 2002). This was evident in the interview with respondent five, who noted that the emphasis on big data "comes from the top. The board of directors are quite aggressive, and we have clear direction from the board. Our vice-president, we get it right from the top." Yet, according to the *2014 State of the Canadian Web Nation Benchmark Report,* 60 percent of respondents noted that the web was not valued by their organizational leaders.

Although there have been interesting signs of growth and development within the non-profit sector, the adaptation to new digital technologies has not been seamless. Non-profit organizations – whether front end of innovation or not – continue to be saddled with legacy software out of date or in need of repair. For example, one of the organizations interviewed, though it has been in existence for only eight years, reported that it has to overhaul its website because it is no longer functional at the back end. The respondent noted "so many things that we want to do, and we are weighted down by the amount of stuff on there." The back end of a website matters because, once a person has entered information on a website, it gets stored in a database on a server. This technology enables an organization to manage content and track who interacts with the website and how. Thanks to this information, an organization develops targeted campaigns and messages and monitors its levels of engagement with the broader community. However, when an organization changes platforms, it is a huge investment of resources, time, and energy.

Ultimately, all respondents agreed that social media and digital tools are facilitators but remain side stories to the actual missions of the organizations. Most reiterated the importance of relationship building. Respondent three indicated that, "before we make something public, we reach out and compel them to share it with other people. It's time consuming to reach out to all [who are] emotionally invested. It's 200 direct messages, but it's important." The non-profit organizations interviewed also maintained the importance of formal, face-to-face interaction with the public. Respondent two insisted that, "as much as we have [a] social media profile, 28,000 Twitter followers, when we have a conversation with people, and something serious, it has to be in person." Hence, digital technologies are not seen as substitutes for direct engagement with the broader public; rather, they facilitate an expansion of outreach.

Political Elites in Canada in the Digital Age

As these examples suggest, digital technologies have had notable impacts on Canadian non-profit organizations on an organizational front. Although the core functions and activities of non-profits remain the same, how they execute those functions and which tools they use have changed in the digital era. Getting non-profit organizations to focus on the type of organizational change required to accommodate new digital technologies will be difficult because non-profits are mission driven. They exist to promote particular values, allow societal groups to express their views, and protect those interests. Because they seek to maximize the societal interests that they represent, their energy is dedicated to that set of goals. This organizational structure sets them apart from public or private organizations. This reality is also reflected in their hiring practices; very few non-profit organizations employ someone with a computer science background, and that is where other industries have invested heavily. To stay up to date, non-profit organizations need to attract new employees or provide current employees with opportunities to gain the skills necessary to adapt to the digital era. With a lack of predictable and stable funding flowing to the non-profit sector, change will likely be slow, and this sector will likely be vastly outpaced by the corporate sector, leading to a greater discrepancy over time.

So far, most of the analysis has focused on internal organizational dynamics and on the relationship between citizens and non-profit organizations. If we are to delve into broader issues of representation, decision making, and accountability, then we need to turn our attention to the state and the relationship between non-profit organizations and formal power.

The question of who shapes public policies under which conditions is an important and complex one for the study of political elites, particularly when the subject matter is the non-profit sector – distinct for its size and scope. We should be concerned about whether a healthy balance of groups and interests exists. The data point to important power imbalances to which we should be attentive. Clear disparities remain within the non-profit sector with regard to organizational capacity. Skills and resources are not distributed evenly. Mid-sized and large organizations appear to be in stronger positions to invest in the development of digital strategies. In particular, organizations that receive funding from foundations and corporations have the flexibility to invest in developing the technological infrastructure to advance their agendas. If our democratic system is to foster greater pluralism in political interests, then we need to ensure that all non-profit organizations can take advantage of the digital revolution.

From a democratic perspective, digital technologies have brought in more transparency in terms of communications practices because everything is out in public view. Non-profit organizations can produce and share vast amounts of information with the public. They can foster high levels of engagement, as the case studies attest. But these instances remain episodic and issue specific. With Twitter and Facebook, it is also not as easy for a non-profit organization to control its messages on the internet. Digital traces are left behind by the organization, and they empower citizens to monitor and hold it to account. This can ensure that non-profits, as political elites, truly represent the interests of citizens in the political arena.

The paradox, however, is that digital technologies have also rendered opaque the representational links between organizations and the public. Organizations are moving away from formal membership and are not non-profit organizations in the traditional sense, with clear lines of accountability back to members. Although new communications technologies can facilitate and accelerate communications, democracy cannot be enhanced if the model of engagement is one of atomized individuals, with latent interests just waiting to be activated in the political arena at the click of a button. Here new digital technologies have complicated and obscured the process of mobilization and representation.

These new technologies have impacts on the political issues advocated to the state and can have significant influences on political debates. Algorithms and human filtering have become new curators of ideas and interests, thereby affecting what is taken up and articulated to the state. These bots can affect how content inspires action, yet they are indifferent to the cause. They follow the media cycle and what is trending through new technologies. As such, they have the power to increase inequality and threaten democracy by distorting the policy process. The decision regarding which cause should move forward and gain traction is no longer made by humans. Bots determine how information is shaped, how claims are articulated, and how interests are represented. This can further reinforce the politicization and centralization of policy agendas – a process that has been gradually increasing in recent decades.

Non-profit organizations are central institutions for the transmission of citizens' interests and preferences into the policy arena. It is too early to tell to what extent these shifts will affect the practices of political representation and the nature of elite communication. In the 1980s, states around the world delegitimized non-profit organizations by using the narrative of "special interest groups" and arguing that they represented only parochial interests (Laforest 2011). Many organizations saw their funding cut and could not fight back. It is clear that in the new digital era governments will no longer be able to dismiss an organization that can mobilize 20,000 Twitter followers. Just as digital technologies are changing the culture within organizations, so too they will change political culture, and the nature of power, as we start to grapple with these important societal questions.

NOTE

1 Federal government spending (CANSIM table 385–0032) divided by GDP (CANSIM table 380–0064) first quarter 1992: 23.4 percent and first quarter 2013: 14.6 percent.

REFERENCES

Care2. 2015. *2015 Digital Outlook Report.* http://www.care2services.com/hubfs/White_Papers/2015_Digital_Outlook_Report.pdf?submissionGuid=13159625-5ae8-4996-a342-d11eaa9cda37.

Castells, Manuel. 2015. *Networks of Outrage and Hope: Social Movements in the Internet Age.* Cambridge, UK: Polity Press.

Gerbaudo, Paolo. 2012. *Tweets and the Streets: Social Media and Contemporary Activism.* London: Pluto Press. https://doi.org/10.2307/j.ctt183pdzs.

Gersick, Connie. 1991. "Revolutionary Change Theories: A Multilevel Exploration of the Punctuated Equilibrium Paradigm." *Academy of Management Review* 16, 1: 10–36. https://doi.org/10.5465/AMR.1991.4278988.

Good Works. 2014. *2014 State of the Canadian Web Nation Benchmark Report.* http://www.goodworksco.ca/2014-canadian-web-benchmark-report/.

Grosenick, Georgina. 2014. "Opportunities Missed: Non-Profit Public Communication and Advocacy in Canada." In *Political Communication in Canada*, edited by Alex Marland, Thierry Giasson, and Tamara Small, 179–93. Vancouver: UBC Press.

Hall, Michael, Margaret L. de Wit, David Lasby, David McIver, Terry Evans, Chris Johnston, Julie McAuley, et al. 2004. *Cornerstones of Community: Highlights of the National Survey of Non-Profit and Voluntary Organizations*. Ottawa: Statistics Canada.

Imagine Canada. 2010. *Sector Monitor* 1, 1.

Laforest, Rachel. 2011. *Voluntary Sector Organizations and the State*. Vancouver: UBC Press.

—, ed. 2013. *Government-Non-Profit Relations in Times of Recession*. Kingston: McGill-Queen's University Press.

Levasseur, Karine. 2012. "In the Name of Charity: Institutional Support and Resistance for Redefining the Meaning of Charity in Canada." *Canadian Public Administration* 55, 2: 181–202. https://doi.org/10.1111/j.1754-7121.2012.00214.x.

Levesque, Mario. 2017. "Vulnerable Populations and the Permanent Campaign: Disability Organizations as Policy Entrepreneurs." In *Permanent Campaigning in Canada*, edited by Alex Marland, Thierry Giasson, and Anna Esselment, 278–97. Vancouver: UBC Press.

Meyer, John, and Brian Rowan. 1977. "Institutional Organizations: Formal Structure as Myth and Ceremony." *American Journal of Sociology* 83, 2: 340–63. https://doi.org/10.1086/226550.

Pfeffer, Jeffrey, and Gerald Salancik. 1978. *The External Control of Organizations: A Resource Dependence Perspective*. New York: Harper and Row.

Powell, Walter W., and Paul J. DiMaggio, eds. 1991. *The New Institutionalism in Organizational Analysis*. Chicago: University of Chicago Press.

Sahlin-Andersson, Kerstin, and Lars Engwall, eds. 2002. *The Expansion of Management Knowledge: Carriers, Flows, and Sources*. Stanford, CA: Business Books.

Saidel, Judith. 1991. "Resource Interdependence: The Relationship between State Agencies and Non-Profit Organizations." *Public Administration Review* 51, 6: 543–53. https://doi.org/10.2307/976605.

Shirky, C. 2009. *Here Comes Everybody: The Power of Organizing without Organizations*. New York: Penguin Books.

Skocpol, Theda. 2003. *Diminished Democracy: From Membership to Management in American Civic Life*. Norman: University of Oklahoma Press.

Small, Tamara, Harold Jansen, Frédérick Bastien, Thierry Giasson, and Royce Koop. 2014. "Online Political Activity in Canada: The Hype and the Facts." *Canadian Parliamentary Review* 37, 4: 9–16.

Statistics Canada. 2015. *Civic Engagement and Political Participation in Canada*. Ottawa: Minister of Industry.

Thelen, Kathleen. 1999. "Historical Institutionalism in Comparative Politics." *Annual Review of Political Science* 2, 1: 369–404. https://doi.org/10.1146/annurev.polisci.2.1.369.

PART 4

Conclusion . . . .

14
Emerging Voices, Evolving Concerns

•••• *Andrea Lawlor, Alex Marland, and Thierry Giasson*

When Justin Trudeau was ascending to power, interim leader of the Liberal Party of Canada Bob Rae rushed to catch an Air Canada flight at Pearson International Airport in Toronto. Lingering passengers were told that the airplane was full and that they would have to wait to catch the next flight. Rae, a former premier of Ontario, reportedly approached the customer service desk. He was informed by the agent that there were no more seats. Unlike the other delayed passengers, he remarked "I am Super Elite" as he pulled a card from his wallet and laid it on the counter. Rae was referring to the highest level of privilege accorded by Air Canada to its customers, a label reserved exclusively for frequent flyers, those typically seated comfortably in the executive class at the front of the aircraft. The status entitles them to special services such as the serenity of gated lounges at bustling airport terminals and the ability to bypass lineups at security clearance during boarding and disembarking and when picking up luggage. Rae was issued a boarding pass moments after differentiating himself, leaving the regular travellers behind (Harvey 2011).

This anecdote does more than evoke Susan Delacourt's recollection in this book's foreword about class divisions on a flight in the early 1990s. It reminds us that classism and elitism run throughout Canadian society and political life. In Chapter 1, we presented a typology of elites in the Canadian polity. We remarked that the more spheres any individual occupies the greater the power and influence of that individual, particularly if the person has a high public profile.

In Table 1.1, we notionally categorized fifteen different types of elites. In practice, the categorization is not so tidy. Individuals often straddle multiple positions at the same time or over their careers. Where practices are not codified or there is a sufficient amount of autonomy in a position, individual elites can behave differently in similar situations, resulting in some variation across interactions with the public. Social changes, such as the incorporation of a greater number of women, visible minorities, and other previously excluded groups into sectors of the elite, have resulted not only in compositional changes but also in a corresponding evolution of norms and practices among elites. In short, the past sixty years have produced a tremendous progression in the number and type of elites whom Canadians have come to know in the public sphere.

By enumerating the types of elites, their roles, and their abilities to influence politics and policy outcomes, we highlight how the Canadian political process is subject to the direction of a relatively small group of citizens with a comparatively large set of powers. In this volume, we highlighted that the variety of elite actors in the political arena is much broader than it might appear initially. The *political* roles of corporate and social elites studied by Mills (1957) and Clement (1975) are of less concern here than those of the government elites described by Porter (1965) and Presthus (1973). The introduction of digital communications technologies has resulted in a flattening of political elite structures. Thus, we have cause to think beyond the three branches of government, public administration, a political party's extraparliamentary wing, and interest groups. Many participants in the public sector today are individuals and organizations that would not warrant study were it not for their use of social media to disrupt officialdom. For example, "advocacy," as an activity, is now less a product of formal organizations and available to any person or group who can master the use of digital technologies in public spaces.

In the following pages, we reflect on the rise of the new segment of elites and a corresponding anti-elite sentiment sweeping through Canada and beyond. As recent campaigns around the world remind us, elite influence and anti-elite discourse go hand in hand, as two opposing ends of a spectrum of political strategy. We then render observations on each set of actors and its ability to shape politics as evolving with communications technologies. We weave in knowledge gained from contributors and observations from contemporary politics in Canada. We then return to the core questions of this book pertaining to representation, decision making, and accountability of political elites in the digital age.

Anti-Elitism in Canada and Beyond

Being part of the upper social strata historically denotes a fairly simple set of dichotomies: wealthy versus not, powerful versus not. In Canada and other

Western liberal democracies, the rise of social welfare programs in the post-war era resulted in the emergence of a solid middle class. In recent years, the fallout from a weakening industrial sector and the Great Recession that began in 2008 eroded the security, real or perceived, of a comfortable middle-class existence. The economic uncertainties for some have been coupled with momentous societal changes for all. Some previously silenced groups, such as Indigenous groups or individuals with disabilities, have found stronger voices in this upheaval. Some political elites, notably the courts, are applying the Charter of Rights and Freedoms to propel changes on topics that befuddle Parliament, including laws on and practices in matters such as gender identity and physician-assisted death. Partisanship threatens to tear communities apart by positioning these issues as fodder for the adversarial ideological gristmill. Social justice advocates organize protests to call for greater equality and diversity; conservatives stoke nativism by blaming media elites and liberal bias for promoting a politically correct orthodoxy; far-right or "alt-right" groups mobilize against the perceived liberalization of societal norms. Ideological controversies feed public debate and polarization. On any given day, even cursory exposure to the news or social media will suggest that we live in a society of malcontents and that those in positions of power are to blame for being out of touch or ill-willed.

The dichotomy that differentiates elites from non-elites with which we are most concerned is the possession of political influence and power. Many Canadians feel separated from their political representatives and isolated from their peers in civil society. With some exceptions, such as the Quebec student strikes of 2012 or the Idle No More campaign, these technology-enabled winds of change are not producing large-scale civil unrest domestically. Outside Canada, elections and referendums such as the Scottish referendum on independence and the Brexit vote suggest that traditional expressions of political representation are being rejected and replaced by protest voting, populism, and even demagoguery. All are attempts to overcome powerlessness with bold change, even when that change comes with substantial risk to individual well-being. Few have produced such change with a clear view of what it will mean for civil and human rights, economic stability, and advancement of global peace.

Unrest and political tumult are more prevalent in the United States, the United Kingdom, and the European Union. In America, the politics of race and class conflict has reached a level of discontent unseen since the civil rights conflicts of the 1960s. Disenfranchisement and a loss of income security have produced a climate in which citizens are experiencing difficulty adapting to socio-economic transformations. The Black Lives Matter movement and the riots resulting from digital video evidence of some police officers' brutality against African Americans, and the inflammatory rhetoric of Republican President Donald Trump, are just some examples of how digital media can capture discontent.

In the United Kingdom, the Brexit referendum vote in June 2015 reverberated as a signal that an anti-elite sentiment bubbling below the surface for decades had finally erupted. Largely galvanized over the issue of immigration and refugee support, a slim majority of voters articulated dissatisfaction with status quo policies, registering strong discontent with the European Union bureaucracy making policy decisions for Britain. This anti-elite sentiment was encapsulated by the Leave campaign advocate Michael Gove's (perhaps unplanned) viral quip that "people in this country have had enough of experts" and by his Leave campaign ally, Labour MP Gisela Stuart, who corroborated that "there is only one expert that matters, and that's you, the voter" (quoted in Clarke and Newman 2017). Rarely have this depth of disenchantment with elites and a corresponding appropriation of claims to expertise been so wholeheartedly embraced by the public.

Canadians seem to be perplexed by these displays of anti-elite sentiment yet themselves sometimes hold conflicting views on divisive issues. Most identify equality and tolerance as core Canadian values and believe in the freedom of women to choose their clothing. Yet many oppose Islamic religious clothing and agree that potential immigrants should be screened for "anti-Canadian values" (Forum Research 2016). Little wonder that some politicians, such as MP Kellie Leitch (a medical doctor and elite politician), have sought to stir patriotism and nationalism as well as a rhetoric of fear for political gain. A strategist on her Conservative Party leadership campaign explained her public scolding of elites as a tactic to attract media attention and rile up the party's grassroots. "Elitism is not a function of income or education. It's about being out of touch with average people," he explained (quoted in Macdonald 2016). Quebec's polarized debates on reasonable accommodation practices in the public service, which culminated with the Parti Québécois's project to impose a charter on secularism, is another instance of political manoeuvring feeding on and potentially contributing to societal xenophobia. For his part, Prime Minister Justin Trudeau promotes diversity and inclusivity, and he connects global anti-elitism with middle-class frustration with a capitalist system perceived to unjustly favour the wealthy (Curry 2017).

Anti-elitism is not a new phenomenon; neither are efforts of political leaders to show that they are onside with public opinion. To wit, the Harper Conservatives were fond of blaming urban elites for social problems (e.g., CBC News 2010). Before them, Paul Martin chastised Jean Chrétien's government for an operating culture in which power brokers were based on "who you know in the PMO." Presumably to enhance credibility, Chrétien promoted an image of himself as the "little guy from Shawinigan." Kim Campbell sought to distance herself from Brian Mulroney's image as being cozy with corporate elites. Mulroney rebuked John Turner in the 1984 leaders' debates for approving a slew of Liberal patronage appointments. And so on throughout Canadian history.

To some extent, anti-elite tendencies have ebbed and flowed with electoral cycles. The resentment felt by western Canada about the so-called Laurentian elites and the concentration of power running along the Toronto–Ottawa–Montreal corridor might have temporarily receded when Harper, a Calgary MP, became prime minister. The Conservatives were returned to office twice after hard-hitting negative advertising that branded Liberal leaders (and former political science professors) Stéphane Dion and Michael Ignatieff as out-of-touch urbanites, too bound up with the liberal intelligentsia to understand the plight of regular working citizens. The same formula failed in 2015, by which time the Conservatives firmly represented the Ottawa establishment, at odds with Harper's opinion that "you cannot govern well, and you cannot govern properly, unless you understand the values and realities of ordinary Canadians" (quoted in Cross 2015). This time flippant advertising was unable to dislodge Canadians' parasocial attachment to a more telegenic and surprisingly astute leader who had grown up in the public eye. Cognizant of his privileged status, Justin Trudeau democratized his celebrity by mingling with crowds eagerly seeking selfies and by positioning himself as a champion of the middle class and women. Yet, as happens with all who assume office, the anti-establishment message is slowly replaced by that of officialdom. The governing Liberals have been rebuked for taking advantage of their position, for instance the most senior PMO personnel billing $200,000 for their personal moving expenses (Boutilier 2016). In 2016, Prime Minister Trudeau was celebrated as an international star at the World Economic Forum's annual summit in Switzerland, where he mingled with high-ranking political and economic elites from around the globe. But in 2017, under criticism for travelling by private helicopter to vacation on a private Bahamian island owned by the Aga Khan – a trip reported to have cost more than $215,000 to Canadian taxpayers (Thompson 2017) – the prime minister skipped the economic summit in favour of embarking on a cross-country listening tour with Canadians.

Leaders are mindful that public resentment of those in high office provides an opening for critics and opposition leaders to seek power by using their own anti-elitist messages. It is a continuing cycle, periodically interrupted by crusading populists. These political leaders simultaneously advocate greater citizen influence through direct democracy and by limiting the authority of experts and elites. Meanwhile, they themselves amass personal power by eschewing established norms and fostering paranoia about elites. This paradoxical populist posture has been used across the political spectrum, from conservatives to progressives, with varying success. It has generated protest votes that profoundly modified partisan and institutional alignments, such as the 1993 and 2011 Canadian federal elections. Populism brought to power new formations that ran on promises of transformational governance following decades of single-party dominance in government, such as the 1976 election in Quebec of the Parti Québécois and the 2015 election in Alberta of the NDP. Parliamentarians bristle under the weight of strict party discipline and executive dominance, expressing their own anti-elitism by voting in the legislature against their house leader's instructions and sometimes pressuring a sitting first minister to make way for new blood. An anti-elite mood is a constant threat to those in power.

More so now than ever, branding oneself as a member of the elite or critiquing the middle/working class is political suicide. Elitism is perceived to be normatively wrong and politically tone deaf, particularly with respect to governance. This negative perception exists even though leadership and organizational hierarchy is necessary for governments to operate. It overlooks that widespread public consultation is unwieldy and often leads to muddled political outcomes. The separation of a privileged few to rule over the masses is nevertheless at odds with current perceptions of democracy, focused on citizen consultation and direct relay of preferences. Elections remain the central mechanism to hold rulers to account, but with the ubiquity of low-cost digital media politics operates in a state of 24/7 live democracy. Public trust in politicians is extremely low, their occupation ranking among the least trustworthy in Canada (see Table 14.1). Confidence in the

TABLE 14.1

Most and least trustworthy professions in Canada, 2014

Profession	Rating of trust (%)
Emergency services and medicine	Firefighters 77, ambulance drivers/paramedics 74, pharmacists 70, nurses 69, doctors 65, veterinarians 51, dentists 50, psychologists/counsellors 35, chiropractors 30
Public safety/security	Airline pilots 65, Canadian soldiers 58, police officers 46, food safety inspectors 37, airport security guards 29, airport baggage handlers 12
Farming	Farmers 58
Educators/childcare	Teachers 52, daycare workers 39
Law	Judges 42, lawyers 16
Skilled trades	Electricians 37, plumbers 28, auto mechanics 16
Finance/business	Accountants 34, financial advisers 22, CEOs 11
Religious	Church leaders 24
Media	Journalists 18, television and radio personalities 17, bloggers 6
Politicians	Local politicians 6, national politicians 6
Sales	Car salespeople 5, telemarketers 4

NOTE: Ipsos Reid survey of 4,026 Canadians administered in September 2014. The figures are proportions of who ranked the profession as a 6 or 7 on a seven-point scale, where 7 is "extremely trustworthy."
SOURCE: Compiled from Tencer (2015).

media does not fare much better, with bloggers less trusted than mainstream journalists, on par with politicians. Yet many individual politicians are popular with their constituents, particularly those who try to set themselves apart from the machinery of government or their party. So perhaps the prevailing distaste for politics is a reflection of Hollywood portrayals of a nefarious and cynical vocation rather than of some Canadian office holders themselves. This suggests that we need to continue to unpack the concept of political elites in Canada to understand how they are changing in a digital landscape.

High-Profile and Low-Profile Political Elites

This book situates political elites in a digital space. We have not delved into actors who operate in the political grey space that often goes undetected.

Rather, we treat political elites as dynamic *public* actors increasingly forced to justify their positions of power to a skeptical public. Elitism might imply power, but it does not necessarily convey stability. Elites are displaced with increasing ease by those who wield the power to publicly blame or shame. Before addressing the three main research questions that we posed in the introductory chapter, it is instructive to juxtapose our Table 1.1 typology with how an Ottawa-based political news magazine identifies the "most powerful and influential people in government" (Burgess 2016). We resist being drawn here into the pitfalls of a methodological battle over the construction of lists and taxonomies. Rather, we seek some external validity on the political movers and shakers in Ottawa circles.

The *Hill Times* publishes twice weekly about news on Parliament Hill and the Ottawa public sector. Its website boasts about the heavy hitters in Canadian politics whom it counts among its readers. It is immediately interesting that only traditional elite structures are promoted, namely "Cabinet ministers, MPs, Senators, political staffers, lobbyists, backroomers, political junkies, lots of influential players in Parliament, Cabinet, the Prime Minister's Office, the Privy Council, the Finance Department, Treasury Board, the Department of National Defence, the Justice Department, and more" (*Hill Times* 2016). This is a conventional way of looking at the top of the pyramid of parliamentary governance. On the basis of this description, we believe that the proximity to power is how Donald Savoie (1999) described it in *Governing from the Centre: The Concentration of Power in Canadian Politics* before the onset of social media. Namely, that power is concentrated in the Prime Minister's Office and central agencies. A similar argument could be made for provincial premiers and their inner circles.

So who tops the pyramid of the politically powerful in Canada? According to the *Hill Times Power & Influence* magazine, the top three soon after the Liberals formed the government were Prime Minister Trudeau, his chief of staff Katie Telford, and his principal secretary Gerald Butts. So firm was their perch atop the government that the magazine dubbed them "the three musketeers" (Foster 2017). Historically, the media attention accorded to political personnel has fluctuated. Some, such as Liberal Senator Keith Davey and Progressive Conservative Party President Dalton Camp roughly half a century ago, become well known. Others, such as Conservative PMO Deputy Chief of Staff Patrick Muttart a decade ago, were familiar only to those trying to comprehend political marketing. What is different about Trudeau's team from predecessors is that they came to office with active social media profiles that remain so today. Butts, in particular, is known for a combative online style, acting as the government's chief spin doctor (e.g., Farooq 2016). In comparison, the social media accounts belonging to other Liberals went dark once they began working in the PMO.

Other senior PMO personnel on the *Power and Influence* list included the deputy chief of staff, the director of policy, and Kate Purchase, the director of communications. The top non-PMO political staffer was the chief of staff to Minister of Finance Bill Morneau. Others included ministers of the traditionally powerful central agencies of Finance and Treasury Board and some individual ministers known to have long-standing personal ties to Trudeau. The powerful regional ministers who characterized politics in the twentieth century (Bakvis 1991) have been less obvious in recent years, which might be a function of their public endorsements of the prime minister. A case in point is Judy Foote, the former Liberal minister for public services and procurement, the regional minister for Canada's easternmost province, and the minister who shared a House of Commons desk with Prime Minister Trudeau. "A lot of what we do on behalf of Newfoundland and Labrador would not happen without the prime minister's intervention," she has publicly explained (Cowan 2016). In comparison, the inclusion of Ontario Liberal Premier Kathleen Wynne reflects the size of that province's population and economy as well as the close connections between the national and Ontario Liberal parties (e.g., Esselment 2010). Rounding out the upper tranche were the Conservative leader of the official opposition; in the public service, the clerk of the Privy Council Office, the secretary of the Treasury Board, and the chief of the defence staff; and the chief justice of the Supreme Court. Outside the government, it is notable that the national chief of the Assembly of First Nations (AFN), Perry Bellegarde, was identified as being highly influential.

After the top twenty-five, this particular list included politicians (ministers, premiers, MPs, mayors of large cities), political staff (members of the PMO, chiefs of staff to ministers and the leader of the official opposition, and the managing director of the Liberal Caucus Research Bureau), public servants (ranging from the auditor general to deputy ministers), and high-profile members of the Ottawa press gallery, of which only two were affiliated with online publications (National Newswatch and the *Huffington Post*). It concluded with a cluster of four others with substantial political capital: the Liberal Party president, the party's lead fundraiser and interim national director, a Conservative Party executive director, and Sophie Grégoire-Trudeau.

Her ascendancy and that of her husband as political celebrities and their connectivity through digital media are worthy of attention among those studying gendered media and those interested in PMO resources deployed to maintain their online presence (J. Smith 2016).

Although we recognize the limits of this exercise, it serves to illustrate who is considered a political elite. Indeed, this categorization represents a list of elites as compiled by other elites. Compared with our own categorization, those judging who has "power and influence" appear to believe that the governor general and Supreme Court justices other than the chief justice are not considered prominent political actors. There is thought to be more political influence among partisans who have transitioned from the campaign trail to fill key roles within the PMO. The average parliamentarian/local party representative holds little sway outside an electoral district, and members of the intelligentsia have clout only if they have a significant media presence and are known by other government elites. With the exceptions of the chief of the AFN and members of the press gallery, the *Hill Times* makes no mention of external political, corporate, or societal figures. The leaders of interest groups, large corporations, and social movements mobilizing change through digital media are seen to be less consequential than the ideas that they promote. Perhaps they are viewed as more transient and less entrenched in the political system than the people who occupy the institutions of Parliament; perhaps they are succeeding in occupying the grey space mentioned earlier. Equally, the influential lobbyists and public affairs personnel who work through back channels remain obscure, as do for-hire political strategists. They constitute a class of elites worthy of scrutiny in their own right.

If transformation is occurring in Canadian politics, much of it is happening through traditional institutions and processes, even when the actors are increasingly diverse. That is, non-traditional political actors with large online followings do not seem to register among the powerful, at least to the *Hill Times*. The adage of "power in the backrooms" has purchase here as well. Other than the prime minister, who has undeniable agenda-setting power, and the occasional cabinet minister or even chief justice of the Supreme Court, policy-making authority is less evident on this list than we might otherwise assume. The *Hill Times* captures a great deal of what we refer to in our introduction as the representative power of elites but perhaps less of the explicit authority to make decisions and an indeterminate amount of accountability. The challenge of looking for the locus of power in known entities is that it risks ignoring what we do not know (and, as external observers, might not be able to know) about where power resides in Ottawa. A number of the chapters in our book push beyond what the *Hill Times* list can do to present a broader categorization of political actors and an in-depth look at their motivations, capabilities, and limitations.

We can further group the cohorts in Table 1.1 into whether they are public figures or largely backroom actors and hypothesize about the extent of their political influence (Table 14.2). As before, these cohorts are indicative rather than definitive, and they are presented with the objective of stimulating conversation. We leave off interest groups, social movements, lobbyists, public affairs personnel, and professional political consultants because their influence is too varied to treat their kind as a monolith. We do recognize that, historically, some interest groups – whether socially/culturally driven or economically motivated – have tremendous power in influencing the decision-making patterns of elected elites (Nevitte 1996; Pross 1992). Some individuals, families, and organizations have been well connected and play activist roles, passing through ebbs and flows depending on the issues of the day and the government's agenda, by gaining privileged access to party leaders, ministers, and prime ministers. Similarly, advocacy groups of all types – ranging from unions to issue-based organizations – make indelible marks on aspects of provincial and federal politics when windows of opportunity permit them to do so. Although we are unable to render a definitive judgment on online influencers, it is becoming clear that, from time to time, they can make significant contributions to high-stakes campaigns by creating the right conditions for focusing events and galvanizing public opinion (Poell and Borra 2012; see also Chapters 10 and 11 in this book). In this way, we recognize that the rapidly evolving technological context can elevate and displace elite actors faster than we can study them. All told, the individuals in the column on the right of Table 14.2 – not all of whom we have been able to tackle in this volume – warrant deeper study. Such research can be assisted by using the data collection tips presented in Chapter 2.

This categorization illustrates our impression that political power is distributed in an uneven manner and that this distribution does not constitute an exemplary model of democratic governance. Harkening back to our earlier discussion of the contemporary understanding of electoral representation, this observation is tempered by the fact that politicians elected to

Table 14.2

Influence of high- and low-profile Canadian political elites

Less political influence	More political influence
High-profile elites	
Formal executive (monarch, governor general, lieutenant governors)	First ministers (PM/premiers)
	Ministers of key portfolios
Ministers of minor portfolios	Press gallery
Opposition leaders and members of shadow cabinets	Chief justice of the Supreme Court
	Auditor general
Pollsters	Parliamentary budget officer
Pundits, online influencers	CEOs/presidents of large Canadian corporations
	Heads of large labour unions
	National media personalities
Low-profile elites	
Parliamentary secretaries	Political staff and party strategists working with high-profile elites (particularly those in the PMO)
Most senators	
Most backbenchers	Judiciary, particularly Supreme Court justices
Most political staff working for legislators	Public servants in central agencies
Most candidates standing for election	Senior civil service
Members of political parties' electoral district associations	Political parties' central executives (e.g., national directors, chairs)
Other officers of the legislature	Political party fundraisers
Heads of small non-governmental organizations and interest groups	CEOs/directors of the largest non-governmental organizations and interest groups
Most public servants	Members of wealthy Canadian families and political or economic "dynasties"
Intelligentsia	Lobbyists representing large national clients from strategic sectors (e.g., energy, finance, health)

NOTE: This table builds on Table 1.1 in Chapter 1 and is not intended to be definitive. Exceptions exist in every grouping. For instance, a backbench MP with a national profile has more political power than a weak minister overseeing a small portfolio.

represent Canadians' views are firmly categorized as public figures with little power. It is a far cry for the Burkean logic that informs much of the undergraduate teaching of political representation. Parliamentarians' influence is typically limited to a minimal number of issues and short bursts of attention. At times, their presence might be of greater importance – for example, on the campaign trail, as shown in Chapter 12. Yet noteworthy MPs are as often liabilities as assets to their parties. In many cases, attention yields scrutiny, and the level of scrutiny that comes with media attention and investigative journalism is often not something that the average person can sustain. There are exceptions, of course, including those who actively communicate and mobilize support through social media. Nevertheless, all parliamentarians are confronted by constraining factors such as available time and resources and the challenges posed by balancing their personal life with constituency and parliamentary work (Koop, Farney, and Loat 2013). This understanding challenges the conventional notion that lower-level elected representatives must be the true voices of the public because their connection to the electorate makes them more likely to pursue policies in line with constituents' preferences (Jervis 1992).

Similarly, the age-old grievances produced by executive-driven appointment procedures and patronage positions continue to mount. The independence of officers of Parliament comes into question when they are tasked with monitoring the actions of the government that appointed them. Only in cases in which a maverick appointee – former Parliamentary Budget Officer Kevin Page, for example – specifically opposes the appointer do we see an element of political independence. But this seems to be largely reflective of the person, not the office. Similarly, recent changes to appointment processes for the Senate might represent little more than a public relations exercise by the Liberals. "It's elites and bureaucrats that seem to be getting all the jobs," lamented a hotdog vendor about the spate of twenty-one so-called independent senators appointed to the red chamber through that process. "I meet every kind of person. White-collar, blue-collar, no collar at all ... They're tired of hearing of the VIPs getting all the big jobs" (M.-D. Smith 2016). Position this narrative alongside the discourse on the need for merit-based appointments and it becomes difficult to disentangle which set of considerations Canadians want to be paramount in their representatives.

News media are another channel through which political power is articulated. Although the business models of traditional and digital media operations are under stress (e.g., Ryckewaert 2016), journalists perform an important watchdog function. Most importantly, they serve as the primary source of political information for citizens and therefore have the added privilege of gatekeeping and framing political information for the public (Chong and Druckman 2007). Of course, the most formidable recent change to media has been the incorporation of digital technology to capture information and tell more interactive stories. Traditional media have felt the pressures of citizen and activist journalists closing in on their sphere of influence, as illustrated in Chapter 10. This has had the questionable effect of pushing the fourth estate into a highly competitive model of live real-time information capture and distribution, in which opportunities to engage in verification and contextualization processes have diminished (Chacon, Giasson, and Brin 2015). The result is often a thinning of content quality and depth. The fracturing of the media landscape therefore presents a potential cost for time-consuming investigative journalism and fact-checking routines, rendering political information potentially less credible and useful. This competition produces hyper-sensationalism in political news, a focus on journalistic exposé of scandal in lieu of policy discussion, and opinionated, event-driven news rather than sustained, sober discussion (Boydstun 2013). All of this contributes to public cynicism about media elites.

Where Canadian political actors appear to be disconnected from evolving public expectations is the relative obscurity of insiders involved in policy decisions. The operations of the Supreme Court of Canada and its nine justices warrant more public scrutiny as a matter of democratic accountability (Macfarlane 2013). Yet Canadians appear to be sensitive to politicians who try to constrain judges, as became evident in the skirmish between Chief Justice Beverley McLachlin and Prime Minister Stephen Harper (Manfredi 2014; see also Chapter 7 in this book). When senior political staff such as Telford and Butts participate in public conversations, their power magnifies. But the public sector bargain that offers up the minister to shield the senior civil service from public scrutiny is increasingly incompatible with evolving public expectations. In fact, the public service is drawn into politicized communication activities, turning non-partisans into cogs in a partisan machine (Aucoin 2012; also see Chapter 3). Conversely, political parties are shells of their former selves for reasons that range from the considerable authority of their leaders (see Chapter 8) to citizens who turn to non-traditional forms of political engagement such as boycotts and clicktivism (e.g., Halupka 2014). Membership in those parties, of course, is one part heuristic for the public and one part electoral ticket for an unknown MP. Yet parties are so rarely considered to be vehicles for citizen expression (Young 2013) that it makes one question their role. Perhaps more so than any other set of political institutions, the political party has become bureaucratic, having transitioned fully from a mode of citizen representation, driven by its member base, to a place where elites can shield themselves entirely from the demands of public participation.

Elites and Non-Elites: The Digital Turn in Canadian Politics

In all cases, traditional political elites have fallen into two camps: those who have seen their power eroded by the changing norms of political participation and the democratization of technological advances and those who have used the transition to this new set of norms to consolidate their power. When we set about to organize this volume, we asked contributors to consider our main research questions, articulated in Chapter 1, on the themes of political elite representation, decision making, and accountability in a digital environment. As the project unfolded, it became apparent that digital communication is playing an ever more significant role in major political events. Chances are that, as this very sentence is being read, there is further evidence of the political implications of the digital turn.

Worldwide, the use of information and communication technologies contributes to propelling political conversations and spurring political actions. The early days of one-way, single-mode, plain-format messaging have long been displaced. Today there are sophisticated multimedia platforms that permit elites to communicate slick, targeted, convincing messages, relying on technologies and tactics typically reserved for marketers. The conversion of social media software and smartphone hardware enables portable, non-stop, quick, and inexpensive communications among multitudes of previously diverse interests. Websites, Facebook, Twitter, Instagram, YouTube, and an array of mobile applications are helping political actors to build their personal brands and promote calls to action. Sophisticated back-end technologies that facilitate the gathering of voter information in outreach databases and automated access to voters through robocalls are the institutional counterparts that further strengthen elites' access to the public. This increase in dynamic, two-way interaction between elites and non-elites has a further consequence: entrenched institutions and processes are subject to critique. As more information is released to the public, and as there is more real-time interaction among elites and non-elites alike, the masses call for greater democratization of governance and for enhanced accountability, even when there is little consensus on what it would look like.

Some readers could find such assertions technologically deterministic. Contributors to this volume apprehend digital platforms and technologies as tools that humans – politicians, strategists, citizens, and reporters alike – mobilize and use for political purposes. Not unlike previous technological innovations, such as the printing press, radio, and television, these digital tools have been developed by communities of individuals, software or computer engineers, who share values, organizational cultures, and attitudes that contribute to shaping the technologies (Howard 2006). Developers create platforms to attain certain goals, for instance enhancing unmediated communications between message producers and receivers or facilitating collaboration in message (co)production. On their own, online platforms have no impact on politics: it is their strategic use by elite and non-elite political actors that generates political transformations. All of the chapters in this volume reveal how these tools are used for political reasons and how these practices are reshaping elite status and influence in Canada.

What can we glean from this book's case studies to shed light on how changes in digital technology use, management, and strategy affect how citizens participate in and monitor politics? Themes that cross all chapters are an expansion of access, a displacement of traditional elites, and a bridging of elite and non-elite political communities. These themes capture this volume's overall foci: representation, decision making, and accountability, each of which is visible in these changes.

The use of digital technologies for both direct communication with elites and monitoring of elite behaviour has changed the extent to which citizens can articulate their concerns. The public is now better equipped to hold decision makers accountable if they stray from those priorities. We see evidence of greater access in the chapter by Melanee Thomas and her colleagues that points to the increased representation of women elites in social and traditional media, albeit prompting a set of gendered observations that can be exaggerated by each platform. Equally, J.P. Lewis and Stéphanie Yates point to how premiers use video posts on social media to represent issues to attentive constituents but also acknowledge that the availability of this type of content is not necessarily reflective of consumption by the public. Erin Crandall's work on the sparring between the former prime minister and the former chief justice takes a slightly different approach to the subject of access. Crandall points to the outward attempts of elites to present their versions of issues to the public across various forms of communication on digital media. Finally, Robert Shepherd and Bryan Evans reveal the evolution of intra-organization communication strategies in response to increased public input facilitated by the federal government's 2016 communications policy calling for an expanded use of digital tools and technologies. All of these authors note that the key ingredient of this novel form of instantaneous access is that digital technologies, mobile platforms, and social media have become non-negotiable staples of elite messaging. Equally, many of them recognize that the largely unidirectional nature of these strategic communications does not necessarily add up to greater engagement, merely greater accessibility of curated information.

Another theme that this book examines is the displacement of political influence in novel spaces. Chapters by Geneviève Chacon and her colleagues, as well as by Fenwick McKelvey and his co-authors, identify and contextualize how the societal adoption of online technologies contributes to the emergence of new elites. They show that bloggers, social media users, hacktivists, and citizen journalists are on the rise in number, popularity, and influence. These actors occupy positions that were previously unheard of and potentially even untenable in mainstream politics around the time that the Harper Conservatives came to power. The use of digital platforms, especially Twitter, provides citizens with direct access to traditional elites and to large audiences of politically minded citizens who relay their opinions and questions in a viral manner. Where past analyses have questioned the influence of political bloggers in Canada (e.g., Giasson, Jansen, and Koop 2014), these two chapters reveal the increased potential for direct influence by internet users who count thousands of followers and see their online postings shared hundreds of times. Already online organizations such as Anonymous, WikiLeaks, and the ill-identified Russian hackers have altered the courses of political events by revealing confidential information online. They represent a displacement of the mainstream traditional news production cycle because of their rapid-fire nature and ability to source and publish news with so few institutional constraints. Furthermore, they represent an unprecedented check on elites by exposing fraud and corruption at the source, or by manufacturing information to meet their own political ends.

In their respective chapters, Julie Killin and Tamara Small, as well as Cristine de Clercy, take different approaches to the subject of displacement. By accounting for the asymmetrical presence of local party candidates on Twitter during the 2015 federal campaign, Killin and Small remind us that some candidates are better than others at cultivating a personal vote, for instance by actively using microblogging with potential voters in their ridings. Their finding that local candidates tweet frequently about local issues highlights how social media provide them with platforms to directly access voters, tailoring party messages to local conditions. Yet, since candidates are also constrained by party-led messages during campaigns, we are left with important questions regarding the real impact of this communication. Does it really reach an audience? Does it change the informational status quo? Or does it merely amount to more partisan noise with no corresponding message? On this, the authors exert caution but nevertheless mention that candidates in their sample who engaged in more active and dialogical tweeting did fare better on polling day.

This analysis is complemented by de Clercy's contribution, which investigates the other end of the representational spectrum in party politics. It looks at the augmentation of the role of the party leader at the expense of the party brass and parliamentary caucus members. Although this is not a new phenomenon, it is a profound example of the displacement of the traditional party organization in favour of a direct connection between the party leader and the grassroots. Investigating recent transformations to the inner governance of the Liberal Party of Canada under Trudeau's direction, de Clercy's analysis of the party's constitution and of the role of the parliamentary caucus reveals how the leader exerts considerable influence in the organization, raises money on behalf of the party, and makes decisions. Party loyalists, in turn, monitor those actions. Her analysis of the interactions between leader and followers (caucus members, party brass, rank-and-file members) outlines Trudeau's fearless and somewhat unilateral leadership approach, making the most of a party constitution that gave the leader decision-making power over his organization. In line with the conclusions of Killin and Small, the chapter outlines how caucus members use digital technologies, such as Facebook, to engage with constituents. Although the nature of this communication might be largely unidirectional, with candidates broadcasting messages to the public, we can see how the emergence of digital technologies has started to undermine the monopoly that party elites have on campaign messaging. Together these chapters seem to indicate that organizational adaptation to digital technologies is the source of displacement. This finding can be contrasted with the contributions of Chacon and colleagues and McKelvey and co-authors suggesting that such changes might be the products of citizens' reactions to or antipathy toward elites.

A further theme is the bridging of traditional elite and emerging communities of political influencers directly engaged with the government. Although the distinction between elites and average citizens might have appeared somewhat stark just a few decades ago, the rise of digital communications has led a series of actors to bridge this divide. The result is arguably an emerging slate of contributors to the political decision-making process. Rachel Laforest's chapter illustrates how lesser-heard interest organizations leverage online technologies to enhance their roles in issue-based conversations and debates with both elites and non-elites. Jamie Gillies and David Coletto's exploration of the rise of the strategic adviser class is evidence of the enlarging of the party-bureaucrat connection. Their chapter reminds readers that, though there is not a professional political consulting industry in Canada, campaign strategists have been key figures in campaign organizations in our country for decades. Their account reveals the recent centralization of the role of digital strategists and data engineers in federal parties. Where they once operated at the fringe of electoral communications by designing websites, they have moved to the centre of strategic operations, contributing knowledge and expertise on market research, data analysis, voter segmentation and targeting, as well as fundraising and message design. These digital-savvy politicos are first and foremost party loyalists, a finding that complements the work of Jennifer Robson and R. Paul Wilson, who document the relationship between public servants and political staffers working in ministerial cabinets. Their chapter demonstrates how bridges are built and burned between these two classes of backroom players when assisting ministers in their duties. Looking at Harper's tenure from 2006 to 2015, during which social media gained influence, Robson and Wilson reveal how shorter reaction times and faster approaches to government communications became central concerns in cabinets. At times, this development strains the working relationships between political staffers and public servants.

Each of these themes captures some dimension of the evolving composition and communications strategies of political elites in Canada. We expect these observed tendencies to become stronger. Centripetal forces in the technological world will likely make communications easier for governments to make information available and to monitor public happenings. If they choose not to do so, then the rise of technological know-how will make the media, activists, and citizens more likely to seek this information through unconventional means. Moreover, at each general election, a new generation of parliamentarians is elected, and they are comfortable operating in the digital world. The result is that elites and non-elites in Canada and beyond must come to a new understanding of how to treat government information: whether it is a mechanism for maintaining accountability or a mode of advancement for certain interests over others.

Political Elites and the State of Canadian Democracy

Political Elites in Canada provides the basis for determining who these individuals are and how they behave in an environment of instant communication. To be considered an elite is a dubious honour. Elite status is increasingly under fire for its privilege, and its members risk losing influence in favour of more populist advocacy. In the past, this might have afforded prestige and career advancement; for some, it still does. A substantial number of high-ranking individuals still continue to marshal their political and economic acumen to consolidate positions of power. Some, such as senior civil servants, industry leaders, and wealthy citizens with private channels of political influence, do so by staying firmly in the shadows and not attracting public attention or criticism. Others take a riskier path by publicly rejecting elites and drawing lines between their success and what it truly means to be elite. This points to a further dimension of elitism in the twenty-first century: has the term been altered so significantly that it now only signifies cultural, societal, or insider status rather than capturing its traditional political and economic dimensions? Either way the growth of instant forms of communication and the reduction of cost barriers to these technologies will assist everyday citizens in monitoring elite behaviour and becoming informed on subjects of interest.

The extent to which this technological change is advantageous to Canadian democracy remains to be seen. The trend in citizen engagement with political information points toward deeper access to fewer sources. News intake habits tend to be preference reinforcing. News that is inconsistent with an individual's overall understanding of an issue or that is out of line with that person's existing set of political preferences appears to be deprioritized or ignored altogether (Prior 2013). Moreover, social media algorithms are designed to further limit the probability that users will be exposed to politically dissonant information and news. There is also the not-so-small matter of dubious information circulating online that can be mistaken as credible, leading to justified anxieties about "fake news" (Ballingall 2017).

In sum, the fact that citizens can access more information using digital technology does not necessarily mean that they are accessing better-quality and more useful information from a wider variety of sources (Dilliplane 2011). This sort of informational isolationism or echo chamber information gathering does little to move citizens from their entrenched preferences or promote critical deliberation. Rather, it polarizes the public sphere and subjects political actors to online mobs when citizens take a letter-of-the-law approach to evaluating public sector decisions. Members of the political elite can expect considerable controversy when a decision is out of step with something previously said or if they change their minds when presented with new information. Worse, the announcement of a thoughtful decision can be derailed by a minor gaffe that goes viral online, potentially upsetting good public policy and causing irreparable damage to a politician's career. The permanent record created by a digital media footprint can simultaneously be a useful tool and a liability for thoughtful policy development.

The fast-evolving technological context warrants some caution in applying our findings. However, there are many observations here that scholars and practitioners cannot afford to overlook. At a minimum, social forces, coupled with technological advances, have disrupted the conventional concept of the political elite. The categories that we and others rely on to conceptualize who belongs in the elite are subject to change and largely dependent on how traditional elites adapt to the evolving information environment. Access to elite status appears to be more permeable than ever before. Amid constant cries for merit over patronage, Canadians who demonstrate the skill to use digital technologies to advance their positions and preferences might find themselves among the new political elite, celebrated (or critiqued) for their agile approaches to communication and information sharing. As well, the skilled use of digital communication is necessary for elites, but it is not sufficient to maintain elite status. Narrow or unskilled use of social media will do little to improve a brand. Indeed, it can present a liability. Moreover, unidirectional communication, a common refrain in this volume among the traditional elite, can advance a political career only so far. Although two-way, real-time communication might pose an enhanced risk of gaffes, mistakes, and loss of message control, increased engagement appears to be the new frontier that the traditional political elite must conquer, risks and all.

Looking ahead, Canadian political elites should be mindful of populist arguments that citizens are the true experts on policy matters. Increased public access to information typically reserved for elites under policies of transparency and freedom of information has become a priority for governments who wish to promote accountability. Whereas this is generally advantageous for democratic citizenship, its use by anti-elite advocates can link the production of knowledge to the manufacturing of ideological positions. Such concerns are of paramount importance to how scholars perceive the relationship between elite actors and the wider public.

Few readers will have heard about the elite actor story with which we opened this concluding chapter. The Bob Rae incident warranted a fleeting report in the *Globe and Mail* authored by a community contributor, a source of information that in itself marks one of the many transformations of mainstream media. The former interim Liberal leader escaped online ridicule and outrage in 2011. If such a minor event occurred today involving another well-known parliamentarian at an overcrowded airport gate, chances are that many more people would be exposed to it, to the point that it could become imprinted on the public mindset. The episode would be surreptitiously recorded on a smartphone by other waiting passengers, the video would be rapidly shared on social media, the mainstream media would repeat the clip many times, there would be internet memes and online vitriol circulating, and all of this would be egged on by political opponents – possibly dredged up on the floor of the House of Commons, though we suspect that fewer people would take notice by the time that it arose in such a formal forum. In the right circumstances, it is conceivable that an elected official would face public pressure to step down for using Super Elite entitlements to board an oversold flight.

At every turn, office holders at all levels of government face new realities in public and private interactions. The new norm for elite behaviour is to publicly disown such trappings of power. Those who embody officialdom face a perpetual predicament. Should they isolate themselves? Or should they more closely align themselves with public interests? In comparison, society as a whole is confronting new realities. How will elites be leveraged to advance public interests in a manner reflective of new norms of representational behaviour? We suspect that these tensions will drive the politics of the coming decades in Canada and undoubtedly be influenced by further advances in communication technologies.

REFERENCES

Aucoin, Peter. 2012. "New Political Governance in Westminster Systems: Impartial Public Administration and Management Performance at Risk." *Governance: An International Journal of Policy, Administration, and Institutions* 25, 2: 177–99. https://doi.org/10.1111/j.1468-0491.2012.01569.x.

Bakvis, Herman. 1991. *Regional Ministers: Power and Influence in the Canadian Cabinet.* Toronto: University of Toronto Press.

Ballingall, Alex. 2017. "Google, Facebook Tell Government They Take 'Fake News' Seriously." *Toronto Star,* February 15. https://www.thestar.com/news/canada/2017/02/15/google-facebook-tell-government-they-take-fake-news-seriously.html.

Boutilier, Alex. 2016. "Trudeau's Top Staff to Repay Some Moving Expenses." *Toronto Star,* September 22. https://www.thestar.com/news/canada/2016/09/22/liberal-aides-gerald-butts-katie-telford-apologize-over-moving-expenses.html.

Boydstun, Amber E. 2013. *Making the News: Politics, the Media, and Agenda Setting.* Chicago: University of Chicago Press. https://doi.org/10.7208/chicago/97802260 65601.001.0001.

Burgess, Mark. 2016. "The Top 100 Most Powerful and Influential People in Government and Politics in 2016: List." *Hill Times,* January 25. https://www.hilltimes.com/2016/01/25/the-top-100-most-powerful-and-influential-people-in-government-and-politics-in-2016-list/49204.

CBC News. 2010. "Baird Slams 'Toronto Elites' over Gun Registry." September 16. http://www.cbc.ca/news/politics/baird-slams-toronto-elites-over-gun-registry-1.883606.

Chacon, Geneviève, Thierry Giasson, and Colette Brin. 2015. "Le journalisme politique en 140 caractères: Le cas du Québec." *Sur le journalisme, About Journalism, Sobre jornalismo* 4, 1: 34–49.

Chong, Dennis, and James N. Druckman. 2007. "Framing Theory." *Annual Review of Political Science* 10, 1: 103–26. https://doi.org/10.1146/annurev.polisci.10.072805.103054.

Clarke, John, and Janet Newman. 2017. "'People in This Country Have Had Enough of Experts': Brexit and the Paradoxes of Populism." *Critical Policy Studies* 11, 1: 101–16. https://doi.org/10.1080/19460171.2017.1282376.

Clement, Wallace. 1975. *The Canadian Corporate Elite.* Toronto: McClelland and Stewart.

Cowan, Peter. 2016. "The Newfoundlander with the Ear of the Prime Minister." *CBC News,* November 7. http://www.cbc.ca/news/canada/newfoundland-labrador/judy-foote-support-nl-1.3839328.

Cross, Jessica Smith. 2015. "Full Transcript: Metro's Q&A with Prime Minister Stephen Harper." *Metro* [Toronto], September 29. http://www.metronews.ca/news/canada/2015/09/29/q-a-metro-interviews-prime-minister-stephen-harper.html.

Curry, Bill. 2017. "Trudeau Blames Corporate Elites for Rise in Public Anger." *Globe and Mail,* February 17. https://www.theglobeandmail.com/news/politics/trudeau-merkel-germany-nato-spending/article34065401/.

Dilliplane, Susanna. 2011. "All the News You Want to Hear: The Impact of Partisan News Exposure on Political Participation." *Public Opinion Quarterly* 75, 2: 287–316. https://doi.org/10.1093/poq/nfr006.

Esselment, Anna. 2010. "Fighting Elections: Cross-Level Political Party Integration in Canada." *Canadian Journal of Political Science* 43, 4: 871–92. https://doi.org/10.1017/S0008423910000727.

Farooq, Ramisha. 2016. "Gerald Butts, Trudeau's Principal Secretary, Ignites Twitter Skirmish over ISIS Policy." *CBC News,* February 9. http://www.cbc.ca/news/politics/trudeau-twitter-butts-isis-policy-1.3440155.

Forum Research. 2016. "Voters Agree with Screening for 'Anti-Canadian Values.'" News release, September 9. http://poll.forumresearch.com/post/2587/voters-agree-with-screening-for-anti-canadian-values/.

Foster, Ally. 2017. "The Top 100: The Top 25." *Power and Influence,* February 8. https://www.hilltimes.com/2017/02/08/top-100-top-25/95426.

Giasson, Thierry, Harold Jansen, and Royce Koop. 2014. "Blogging, Partisanship, and Political Participation in Canada." In *Political Communication in Canada: Meet the Press and Tweet the Rest,* edited by Alex Marland, Thierry Giasson, and Tamara A. Small, 194–211. Vancouver: UBC Press.

Halupka, Max. 2014. "Clicktivism: A Systematic Heuristic." *Policy and Internet* 6, 2: 115–32. https://doi.org/10.1002/1944-2866.POI355.

Harvey, Kenneth. 2011. "Thank You, Bob Rae, for Stealing My Plane Seat." *Globe and Mail,* July 22. https://www.theglobeandmail.com/news/politics/thank-you-bob-rae-for-stealing-my-plane-seat/article587816/.

Hill Times. 2016. "About Us." https://www.hilltimes.com/about-us.

Howard, Philip. 2006. *New Media Campaigns and the Managed Citizen.* New York: Cambridge University Press.

Jervis, R. 1992. "Political Implications of Loss Aversion." *Political Psychology* 13, 2: 187–204. https://doi.org/10.2307/3791678.

Koop, Royce, Jim Farney, and Allison Loat. 2013. "Balancing Family and Work: Challenges Facing Canadian MPs." *Canadian Parliamentary Review* 36, 1: 37–42.

Macdonald, Neil. 2016. "Reaching for the Top while Bashing the Elites: Kellie Leitch Picks Up the Cudgel." *CBC News,* October 7. http://www.cbc.ca/news/politics/leitch-elite-surgeon-minister-scholar-1.3795074.

Macfarlane, Emmett. 2013. *Governing from the Bench: The Supreme Court of Canada and the Judicial Role.* Vancouver: UBC Press.

Manfredi, Christopher. 2014. "Conservatives, the Supreme Court of Canada, and the Constitution: Judicial-Government Relations, 2006–2015." *Osgoode Hall Law Journal* 52: 951–83.

Mills, Charles W. 1957. *The Power Elite.* New York: Oxford University Press.

Nevitte, Neil. 1996. *The Decline of Deference: Canadian Value Change in Cross-National Perspectives.* Toronto: University of Toronto Press.

Poell, Thomas, and Erick Borra. 2012. "Twitter, YouTube, and Flickr as Platforms of Alternative Journalism: The Social Media Account of the 2010 Toronto G20 Protests." *Journalism* 13, 6: 695–713. https://doi.org/10.1177/1464884911431533.

Porter, John. 1965. *The Vertical Mosaic: An Analysis of Social Class and Power in Canada.* Toronto: University of Toronto Press. https://doi.org/10.3138/9781442683044.
Presthus, Robert. 1973. *Elite Accommodation in Canada.* Toronto: Macmillan.
Prior, Marcus. 2013. "Media and Political Polarization." *Annual Review of Political Science* 16, 1: 101–27. https://doi.org/10.1146/annurev-polisci-100711-135242.
Pross, A. Paul. 1992. *Group Politics and Public Policy.* Toronto: Oxford University Press.
Ryckewaert, Laura. 2016. "'The Biggest Challenge Is the CBC,' as Other Media Cuts Continue, Questions Raised over Impact of Mother Corp." *Hill Times,* November 7, 4.
Savoie, Donald. 1999. *Governing from the Centre: The Concentration of Power in Canadian Politics.* Toronto: University of Toronto Press.
Smith, Joanna. 2016. "Sophie Grégoire Trudeau Now on Facebook, Instagram." *CTV News,* October 11. http://www.ctvnews.ca/politics/sophie-gregoire-trudeau-now-on-facebook-instagram-1.3110870.
Smith, Marie-Danielle. 2016. "'Regular' Canadians Hoped to Become Senators under the New System – until They Saw the 'Elites' Trudeau Chose." *National Post,* November 6. http://nationalpost.com/news/canada/canadian-politics/regular-canadians-hoped-to-become-senators-under-new-system-until-they-saw-the-elites-trudeau-chose.
Tencer, Daniel. 2015. "Canada's Most and Least Trusted Professions: Sorry, CEOs and Politicians." *Huffington Post,* January 20. http://www.huffingtonpost.ca/2015/01/20/most-least-trusted-professions-canada_n_6510232.html.
Thompson, Elizabeth. 2017. "Trudeau's Bahamas Vacation Cost over $215K – Far More than Initially Disclosed." *CBC News,* September 13. http://www.cbc.ca/news/politics/trudeau-bahamas-vacation-rcmp-1.4286033.
Young, Lisa. 2013. "Party Members and Intra-Party Democracy." In *The Challenges of Intra-Party Democracy,* edited by W.P. Cross and R.S. Katz, 60–85. Oxford: Oxford University Press. https://doi.org/10.1093/acprof:oso/9780199661879.003.0005.

Glossary

The following key communication-related concepts are used in *Political Elites in Canada*. This list provides important contextual relevance. It is partially derived from recent books in the Communication, Strategy, and Politics series, including *Permanent Campaigning in Canada* (UBC Press, 2017, 322–31).

access to information (or freedom of information): The legislated provision that citizens have the right to request and obtain records from their government within a reasonable period, subject to reasonable limitations. Among the limitations are files received from other governments in confidence, files that might harm diplomatic or military activities, files that might injure a person, or files that might harm the jurisdiction's economic interests. Advice and recommendations prepared for senior government officials, including ministers, are normally exempt, as are most orders-in-council to emerge from cabinet. Coordinators interpret the legislation to determine what must be released verbatim, what must be redacted, and what must be withheld.

advertising: Any controlled, mediated (print, television, radio, and internet), and paid form of communication whose objective is to influence the opinion, choice, or behaviour of its destined audience. See also *government advertising*.

agenda setting: Agenda setting occurs when extensive focus on an issue increases the public's perceptions of its importance. Both governments and the media can be responsible for agenda-setting effects.

anti-elitism: A private or public sentiment that those in positions of power have an excess of decision-making authority and are perceived to be overly disconnected from the general public. See *political elites*.

backrooms: A term used to refer to decisions and activities among political elites that occur away from the public eye.

blog: Short for "weblog," a low-cost, publicly available, single- or multi-authored web publication that has limited external editorial oversight. It provides updated mixed-media information, comments, and opinions archived in reverse chrono-logical order, and it regularly comprises interactive elements such as hyperlinks. Blog writers (bloggers) post content on a wide variety of subjects, including pol-itics. The aggregation of all blogs is known as the blogosphere. See also *social media*.

branding: The overall perception of a product or organization. It often employs familiar logos or slogans to evoke meanings, ideas, and associations in the con-sumer. In politics, branding involves creating a trustful, long-term relationship with electors. A political brand is deeper than a political image because brands comprise tangible and non-tangible components, including personal experien-ces, emotional attachments, and partisan loyalties. See also *image*.

central agencies: The main interconnected coordinating and decision-making organizations at the apex of the government. In the government of Canada, this includes the Prime Minister's Office, the Privy Council Office, the Department of Finance, and the Treasury Board Secretariat. Depending on circumstances, other central actors can be engaged, most commonly the Department of Justice.

centralization: This concept posits that information, power, and communication strategy are clustered among core decision makers. In the federal government, centralization normally refers to central agencies. Within political parties, it nor-mally refers to a leader's concentration of power and inner circle. Centralization constrains the independence of line departments, junior ministers, parliamen-tarians, and election candidates.

database marketing: Quantitative data on electors stored in a database and used to create targeted marketing messages. In Canada, political parties begin with information obtained from the list of electors, to which they add information collected when people contact the party, take out a membership, make a dona-tion, put up a lawn sign, or respond to get-out-the-vote contact efforts, along with other data sources. Information can also be obtained from Statistics Canada, telemarketing companies, and list providers. Increasingly, database marketing is supplemented by scouring the web and social media for information on electors.

democracy: A system of government whereby citizens elect representatives and governing officials, who in turn are responsive to the public. The concept of democracy is evolving in the digital age with growing expectations for public engagement in transparent decision making irrespective of elections or the traditional role of members of the legislature. See *pluralism*.

digital communication: Any form of information creation, storage, or transfer through computer technology using binary digits, often shared through the internet. Examples of digital communication include social media applications and cloud computing, used on digital platforms such as smartphones, laptops, tablets, and televisions.

digital government/e-government: The application of digital technologies to the functions of the public sector.

election platform/manifesto: A document identifying a political party's commitments and policy proposals that, should the party form the government, will guide the government's agenda.

frames: Heuristic shortcuts or interpretive cues used to present and give meaning to social and political issues by emphasizing or excluding specific elements. The political elite and the media develop frames to define political debates. Frames provide targeted audiences with definitions of social and political problems or issues along with the agendas of political actors involved in the debates and their proposed solutions or potential outcomes. See also *framing; image*.

framing: A strategic communicative process and an effect of the mediatization of politics. As a strategic process, it is the act of shaping or presenting issues, such as political ones, by using frames to reflect particular agendas and influence public opinion. As an effect, it is the indirect consequence of exposure to media coverage of politics over public opinion. The frames used by media to depict political issues lead citizens to cast different forms of responsibility on policy makers or interpret political and social issues in varying ways. The public's understanding of political issues is therefore influenced by the dominant frames used to define them. See also *frames; image*.

gatekeeping: A process in which news editors select and favour certain types of stories over others, thereby controlling the flow and content of information, political or otherwise, and ultimately determining the news. Gatekeeping is highly influenced by the subjective attitudes or biases of journalists and editors and results in a hierarchy of news stories presented to the public. See also *agenda setting*.

gendered media coverage: The different media treatment of people on the basis of their gender, such as by applying role stereotypes.

government advertising: Political communications by a government to its citizens about public programs and services through various media, including print, television, radio, and online. Government advertising can be categorized as partisan if, according to a law in Ontario banning the practice, it is self-congratulatory, timed for political gain, or inappropriately uses the colour associated with the governing party.

hashtag: Use of the "#" symbol on Twitter to group themed posts by keyword, acronym, or phrase. This organizational tool enables contribution to a larger conversation and facilitates a search for tweets on a similar topic. See *tweets.*

image: The mental impression or perception of an object, being, or concept, such as a politician, political party, or public policy. Images are subjective because of the ways in which their target audiences receive, absorb, process, and evoke political messages. The public images of political actors are actually imaginary constructs shaped by information and visuals controlled and filtered by political parties, public relations personnel, the media, pundits, and others. See also *branding; framing.*

information and communication technologies (ICTs): A broad term referring to electronic communications software and hardware, ranging from broadcast media to handheld devices. See *digital communication.*

interest group: A voluntary or non-profit organization that forms because of a shared connection or cause by its members. Interest groups seek to influence legislation by meeting with, and persuading, government policy makers about their common interests.

issues management: The way in which political parties or governments (particularly the Prime Minister's Office) identify potentially harmful stories and rapidly develop a response to combat them.

lobbying: The act of communicating with public office holders about issues or legislation on behalf of a client, corporation, or organization.

lobbyists: Unelected people who leverage knowledge of the political system to influence the views of those with political power, in an attempt to achieve a desired public policy outcome in the name of interest groups or corporate clients.

Although viewed as legitimate actors, lobbyists in Canada who work for compensation must register with the government and track their interactions with politicians and public servants.

market intelligence: Empirical data on the political marketplace and public views, also known as "market research." Collecting market intelligence involves quantitative and qualitative methods such as polls, opinion surveys, focus groups, role playing, consultation, and analysis of existing public census data and election records. A political party relies on market intelligence to prioritize issues, develop and refine communication strategies, and present itself as the most competent party to address those issues.

mass media/news media: Print and broadcast news outlets that reach a mass audience, such as newspapers, magazines, radio, and television. They are also referred to as mainstream/traditional/conventional/legacy media because of the growing presence of alternative information platforms, including blogs, online media, community news outlets, transit publications, and social media.

media logic: The theory that institutional actors change their behaviour in response to how journalists gather and report news.

media management: The strategies and techniques employed by public relations personnel in their interactions with the media, particularly tactics designed to control the message and frame. See *public relations.*

media relations: Activities undertaken to manage and optimize interactions with the news media, such as news releases, pseudo-events, and questions from journalists. See *public relations.*

mediation: The interpretation of information through the media and the subsequent relay of this information to the public.

narrowcasting: The act of selecting media, based on the nature of the communication, most likely to reach targeted market segments – for example, communicating with target groups by advertising on sports or lifestyle specialty channels instead of via the broader mass media.

New Political Governance: A model of public sector management in which the governing party's pursuit of partisan gain leads to practices that betray the principles of impartial public administration in Westminster systems. See also *permanent campaign.*

online influencers: Social media users who are especially active online, who are considered to have specialized knowledge, whose posts reach a high number of people, and whose online comments can affect other users' opinions.

opposition research: Involves the collection of information on political opponents to discredit a target or defend oneself. Online platforms have increased the ability to gather details and opportunities to disseminate the findings of "oppo."

partisanship: A person's psychological ties to a political party. Every party has a core of strong partisans who might or might not publicly self-identify as such.

permanent campaign: Electioneering throughout governance, which often involves leveraging public resources. This is more prevalent with fixed-date election legislation because all political parties maintain a state of election readiness that builds as the election approaches. Non-stop campaigning is most pronounced in the final year of a four-year cycle, during by-elections, and during the uncertainty of a minority government when the possibility of a sudden election campaign is ever present.

personalization: The self-disclosure of private and personal details by politicians and the increased attention from the news media on the private lives of politicians, such as their families.

pluralism: The concept that a democratic society must have a vibrant public sphere that welcomes a diversity of political views from across the political spectrum.

political communication: The role of communication in politics, including the generation of messages by political actors (political organizations, non-profits, citizens, the media) and their transmission as well as reception. Communication occurs in a variety of forms (formal and informal), in a number of venues (public and private), and through a variety of media (mediated or unmediated content).

political elites: Individuals who hold public office, who act as agents of those who do, or who otherwise have greater political influence and power than other citizens do.

political marketing: The application of business marketing concepts to the practice and study of politics and government. With political marketing, a political organization uses business techniques to inform and shape its strategic behaviour, designed to satisfy citizens' needs and wants. Strategies and tools include branding, e-marketing, delivery, focus groups, get out the vote, internal marketing, listening exercises, opposition research, polling, public relations, segmentation, strategic product development, volunteer management, voter-driven communication, voter expectation management, and voter profiling.

political power: The ability to get other political actors or citizens to believe or do something that they might not have otherwise.

political strategists: Individuals who advise those with political power. Strategists draw on their knowledge, experience, and available resources, including market intelligence, as they make political calculations for their clients to achieve desired objectives.

press gallery: An organization composed of journalists accredited to cover the activities of the legislature, notably the Ottawa-based parliamentary press gallery.

Prime Minister's Office (PMO): The central agency of roughly seventy to ninety party personnel on the government payroll who provide support to the prime minister. PMO staff direct the business of government by liaising with the Privy Council Office, ministers, and members of the governing party caucus. In addition to their access to considerable resources, PMO personnel use a network of staff working for the ruling party in the executive branch, the legislative branch, and the party's extraparliamentary wing. See *centralization.*

priming: Communication tactic that seeks to influence the criteria that journalists and citizens employ when evaluating subject matter.

Privy Council Office (PCO): The bureaucratic arm of the Prime Minister's Office headed by the clerk of the Privy Council, the top public servant in the government. Staff in the PCO liaise with the PMO, deputy ministers, and other senior public servants. See *central agencies.*

professionalism: Refers to the media's treatment of political actors' communication as a proxy for amateurism or political prowess.

public relations (PR): The strategic use of communication tools and media-relations techniques to optimize interactions between an organization and its stakeholders.

publicity: The use of media relations and/or other communications to generate public awareness of a subject or topic.

social media: Internet-based applications in which users create and share content. Includes applications such as social networking (Facebook, Google+, Instagram, LinkedIn), blogs, microblogs (Tumblr, Twitter), online videos (YouTube), wikis (Wikipedia), and social bookmarking (Digg). They are also known as Web 2.0.

spin: The framing of information to reflect a bias favourable to the sender, ideally without receivers noticing.

strategic communication: The proactive coordination of a communication strategy to help an organization stay on message and highlight what it is delivering to its targeted audience (clients, customers, citizens, voters). In the government, this usually occurs within the Prime Minister's Office and takes into account all aspects of communication, including government announcements, advertising, speech writing, market research, ethnic outreach, and stakeholder relations.

Treasury Board Secretariat (TBS): The bureaucratic arm of the Treasury Board cabinet committee tasked with implementing central policies and directives across the government, such as its communications policy. See *central agencies.*

tweets: Short messages or contributions posted to Twitter, a microblogging website. Tweets may be up to 280 characters long and may include digital photos, video clips, or website links. See *hashtag.*

whole of government (WOG): An umbrella approach to governing that seeks to unify the disparate departments and agencies into a cohesive agenda.

Contributors

GENEVIÈVE CHACON (Université Laval) researches political communication, journalism practice, and digital media. Her work on recent transformations in political journalism has been published in *Sur le journalisme/About Journalism/Sobre jornalismo* and *Le temps des médias*.

DAVID COLETTO (Abacus Data and Carleton University) is an adjunct professor at Carleton University and the CEO and founding partner of Abacus Data.

MARIANNE CÔTÉ (Concordia University) completed a master's degree in media studies in communication studies. She wrote her thesis on the smart city concept, using the case of Montreal to discuss the technological sublime and the future of cities.

ERIN CRANDALL (Acadia University) researches Canadian politics, courts, and constitutional law. Her work has appeared in the *Canadian Journal of Political Science, Canadian Journal of Women and the Law,* and *Canadian Public Administration,* among others.

CRISTINE DE CLERCY (University of Western Ontario) specializes in studying political leadership using several different methodologies. Her fields of research expertise include Canadian politics, comparative politics, executive studies, political economy, and women in politics.

SUSAN DELACOURT (iPolitics and *Toronto Star*) has been reporting on Canadian politics since the late 1980s. Her most recent book, *Shopping for Votes: How Politicians Choose Us and We Choose Them,* 2nd edition (Douglas and McIntyre, 2016), looks at how consumer culture has mixed with Canadian political culture.

ANNA ESSELMENT (University of Waterloo) researches Canadian political parties, campaigns, institutions, and the role of partisanship in intergovernmental relations. She co-edited *Permanent Campaigning in Canada* (UBC Press, 2017).

BRYAN EVANS (Ryerson University) is the co-editor, with Stephen McBride, of *Austerity: The Lived Experience* and of *The Austerity State*, both of which were published by the University of Toronto Press in 2017. His recent research has looked at policy analysis and advocacy in the Canadian labour movement.

THIERRY GIASSON (Université Laval) is the co-editor, with Alex Marland, of the series Communication, Strategy, and Politics at UBC Press. His research investigates online forms of political campaigning and citizenship, transformations in political journalism, the mediatization of social crises, as well as political marketing practices in Canada and Quebec.

JAMIE GILLIES (St. Thomas University) is executive director of the Frank McKenna Centre for Communications and Public Policy and has research interests in American and Canadian politics and public policy, political communications, and executive leadership in advanced industrial democracies. He edited *Political Marketing in the 2016 U.S. Presidential Election* (Palgrave Pivot, 2017).

TANIA GOSSELIN (Université du Québec à Montréal) is a co-founder and co-director of the Public Opinion and Political Communication Lab at the Université du Québec à Montréal. She is a co-investigator of the expert survey European Media Systems Survey.

ALLISON HARELL (Université du Québec à Montréal) holds the UQAM research chair in the political psychology of social solidarity at the Université du Québec à Montréal. Her work appears in the *Canadian Journal of Political Science, Politics and Gender,* and *Political Research Quarterly.*

JULIE KILLIN (University of Calgary) researches political campaigns, with a special focus on how gender affects the content and delivery of campaign messages. She also studies local campaign strategies and candidate recruitment.

RACHEL LAFOREST (Queen's University) studies non-profits in Canadian politics. She authored *Voluntary Sector Organizations and the State* (UBC Press, 2011) and edited *Government-Nonprofit Relations in Times of Recession* (MQUP,

2013) and *The New Federal Policy Agenda and the Voluntary Sector: On the Cutting Edge* (MQUP, 2009).

ANDREA LAWLOR (King's University College at Western University) studies the role of media in the policy process. Her work can be found in the *Canadian Journal of Political Science*, the *Journal of Social Policy*, and *Public Policy and Administration*, among others.

J.P. LEWIS (University of New Brunswick) has published about cabinet and political elites in the *Canadian Journal of Political Science*, *Canadian Public Administration*, *Canadian Parliamentary Review*, and *Governance*. He co-edited, with Joanna Everitt, *The Blueprint: Conservative Parties and Their Impact on Canadian Politics* (University of Toronto Press, 2017).

ALEX MARLAND (Memorial University of Newfoundland) publishes about Canadian politics, political marketing, and political communication. His book *Brand Command: Canadian Politics and Democracy in the Age of Message Control* (UBC Press, 2016) won the Donner Prize for best public policy book by a Canadian.

FENWICK MCKELVEY (Concordia University) studies politics and policies concerning digital infrastructure, with a focus on internet traffic management and political engagement platforms. He is the author of *Internet Daemons: Digital Communications Possessed* (University of Minnesota Press, 2018).

VINCENT RAYNAULD (Emerson College) studies political communication, social media, research methods, e-electioneering, and journalism. His work has appeared in several French- and English-language peer-reviewed academic journals, including *Information, Communication, and Society*, *Journal of Information Technology and Politics*, *French Politics*, *American Behavioral Scientist*, and *Politique et sociétés*.

JENNIFER ROBSON (Carleton University) teaches in political management and public affairs and policy management at Carleton University. She has worked in several political offices, for the federal public service, and spent nearly a decade in the voluntary sector holding senior roles in policy development and research.

Robert P. Shepherd (Carleton University) studies policy and program evaluation systems in comparative perspective, public management reform, and ethics systems with an emphasis on lobbying and whistleblowing regimes. His current research explores Indigenous reconciliation in Canada with an emphasis on community engagement and youth resilience through transformative evaluative techniques.

Tamara A. Small (University of Guelph) researches the use and impact of the internet by Canadian political actors. She co-authored *Fighting for Votes: Parties, the Media, and Voters in an Ontario Election* (UBC Press, 2015) and co-edited *Political Communication in Canada: Meet the Press, Tweet the Rest* (UBC Press, 2014).

Melanee Thomas (University of Calgary) researches gender, stereotypes, and political engagement; gender and political careers; electoral politics; and Canadian politics. She co-edited *Mothers and Others: The Role of Parenthood in Politics* (UBC Press, 2017) and has published in *Politics and Gender, Electoral Studies,* and the *Canadian Journal of Political Science.*

R. Paul Wilson (Carleton University) teaches in the Clayton Riddell Graduate Program in political management. He previously served as the director of policy in the Prime Minister's Office and focuses his research on political staffers within both the core executive and parliamentary offices.

Stéphanie Yates (Université du Québec à Montréal) studies the role of citizens and interest groups in states' and businesses' governance. Using an interdisciplinary approach, she has published on lobbying, public participation, social acceptability, and corporate social responsibility.

Index

Aboriginal peoples. *See* Indigenous peoples

academics: as public intellectuals, 21. *See also* intelligentsia

academics, interviews with political elites: about, 29, 38–39; consent by elites vs other subjects, 31–32, 41; interviewees' research interests, 39; journalistic role of, 44–45; researcher's reputation management, 33, 36–37, 37(f), 38–39, 41; tips on placing requests, 37–38, 37(f). *See also* interviews with political elites, access to

academics, legal. *See* legal elites

Access to Information Act, 83

access to information commissioner, 12(t), 17, 82–83

access to information requests: about, 42–43, 82–83; communications standards, 67–68, 82–83; definition, 288; for emails and instant messages, 82–83; interviews as alternative to, 45n1; before interviews with elites, 38, 42–43; website on responses to, 43. *See also* accountability, political; open-government movement; transparency

accountability, political: about, 6–7, 19–21, 82–83; access to information requests, 82–83; Code of Conduct, 72, 82, 83; digital media's impact on, 6–7, 21, 277–79; of for-profit organizations, 249; government watchdog agencies, 12(t), 14, 275; internal mechanisms for, 67–68, 82–83; key questions on, 6–7; mainstream media's role, 19; of ministers for staff, 82; non-profit organizations, 258; of party leaders and caucuses, 155–56, 164–65; political finance rules, 19, 180–81; of political strategists, 181; premiers' social media videos as, 116–17, 118–19, 120–24; of public servants, 56, 66, 82–83; social media elites' roles in, 218, 284; social media videos on promises, 110; of Supreme Court, 276; transparency, 7, 17; Twitter use in campaigns for, 238–39. *See also* access to information requests; decision making, political; Federal Accountability Act (2006); open-government movement; representation, political; transparency

Accountability Act. *See* Federal Accountability Act (2006)

activists in social media. *See* citizen journalists; hackers and hactivists; Twitter, social media elites in 2015 election

advertising, government: definitions, 288, 291

advocacy, 18–19, 244, 246, 264. *See also* interest groups; non-profit organizations

agenda setting, 208, 288. *See also* gatekeepers and gatekeeping

aggregators, media: National Newswatch, 211, 212, 214, 272; as political elites, 13(t). *See also* social media elites;

Twitter, social media elites and hashtags in 2015 election

Albaugh, Quinn, 187

Alberta: candidates' Twitter use in 2015 election, 226–27; Notley's election (2015), 268. *See also* Notley, Rachel, gendered media coverage; Notley, Rachel, social media videos; Prentice, Jim, gendered media coverage; Twitter, candidates' use in 2015 election

Albinati, Chris, 230(t)

Aldrich, John, 153

Allen, George, 112

alternative media. *See* blogs and bloggers; citizen journalists; social media

Ambrose, Rona, 36

Anonymous (hacker collective), 204, 209–10, 212–13, 217–18, 279. *See also* Operation Anon Down (OpAnonDown, Anonymous collective)

anti-elitism: about, 264–70, 284; definition, 288; global forms, 265–66; historical background, ix–x, 267–68; ideological controversies, 265, 284; political power, 265; populism, 268; public trust in politicians, ix–x, 269–70, 269(t). *See also* political elites

As It Happens (CBC), 214

Assembly of First Nations, 272

assistant deputy ministers. *See* deputy ministers and assistants; public policy, senior public servants, and digital media; public servants, senior

astroturfing, 59

Aucoin, Peter, 17, 72–73

auditor general: as political elite, 12(t), 14, 17, 272, 274(t)

backbenchers, 15, 16, 36, 274(t). *See also* MPs (members of Parliament)

backrooms: definition, 288

Baird, John, 215

Ball, Dwight, social media videos: about, 114–18; accountability, decision making, and representation, 116–23; number

and view counts, 115(t); styles of videos, 119–20, 120(t), 123. *See also* premiers and social media videos

Bance, Jerry, 214

Barlow, John, 231(t), 232–33

Bateman, Joyce, 231(t), 232

B-corporations, 249

Begg, Gary, 231(t), 233

Bellegarde, Perry, 272

Bloc Québécois, 227, 267

blogs and bloggers: about, 205–6; definition of blog, 289; opposition research by, 206, 213–14; as political elites, 13(t), 20, 205–7; political influence of, 20, 204–5, 207–9, 279; public trust in, 269(t), 270; reputation management by, 123, 131; trends, 255. *See also* Jago, Robert; social media elites; Twitter, social media elites in 2015 election

Blumler, Jay, 186

Boolert, Thana, 230(t)

branding and image management: campaign strategies (2015), 179, 216; comparison of brand and image, 289, 291; decision-making styles, 116–17; definitions, 289, 291; image management, 113, 291; marital and parental status, 91–92; message control, 112–13; by political parties, 153, 158, 216–17; resignation of CPC candidates (2015), 214–15, 216–17; Senate caucus reforms (LPC), 158; social media videos, 109, 112–13, 120–24. *See also* frames and framing; gender; marketing, political; premiers and social media videos; scandals, leaks, and gaffes

British Columbia: candidates' Twitter use in 2015 election, 226–27; first woman premier, 90. *See also* Campbell, Gordon, gendered media coverage; Clark, Christy, gendered media coverage; Clark, Christy, social media videos; Twitter, candidates' use in 2015 election

broadcast media. *See* media, mainstream

295. *See also* branding and image management; gender; public policy areas and gendered media

Framework, website audits, 249, 251

Fraser, Sean, 230(t)

freedom of information. *See* access to information requests; open-government movement

Freeland, Chrystia, 229, 231(t), 234

Froomkin, Michael, 60

gaffes. *See* scandals, leaks, and gaffes

Gallant, Brian, social media videos: about, 114–18; accountability, decision making, and representation, 116–23; number and view counts, 115(t); styles of videos, 119–21, 120(t). *See also* premiers and social media videos

gatekeepers and gatekeeping: about, xi, 33; access to political elites, 33–34, 36; agenda setting by, 208, 288; definitions, 290; by mainstream media, 19–20, 184, 276; phone calls to gatekeepers, 40; social media's disruption of, 10, 111, 185–86, 188, 200, 205–6, 264; timing of requests to gatekeepers, 41. *See also* interviews with political elites, access to

gender: bias and sexism in online comments, 104–5; definition of gendered media coverage, 291; gendered media coverage, 90–94, 291; images and branding, 91–92; marital and parental status, 91–92; politics as masculine, 90, 91; power elites in twentieth century, 7–8; tone and volume of gendered coverage, 90–92; underrepresentation of women in government, 89–91. *See also* political elites and gender; premiers and gendered media coverage; public policy areas and gendered media; women

Gerbaudo, Paolo, 243

Gersick, Connie, 245

Global News: Twitter activity (2015), 194–98, 195(t), 197(t)

Globe and Mail: gendered coverage of premiers, 95, 96; historical background, x–xi; SCC and Nadon controversy, 136–37, 138

Globe and Mail and social media: about, 196–98, 197(t); coverage of social media elites, 211, 214(t); followers, 95; Twitter activity (2015), 196–98, 197(t)

glossary, 288–95

Good Works, 249

Google+, 215, 295. *See also* social media

Governing from the Centre (Savoie), 30–31, 270

government advertising: definitions, 288, 291

government elites, definition, 10

governors general: as political elites, 12(t), 13–14, 272, 274(t)

grassroots organizations. *See* interest groups; non-profit organizations

Green Party: access to interviews with elites, 36; digital media's impact on, 40. *See also* political parties

Green Party, federal election (2015): candidate tweets, 226–27, 229–33, 230(t)–31(t); personal-local vs party-national campaigns, 236. *See also* Twitter, candidates' use in 2015 election

Grégoire Trudeau, Sophie, 193–94, 271–72

Grewal, Nina, 231(t), 232

grey literature, definition, 249

Grosenick, Georgina, 246

Guibord, Gilles, 214

Hachey, David, 230(t)

hackers and hactivists: about, 206–7, 279; Anonymous (collective), 204, 209–10, 212–13, 217–18, 279. *See also* social media elites

Hagar, Douglas, 235

Hardie, Ken, 231(t), 233

Harper, Stephen: negative campaigning, 172; views on ordinary Canadians, 267–68. *See also* Conservative Party of Canada (CPC), federal election (2015)

literature review, 72–74; methods of study, 74–76; permanent campaign, 71; personality factors, 78–79; political staffers, 71–72, 82–84; public servants, 71–72; roles of, 71–72, 84–86; surveys of public servants (2008, 2014), 74–75, 86nn1–2; time period of study (2015), 76; training of, 83–84

Mishler, William, 29–30

monarchy: as political elites, 12(t), 13–14

Monsef, Maryam, 36

Morneau, Bill, 18, 271

MPs (members of Parliament): access to interviews with, 36; backbenchers, 15, 36, 274(t); as political elites, 12(t), 15–16, 274(t), 275; underrepresentation of women, 90. See also interviews with political elites, access to

Muttart, Patrick, 179, 180, 270

Nadon, Marc: SCC appointment and nullification, 17, 132–36, 135(t). See also Supreme Court: digital media and traditional elites

narrowcasting: definitions, 113, 292. See also targeting and database marketing

NationBuilder, 254

National Newswatch, 211, 212, 214, 272

National Post: coverage of social media elites, 211, 214(t), 217; gendered coverage of premiers, 95, 96; SCC and Nadon controversy, 134, 135(t), 138; social media followers, 95; Twitter activity (2015), 196–98, 197(t)

NDP. See New Democratic Party (NDP)

neo-institutionalist theory, 244–45

New Brunswick, premiers. See Gallant, Brian, social media videos

New Democratic Party (NDP): access to interviews with elites, 36; bloggers, 206; political strategists, 179; union and activist culture, 9, 179. See also political parties

New Democratic Party (NDP), federal election (2015): candidate tweets, 226–

27, 229–33, 230(t)–31(t); retweeting of national tweets, 236. See also Twitter, candidates' use in 2015 election

New Political Governance (NPG): about, 52; definition, 292–93; federal communications policy (2016), 58, 61; ministers' political staffers, 73; NGOs' influence on policy process, 52; politicization of public administrations, 17; public input by vulnerable people, 58. See also partisanship; permanent campaign

Newfoundland and Labrador: candidates' Twitter use in 2015 election, 226–27; PMO centralization of power, 271. See also Ball, Dwight, social media videos; Twitter, candidates' use in 2015 election

news cycles: and public policy cycle, 53(f), 54–55, 58–59, 67; traditional vs political information cycles, 186, 207–8

news media. See media, mainstream

newsletters, digital, 255

newspapers: coverage of SCC and Nadon controversy, 138–45, 139(t), 143(f); historical background, x–xi. See also media, mainstream; premiers and gendered media coverage; Supreme Court: digital media and traditional elites

Nicholas, Holly, 212

Nichols, Kevin, 230(t), 232, 233

non-professional social media elites. See blogs and bloggers; citizen journalists; hackers and hacktivists; social media elites

non-profit organizations: about, 243–45, 257–59; advocacy by, 244, 246; astroturfing (false organizations), 59; charities and CRA registrations, 249; definitions, 243, 248; funding pressures, 245–46, 257–59; fundraising, 250–51, 252–53; historical background, 245; horizontal vs hierarchical structures, 255; membership trends, 247, 253–54, 258; neo-institutionalist theory, 244–45; as political elites, 244; scholarly

populism, 268. *See also* anti-elitism
Porter, John, 8, 10, 264
positive political theory, 152
power elite. *See* political elites
Power and Influence: list of political elites, 271–73
Power Elite, The (Mills), 7–8, 10
power relations: about, 21, 270–71; anti-elitism, 264–70; constitutions as power structures, 154; convergence of elite roles, 13; definition of political power, 294; digital media's impact on, 52, 243; flattening of hierarchies, 6, 264; in interviews with elites, 31; non-profit organizations, 258; in political parties, 152–53; uneven distribution, 273–75. *See also* political elites
premiers: about, 109; centralization, 15, 109, 110, 114; first openly lesbian premier, 96, 98–99, 103; as political elites, 12(t), 14–15, 109, 271, 272, 274(t); social media videos, 109–10, 114; underrepresentation of women, 90, 91; women premiers, increase, 93, 94
premiers and gendered media coverage: about, 89–94, 102–5; content of coverage, 93; data sources and analysis, 94–95, 105n5, 106n6; findings of study, 95–105, 97(t); future research, 102, 104–5; gendered media coverage, definition, 291; hypotheses of study, 93–94, 104, 105n3; limitations of study, 104–5, 106n6; methods of study, 94–95, 106n7; policy areas, 93, 99–104, 101(t), 102, 103–4, 105n2; premiers, 94, 105n4; prominence, tone, and volume of coverage, 93, 95–99, 97(t), 100(f), 103; reader comments in online news, 104–5; time period of study, 94–95; trends in media, 93, 104–5. *See also* gender
premiers and social media videos: about, 114, 120–24; accountability, 116–17, 120, 123; branding and image management, 109; data sources and analysis, 114–17, 115(t); decision making

(collegial vs authoritative), 116–17, 118, 120–22; findings of study, 117–24; key questions of study, 116–17; methods of study, 114–17; policy areas, 118; representation, 116–18, 120–22; styles (message, news, outreach, press, speech), 119–22, 120(t); targeted messages, 117–18; time period of study (2016), 114; view counts, 114–16, 115(t)
Prentice, Jim, gendered media coverage: about, 94, 105n4; policy areas, 99–104, 101(t); prominence and volume of coverage, 95–98, 97(t), 103; tone of media coverage, 97(t), 98–99, 100(f), 103. *See also* premiers and gendered media coverage
press coverage. *See* media, mainstream
press gallery: definition, 294; proposal for academics in, 44–45. *See also* journalism
Presthus, Robert, 10–11, 29, 264
prime minister: access to interviews with, 36; centralization, 15, 18, 68, 289; as political elite, 12(t), 14–15, 271, 274(t); SCC appointments, 132–33; social media use, 15; underrepresentation of women, 90, 91. *See also* Harper, Stephen; Trudeau, Justin
Prime Minister's Office (PMO): centralization, 15, 68, 109, 270–71; definition, 294; message control, 62–63; political communicators, 62–63; as political elites, 12(t), 14, 16, 274(t); political staff, 14, 62–63; social media's use by, 16; strategic communications, definition, 295. *See also* Harper, Stephen, government; Trudeau, Justin, government
priming of news reception, 208, 294
Prince Edward Island, premiers. *See* MacLauchlan, Wade, social media videos
print media: historical background, x–xi. *See also* media, mainstream
private citizens as journalists. *See* blogs and bloggers; citizen journalists

public servants, senior: accountability, 66; digital media's effects on, 51, 66–69; employee confidence in, 75–77, 77(t); employee job satisfaction, 75–82, 77(t), 78(t); permanent campaigns, 75, 81; as political elites, 12(t); political influence of, 17–18, 66–69, 274(t); training of, 83–84. *See also* deputy ministers and assistants; ministers' political staff and public servants; Privy Council, clerk of the; public policy, senior public servants, and digital media

Public Service Commission of Canada (PSC), 74

Public Service Employee Survey (Statistics Canada), 74–75

publicity, definition, 294

pundits: as political elites, 13(t), 21, 274(t); social media use, 199

Purchase, Kate, 271

Quebec: anti-elitism, 265, 266, 267; Bloc Québécois, 267; Parti Québécois, 266, 268. *See also* Couillard, Philippe, social media videos

Quebec and Supreme Court of Canada: reference on Nadon appointment, 134. *See also* Supreme Court, digital media and traditional elites

race and ethnicity: racist online comments, 116; white power elites in the twentieth century, 7–8

Rae, Bob, 263, 284

Ramnarine, Sasha, 231(t)

Ratti, Jillian, 230(t)

Rebel: Jago's tweets, 212

Reference re Senate Reform (2014), 134, 135(t)

Reference re Supreme Court Act (2014), 134, 135(t). *See also* Supreme Court, digital media and traditional elites

Reform Party, 267

representation, political: about, 6–7, 21, 277; digital media's impact on, 6, 21,

43–45, 277; excluded voices, 52; flattening of hierarchies, 6, 264; interviews with elites, 43–45; key questions on, 6–7; open-government movement, 18, 52; pluralism, 18–19, 52, 293; social media videos for connection, 110. *See also* accountability, political; decision making, political; democracy and public input

reputation management on social media: by candidates and appointees, 123, 131, 159, 214–15; by researchers, 33, 36–37, 37(f), 38–39, 41

results-based management, 62, 64

retweets, 187, 190. *See also* Twitter

Routledge, Kyle, 231(t), 233

Rowe, Malcolm, 133

Saskatchewan, premiers. *See* Wall, Brad, social media videos

Savoie, Donald, 30, 270–71

Sayers, Anthony, 226

scandals, leaks, and gaffes: about, 216, 283; candidates in election (2015), 159, 214–15; Duffy expenses, 83, 189, 195(t); Harper's plagiarism, 112; influence of social media elites, 216–18; ministerial political staff, 72; viral media on gaffes, 61–62, 112, 284

Scarpaleggia, Francis, 162–63

SCC. *See* Supreme Court

Selinger, Greg, social media videos: about, 114–17; accountability, decision making, and representation, 116–23; number and view counts, 115(t), 117; styles of videos, 119–20, 120(t). *See also* premiers and social media videos

Senate Reform, Reference re (2014), 134, 135(t)

Senate and senators: appointment process, 170, 181, 275; caucus traditions, 151, 156; controversies (CPC), 72, 83, 189; Duffy scandal, 83, 189, 195(t); as political elites, 12(t), 271, 274(t); Senate caucus reforms (LPC), 157–58; Senate

103. *See also* premiers and gendered media coverage

Wynne, Kathleen, social media videos: about, 114–17; accountability, decision making, and representation, 116–23; number and view counts, 115(t), 116, 117, 122; styles of videos, 119–22, 120(t). *See also* premiers and social media videos

YouTube: government self-promotion, 59; premiers' use of videos, 114–16, 115(t); statistics on use, 206; viral media on political gaffes, 112. *See also* premiers and social media videos; social media; videos